THE COMPLETE WORKS OF ROBERT BROWNING, VOLUME V

Portrait of Robert Browning by Dante Gabriel Rossetti, 1855.

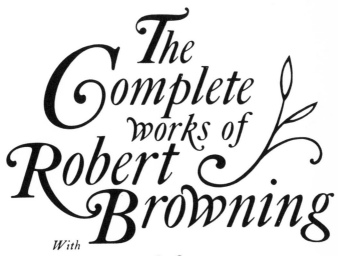

The Complete works of Robert Browning

With Variant Readings & Annotations

EDITORIAL BOARD

ROMA A. KING, JR. *General Editor*

JACK W. HERRING

PARK HONAN

ARTHUR N. KINCAID

ALLAN C. DOOLEY

Volume V

OHIO UNIVERSITY PRESS
ATHENS, OHIO
BAYLOR UNIVERSITY
WACO, TEXAS
1981

Members of the Editorial Staff who have assisted in the preparation of Volume V:
  John Berkey
  Ashby Bland Crowder, Jr.
  Susan Crowl
  Ray Fitch
  Nathaniel Hart

CONTENTS

	Page Number
PREFACE	vii
TABLES	xx
ACKNOWLEDGMENTS	xxiv
A SOUL'S TRAGEDY	3
Act I	9
Act II	25
POEMS (1849)	
Title Page	43
Prefatory Note	45
Contents	47
CHRISTMAS-EVE AND EASTER-DAY	49
Christmas-Eve	53
Easter-Day	97
ESSAY ON SHELLEY	135

MEN AND WOMEN, VOLUME I   153
    Love Among the Ruins   163
    A Lovers' Quarrel   167
    Evelyn Hope   174
    Up at a Villa—Down in the City   177
    A Woman's Last Word   181
    Fra Lippo Lippi   183
    A Toccata of Galuppi's   197
    By the Fire-Side   200
    Any Wife to Any Husband   213
    An Epistle Containing the Strange
      Medical Experience of Karshish,
      the Arab Physician   219
    Mesmerism   230
    A Serenade at the Villa   237
    My Star   240
    Instans Tyrannus   241
    A Pretty Woman   244
    "Childe Roland to the Dark Tower
      Came"   248
    Respectability   257
    A Light Woman   258
    The Statue and the Bust   261
    Love in a Life   272
    Life in a Love   273
    How It Strikes a Contemporary   274
    The Last Ride Together   278
    The Patriot   283
    Master Hugues of Saxe-Gotha   285
    Bishop Blougram's Apology   293
    Memorabilia   331

EDITORIAL NOTES
    A Soul's Tragedy   333
    Christmas-Eve and Easter-Day   339
    Essay on Shelley   350
    Men and Women, Volume I   355

CUMULATIVE INDEX OF TITLES   391

CUMULATIVE INDEX OF FIRST LINES   394

I CONTENTS

This edition of the works of Robert Browning is intended to be complete. It will comprise at least fourteen volumes and will contain:

1. The entire contents of the first editions of Browning's works, arranged in their chronological order of publication. (The poems included in *Dramatic Lyrics, Dramatic Romances and Lyrics,* and *Men and Women,* for example, appear in the order of their first publication rather than in the order in which Browning rearranged them for later publication.)

2. All prefaces and dedications which Browning is known to have written for his own works and for those of Elizabeth Barrett Browning.

3. The two prose essays that Browning is known to have published: the review of a book on Tasso, generally referred to as the "Essay on Chatterton," and the preface for a collection of letters supposed to have been written by Percy Bysshe Shelley, generally referred to as the "Essay on Shelley."

4. The front matter and the table of contents of each of the collected editions (1849, 1863, 1865, 1868, 1888-1889) which Browning himself saw through the press.

5. Poems published during Browning's lifetime but not collected by him.

6. Poems not published during Browning's lifetime which have come to light since his death.

7. John Forster's *Thomas Wentworth, Earl of Strafford,* to which Browning contributed significantly, though the precise extent of his contribution has not been determined.

8. Variants appearing in primary and secondary materials as defined in Section II below.

9. Textual emendations.

10. Informational and explanatory notes for each work.

II PRIMARY AND SECONDARY MATERIALS

Aside from a handful of uncollected short works, all of Browning's works but *Asolando* (1889) went through two or more editions during his lifetime. Except for *Pauline* (1833), *Strafford* (1837), and *Sordello* (1840), all the works published before 1849 were revised and corrected for the 1849 collection. *Strafford* and *Sordello* were revised and corrected for the collection of 1863, as were all the other works in that edition. Though no further poems were added in the collection of 1865, all the works were once again corrected and revised. The 1868 collection added a revised *Pauline* and *Dramatis Personae* (1864) to the other works, which were themselves again revised and corrected. The printing of the last edition of the *Poetical Works* over which Browning exercised control began in 1888, and the first eight volumes are dated thus on their title-pages. Volumes 9 through 16 of this first impression are dated 1889, and we have designated them 1889a to distinguish them from the second impression of all 16 volumes, which was begun and completed in 1889. Some of the earlier volumes of the first impression sold out almost immediately, and in preparation for a second impression, Browning revised and corrected the first ten volumes before he left for Italy in late August, 1889. The second impression, in which all sixteen volumes bear the date 1889 on their title-pages, consisted of a revised and corrected second impression of volumes 1-10, plus a second impression of volumes 11-16 altered by Browning in one instance. This impression we term 1889 (see section III below).

Existing manuscripts and editions are classified as either primary or secondary material. The primary materials include the following:

1. The manuscript of a work when such is known to exist.

2. Proof sheets, when known to exist, that contain authorial corrections and revisions.

3. The first and subsequent editions of a work that preserve evidence of Browning's intentions and were under his control.

4. The collected editions over which Browning exercised control:

1849—*Poems.* Two Volumes. London: Chapman and Hall.

1863—*The Poetical Works.* Three Volumes. London: Chapman and Hall.

1865—*The Poetical Works.* Three Volumes. London: Chapman and Hall.

1868—*The Poetical Works.* Six Volumes. London: Smith, Elder and Company. Reissued in stereotype impressions with varying title pages.

1888-1889—*The Poetical Works.* Sixteen Volumes. London: Smith, Elder and Company. Exists in numerous stereotype impressions, of which two are primary material:

1888-1889a—The first impression, in which volumes 1-8 are dated 1888 and volumes 9-16 are dated 1889.

1889—The corrected second impression of volumes 1-10 and a second impression of volumes 11-16 altered by Browning

only as stated in section III below; all dated 1889 on the title
pages.

5. The corrections in Browning's hand in the Dykes Campbell copy
of 1888-1889a, and the manuscript list of corrections to that impression
in the Brown University Library (see section III below).

Other materials (including some in the poet's handwriting) that
affected the text are secondary. Examples are: the copy of the first edition
of *Pauline* which contains annotations by Browning and John Stuart
Mill; the copies of the first edition of *Paracelsus* which contain correc-
tions in Browning's hand; a very early manuscript of *A Blot in the
'Scutcheon* which Browning presented to William Macready, but not
the one from which the first edition was printed; informal lists of
corrections that Browning included in letters to friends, such as the
corrections to *Men and Women* he sent to D. G. Rossetti; Elizabeth
Barrett's suggestions for revisions in *A Soul's Tragedy* and certain
poems in *Dramatic Romances and Lyrics*; and the edition of *Strafford* by
Emily Hickey for which Browning made suggestions.

The text and variant readings of this edition derive from collation of
primary materials as defined above. Secondary materials are discussed in
the notes and sometimes play a part when emendation is required.

III COPY-TEXT

The copy-text for this edition is Browning's final text: the first ten
volumes of 1889 and the last six volumes of 1888-1889a, as described
above. For this choice we offer the following explanation.

Manuscripts used as printer's copy for twenty of Browning's thirty-
four book publications are known to exist; others may yet become
available. These manuscripts, or, in their absence, the first editions of the
works, might be considered as the most desirable copy-text. And this
would be the case for an author who exercised little control over his text
after the manuscript or first edition stage, or whose text clearly became
corrupted in a succession of editions. To preserve the intention of such
an author, one would have to choose an early text and emend it as
evidence and judgment demanded.

With Browning, however, the situation is different, and our copy-
text choice results from that difference. Throughout his life Browning
continually revised his poetry. He did more than correct printer's errors
and clarify previously intended meanings; his texts themselves remained
fluid, subject to continuous alteration. As the manuscript which he
submitted to his publisher was no doubt already a product of revision, so
each subsequent edition under his control reflects the results of an
ongoing process of creating, revising, and correcting. If we were to

choose the manuscript (where extant) or first edition as copy-text, pre-serving Browning's intention would require extensive emendation to capture the additions, revisions, and alterations which Browning de-monstrably made in later editions. By selecting Browning's final correct-ed text as our copy-text, emending it only to eliminate errors and the consequences of changing house-styling, we present his works in the form closest to that which he intended after years of revision and polish-ing.

But this is true only if Browning in fact exercised extensive control over the printing of his various editions. That he intended and attempt-ed to do so is apparent in his comments and his practice. In 1855, demanding accuracy from the printers, he pointed out to his publisher Chapman, "I attach importance to the mere stops . . ." (DeVane and Knickerbocker, p. 83). There is evidence of his desire to control the details of his text as early as 1835, in the case of *Paracelsus*. The *Paracel-sus* manuscript, now in the Forster and Dyce collection in the Victoria and Albert Museum Library, demonstrates a highly unconventional system of punctuation. Of particular note is Browning's unrestrained use of dashes, often in strings of two or three, instead of more precise or orthodox punctuation marks. It appears that this was done for its rhetorical effect. One sheet of Part 1 of the manuscript and all but the first and last sheets of Part 3 have had punctuation revised in pencil by someone other than Browning, perhaps J. Riggs, whose name appears three times in the margins of Part 3. In addition to these revisions, there are analogous punctuation revisions (in both pencil and ink) which appear to be in Browning's hand, and a few verbal alterations obviously in the poet's script.

A collation of the first edition (1835) with the manuscript reveals that a major restyling of punctuation was carried out before *Paracelsus* was published. However, the revisions incorporated into the first edition by no means slavishly follow the example set by the pencilled revisions of Parts 1 and 3 of the manuscript. Apparently the surviving manuscript was not used as printer's copy for the first edition. Browning may have submitted a second manuscript, or he may have revised extensively in proof. The printers may have carried out the revisions to punctuation, with or without the poet's point by point involvement. With the present evidence, we cannot be conclusive about the extent of Browning's control over the first edition of *Paracelsus*. It can be stated, however, in the light of the incompleteness of the pencilled revisions and the fre-quent lack of correspondence between the pencilled revisions and the lines as printed in 1835, that Browning himself may have been responsi-ble for the punctuation of the first edition of *Paracelsus*. Certainly he was responsible for the frequent instances in the first and subsequent editions where the punctuation defies conventional rules, as in the following examples:

> What though
> It be so?—if indeed the strong desire
> Eclipse the aim in me?—if splendour break
>> (Part I, 11. 329-331)

> I surely loved them—that last night, at least,
> When we . . . gone! gone! the better: I am saved
>> (Part II, 11. 132-133)

> Of the body, even,)—what God is, what we are,
>> (Part V, 1. 642, 1849 reading)

The manuscripts of *Colombe's Birthday* (1844) and *Christmas-Eve and Easter-Day* (1850) were followed very carefully in the printing of the first editions. There are slight indications of minor house-styling, such as the spellings *colour* and *honour* for the manuscripts' *color* and *honor*. But the unorthodox punctuation, used to indicate elocutionary and rhetorical subtleties as well as syntactical relationships, is carried over almost unaltered from the manuscripts to the first editions. Similar evidence of Browning's painstaking attention to the smallest details in the printing of his poems can be seen in the manuscript and proof sheets of *The Ring and the Book* (1868-69). These materials reveal an interesting and significant pattern. It appears that Browning wrote swiftly, giving primary attention to wording and less to punctuation, being satisfied to use dashes to indicate almost any break in thought, syntax, or rhythm. Later, in the proof sheets for Books 1-6 of the poem and in the manuscript itself for Books 7-12, he changed the dashes to more specific and purposeful punctuation marks. The revised punctuation is what was printed, for the most part, in the first edition of *The Ring and the Book*; what further revisions there are conform to Browning's practice, though hardly to standard rules. Clearly Browning was in control of nearly every aspect of the published form of his works, even to the "mere stops."

Of still greater importance in our choice of copy-text is the substantial evidence that Browning took similar care with his collected editions. Though he characterized his changes for later editions as trivial and few in number, collations reveal thousands of revisions and corrections in each successive text. *Paracelsus*, for example, was extensively revised for the 1849 *Poems*; it was again reworked for the *Poetical Works* of 1863. *Sordello*, omitted in 1849, reappeared in 1863 with 181 new lines and short marginal glosses; Browning admitted only that it was "corrected *throughout*" (DeVane and Knickerbocker, p. 157). The poems of *Men and Women* (1855) were altered in numerous small but meaningful ways for both the 1863 and 1865 editions of the *Poetical Works* (See Allan C. Dooley, "The Textual Significance of Robert Browning's 1865 *Poetical Works*," *PBSA* 71 [1977], 212-18). Professor Michael Hancher, editor of Browning's correspondence with his publisher, George Smith, has cited evidence of the poet's close supervision of the 1868 collected edition ("Browning and the *Poetical Works* of 1888-1889," *Browning Newsletter*, Spring, 1971, 25-27). Mrs. Orr, writing of the same period in Browning's life, reports his resentment of those who garbled his text by misplacing his stops (*Life*, pp. 357-58).

There is plentiful and irrefutable evidence that Browning controlled, in the same meticulous way, the text of his last collected edition, that which we term 1888-1889. Hancher has summarized the relevant information:

> The evidence is clear that Browning undertook the 1888-1889 edition of his *Poetical Works* intent on controlling even the smallest minutiae of the text. Though he at one time considered supplying biographical and explanatory notes to the poems, he finally decided against such a scheme, concluding, in his letter to Smith of 12 November 1887, "I am correcting them carefully, and *that* must suffice." On 13 January 1888, he wrote, regarding the six-volume edition of his collected works published in 1868 which was to serve as the printer's copy for the final edition: "I have thoroughly corrected the six volumes of the Works, and can let you have them at once." . . . Browning evidently kept a sharp eye on the production of all sixteen of the volumes, including those later volumes. . . . Browning returned proof for Volume 3 on 6 May 1888, commenting, "I have had, as usual, to congratulate myself on the scrupulous accuracy of the Printers"; on 31 December he returned proofs of Volume 11, "corrected carefully"; and he returned "the corrected Proofs of Vol. XV" on 1 May 1889.

Throughout his long career, then, Browning continuously revised and corrected his works. Furthermore, his publishers took care to follow his directions exactly, accepting his changes and incorporating them into each successive edition. This is not to say that no one else had any effect whatsoever on Browning's text: Elizabeth Barrett made suggestions for revisions to *A Soul's Tragedy* and *Dramatic Romances and Lyrics*. Browning accepted some suggestions and rejected others, and those which he accepted we regard as his own. Mrs. Orr reports that Browning sent proof sheets to Joseph Milsand, a friend in France, for corrections (*Life*, p. 265), and that Browning accepted suggestions from friends and readers for the corrections of errors in his printed works. In some of the editions, there are slight evidences of minor house-styling in capitalization and the indication of quotations. But the evidence of Browning's own careful attention to revisions and corrections in both his manuscripts and proof sheets assures us that other persons played only a very minor role in the development of his text. We conclude that the vast majority of the alterations in the texts listed above as Primary Materials are Browning's own, and that only Browning's final corrected text, the result of years of careful work by the poet himself, reflects his full intentions.

The first impression of Browning's final collected edition (i.e., 1888-1889a) is not in and of itself the poet's final corrected text. By the spring of 1889 some of the early volumes of the first impression were already sold out, and by mid-August it was evident that a new one would be required. About this time James Dykes Campbell, Honorary Secretary of the London Browning Society, was informed by Browning that he was making further corrections to be incorporated into the new impression. According to Dykes Campbell, Browning had corrected the first ten volumes and offered to transcribe the corrections into Dykes Campbell's copy of 1888-1889a before leaving for Italy. The volumes altered in Browning's hand are now in the British Library and contain on the flyleaf of Volume 1 Dykes Campbell's note explaining precisely what happened. Of course, Dykes Campbell's copy was not the one used by the printer for the second impression. Nevertheless, these changes are indisputably Browning's and are those which, according to his own statement, he proposed to make in the new impression. This set of corrections carries, therefore, great authority.

Equally authoritative is a second set of corrections, also in Browning's hand, for part of 1888-1889a. In the poet's possession at the time of his death, this handwritten list was included in lot 179 of Sotheby, Wilkinson, and Hodge's auction of Browning materials in 1913; it is today located in the Brown University Library. The list contains corrections only for Volumes 4-10 of 1888-1889a. We know that Browning, on 26 July 1889, had completed and sent to Smith "the corrections for Vol. III in readiness for whenever you need them." By the latter part of August, according to Dykes Campbell, the poet had finished corrections for Volumes 1-10. Browning left for Italy on 29 August. The condition of the Brown University list does not indicate that it was ever used by the printer. Thus we surmise that the Brown list (completing the corrections through volume 10) may be the poet's copy of another list sent to his publisher. Whatever the case, the actual documents used by the printers—a set of marked volumes or handwritten lists—are not known to exist. A possible exception is a marked copy of *Red Cotton Night-Cap Country* (now in the Berg Collection of the New York Public Library) which seems to have been used by printers. Further materials used in preparing Browning's final edition may yet appear.

The matter is complicated further because neither set of corrections of 1888-1889a corresponds exactly to each other nor to the 1889 second impression. Each set contains corrections the other omits, and in a few cases the sets present alternative corrections of the same error. Our study of the Dykes Campbell copy of 1888-1889a reveals fifteen discrepancies between its corrections and the 1889 second impression. The Brown University list, which contains far fewer corrections, varies from the second impression in thirteen instances. Though neither of these sets of corrections was used by the printers, both are authoritative; we consider them legitimate textual variants, and record them as such. The lists are, of course, useful when emendation of the copy-text is required.

The value of the Dykes Campbell copy of 1888-1889a and the Brown University list is not that they render Browning's text perfect. The corrections to 1888-1889a must have existed in at least one other, still more authoritative form: the documents which Browning sent to his publisher. The significance of the existing sets of corrections is that they clearly indicate two important points: Browning's direct and active interest in the preparation of a corrected second impression of his final collected edition; and, given the high degree of correspondence between the two sets of corrections and the affected lines of the second impression, the concern of the printers to follow the poet's directives.

The second impression of 1888-1889 incorporated most of Browning's corrections to the first ten volumes of the first impression. There is no evidence whatever that any corrections beyond those which Browning sent to his publisher in the summer of 1889 were ever made. We choose, therefore, the 1889 corrected second impression of volumes 1-10 as copy-text for the works in those volumes. Corrections to the first impression were achieved by cutting the affected letters of punctuation out of the stereotype plates and pressing or soldering in the correct pieces of type. The corrected plates were then used for many copies, without changing the date on the title pages (except, of course, in volumes 17 [*Asolando*] and 18 [*New Poems*], added to the set by the publishers in 1894 and 1914 respectively). External evidence from publishers' catalogues and the advertisements bound into some volumes of 1889 indicate that copies of this impression were produced as late as 1913, although the dates on the title pages of volumes 1-16 remained 1889. Extensive plate deterioration is characteristic of the later copies, and use of the Hinman collator on early and late examples of 1889 reveals that the inserted corrections were somewhat fragile, some of them having decayed or disappeared entirely as the plates aged.

We do not use as copy-text volumes 11-16 of 1889, because there is no present evidence indicating that Browning exercised substantial control over this part of the second impression of 1888-1889. We do know that he made one correction, which he requested in a letter to Smith quoted by Hancher:

> I have just had pointed out to [me] that an error, I supposed corrected, still is to be found in the 13th Volume—(Aristophanes' Apology) page 143, line 9, where the word should be Opora—without an i. I should like it altered, if that may be possible.

xiv

This correction was indeed made in the second impression. Our collations of copies of volumes 11-16 of 1889a and 1889 show no other intentional changes. The later copies do show, however, extensive type batter, numerous scratches, and irregular inking. Therefore our copy-text for the works in the last six volumes of 1888-1889 is volumes 11-16 of 1888-1889a.

IV VARIANTS

In this edition we record, with a very few exceptions discussed below, all variants from the copy-text appearing in the manuscripts and in the editions under Browning's control. Our purpose in doing this is two-fold.

1. We enable the reader to reconstruct the text of a work as it stood at the various stages of its development.

2. We provide the materials necessary to an understanding of how Browning's growth and development as an artist are reflected in his successive revisions to his works.

As a consequence of this policy our variant listings inevitably contain some variants that were not created by Browning; printer's errors and readings that may result from house-styling will appear occasionally. But the evidence that Browning assumed responsibility for what was printed, and that he considered and used unorthodox punctuation as part of his meaning, is so persuasive that we must record even the smallest and oddest variants. The following examples, characteristic of Browning's revisions, illustrate the point:

> *Pauline*, l. 700:
> > 1833: I am prepared—I have made life my own—
> > 1868: I am prepared: I have made life my own.
> "Evelyn Hope," l. 41:
> > 1855: I have lived, I shall say, so much since then,
> > 1865: I have lived (I shall say) so much since then,
> "Bishop Blougram's Apology," l. 267:
> > 1855: That's the first cabin-comfort I secure—
> > 1865: That's the first-cabin comfort I secure:

We have concluded that Browning himself is nearly always responsible for such changes. But even if he only accepted these changes (rather than originating them), their effect on syntax, rhythm, and meaning is so significant that they must be recorded in our variant listings.

The only variants we do not record are those which strongly appear to result from systematic house-styling. For example, Browning nowhere indicated that he wished to use typography to influence meaning, and our inference is that any changes in line-spacing, depth of paragraph indentation, and the like, were the responsibility of the printers of the various editions, not the poet himself. House-styling was also very probably the cause of certain variants in the apparatus of Browning's plays, including variants in stage directions which involve a change only in manner of statement, such as *Enter Hampden* instead of *Hampden enters*; variants in the printing of stage directions, such as *Aside* instead of *aside*, or *[Aside.]* instead of *[Aside]*, or *[Strafford.]* instead of *[Strafford]*; variants in character designations, such as *Lady Carlisle* instead of *Car* or *Carlisle*. Browning also accepted current convention for indicating quotations (see section V below). Neither do we list changes in type face (except when used for emphasis), nor the presence or absence of a period at the end of the title of a work.

V ALTERATIONS TO THE COPY-TEXT

We have rearranged the sequence of works in the copy-text, so that they appear in the order of their first publication. This process involves the restoration to the original order of the poems included in *Dramatic Lyrics, Dramatic Romances and Lyrics,* and *Men and Women*. We realize, of course, that Browning himself was responsible for the rearrangement of these poems in the various collected editions; in his prefatory note for the 1888-1889 edition, however, he indicates that he desired a chronological presentation:

> The poems that follow are again, as before, printed in chronological order; but only so far as proves compatible with the prescribed size of each volume, which necessitates an occasional change in the distribution of its contents.

We would like both to indicate Browning's stated intentions about the placement of his poems and to present the poems in the order which suggests Browning's development as a poet. We have chosen, therefore, to present the poems in order of their first publication, with an indication in the notes as to their respective subsequent placement. We also include the tables of contents of the editions listed as Primary Materials above.

We have regularized or modernized the copy-text in the following minor ways:

1. We do not place a period at the end of the title of a work, though the copy-text does.

2. In some of Browning's editions, including the copy-text, the first word of each work is printed in capital letters. We have used the modern practice of capitalizing only the first letter.

3. The inconsistent use of both an ampersand and the word *and* has been regularized to the use of *and*.

4. We have eliminated the space between the two parts of a contraction; thus the copy-text's *it 's* is printed as *it's*, for example.

5. We uniformly place periods and commas within closing quotation marks.

6. We have employed throughout the modern practice of indicating quoted passages with quotation marks only at the beginning and end of the quotation. Throughout Browning's career, no matter which publisher or printer was handling his works, this matter was treated very inconsistently. In some of the poet's manuscripts and in most of his first editions, quotations are indicated by quotation marks only at the beginning and end. In the collected editions of 1863 and 1865, issued by Chapman and Hall, some quoted passages have quotation marks at the beginning of each line of the quotation, while others follow modern practice. In Smith, Elder's collected editions of 1868 and 1888-1889, quotation marks appear at the beginning of each line of a quotation. We have regularized and modernized what seems a matter of house-styling in both copy-text and variants.

The remaining way in which the copy-text is altered is emendation. Our policy is to emend the copy-text to eliminate apparent errors of either Browning or his printers. It is evident that Browning did make errors and overlook mistakes, as shown by the following example from "One Word More," the last poem in *Men and Women*. Stanza sixteen of the copy-text opens with the following lines:

> What, there's nothing in the moon noteworthy?
> Nay: for if that moon could love a mortal,
> Use, to charm him (so to fit a fancy,
> All her magic ('tis the old sweet mythos)
> She . . .

Clearly the end punctuation in the third line is incorrect. A study of the various texts is illuminating. Following are the readings of the line in each of the editions for which Browning was responsible:

MS:	fancy)
P:	fancy)
1855:	fancy)
1863:	fancy)
1865:	fancy)
1868:	fancy)
1888:	fancy
1889:	fancy,

The omission of one parenthesis in 1888 was almost certainly a printer's error. Browning, in the Dykes Campbell copy corrections to 1888-1889a, missed or ignored the error. However, in the Brown University list of corrections, he indicated that *fancy* should be followed by a comma. This is the way the line appears in the corrected second impression of Volume 4, but the correction at best satisfies the demands of syntax only partially. Browning might have written the line:

> Use, to charm him, so to fit a fancy,

or, to maintain parallelism between the third and fourth lines:

> Use, to charm him (so to fit a fancy),

or he might simply have restored the earlier reading. Oversights of this nature demand emendation, and our choice would be to restore the punctuation of the manuscript through 1868. All of our emendations will be based, as far as possible, on the historical collation of the passage involved, the grammatical demands of the passage in context, and the poet's treatment of other similar passages. Fortunately, the multiple editions of most of the works provide the editor with ample textual evidence to make an informed and useful emendation.

All emendations to the copy-text are listed at the beginning of the Editorial Notes for each work. The variant listings for the copy-text also incorporate the emendations, which are preceded and followed there by the symbol indicating an editor's note.

VI APPARATUS

1. *Variants.* In presenting the variants from the copy-text, we list at the bottom of each page readings from the known manuscripts, proof sheets of the first editions when we have located them, and the first and subsequent editions.

A variant is generally preceded and followed by a pickup and a drop word (Example a). No note terminates with a punctuation mark unless the punctuation mark comes at the end of the line; if a variant drops or adds a punctuation mark, the next word is added (example b). If the normal pickup word has appeared previously in the same line, the note begins with the word preceding it. If the normal drop word appears subsequently in the line, the next word is added (example c). If a capitalized pickup word occurs within the line, it is accompanied by the preceding word (example d). No pickup or drop words, however, are used for any variant consisting of an internal change, for example a hyphen in a compounded word, an apostrophe, a tense change or a spelling change (example e). A change in capitalization within a line of poetry will be preceded by a pickup word, for which, within an entry containing other variants, the $<>$ is suitable (example f). No drop word is used when the variant comes at the end of a line (example g). Examples from *Sordello* (all from Book 1 except c [2] which is from Book 4):

a. ⁶¹¹| *1840:*but that appeared *1863:*but this appeared

b. variant at end of line: ¹⁰⁹| *1840:*intrigue:" *1863:* intrigue.

   variant within line: ⁸²| *1840:*forests like *1863:*forests, like

c. ¹³²| *1840:*too sleeps; but 1863:too sleeps: but ⁷⁷| *1840:*that night by *1863:*that, night by night, *1888:*by night

d. ²⁹⁵| *1840:*at Padua to repulse the *1863:*at Padua who repulsed the

e. ²⁸⁴| *1840:*are *1863:*were

   ³⁴⁴| *1840:*dying-day, *1863:*dying day,

f. capitalization change with no other variants: ⁷⁴¹| *1840:* retaining Will, *1863:*retaining will,

   with other variants: ⁸⁴³| *1840:*Was $<>$ Him back! Why *1863:* Is $<>$ back!" Why *1865:*him

g. ⁴²⁷| *1840:*dregs; *1863:*dregs.

Each recorded variant will be assumed to be incorporated in the next edition if there is no indication otherwise. This rule applies even in cases where the change occurs between 1888-1889a, although it means that the variant note duplicates the copy-text. A variant listing, then, traces the history of a line and brings it forward to the point where it matches the copy-text.

In Browning's plays, all character designations which happen to occur in variant listings are standardized to the copy-text reading. In listing variants in the plays, we ignore character designations unless the designation comes within a numbered line. In such a case, the variant is treated as any other word, and can be used as a pickup or drop word. When a character designation is used as a pickup word, however, the rule excluding capitalized pickup words (except at the beginning of a line) does not apply, and we do not revert to the next earliest uncapitalized pickup word.

2. *Line numbers.* Poetic lines are numbered in the traditional manner by considering one complete poetic line as one unit of counting. In prose passages the unit of counting is the type lines of this edition.

3. *Table of signs in variant listings.* We have avoided all symbols and signs used by Browning himself. The following is a table of the signs needed to read the variant notes:

§ . . . §	Editor's note
$<>$	Words omitted
/	Line break
$//$, $///$, . . .	Line break plus one or more lines without internal variants

4. *Annotations.* In general principle, we have annotated proper names, phrases that function as proper names, and words or groups of words the full meaning of which requires factual, historical, or literary background. Thus we have attempted to hold interpretation to a minimum, although we realize that the act of selection itself is to some extent interpretative.

Notes, particularly on historical figures and events, tend to fullness and even to the tangential and unessential. As a result, some of the information provided may seem unnecessary to the scholar. On the other hand, it is not possible to assume that all who use this edition are fully equipped to assimilate unaided all of Browning's copious literary, historical, and mythological allusions. Thus we have directed our efforts toward a diverse audience.

TABLES

1. *Manuscripts.* We have located manuscripts for the following of Browning's works; the list is chronological.

Paracelsus
>   Forster and Dyce Collection,
>   Victoria and Albert Museum, London

Colombe's Birthday
>   New York Public Library

Christmas-Eve and Easter-Day
>   Forster and Dyce Collection,
>   Victoria and Albert Museum, London

"Love Among the Ruins"
>   Lowell Collection,
>   Houghton Library, Harvard University

"The Twins"
>   Pierpont Morgan Library, New York

"One Word More"
>   Pierpont Morgan Library, New York

Dramatis Personae
>   Pierpont Morgan Library, New York

The Ring and the Book
>   British Library, London

Balaustion's Adventure
>   Balliol College Library, Oxford

Prince Hohenstiel-Schwangau
>   Balliol College Library, Oxford

Fifine at the Fair
>   Balliol College Library, Oxford

Red Cotton Night-Cap Country
    Balliol College Library, Oxford
Aristophanes' Apology
    Balliol College Library, Oxford
The Inn Album
    Balliol College Library, Oxford
Of Pacchiarotto, and How He Worked in Distemper
    Balliol College Library, Oxford
The Agamemnon of Aeschylus
    Balliol College Library, Oxford
La Saisaiz and The Two Poets of Croisic
    Balliol College Library, Oxford
Dramatic Idylls
    Balliol College Library, Oxford
Dramatic Idylls, Second Series
    Balliol College Library, Oxford
Jocoseria
    Balliol College Library, Oxford
Ferishtah's Fancies
    Balliol College Library, Oxford
Parleyings With Certain People of Importance in Their Day
    Balliol College Library, Oxford
Asolando
    Pierpont Morgan Library, New York

We have been unable to locate manuscripts for the following works, and request that persons with information about any of them communicate with us.

Pauline	*The Return of the Druses*
Strafford	*A Blot in the 'Scutcheon*
Sordello	*Dramatic Romances and Lyrics*
Pippa Passes	*Luria*
King Victor and King Charles	*A Soul's Tragedy*
"Essay on Chatterton"	"Essay on Shelley"
Dramatic Lyrics	*Men and Women*

    2. *Editions referred to in Volume V.* The following editions have been used in preparing the text and variants presented in this volume. The dates given below are used as symbols in the variant listings at the bottom of each page.

1846   *Bells and Pomegranates*, No. VIII. and Last.
        London: Edward Moxon.

1849   *Poems.*
          Two Volumes. London: Chapman and Hall.
1850   *Christmas-Eve and Easter-Day.*
          London: Chapman and Hall.

       Letters of Percy Bysshe Shelley, with an Introductory Essay by Robert Browning.
          London: Edward Moxon, 1852.
1855   *Men and Women.*
          London: Chapman and Hall.
1863   *The Poetical Works.*
          Three Volumes. London: Chapman and Hall.
1865   *The Poetical Works.*
          Three Volumes. London: Chapman and Hall.
1868   *The Poetical Works.*
          Six Volumes. London: Smith, Elder and Company.
1888   *The Poetical Works.*
          Volumes 1-8. London: Smith, Elder and Company.
1889a *The Poetical Works.*
          Volumes 9-16. London: Smith, Elder and Company.
1889   *The Poetical Works.*
          Sixteen Volumes. London: Smith, Elder and Company.
          (second impression of 1888-1889a)

   3. *Short titles and abbreviations.* The following short forms of reference have been used in notes for this edition.

B	Browning
BrU	Browning's list of corrections located at Brown University
DC	Browning's corrections in James Dykes Campbell's copy of 1888-1889a
DeVane, *Hbk.*	William Clyde DeVane. *A Browning Handbook.* New York: Appleton-Century-Crofts, 1955.
DeVane and Knickerbocker	*New Letters of Robert Browning,* ed. William Clyde DeVane and Kenneth L. Knickerbocker. New Haven: Yale University Press, 1950.
EBB	Elizabeth Barrett Browning
Griffin and Minchin	W. H. Griffin and H. C. Minchin. *The Life of Robert Browning.* New York: Macmillan, 1910.

Ohio University Press
Swallow Press

The editors take pleasure in sending you a copy of

THE COMPLETE WORKS OF ROBERT BROWNING
VOLUME V
With Variant Readings & Annotations

Edited by Roma A. King, Jr., et al

ISBN 0-8214-0220-X $35.00

Publication date: August 31, 1981

*We would appreciate receiving two copies of any published
review or mention of this book.*

Scott Quadrangle / Athens, Ohio 45701

Heydon and Kelley	*Elizabeth Barrett Browning's Letters to Mrs. David Ogilvy*, ed. Peter N. Heydon and Philip Kelley. London: Murray, 1974.
Hood, *Ltrs.*	*Letters of Robert Browning Collected by T. J. Wise*, ed. Thurman L. Hood. New Haven: Yale University Press, 1933.
Irvine and Honan	William Irvine and Park Honan. *The Book, the Ring, and the Poet*. New York: McGraw-Hill, 1974.
Landis and Freeman	*Letters of the Brownings to George Barrett*, ed. Paul Landis and Ronald E. Freeman. Urbana: University of Illinois Press, 1958.
Letters of EBB	*The Letters of Elizabeth Barrett Browning*, ed. F. G. Kenyon. 2 vols. New York: Macmillan, 1897.
New Poems	*New Poems by Robert Browning and Elizabeth Barrett Browning*, ed. F. G. Kenyon. New York: Macmillan, 1915.
Orr, *Hbk.*	Mrs. Sutherland Orr. *Handbook to the Works of Robert Browning*. New Edition. Revised and in Part Rewritten by F. G. Kenyon. Boston and New York: Houghton Mifflin, 1891.
Orr, *Life*	Mrs. Sutherland Orr. *Life and Letters of Robert Browning*. Second Edition. London: Smith, Elder, 1891.
RB-EBB, ed. Kintner	*The Letters of Robert Browning and Elizabeth Barrett Barrett*, 1845-1846, ed. Elvan Kintner. Cambridge, Mass.: The Belknap Press of Harvard University Press, 1969.
Vasari	Giorgio Vasari. *Lives of the Painters, Sculptors and Architects*, ed. and tr. A. B. Hinds. Intro. by William Gaunt. 4 vols. London: Dent (Everyman's Library), 1963.

Citations and quotations from the Bible refer to the King James Version.

Citations and quotations from Shakespeare refer to *The Riverside Shakespeare*, ed. G. B. Evans, et. al. Boston: Houghton Mifflin, 1974.

For providing money and services which have made it possible for us to assemble the vast materials required for the preparation of this edition, the following institutions have our especial appreciation: the Ohio University Press, the Ohio University Library, the Ohio University English Department; Baylor University and the Armstrong Browning Library of Baylor University; the Kent State University Library and its Bibliographical and Textual Center, the Kent State University Research Council, the Kent State University English Department.

We also thank the following for making available to us materials under their care: the Armstrong Browning Library; the Balliol College Library, Oxford, and its librarian Mr. E. V. Quinn; the Beinecke Rare Book and Manuscript Library, Yale University, and its director Mr. H. W. Liebert; the British Library; the John Hay Library, Brown University; the Houghton Library, Harvard University; the Henry E. Huntington Library; the Department of Special Collections, Kent State University, and its director Mr. Dean H. Keller; Mr. Philip Kelley, New York; Mr. John Murray, London; the Library of the Victoria and Albert Museum.

Of the many scholars who have assisted in the preparation of this edition, the following deserve our thanks for their parts in compiling the present volume: Pat Elisar, Bruce Harkness, Ruth Nurmi, Sidney Reid, John Parks, Louis Paskoff, Susan Shulman, Charles Flint Thomas. Special gratitude is due to Professor Frederick E. Faverty, whose influence on the study of Victorian poetry is greater than he can know. The frontispiece is reproduced by permission of the Syndics of the Fitzwilliam Museum, Cambridge.

A SOUL'S TRAGEDY

Edited by Allan C. Dooley

CHRISTMAS-EVE AND EASTER-DAY

Edited by Harry Krynicky

ESSAY ON SHELLEY

Edited by Donald Smalley

MEN AND WOMEN, VOLUME I

Edited by Allan C. Dooley

BELLS AND POMEGRANATES, NUMBER VIII. AND LAST

A SOUL'S TRAGEDY

Edited by Allan C. Dooley

Here ends my first series of "Bells and Pomegranates;" and I take the opportunity of explaining, in reply to inquiries, that I only meant by that title to indicate an endeavour towards something like an alternation, or mixture, of music with discoursing, sound with sense, poetry with thought; which looks too ambitious, thus expressed, so the symbol was preferred. It is little to the purpose, that such is actually one of the most familiar of the many Rabbinical (and Patristic) acceptations of the phrase; because I confess that, letting authority alone, I supposed the bare words, in such juxtaposition, would sufficiently convey the desired meaning. "Faith and good works" is another fancy, for instance, and perhaps no easier to arrive at; yet Giotto placed a pomegranate fruit in the hand of Dante, and Raffaelle crowned his Theology (in the *Camera della Segnatura*) with blossoms of the same; as if the Bellari and Vasari would be sure to come after, and explain that it was merely *"simbolo delle buone opere—il qual Pomo granato fu però usato nelle vesti del Pontefice appresso gli Ebrei."*

R. B.

§ appears on verso of half title, 1846 only §

4

A SOUL'S TRAGEDY

ACT FIRST,
BEING WHAT WAS CALLED THE POETRY OF CHIAPPINO'S LIFE: AND ACT SECOND, ITS PROSE.

*1846:*PART FIRST < > AND PART SECOND   *1868:*ACT FIRST < > AND ACT SECOND

PERSONS

Luitolfo *and* Eulalia, *betrothed lovers*
Chiappino, *their friend*
Ogniben, *the Pope's Legate*
Citizens of Faenza
Time, 15—
Place, *Faenza*

§ appears 1865-1889 only §   *1865*:§ printed in running form § *lovers*:
Chiappino < > *friend*:Ogniben, *the Legate*: Citizens   *1868*:lovers. /
Chiappino < > the Pope's Legate. / Citizens

A SOUL'S TRAGEDY

1846

ACT I.

SCENE—*Inside* LUITOLFO's *house.*
CHIAPPINO, EULALIA.

    EULALIA   What is it keeps Luitolfo? Night's fast falling,
    And 'twas scarce sunset . . . had the ave-bell
    Sounded before he sought the Provost's house?
    I think not: all he had to say would take
5   Few minutes, such a very few, to say!
    How do you think, Chiappino? If our lord
    The Provost were less friendly to your friend
    Than everybody here professes him,
    I should begin to tremble—should not you?
10 Why are you silent when so many times
    I turn and speak to you?
    CHIAPPINO   That's good!
    EULALIA   You laugh!
    CHIAPPINO   Yes. I had fancied nothing that bears price
    In the whole world was left to call my own;
    And, may be, felt a little pride thereat.
15 Up to a single man's or woman's love,
    Down to the right in my own flesh and blood,
    There's nothing mine, I fancied,—till you spoke:
    —Counting, you see, as "nothing" the permission
    To study this peculiar lot of mine
20 In silence: well, go silence with the rest
    Of the world's good! What can I say, shall serve?

---

§Ed. 1846, 1849, 1863, 1865, 1868, 1888, 1889. No MS extant.§
Part title| *1846:*PART I. *1868:*ACT I.   Stage directions| *1846:house at Faenza.*
CHIAPPINO *1865:house.* CHIAPPINO   ²| *1846:*the Ave-bell *1868:*the ave-bell
³| *1846:*the Provost's House? *1865:*the Provost's house?   ¹¹| *1846:*laugh? *1888:*
laugh!   ¹³| *1846:*own, *1863:*own;   ¹⁴| *1846:*thereat: *1863:*thereat.
¹⁷| *1846:*spoke! *1868:*spoke: ²¹| *1846:*say shall *1849:*say, shall

EULALIA   This,—lest you, even more than needs, embitter
Our parting: say your wrongs have cast, for once,
A cloud across your spirit!

CHIAPPINO   How a cloud?

25   EULALIA   No man nor woman loves you, did you say?

CHIAPPINO   My God, were't not for thee!

EULALIA   Ay, God remains,
Even did men forsake you.

CHIAPPINO   Oh, not so!
Were't not for God, I mean, what hope of truth—
Speaking truth, hearing truth, would stay with man?

30   I, now—the homeless friendless penniless
Proscribed and exiled wretch who speak to you,—
Ought to speak truth, yet could not, for my death,
(The thing that tempts me most) help speaking lies
About your friendship and Luitolfo's courage

35   And all our townsfolk's equanimity—
Through sheer incompetence to rid myself
Of the old miserable lying trick
Caught from the liars I have lived with,—God,
Did I not turn to thee! It is thy prompting

40   I dare to be ashamed of, and thy counsel
Would die along my coward lip, I know.
But I do turn to thee. This craven tongue,
These features which refuse the soul its way,
Reclaim thou! Give me truth—truth, power to speak—

45   And after be sole present to approve
The spoken truth! Or, stay, that spoken truth,
Who knows but you, too, may approve?

22|*1846:*This, lest *1849:*This,—lest   26| *1863:*for Thee *1868:*for thee
27| *1846:*did Men *1863:*did men   29| *1846:*with Man? *1863:*with man?
30| *1846:*homeless, friendless, penniless, *1868:*homeless friendless penniless
31|*1846:*you, *1863:*you,—   34| *1846:*friendship, and <> courage, *1868:*
friendship and <> courage   35| *1846:*equanimity,— *1868:*equanimity—
39| *1849:*thee! it *1863:*to Thee <>Thy *1865:*to Thee! It *1868:*to thee!<> thy
40| *1863:*and Thy *1868:*and thy   41| *1846:*know— *1868:*know.   42| *1846:*
thee! This *1863:*to Thee *1868:*to thee. This   44| *1846:*Reclaim Thou <> speak
*1868:*Reclaim thou *1888:*speak—   45| *1846:*—And *1888:*And
46| *1846:*truth!—or *1868:*truth! Or   47| *1846:*might *1868:*may

EULALIA   Ah, well—
Keep silence then, Chiappino!
CHIAPPINO   You would hear,
You shall now,—why the thing we please to style
50 My gratitude to you and all your friends
For service done me, is just gratitude
So much as yours was service: no whit more.
I was born here, so was Luitolfo; both
At one time, much with the same circumstance
55 Of rank and wealth; and both, up to this night
Of parting company, have side by side
Still fared, he in the sunshine—I, the shadow.
"Why?" asks the world. "Because," replies the world
To its complacent self, "these playfellows,
60 Who took at church the holy-water drop
Each from the other's finger, and so forth,—
Were of two moods: Luitolfo was the proper
Friend-making, everywhere friend-finding soul,
Fit for the sunshine, so, it followed him.
65 A happy-tempered bringer of the best
Out of the worst; who bears with what's past cure,
And puts so good a face on't—wisely passive
Where action's fruitless, while he remedies
In silence what the foolish rail against;
70 A man to smooth such natures as parade
Of opposition must exasperate;
No general gauntlet-gatherer for the weak
Against the strong, yet over-scrupulous
At lucky junctures; one who won't forego
75 The after-battle work of binding wounds,
Because, forsooth he'd have to bring himself

48| *1846*:silence, then *1865*:silence then   49| *1846*:And shall < > we're pleased to
1868:You shall < > we please to   52| *1846*:service—and no more. *1888*:service: no
whit more.   53| *1846*:Luitolfo,—both *1868*:Luitolfo; both   57| *1846*:shadow:
1863:shadow.   58| *1846*:world: "Because *1868*:world. "Because   59| *1863*:
playfellows. *1865*:playfellows,   61| *1846*:One from *1865*:Each from   64| *1846*:so
it < > him; *1863*:so, it < > him.   66| *1846*:cure *1849*:cure,   71| *1846*:
exasperate— *1868*:exasperate;   76| *1846*:forsooth, he'd *1868*:forsooth he'd

11

To side with wound-inflictors for their leave!"
—Why do you gaze, nor help me to repeat
What comes so glibly from the common mouth,
80 About Luitolfo and his so-styled friend?
EULALIA Because that friend's sense is obscured . . .
CHIAPPINO   I thought
You would be readier with the other half
Of the world's story, my half! Yet, 'tis true.
For all the world does say it. Say your worst!
85 True, I thank God, I ever said "you sin,"
When a man did sin: if I could not say it,
I glared it at him; if I could not glare it,
I prayed against him; then my part seemed over.
God's may begin yet: so it will, I trust.
90 EULALIA If the world outraged you, did we?
CHIAPPINO   What's "me"
That you use well or ill? It's man, in me,
All your successes are an outrage to,
You all, whom sunshine follows, as you say!
Here's our Faenza birthplace; they send here
95 A Provost from Ravenna: how he rules,
You can at times be eloquent about.
"Then, end his rule!"—"Ah yes, one stroke does that!
But patience under wrong works slow and sure.
Must violence still bring peace forth? He, beside,
100 Returns so blandly one's obeisance! ah—
Some latent virtue may be lingering yet,
Some human sympathy which, once excite,
And all the lump were leavened quietly:
So, no more talk of striking, for this time!"

77| *1846*:with their inflictors *1863*:with wound-inflictors   79| *1846*:mouth
1849:mouth,   81| *1849*:Because, that *1888*:Because that   83| *1846*:story,—my
half!—Yet, 'tis true, *1868*:story, my half! Yet *1888*:true.   84| *1846*:it! say *1849*:it!
Say *1868*:it. Say   87| *1846*:him,—if *1868*:him; if   88| *1846*:him,—then
<> over; *1868*:him; then <> over.   89| *1846*:yet—so <> trust! *1865*:yet: so
1868:trust.   91| *1846*:ill? It's Man *1868*:ill? It's man   94| *1846*:birthplace—they
1863:birthplace; they   95| *1846*:from Ravenna—how *1863*:from Ravenna: how
1868:A provost § emended to § A Provost § see Editorial Notes §   96| *1846*:about—
1863:about.   97| *1846*:rule"! ah *1849*:rule!" ah *1863*:rule!"—"Ah   98| *1846*:
sure: *1863*:sure.   100| *1846*:obeisance—ah— *1863*:obeisance! ah—   103| *1846*:
quietly— *1865*:quietly: 104| *1846*:striking for <> time! *1849*:striking, for

105 But I, as one of those he rules, won't bear
     These pretty takings-up and layings-down
     Our cause, just as you think occasion suits.
     Enough of earnest, is there? You'll play, will you?
     Diversify your tactics, give submission,
110 Obsequiousness and flattery a turn,
     While we die in our misery patient deaths?
     We all are outraged then, and I the first:
     I, for mankind, resent each shrug and smirk,
     Each beck and bend, each . . . all you do and are,
115 I hate!
     EULALIA We share a common censure, then.
     'Tis well you have not poor Luitolfo's part
     Nor mine to point out in the wide offence.
     CHIAPPINO Oh, shall I let you so escape me, lady?
     Come, on your own ground, lady,—from yourself,
120 (Leaving the people's wrong, which most is mine)
     What have I got to be so grateful for?
     These three last fines, no doubt, one on the other
     Paid by Luitolfo?
     EULALIA   Shame, Chiappino!
     CHIAPPINO   Shame
     Fall presently on who deserves it most!
125 —Which is to see. He paid my fines—my friend,
     Your prosperous smooth lover presently,
     Then, scarce your wooer,—soon, your husband: well—
     I loved you.
     EULALIA   Hold!
     CHIAPPINO   You knew it, years ago.

---

*1863:*time!"   106| *1846:*layings down *1863:*layings-down   107| *1846:*suits! *1868:*
suits.   109| *1846:*tactics,—give *1868:*tactics, give   112| *1846:*first! *1868:*first:
113| *1846:*for Mankind *1863:*for mankind   114| *1846:*each . . all *1888:*each . . . all
115| *1846:*then! *1863:*then.   116| *1888:*Tis § emended to § 'Tis § see Editorial Notes §
117| *1846:*Or *1863:*Nor   118| *1846:*me, Lady? *1865:*me, lady?   119| *1846:*ground,
Lady *1865:*ground, lady   120| *1846:*Leaving < >mine, *1849:*(Leaving < >mine,)
*1868:*mine)   125| *1846:*Which < >see: he *1849:*see. He *1863:*—Which
126| *1846:*smooth husband presently, *1863:*smooth lover presently,
127| *1846:*wooer,—now your lover: well— *1849:*now, your *1863:*wooer,—
soon, your husband: well—   128| *1846:*you! EULALIA < >ago; *1863:*you. EULALIA < >

When my voice faltered and my eye grew dim
130   Because you gave me your silk mask to hold—
My voice that greatens when there's need to curse
The people's Provost to their heart's content,
—My eye, the Provost, who bears all men's eyes,
Banishes now because he cannot bear,—
135   You knew . . . but you do your parts—my part, I:
So be it! You flourish, I decay: all's well.
EULALIA I hear this for the first time.
CHIAPPINO   The fault's there?
Then my days spoke not, and my nights of fire
Were voiceless? Then the very heart may burst,
140   Yet all prove nought, because no mincing speech
Tells leisurely that thus it is and thus?
Eulalia, truce with toying for this once!
A banished fool, who troubles you to-night
For the last time—why, what's to fear from me?
145   You knew I loved you!
EULALIA   Not so, on my faith!
You were my now-affianced lover's friend—
Came in, went out with him, could speak as he.
All praise your ready parts and pregnant wit;
See how your words come from you in a crowd!
150   Luitolfo's first to place you o'er himself
In all that challenges respect and love:
Yet you were silent then, who blame me now.
I say all this by fascination, sure:

---

ago.   129| *1846:*eyes *1865:*eye   132| *1863:*The People's *1868:*The people's
133| *1846:*—My eyes *1865:*—My eye   134| *1846:*bear! *1863:*bear,—   135| *1846:*
knew . . but <> I! *1863:*part, I: *1888:*knew . . . but   136| *1846:*it! you
flourish—I decay! All's well! *1863:*decay. All's *1865:*flourish, I *1868:*it! You <> decay:
all's well.   137| *1846:*time! CHIAPPINO Oh, the fault was there? *1849:*CHIAPPINO The
fault's there? *1863:*time. CHIAPPINO   138| *1846:*not and *1849:*Then, my <> not, and
*1865:*Then my   139| *1846:*burst *1849:*voiceless? Then, the *1865:*voiceless? Then the
*1888:*burst,   142| *1846:*Eulalia—truce <> once— *1863:*Eulalia! truce <> once!
*1868:*Eulalia, truce   143| *1846:*to night *1849:*to-night   144| *1846:*time—Oh,
what's *1863:*time—why, what's   147| *1846:*he; *1863:*he.   151| *1846:*love—
*1863:*love: 152| *1846:*now! *1863:*now.   153| *1846:*sure— *1868:*sure:

I, all but wed to one I love, yet listen!
155 It must be, you are wronged, and that the wrongs
Luitolfo pities . . .
CHIAPPINO   —You too pity? Do!
But hear first what my wrongs are; so began
This talk and so shall end this talk. I say,
Was't not enough that I must strive (I saw)
160 To grow so far familiar with your charms
As next contrive some way to win them—which
To do, an age seemed far too brief—for, see!
We all aspire to heaven; and there lies heaven
Above us: go there! Dare we go? no, surely!
165 How dare we go without a reverent pause,
A growing less unfit for heaven? Just so,
I dared not speak: the greater fool, it seems!
Was't not enough to struggle with such folly,
But I must have, beside, the very man
170 Whose slight free loose and incapacious soul
Gave his tongue scope to say whate'er he would
—Must have him load me with his benefits
—For fortune's fiercest stroke?
EULALIA   Justice to him
That's now entreating, at his risk perhaps,
175 Justice for you! Did he once call those acts
Of simple friendship—bounties, benefits?
CHIAPPINO No: the straight course had been to call them thus.
Then, I had flung them back, and kept myself
Unhampered, free as he to win the prize
180 We both sought. But "the gold was dross," he said:
"He loved me, and I loved him not: why spurn

154| *1846:*I am all < > listen— *1863:*listen! *1888:*I, all   159| *1846:*strive, I saw,
*1863:*strive (I saw)   161| *1846:*As to contrive *1863:*as next contrive   162| *1846:*
too little—for *1888:*too brief—for   163| *1846:*to Heaven—and there is Heaven
*1865:*to Heaven; and *1868:*to heaven < > is heaven *1888:*there lies heaven   164| *1846:*
us—go there *1865:*us: go there   166| *1846:*for Heaven?—Even so, *1868:*for heaven?
Even *1888:*heaven? Just so,   167| *1846:*speak—the *1863:*speak: the   170| *1846:*
slight, free, loose *1868:*slight free loose   173| *1846:*For < > stroke! EULALIA *1863:*
stroke? EULALIA *1888:*—For   177| *1846:*No—the < > them so— *1865:*so; *1868:*No:
the < > so. *1888:*them thus.   180| *1846:*sought—but < > said, *1865:*sought: but
*1868:*sought. But < > said: 181| *1846:*not—to spurn *1865:*not: why spurn

A trifle out of superfluity?
He had forgotten he had done as much."
So had not I! Henceforth, try as I could
185 To take him at his word, there stood by you
My benefactor; who might speak and laugh
And urge his nothings, even banter me
Before you—but my tongue was tied. A dream!
Let's wake: your husband . . . how you shake at that!
190 Good—my revenge!
EULALIA   Why should I shake? What forced
Or forces me to be Luitolfo's bride?
CHIAPPINO There's my revenge, that nothing forces you.
No gratitude, no liking of the eye
Nor longing of the heart, but the poor bond
195 Of habit—here so many times he came,
So much he spoke,—all these compose the tie
That pulls you from me. Well, he paid my fines,
Nor missed a cloak from wardrobe, dish from table;
He spoke a good word to the Provost here,
200 Held me up when my fortunes fell away
—It had not looked so well to let me drop—
Men take pains to preserve a tree-stump, even,
Whose boughs they played beneath—much more a friend.
But one grows tired of seeing, after the first,
205 Pains spent upon impracticable stuff
Like me. I could not change: you know the rest.
I've spoke my mind too fully out, by chance,
This morning to our Provost; so, ere night
I leave the city on pain of death. And now
210 On my account there's gallant intercession
Goes forward—that's so graceful!—and anon

182| *1846*:superfluity: *1865*:superfluity?   183| *1846*:much"! *1849*:much!" *1863*:
much."   184| *1846*:not I!—Henceforth *1865*:not I! Henceforth   186| *1846*:
benefactor—who *1865*:benefactor; who   187| *1846*:nothings—even *1865*:nothings,
even   190| *1846*:shake? what forced, *1849*:shake? What *1865*:forced   192| *1846*:
you! *1863*:you.   193| *1846*:eye, *1863*:eye   197| *1846*:me! Well *1863*:me.
Well   198| *1846*:table— *1865*:table;   199| *1846*:—He <> here— *1865*:He
1868:here,   203| *1846*:friend! *1863*:friend.   206| *1846*:me: I <> change—
you *1868*:me. I <> change: you   207| *1846*:out, for once, *1868*:out, by chance,
208| *1846*:so ere *1863*:so, ere   209| *1846*:death—and *1863*:death:and *1868*:death.

He'll noisily come back: "the intercession
Was made and fails; all's over for us both;
'Tis vain contending; I would better go."
215 And I do go—and straight to you he turns
Light of a load; and ease of that permits
His visage to repair the natural bland
Œconomy, sore broken late to suit
My discontent. Thus, all are pleased—you, with him,
220 He with himself, and all of you with me
—"Who," say the citizens, "had done far better
In letting people sleep upon their woes,
If not possessed with talent to relieve them
When once awake;—but then I had," they'll say,
225 "Doubtless some unknown compensating pride
In what I did; and as I seem content
With ruining myself, why, so should they be."
And so they are, and so be with his prize
The devil, when he gets them speedily!
230 Why does not your Luitolfo come? I long
To don this cloak and take the Lugo path.
It seems you never loved me, then?

EULALIA   Chiappino!

CHIAPPINO Never?

EULALIA   Never.

CHIAPPINO   That's sad. Say what I might,
There was no help from being sure this while
235 You loved me. Love like mine must have return,
I thought: no river starts but to some sea.
And had you loved me, I could soon devise
Some specious reason why you stifled love,

And   212| *1846:*back: the *1863:*back: "the   213| *1846:*fails—all's <> both—
*1868:*fails; all's <> both: *1888:*both;   214| *1846:*contending—I had better go:
*1863:*contending—I would better go." *1868:*contending; I   215| *1846:*go—and
so to *1863:* so, to *1868:*go—and straight to   216| *1846:*load, and *1863:*load; and
217| *1846:*repair its natural *1868:*repair the natural   219| *1846:*discontent: so all *1849:*so,
all *1863:*discontent. Thus, all   221| *1846:*—Who, say the citizens, had *1865:*—
"Who," say the citizens, "had   224| *1846:*once they woke;—but <> had, they'll
*1865:*had," they'll *1868:*once awake;—but   225| *1846:*Doubtless *1865:*"Doubtless
226| *1846:*did—and *1863:*did; and   227| *1846:*why so <> be, *1863:*why, so <> be:
*1865:*be:" *1868:*be."   229| *1846:*devil when *1849:*devil, when   233| *1846:*sad—
say *1863:*sad: say *1868:*sad. Say   234| *1846:*no helping being *1865:*no help
from being   235| *1846:*me—love *1865:*me; love *1868:*me. Love   236| *1846:*

17

Some fancied self-denial on your part,
240 Which made you choose Luitolfo; so, excepting
From the wide condemnation of all here,
One woman. Well, the other dream may break!
If I knew any heart, as mine loved you,
Loved me, though in the vilest breast 'twere lodged,
245 I should, I think, be forced to love again:
Else there's no right nor reason in the world.
EULALIA "If you knew," say you,—but I did not know.
That's where you're blind, Chiappino!—a disease
Which if I may remove, I'll not repent
250 The listening to. You cannot, will not, see
How, place you but in every circumstance
Of us, you are just now indignant at,
You'd be as we.
CHIAPPINO   I should be? . . . that; again!
I, to my friend, my country and my love,
255 Be as Luitolfo and these Faentines?
EULALIA As we.
CHIAPPINO   Now, I'll say something to remember.
I trust in nature for the stable laws
Of beauty and utility.—Spring shall plant,
And Autumn garner to the end of time:
260 I trust in God—the right shall be the right
And other than the wrong, while he endures:
I trust in my own soul, that can perceive
The outward and the inward, nature's good
And God's: so, seeing these men and myself,

---

thought—no < > sea! 1863:sea. 1865:thought: no   239| 1846:part 1849:part,
240| 1846:so excepting 1849:so, excepting   242| 1846:woman! Well 1863:woman.
Well   244| 1846:tho' 1865:though 245| 1846:again— 1863:again: 246| 1846:
world! 1863:world.   247| 1846:know— 1863:know: 1868:know.   248| 1846:
blind, Chiappino! a 1849:blind, Chiappino!—a   250| 1846:to: you 1863:to. You
253| 1846:should be? . . that again! 1849:that, again! 1888:should be? . . . that;
again!   254| 1846:my Friend, my Country and my Love, 1868:my friend, my country
and my love,   256| 1846:CHIAPPINO Now I'll < > remember! 1849:CHIAPPINO Now,
I'll 1868:remember.   257| 1846:in Nature 1863:in nature   258| 1846:Of
Beauty and Utility—Spring 1863:Of beauty and utility 1888:utility.—Spring
260| 1846:the Right < > Right 1863:the right < > right   261| 1846:the
Wrong while He endures— 1849:the Wrong, while 1863:the wrong < > endures:
1868:while he   262| 1846:soul that 1849:soul, that   264| 1846:And God's—So—

265 Having a right to speak, thus do I speak.
I'll not curse—God bears with them, well may I—
But I—protest against their claiming me.
I simply say, if that's allowable,
I would not (broadly) do as they have done.
270 —God curse this townful of born slaves, bred slaves,
Branded into the blood and bone, slaves! Curse
Whoever loves, above his liberty,
House, land or life! and . . . [*A knocking without.*
　　　　　　　　　　　　　　—bless my hero-friend,
Luitolfo!
EULALIA How he knocks!
CHIAPPINO　　　　　　　The peril, lady!
275 "Chiappino, I have run a risk—a risk!
For when I prayed the Provost (he's my friend)
To grant you a week's respite of the sentence
That confiscates your goods, exiles yourself,
He shrugged his shoulder—I say, shrugged it! Yes,
280 And fright of that drove all else from my head.
Here's a good purse of *scudi:* off with you,
Lest of that shrug come what God only knows!
The *scudi*—friend, they're trash—no thanks, I beg!
Take the north gate,—for San Vitale's suburb,
285 Whose double taxes you appealed against,
In discomposure at your ill-success
Is apt to stone you: there, there—only go!
Beside, Eulalia here looks sleepily.
Shake . . . oh, you hurt me, so you squeeze my wrist!"

---

seeing *1863:*And God's: so, seeing　　265| *1846:*speak: *1863:*speak.—　*1888:*speak.
266| *1846:*curse . . . God <> them—well　*1868:*curse—God <> them, well
267| *1846:*me! *1863:*me.　　269| *1846:*not . . broadly . . . do <> done—　*1863:*done.
*1868:*not (broadly) do　　271| *1846:*bone slaves *1849:*bone, slaves　　272| *1846:*loved
*1868:*loves　　273| *1846:without . . . Bless *1863:without.*—bless　　274| *1846:*peril,
Lady! *1865:*peril, lady!　　275| *1846:*run a risk! My God! *1868:*run a risk—a risk!
276| *1846:*How when <> Provost—(he's my friend)—　*1868:*For when <> Provost
(he's my friend)　　277| *1846:*of his sentence *1868:*of the sentence　　278| *1846:*
goods, and exiles you, *1868:*goods, exiles yourself,　　279| *1846:*shoulder . . I
*1863:*shoulder—I　　281| *1846:*scudi—off with you! *1865:scudi:* off with you,
282| *1846:*come—what *1863:*come what　　283| *1846:*beg— *1863:*beg!
284| *1846:*the North <> suburb *1863:*the north *1868:*suburb,　　288| *1846:*

　—Is it not thus you'll speak, adventurous friend?

> [*As he opens the door,* LUITOLFO *rushes in, his garments disordered.*

EULALIA Luitolfo! Blood?

LUITOLFO　　　　　There's more—and more of it!
Eulalia—take the garment! No—you, friend!
You take it and the blood from me—you dare!

EULALIA Oh, who has hurt you? where's the wound?

CHIAPPINO　　　　　　　　　　　"Who," say you?

295　The man with many a touch of virtue yet!
The Provost's friend has proved too frank of speech,
And this comes of it. Miserable hound!
This comes of temporizing, as I said!
Here's fruit of your smooth speeches and soft looks!

300　Now see my way! As God lives, I go straight
To the palace and do justice, once for all!

LUITOLFO What says he?

CHIAPPINO　　　　　I'll do justice on him.

LUITOLFO　　　　　　　　　　Him?

CHIAPPINO The Provost.

LUITOLFO　　　　I've just killed him.

EULALIA　　　　　　　　　Oh, my God!

LUITOLFO My friend, they're on my trace; they'll have me—now!

305　They're round him, busy with him: soon they'll find
He's past their help, and then they'll be on me!
Chiappino, save Eulalia! I forget . . .
Were you not bound for . . .

CHIAPPINO　　　　　Lugo?

LUITOLFO　　　　　　　　Ah—yes—yes!
That was the point I prayed of him to change.

310　Well, go—be happy! Is Eulalia safe?

---

sleepily— *1863:*sleepily.　²⁹²| *1846:*garment . . no . . you *1868:*garment!
No—you　²⁹⁶| *1846:*speech *1863:*speech,　²⁹⁸| *1849:*temporising *1863:*
temporizing　²⁹⁹| *1846:*and fair looks! *1868:*and soft looks!　³⁰²| *1846:*him!
LUITOLFO *1863:*him. LUITOLFO　³⁰³| *1846:*him! EULALIA *1863:*him. EULALIA
³⁰⁴| *1846:*trace—they'll *1868:*trace; they'll　³⁰⁷| *1846:*Chiappino! save Eulalia . .
I forget . . *1849:*forget . . . *1865:*forgot . . . *1868:*Chiappino, save Eulalia! I
forget . . .　³⁰⁸| *1846:*bound . . for <> Lugo! LUITOLFO Ah—yes—yes— *1868:*
bound for <> Lugo? LUITOLFO Ah—yes—yes!　³¹⁰| *1846:*Well—go <> happy . . is

They're on me!

CHIAPPINO   'Tis through me they reach you, then!
Friend, seem the man you are! Lock arms—that's right!
Now tell me what you've done; explain how you
That still professed forbearance, still preached peace,
315 Could bring yourself . . .

LUITOLFO   What was peace for, Chiappino?
I tried peace: did that promise, when peace failed,
Strife should not follow? All my peaceful days
Were just the prelude to a day like this.
I cried "You call me 'friend': save my true friend!
320 Save him, or lose me!"

CHIAPPINO   But you never said
You meant to tell the Provost thus and thus.

LUITOLFO Why should I say it? What else did I mean?

CHIAPPINO Well? He persisted?

LUITOLFO   —"Would so order it
You should not trouble him too soon again."
325 I saw a meaning in his eye and lip;
I poured my heart's store of indignant words
Out on him: then—I know not! He retorted,
And I . . . some staff lay there to hand—I think
He bade his servants thrust me out—I struck . . .
330 Ah, they come! Fly you, save yourselves, you two!
The dead back-weight of the beheading axe!
The glowing trip-hook, thumbscrews and the gadge!

EULALIA They do come! Torches in the Place! Farewell,
Chiappino! You can work no good to us—

_1868_:Well, go <> happy! Is   ³¹²| _1846_:right.   _1865_:right!   ³¹⁶| _1846_:tried
peace—did that say that when <> failed   _1863_:did that promise, when <> failed,
_1868_:tried peace: did   ³¹⁹| _1846_:'friend'—save   _1868_:'friend': save   ³²¹| _1846:_
and thus!   _1868_:and thus.   ³²³| _1846_:LUITOLFO . . Would   _1863_:LUITOLFO
"Would   _1868_:LUITOLFO—"Would   ³²⁴| _1846_:again—   _1863_:again."
³²⁵| _1846_:lip—   _1863_:lip;   ³²⁷| _1846_:him—then,—I <> not.—He retorted—
_1849_:then—I   _1863_:him: then <> not! He retorted,   ³²⁸| _1846_:And I . . some
_1888_:And I . . . some   ³²⁹| _1846_:struck—   _1863_:struck . . .   ³³⁰| _1846_: . .
Ah   _1863_:Ah   ³³³| _1846_:the Place! Farewell—   _1863_:the Place! Farewell,

335 Much to yourself; believe not, all the world
Must needs be cursed henceforth!
CHIAPPINO   And you?
EULALIA   I stay.
CHIAPPINO Ha, ha! Now, listen! I am master here!
This was my coarse disguise; this paper shows
My path of flight and place of refuge—see—
340 Lugo, Argenta, past San Nicolo,
Ferrara, then to Venice and all's safe!
Put on the cloak! His people have to fetch
A compass round about. There's time enough
Ere they can reach us, so you straightway make
345 For Lugo . . . nay, he hears not! On with it—
The cloak, Luitolfo, do you hear me? See—
He obeys he knows not how. Then, if I must—
Answer me! Do you know the Lugo gate?
EULALIA The north-west gate, over the bridge?
LUITOLFO   I know.
350 CHIAPPINO Well, there—you are not frightened? all my route
Is traced in that: at Venice you escape
Their power. Eulalia, I am master here!

      [*Shouts from without. He pushes out* LUITOLFO, *who complies*
        mechanically.

In time! Nay, help me with him—so! He's gone.
EULALIA What have you done? On you, perchance, all know
355 The Provost's hater, will men's vengeance fall
As our accomplice.
CHIAPPINO   Mere accomplice? See!

                  [*Putting on* LUITOLFO's *vest.*

Now, lady, am I true to my profession,

335| *1846:*not all *1849:*not, all   337| *1846:*Ha, ha! now listen *1849:*Ha, ha! Now,
listen   338| *1846:*disguise—this *1863:*disguise; this   340| *1846:*Lugo—
Argenta—past San Nicolo— *1865:*Lugo, Argenta, past San Nicolo,   343| *1846:*
about.—There's *1863:*about. There's   344| *1846:*us—so *1865:*us, so
345| *1846:*For Lugo . . Nay *1865:*For Lugo . . nay *1888:*For Lugo . . . nay
347| *1846:*how.—Then <> must . . . *1863:*how. Then *1868:*must—   349| *1846:*
bridge! LUITOLFO I know! *1868:*bridge? LUITOLFO I know.   350| *1846:*frightened?
All *1863:*frightened? all   351| *1846:*that—at Venice you'll escape *1863:*that: at
*1868:*at Venice you escape   352| *1846:*power! Eulalia—I *1863:*power. Eulalia, I
353| *1846:*time! nay <> him—So!—he's *1865:*him—so! He's *1868:*time! Nay
354| *1846:*perchance all *1849:*perchance, all   356| *1846:*accomplice . . CHIAPPINO
*1863:*accomplice. CHIAPPINO   357| *1846:*Now, Lady *1865:*Now, lady

Or one of these?

EULALIA   You take Luitolfo's place?

CHIAPPINO Die for him.

EULALIA   Well done! [*Shouts increase.*

CHIAPPINO   How the people tarry!
360 I can't be silent; I must speak: or sing—
How natural to sing now!

EULALIA   Hush and pray!
We are to die; but even I perceive
'Tis not a very hard thing so to die.
My cousin of the pale-blue tearful eyes,
365 Poor Cesca, suffers more from one day's life
With the stern husband; Tisbe's heart goes forth
Each evening after that wild son of hers,
To track his thoughtless footstep through the streets:
How easy for them both to die like this!
370 I am not sure that I could live as they.

CHIAPPINO Here they come, crowds! They pass the gate? Yes!—No!—
One torch is in the courtyard. Here flock all.

EULALIA At least Luitolfo has escaped. What cries!

CHIAPPINO If they would drag one to the market-place,
375 One might speak there!

EULALIA   List, list!

CHIAPPINO   They mount the steps.

Enter the POPULACE.

CHIAPPINO I killed the Provost!

THE POPULACE [*speaking together.*] 'Twas Chiappino, friends!
Our saviour! The best man at last as first!
He who first made us feel what chains we wore,
He also strikes the blow that shatters them,

359| *1846:*him! EULALIA *1863:*him. EULALIA   360| *1846:*silent . . I <> speak . .
or *1865:*silent . . . I *1868:*silent; I <> speak: or   362| *1846:*die—but *1863:*die;
but   363| *1846:*die— *1863:*die.   368| *1846:*thro' the streets— *1863:*through
the streets: 372| *1846:*court-yard <> all! *1863:*all. *1868:*courtyard   373| *1846:*
escaped!—What *1863:*escaped. What   374| *1846:*market-place *1849:*market-
place,   375| *1846:*steps! *1863:*list! . . . <> steps. *1865:*list! They
377| *1846:*saviour.—The *1868:*saviour! The   378| *1846:*us see what *1868:*us feel

³⁸⁰ He at last saves us—our best citizen!
    —Oh, have you only courage to speak now?
    My eldest son was christened a year since
    "Cino" to keep Chiappino's name in mind—
    Cino, for shortness merely, you observe!
³⁸⁵ The city's in our hands. The guards are fled.
    Do you, the cause of all, come down—come up—
    Come out to counsel us, our chief, our king,
    Whate'er rewards you! Choose your own reward!
    The peril over, its reward begins!
³⁹⁰ Come and harangue us in the market-place!
    EULALIA Chiappino?
    CHIAPPINO   Yes—I understand your eyes!
    You think I should have promptlier disowned
    This deed with its strange unforeseen success,
    In favour of Luitolfo. But the peril,
³⁹⁵ So far from ended, hardly seems begun.
    To-morrow, rather, when a calm succeeds,
    We easily shall make him full amends:
    And meantime—if we save them as they pray,
    And justify the deed by its effects?
⁴⁰⁰ EULALIA You would, for worlds, you had denied at once.
    CHIAPPINO I know my own intention, be assured!
    All's well. Precede us, fellow-citizens!

---

what   ³⁸²| *1846:*since. *1849:*since   ³⁸⁵| *1846:*The City's <> hands.—The
<> fled—   *1863:*The city's <> fled; *1865:*hands. The <> fled.   ³⁸⁶| *1846:*down—
come down—   *1868:*down—come up—   ³⁸⁷| *1846:*Come forth to   *1868:*Come out
to   ³⁹¹| *1846:*Chiappino! CHIAPPINO Yes . . I   *1868:*Chiappino? CHIAPPINO Yes—I
³⁹³| *1846:*success *1863:*success,   ³⁹⁴| *1846:*of Luitolfo—but   *1868:*of Luitolfo. But
³⁹⁵| *1846:*begun! *1863:*begun.   ³⁹⁸| *1846:*meantime . . if *1865:*meantime . . . if
*1868:*meantime—if   ⁴⁰⁰| *1846:*once! *1863:*once.   ⁴⁰²| *1846:*well! Precede
*1868:*well. Precede

24

ACT II.

SCENE—*The Market-place.*

LUITOLFO *in disguise mingling with the* POPULACE *assembled opposite the* PROVOST'S *Palace.*

1ST BYSTANDER [*to* LUITOLFO.] You, a friend of Luitolfo's? Then, your friend is vanished,—in all probability killed on the night that his patron the tyrannical Provost was loyally suppressed here, exactly a month ago, by our illustrious fellow-citizen, thrice-noble saviour, and
5   new Provost that is like to be, this very morning,—Chiappino!

LUITOLFO He the new Provost?

2ND BYSTANDER Up those steps will he go, and beneath yonder pillar stand, while Ogniben, the Pope's Legate from Ravenna, reads the new dignitary's title to the people, according to established custom: for
10   which reason, there is the assemblage you inquire about.

LUITOLFO Chiappino—the late Provost's successor? Impossible! But tell me of that presently. What I would know first of all is, wherefore Luitolfo must so necessarily have been killed on that memorable night?

3RD BYSTANDER You were Luitolfo's friend? So was I. Never, if you will
15   credit me, did there exist so poor-spirited a milksop. He, with all the opportunities in the world, furnished by daily converse with our oppressor, would not stir a finger to help us: and, when Chiappino rose in

---

§ variant listings: see Editorial Notes §
Part title| *1846:*PART II. *1868:*ACT II.   Stage directions| *1846: The Market-place*
*1888:*SCENE—*The Market-place.*   1| *1846:*You a < > Then your   *1849:*You, a < >
Luitolfo's! Then, your *1863:*Luitolfo's? Then   5| *1846:*be this *1849:*be, this
6| *1846:*He *1865:*He   9| *1846:*established usage.—For *1863:*usage: for *1868:*
established custom: for   10| *1846:*reason there *1849:*reason, there   11| *1846:*the
old Provost's *1868:*the late Provost's   12| *1846:*presently—What *1863:*presently.
What   14| *1846:*was I—Never *1863:*was I. Never   15| *1846:*milk-sop! He
*1868:*milk-sop. He *1888:*milksop   17| *1846:*us: so when *1863:*us: and, when

solitary majesty and . . . how does one go on saying? . . . dealt the godlike blow,—this Luitolfo, not unreasonably fearing the indignation
20 of an aroused and liberated people, fled precipitately. He may have got trodden to death in the press at the south-east gate, when the Provost's guards fled through it to Ravenna, with their wounded master,—if he did not rather hang himself under some hedge.

LUITOLFO Or why not simply have lain perdue in some quiet cor-
25 ner,—such as San Cassiano, where his estate was,—receiving daily intelligence from some sure friend, meanwhile, as to the turn matters were taking here—how, for instance, the Provost was not dead, after all, only wounded—or, as to-day's news would seem to prove, how Chiappino was not Brutus the Elder, after all, only the new Provost—and thus
30 Luitolfo be enabled to watch a favourable opportunity for returning? Might it not have been so?

3RD BYSTANDER Why, he may have taken that care of himself, certainly, for he came of a cautious stock. I'll tell you how his uncle, just such another gingerly treader on tiptoes with finger on lip,—how he met his
35 death in the great plague-year: *dico vobis!* Hearing that the seventeenth house in a certain street was infected, he calculates to pass it in safety by taking plentiful breath, say, when he shall arrive at the eleventh house; then scouring by, holding that breath, till he be got so far on the other side as number twenty-three, and thus elude the danger.—And so did he
40 begin; but, as he arrived at thirteen, we will say,—thinking to improve on his precaution by putting up a little prayer to St. Nepomucene of Prague, this exhausted so much of his lungs' reserve, that at sixteen it was clean spent,—consequently at the fatal seventeen he inhaled with a vigour and persistence enough to suck you any latent venom out of the
45 heart of a stone—Ha, ha!

LUITOLFO [*aside.*] (If I had not lent that man the money he wanted last

---

18| *1846:*and . . . . . how <> saying? . . dealt *1863:*and . . . how *1888:*saying? . . .
dealt   20| *1846:*precipitately: he *1863:*precipitately. He   21| *1846:*gate when
*1849:*gate, when   22| *1846:*thro'<>Ravenna with *1849:*Ravenna, with *1863:*
through   24| *1846:perdue 1849:*perdue   27| *1846:*here . . . how <> dead
after *1863:*here—how *1868:*dead, after   28| *1846:*wounded . . or *1863:*
wounded—or   29| *1846:*new Provost . . and *1863:*new Provost—and
30| *1846:*returning— *1868:*returning?   31| *1846:*might *1868:*Might   33| *1846:*
stock.—I'll *1863:*stock. I'll   40| *1846:*begin—but *1863:*begin; but   45| *1865:*
stone. Ha *1868:*stone—Ha   46| *1865:*LUITOLFO [aside.] If *1868:*LUITOLFO [aside.] (If

spring, I should fear this bitterness was attributable to me.) Luitolfo is dead then, one may conclude?

3RD BYSTANDER Why, he had a house here, and a woman to whom he was affianced; and as they both pass naturally to the new Provost, his friend and heir . . .

LUITOLFO Ah, I suspected you of imposing on me with your pleasantry! I know Chiappino better.

1ST BYSTANDER (Our friend has the bile! After all, I do not dislike finding somebody vary a little this general gape of admiration at Chiappino's glorious qualities.) Pray, how much may you know of what has taken place in Faenza since that memorable night?

LUITOLFO It is most to the purpose, that I know Chiappino to have been by profession a hater of that very office of Provost, you now charge him with proposing to accept.

1ST BYSTANDER Sir, I'll tell you. That night was indeed memorable. Up we rose, a mass of us, men, women, children; out fled the guards with the body of the tyrant; we were to defy the world: but, next grey morning, "What will Rome say?" began everybody. You know we are governed by Ravenna, which is governed by Rome. And quietly into the town, by the Ravenna road, comes on muleback a portly personage, Ogniben by name, with the quality of Pontifical Legate; trots briskly through the streets humming a *"Cur fremuere gentes,"* and makes directly for the Provost's Palace—there it faces you. "One Messer Chiappino is your leader? I have known three-and-twenty leaders of revolts!" (laughing gently to himself)—"Give me the help of your arm from my mule to yonder steps under the pillar—So! And now, my revolters and good friends, what do you want? The guards burst into Ravenna last night bearing your wounded Provost; and, having had a little talk with him, I

47| *1846:*me). Luitolfo   *1863:*me.) Luitolfo   *1865:*me. Luitolfo   *1868:*me.) Luitolfo
48| *1846:*conclude!   *1863:*conclude?   52| *1846:*pleasantry—   *1863:*pleasantry!
53| *1846:*better!   *1863:*better.   54| *1846:*bile! after   *1868:*bile! After   56| *1846:*
qualities—.) Pray how   *1849:*qualities—.) Pray, how   *1863:*qualities.) Pray   58| *1846:*
purpose that   *1849:*purpose, that   61| *1846:*memorable—up   *1863:*memorable; up
*1868:*memorable. Up   62| *1846:*children—out   *1868:*children; out   63| *1846:*
tyrant—we   *1868:*tyrant; we   64| *1846:*"what<>say," began everybody—(you   *1849:*
"What   *1863:*say?" began   *1868:*everybody. You   65| *1846:*by Rome). And<>town
by   *1849:*town, by   *1868:*by Rome. And   66| *1846:*road comes   *1849:*road, comes
67| *1846:*of Pontifical Legate—trots<>thro'   *1863:*through   *1868:*of Pontifical Legate;
trots   *1888:*with name, the quality   DC:name, with the quality   *1889:*name, with the
quality   68| *1846:fremuère*   *1865:fremuere*   69| *1846:*you—"One   *1863:*you.
"One   70| *1846:*three and-twenty   *1849:*three-and-twenty   74| *1846:*wounded

27

take on myself to come and try appease the disorderliness, before Rome, hearing of it, resort to another method: 'tis I come, and not another, from a certain love I confess to, of composing differences. So, do you understand, you are about to experience this unheard-of tyranny from me, that there shall be no heading nor hanging, no confiscation nor exile: I insist on your simply pleasing yourselves. And now, pray, what does please you? To live without any government at all? Or having decided for one, to see its minister murdered by the first of your body that chooses to find himself wronged, or disposed for reverting to first principles and a justice anterior to all institutions,—and so will you carry matters, that the rest of the world must at length unite and put down such a den of wild beasts? As for vengeance on what has just taken place,—once for all, the wounded man assures me he cannot conjecture who struck him; and this so earnestly, that one may be sure he knows perfectly well what intimate acquaintance could find admission to speak with him late last evening. I come not for vengeance therefore, but from pure curiosity to hear what you will do next." And thus he ran on, on, easily and volubly, till he seemed to arrive quite naturally at the praise of law, order, and paternal government by somebody from rather a distance. All our citizens were in the snare, and about to be friends with so congenial an adviser; but that Chiappino suddenly stood forth, spoke out indignantly, and set things right again.

LUITOLFO Do you see? I recognize him there!

3RD BYSTANDER Ay but, mark you, at the end of Chiappino's longest period in praise of a pure republic,—"And by whom do I desire such a government should be administered, perhaps, but by one like yourself?"—returns the Legate: thereupon speaking for a quarter of an hour

---

Provost—and *1865:*wounded Provost; and ⁷⁶| *1846:*resorts<>method; 'tis *1849:* resort *1863:*method: 'tis ⁸⁰| *1846:*exile,—I<>yourselves,—and now pray what *1849:*now, pray, what *1868:*exile: I<>yourselves. And ⁸⁴| *1846:*Justice *1863:* justice ⁸⁸| *1846:*him—and *1868:*him; and ⁹⁰| *1846:*him so late that evening—I *1863:*him late last evening. I ⁹¹⁻⁹²| *1846:*next."—And thus ran on,/easily *1849:* thus he ran on,/easily *1868:*next." And<>ran on,/on, easily ⁹³| *1846:* of Law, Order and Paternal Government *1863:*of law, order, and paternal government ⁹⁴| *1846:*distance:all *1863:*distance. All ⁹⁶| *1846:*indignantly and<>again . . . *1849:* indignantly, and *1863:*again. ⁹⁷| *1846:*see?—I recognise *1863:*see? I *1888:*recognize ⁹⁸| *1846:*3RD BYSTANDER Ay, but mark *1865:*3RD BYSTANDER Ay but, mark ⁹⁹| *1846:* pure Republic . . "And *1849:*pure Republic. "And *1863:*pure republic,—"And ¹⁰¹| *1846:*the Legate—thereupon speaking, for *1863:*the Legate: thereupon speaking for

together, on the natural and only legitimate government by the best and wisest. And it should seem there was soon discovered to be no such vast discrepancy at bottom between this and Chiappino's theory, place but
105 each in its proper light. "Oh, are you there?" quoth Chiappino: "Ay, in that, I agree," returns Chiappino: and so on.

LUITOLFO But did Chiappino cede at once to this?

1ST BYSTANDER Why, not altogether at once. For instance, he said that the difference between him and all his fellows was, that they seemed all
110 wishing to be kings in one or another way,—"whereas what right," asked he, "has any man to wish to be superior to another?"—whereat, "Ah, sir," answers the Legate, "this is the death of me, so often as I expect something is really going to be revealed to us by you clearer-seers, deeper-thinkers—this—that your right-hand (to speak by a figure)
115 should be found taking up the weapon it displayed so ostentatiously, not to destroy any dragon in our path, as was prophesied, but simply to cut off its own fellow left-hand: yourself set about attacking yourself. For see now! Here are you who, I make sure, glory exceedingly in knowing the noble nature of the soul, its divine impulses, and so forth; and
120 with such a knowledge you stand, as it were, armed to encounter the natural doubts and fears as to that same inherent nobility, which are apt to waylay us, the weaker ones, in the road of life. And when we look eagerly to see them fall before you, lo, round you wheel, only the left-hand gets the blow; one proof of the soul's nobility destroys simply
125 another proof, quite as good, of the same, for you are found delivering an opinion like this! Why, what is this perpetual yearning to exceed, to subdue, to be better than, and a king over, one's fellows,—all that you so disclaim,—but the very tendency yourself are most proud of, and under another form, would oppose to it,—only in a lower stage of manifesta-
130 tion? You don't want to be vulgarly superior to your fellows after their poor fashion—to have me hold solemnly up your gown's tail, or hand you an express of the last importance from the Pope, with all these bystanders noticing how unconcerned you look the while: but neither

---

102| *1846:*Best *1863:*best   103| *1846:*Wisest—and *1863:*wisest. And   105| *1846:* light—"Oh<>Chiappino:—"In *1863:*light. "Oh *1868:*Chiappino: "Ay, in   106| *1846:*Chiappino, and *1868:*Chiappino: and   108| *1846:*once—for *1863:*once. For   110| *1846:*way,—whereas<>right, *1863:*way,—"whereas<>right,"   111| *1846:*he, has<>another?—whereat, *1863:*he, "has<>another?"—whereat,   112| *1846:*"Ah Sir *1863:*"Ah, Sir *1865:*"Ah sir *1868:*"Ah, sir   114| *1846:*right-hand, (to *1849:* right-hand (to   117| *1846:*left-hand—yourself set<>attacking yourself— *1863:*left-hand: yourself set *1868:*attacking yourself.   118| *1846:*for *1868:*For   121| *1846:* nobility, that are *1888:*nobility, which are   122| *1846:*us the weaker ones in <> Life,—and *1849:*us, the weaker ones, in *1863:*of life. And   123-24| *1846:*left hand *1888:*left-hand   125| *1846:*same,—you *1868:*same, for you   133| *1846:*while—but

does our gaping friend, the burgess yonder, want the other kind of
135   kingship, that consists in understanding better than his fellows this and
similar points of human nature, nor to roll under his tongue this
sweeter morsel still,—the feeling that, through immense philosophy, he
does *not* feel, he rather thinks, above you and me!" And so chatting, they
glided off arm-in-arm.

140   LUITOLFO And the result is . . .

1ST BYSTANDER Why that, a month having gone by, the indomitable
Chiappino, marrying as he will Luitolfo's love—at all events succeed-
ing to Luitolfo's wealth—becomes the first inhabitant of Faenza, and a
proper aspirant to the Provostship; which we assemble here to see
145   conferred on him this morning. The Legate's Guard to clear the way!
He will follow presently.

LUITOLFO [*withdrawing a little.*] I understand the drift of Eulalia's
communications less than ever. Yet she surely said, in so many words,
that Chiappino was in urgent danger: wherefore, disregarding her in-
150   junction to continue in my retreat and await the result of—what she
called, some experiment yet in process—I hastened here without her
leave or knowledge: how could I else? But if this they say be true—if it
were for such a purpose, she and Chiappino kept me away . . . Oh, no,
no! I must confront him and her before I believe this of them. And at the
155   word, see!

Enter CHIAPPINO *and* EULALIA.

EULALIA We part here, then? The change in your principles would seem
to be complete.

CHIAPPINO Now, why refuse to see that in my present course I change no

---

*1863:*while: but   136| *1846:*under the tongue *1863:*under his tongue   137|
*1846:*still, the < > thro' *1863:*still,—the < > through   138| *1846:*me!"—And so chatting
they *1849:*chatting, they *1863:*me!" And   139| *1846:*arm in arm. *1888:*arm-in-arm.
140| *1846:*is . . *1888:*is . . .   141| *1846:*1ST BYSTANDER Why, that a *1865:*1ST
BYSTANDER Why that, a   143| *1846:*Luitolfo's goods,—becomes *1868:*Luitolfo's
wealth—becomes   144| *1846:*the Provostship—which *1863:*the Provostship; which
*1868:*the provostship *1888:*the Provostship   146| *1846:*presently! *1863:*presently.
148| *1846:*ever—yet *1863:*ever. Yet   149-50| *1846:*danger,—wherefore < > injunctions
< > wait < > of, what *1863:*danger: wherefore < > injunction < > await *1888:*of—what
152| *1846:*knowledge—what could I else?—Yet if what they < > true . . if *1863:*
else?—But if < > true—if *1865:*else? But *1868:*knowledge: what < > if this they *1888:*
knowledge: how could   154| *1846:*them—and *1863:*them. And   157| *1846:*
complete! *1863:*complete.   158| *1865:*CHIAPPINO Now why *1868:*CHIAPPINO Now,

principles, only re-adapt them and more adroitly? I had despaired of,
what you may call the material instrumentality of life; of ever being able
to rightly operate on mankind through such a deranged machinery as
the existing modes of government: but now, if I suddenly discover how
to inform these perverted institutions with fresh purpose, bring the
functionary limbs once more into immediate communication with, and
subjection to, the soul I am about to bestow on them—do you see? Why
should one desire to invent, as long as it remains possible to renew and
transform? When all further hope of the old organization shall be
extinct, then, I grant you, it may be time to try and create another.

EULALIA And there being discoverable some hope yet in the hitherto
much-abused old system of absolute government by a Provost here, you
mean to take your time about endeavouring to realize those visions of a
perfect State, we once heard of?

CHIAPPINO Say, I would fain realize my conception of a palace, for
instance, and that there is, abstractedly, but a single way of erecting one
perfectly. Here, in the market-place is my allotted building-ground;
here I stand without a stone to lay, or a labourer to help me,—stand, too,
during a short day of life, close on which the night comes. On the other
hand, circumstances suddenly offer me (turn and see it!) the old Pro-
vost's house to experiment upon—ruinous, if you please, wrongly con-
structed at the beginning, and ready to tumble now. But materials
abound, a crowd of workmen offer their services; here, exists yet a Hall
of Audience of originally noble proportions, there a Guest-chamber of
symmetrical design enough: and I may restore, enlarge, abolish or unite
these to heart's content. Ought I not make the best of such an oppor-
tunity, rather than continue to gaze disconsolately with folded arms on
the flat pavement here, while the sun goes slowly down, never to rise
again? Since you cannot understand this nor me, it is better we should
part as you desire.

---

why   159| *1846:*of *1863:*of,   160| *1846:*Life *1863:*life   161| *1846:*thro'
*1863:*through   162| *1846:*government—but *1863:*government: but   165| *1846:*
to the <>them . . . do *1863:*to, the <>them—do   166| *1846:*invent, so long
*1863:*invent, as long   167| *1849:*organisation *1863:*organization   168| *1846:*it
will be *1863:*it may be   171| *1849:*realise *1863:*realize   173| *1846:*Palace *1849:*
realise *1863:*realize *1865:*palace   175| *1846:*perfectly; here, in *1863:*perfectly. Here,
in   178| *1846:*me . . turn<>it . . the *1868:*me (turn<>it) the *1888:*it!) the
179| *1846:*House *1865:*house   180| *1846:*now—but *1863:*now. But   182| *1846:*
there, a *1868:*there a   183| *1846:*enough; and *1863:*enough: and   184-85| *1846:*
content—ought I not rather make<>opportunity, than *1863:*content. Ought *1865:*not
make<>opportunity, rather than   187| *1846:*again? But you<>me: it *1863:*again?

EULALIA So, the love breaks away too!

190 CHIAPPINO No, rather my soul's capacity for love widens—needs more than one object to content it,—and, being better instructed, will not persist in seeing all the component parts of love in what is only a single part,—nor in finding that so many and so various loves are all united in the love of a woman,—manifold uses in one instrument, as the savage

195 has his sword, staff, sceptre and idol, all in one club-stick. Love is a very compound thing. The intellectual part of my love I shall give to men, the mighty dead or the illustrious living; and determine to call a mere sensual instinct by as few fine names as possible. What do I lose?

EULALIA Nay, I only think, what do I lose? and, one more word—which

200 shall complete my instruction—does friendship go too? What of Luitolfo, the author of your present prosperity?

CHIAPPINO How the author?

EULALIA That blow now called yours . . .

CHIAPPINO Struck without principle or purpose, as by a blind natural

205 operation: yet to which all my thought and life directly and advisedly tended. I would have struck it, and could not: he would have done his utmost to avoid striking it, yet did so. I dispute his right to that deed of mine—a final action with him, from the first effect of which he fled away,—a mere first step with me, on which I base a whole mighty

210 superstructure of good to follow. Could he get good from it?

EULALIA So we profess, so we perform!

Enter OGNIBEN. EULALIA *stands apart.*

OGNIBEN I have seen three-and-twenty leaders of revolts. By your leave, sir! Perform? What does the lady say of performing?

Since you<>me, it   189| *1846:*EULALIA So the   *1863:*EULALIA So, the   193|
*1846:*finding the so many<> loves, united   *1868:*finding that so many<>loves, are all
united   *1888:*loves are   194| *1846:*woman,—finding all uses   *1863:*woman,—manifold
uses   195| *1846:*sword, sceptre   *1888:*sword, staff, sceptre   196| *1846:*thing. I shall
give the intellectual part of my love to Men,   *1865:*thing. The intellectual part of my love
I shall give to men,   197| *1846:*dead, or illustrious   *1868:*dead or the illustrious
199| *1846:*do I love! and   *1849:*do I lose! and   *1863:*lose? and   200| *1846:*does
Friendship go too?—What of   *1863:*does friendship go too? What of   201| *1846:*
Luitolfo—the   *1863:*Luitolfo, the   202| *1846:*author?—   *1888:*author?   205| *1846:*
operation—and to<>thoughts   *1863:*operation—yet to<>thought   *1868:*operation:yet
206| *1846:*not. He   *1865:*not: he   209| *1846:*away—a mere   *1868:*away,—a mere
212| *1846:*revolts!—By   *1868:*revolts! By   *1888:*revolts. By   213| *1846:*Sir <>

32

CHIAPPINO Only the trite saying, that we must not trust profession, only
performance.

OGNIBEN She'll not say that, sir, when she knows you longer; you'll
instruct her better. Ever judge of men by their professions! For though
the bright moment of promising is but a moment and cannot be pro-
longed, yet, if sincere in its moment's extravagant goodness, why, trust
it and know the man by it, I say—not by his performance; which is half
the world's work, interfere as the world needs must, with its accidents
and circumstances: the profession was purely the man's own. I judge
people by what they might be,—not are, nor will be.

CHIAPPINO But have there not been found, too, performing natures, not
merely promising?

OGNIBEN Plenty. Little Bindo of our town, for instance, promised his
friend, great ugly Masaccio, once, "I will repay you!"—for a favour done
him. So, when his father came to die, and Bindo succeeded to the
inheritance, he sends straightway for Masaccio and shares all with
him—gives him half the land, half the money, half the kegs of wine in
the cellar. "Good," say you: and it is good. But had little Bindo found
himself possessor of all this wealth some five years before—on the happy
night when Masaccio procured him that interview in the garden with
his pretty cousin Lisa—instead of being the beggar he then was,—I am
bound to believe that in the warm moment of promise he would have
given away all the wine-kegs and all the money and all the land, and
only reserved to himself some hut on a hill-top hard by, whence he
might spend his life in looking and seeing his friend enjoy himself: he
meant fully that much, but the world interfered.—To our business! Did
I understand you just now within-doors? You are not going to marry
your old friend's love, after all?

Performing?   *1865:*sir < > performing?   214| *1846:*Profession   *1865:*profession
215| *1846:*Performance.   *1865:*performance.   216| *1846:*Sir   *1865:*sir   217| *1846:*
tho'   *1863:*though   220| *1846:*performance—which   *1865:*performance; which
221| *1846:*must with   *1863:*must, with   222| *1846:*circumstances,—the profession < >
own! I   *1863:*own. I   *1865:*circumstances: the profession   226| *1846:*OGNIBEN Plenty:
little   *1863:*OGNIBEN Plenty. Little   227| *1846:*you"!—for   *1849:*you!"—for   228|
*1846:*him: so when < > die and   *1849:*die, and   *1863:*so when   *1868:*him. So   230|
*1846:*him; gives   *1863:*him—gives   231| *1846:*you—and < > good: but   *1863:*is good.
But   *1865:*you: and   236| *1846:*wine-kegs, and all the money, and all   *1868:*wine-kegs
and all the money and all   239| *1846:*interfered!—To our business—did   *1863:*

CHIAPPINO I must have a woman that can sympathize with, and appreciate me, I told you.

OGNIBEN Oh, I remember! you, the greater nature, needs must have a
245 lesser one (—avowedly lesser—contest with you on that score would never do)—such a nature must comprehend you, as the phrase is, accompany and testify of your greatness from point to point onward. Why, that were being not merely as great as yourself, but greater considerably! Meantime, might not the more bounded nature as reasonably
250 count on your appreciation of it, rather?—on your keeping close by it, so far as you both go together, and then going on by yourself as far as you please? Thus God serves us.

CHIAPPINO And yet a woman that could understand the whole of me, to whom I could reveal alike the strength and the weakness—
255 OGNIBEN Ah, my friend, wish for nothing so foolish! Worship your love, give her the best of you to see; be to her like the western lands (they bring us such strange news of) to the Spanish Court; send her only your lumps of gold, fans of feathers, your spirit-like birds, and fruits and gems! So shall you, what is unseen of you, be supposed altogether a
260 paradise by her,—as these western lands by Spain: though I warrant there is filth, red baboons, ugly reptiles and squalor enough, which they bring Spain as few samples of as possible. Do you want your mistress to respect your body generally? Offer her your mouth to kiss: don't strip off your boot and put your foot to her lips! You understand my humour by
265 this time? I help men to carry out their own principles: if they please to say two and two make five, I assent, so they will but go on and say, four and four make ten.

CHIAPPINO But these are my private affairs; what I desire you to occupy yourself about, is my public appearance presently: for when the people
270 hear that I am appointed Provost, though you and I may thoroughly discern—and easily, too—the right principle at bottom of such a move-

---

interfered.—To our business! Did   242| *1846:*with and   *1849:*with, and   246|
*1846:*do!)—such   *1868:*do)—such   247| *1846:*onward: *1863:*onward.   248|*1846:*why
*1863:*Why   252| *1846:*please? So God $<>$ us!   *1863:*please? Thus God   *1865:*us
255| *1865:*Ah my   *1888:*Ah, my   256| *1846:*Love$<>$Western Lands   *1863:*western lands
*1868:*love   257| *1846:*the Spanish Court—send   *1868:*the Spanish Court;send   259|
*1846:*gems—so   *1868:*gems! So   260| *1846:*Paradise$<>$Western$<>$Spain—tho'   *1863:*
these western$<>$though   *1868:*paradise$<>$Spain: though   263| *1846:*kiss—don't
*1863:*kiss:don't   265| *1846:*principle   *1863:*principles   266| *1846:*assent, if they$<>$
on and say four   *1849:*on and say, four   *1863:*assent, so they   267| *1846:*ten!   *1865:*ten.
268| *1846:*affairs—what   *1863:*affairs; what   270| *1846:*tho'   *1863:*though   271|

ment, and how my republicanism remains thoroughly unaltered, only
takes a form of expression hitherto commonly judged (and heretofore by
myself) incompatible with its existence,—when thus I reconcile myself
275   to an old form of government instead of proposing a new one . . .

OGNIBEN Why, you must deal with people broadly. Begin at a distance
from this matter and say,—New truths, old truths! sirs, there is nothing
new possible to be revealed to us in the moral world; we know all we
shall ever know: and it is for simply reminding us, by their various
280   respective expedients, how we do know this and the other matter, that
men get called prophets, poets and the like. A philosopher's life is spent
in discovering that, of the half-dozen truths he knew when a child, such
an one is a lie, as the world states it in set terms; and then, after a weary
lapse of years, and plenty of hard-thinking, it becomes a truth again
285   after all, as he happens to newly consider it and view it in a different
relation with the others: and so he restates it, to the confusion of
somebody else in good time. As for adding to the original stock of
truths,—impossible! Thus, you see the expression of them is the grand
business:—you have got a truth in your head about the right way of
290   governing people, and you took a mode of expressing it which now you
confess to be imperfect. But what then? There is truth in falsehood,
falsehood in truth. No man ever told one great truth, that I know,
without the help of a good dozen of lies at least, generally unconscious
ones. And as when a child comes in breathlessly and relates a strange
295   story, you try to conjecture from the very falsities in it, what the reality
was,—do not conclude that he saw nothing in the sky, because he
assuredly did not see a flying horse there as he says,—so, through the
contradictory expression, do you see, men should look painfully for,
and trust to arrive eventually at, what you call the true principle at bot-
300   tom. Ah, what an answer is there! to what will it not prove applica-
ble?—"Contradictions? Of course there were," say you!

*1846:*easily too   *1849:*easily, too   273| *1846:*judged . . and   *1865:*judged (and
274| *1846:*myself . . incompatible<>existence . . when   *1863:*existence,—when   *1865:*
myself) incompatible   277| *1846:*say,—new<>old truths! why there   *1849:*why, there
*1863:*old truths! sirs, there   *1865:*say,—New   278| *1846:*world—we know   *1868:*world;
we know   279| *1846:*know, and   *1868:*know: and   280| *1849:*do   *1868:*do
281| *1846:*like:a   *1849:*like. A   284| *1846:*hard thinking   *1863:*hard-thinking
286| *1846:*others—and   *1863:*others: and   287| *1846:*time.—As   *1863:*time. As   288|
*1846:*impossible!—So you   *1863:*impossible! Thus, you   290| *1846:*it—which   *1863:*it
which   291| *1846:*imperfect—but<>Truth in Falsehood,   *1863:*truth in falsehood,
*1868:*imperfect. But   292| *1846:*Falsehood in Truth.—No   *1863:*falsehood in truth.
No   294| *1846:*ones: and as   *1868:*ones. And as   297| *1846:*thro'   *1863:*through
300-301| *1846:*applicable!—"Contradictions?"—Of<>were, say you!   *1865:*you?   *1868:*

CHIAPPINO Still, the world at large may call it inconsistency, and what shall I urge in reply?

OGNIBEN Why, look you, when they tax you with tergiversation or duplicity, you may answer—you begin to perceive that, when all's done and said, both great parties in the State, the advocators of change in the present system of things, and the opponents of it, patriot and anti-patriot, are found working together for the common good; and that in the midst of their efforts for and against its progress, the world somehow or other still advances: to which result they contribute in equal proportions, those who spend their life in pushing it onward, as those who give theirs to the business of pulling it back. Now, if you found the world stand still between the opposite forces, and were glad, I should conceive you: but it steadily advances, you rejoice to see! By the side of such a rejoicer, the man who only winks as he keeps cunning and quiet, and says, "Let yonder hot-headed fellow fight out my battle! I, for one, shall win in the end by the blows he gives, and which I ought to be giving"—even he seems graceful in his avowal, when one considers that he might say, "I shall win quite as much by the blows our antagonist gives him, blows from which he saves me—I thank the antagonist equally!" Moreover, you may enlarge on the loss of the edge of party-animosity with age and experience . . .

CHIAPPINO And naturally time must wear off such asperities: the bitterest adversaries get to discover certain points of similarity between each other, common sympathies—do they not?

OGNIBEN Ay, had the young David but sat first to dine on his cheeses with the Philistine, he had soon discovered an abandance of such common sympathies. He of Gath, it is recorded, was born of a father and mother, had brothers and sisters like another man,—they, no more than the sons of Jesse, were used to eat each other. But, for the sake of one broad antipathy that had existed from the beginning, David slung the

applicable?—"Contradictions? Of < >were," say you!   302| 1846:Still the   1849:Still, the   303| 1846:I say in   1863:I urge in   304| 1846:Why look   1863:Why, look   306| 1846:state   1863:State   308| 1846:good, and   1868:good; and   310| 1846: advances—to   1868:advances: to   311| 1846:spent < >onward as < >gave   1868:spend < > onward, as < >give   312| 1846:back—now   1863:back. Now   314| 1846: you—but   1863:you: but   316| 1846:battle; I   1868:battle! I   320| 1846:him, and from   1868:him, blows from   321| 1846:you must enlarge   1863:you may enlarge   322| 1846:experience—   1863:experience . . .   323| 1846:asperities—the   1863:asperities: the   326| 1846:sate   1863:sat   328| 1846:sympathies—He < >Father   1849:father   1863:sympathies. He   329| 1846:Mother   1849:mother   330| 1846:other; but

stone, cut off the giant's head, made a spoil of it, and after ate his cheeses alone, with the better appetite, for all I can learn. My friend, as you, with a quickened eye-sight, go on discovering much good on the worse
335 side, remember that the same process should proportionably magnify and demonstrate to you the much more good on the better side! And when I profess no sympathy for the Goliaths of our time, and you object that a large nature should sympathize with every form of intelligence, and see the good in it, however limited—I answer, "So I do; but preserve
340 the proportions of my sympathy, however finelier or widelier I may extend its action." I desire to be able, with a quickened eye-sight, to descry beauty in corruption where others see foulness only: but I hope I shall also continue to see a redoubled beauty in the higher forms of matter, where already everybody sees no foulness at all. I must retain,
345 too, my old power of selection, and choice of appropriation, to apply to such new gifts; else they only dazzle instead of enlightening me. God has his archangels and consorts with them: though he made too, and intimately sees what is good in, the worm. Observe, I speak only as you profess to think and, so, ought to speak: I do justice to your own
350 principles, that is all.

CHIAPPINO But you very well know that the two parties do, on occasion, assume each other's characteristics. What more disgusting, for instance, than to see how promptly the newly emancipated slave will adopt, in his own favour, the very measures of precaution, which pressed soreliest on
355 himself as institutions of the tyranny he has just escaped from? Do the classes, hitherto without opinion, get leave to express it? there follows a confederacy immediately, from which—exercise your individual right and dissent, and woe be to you!

OGNIBEN And a journey over the sea to you! That is the generous way.
360 Cry—"Emancipated slaves, the first excess, and off I go!" The first time a

---

1863:other. But   ³³³| *1846*:alone with < > appetite for   *1849*:alone, with < > appetite,
for   ³³⁶| *1846*:side—and   *1863*:side. And   *1868*:side! And   ³³⁷| *1846*:the Goliahs
1888:the Goliaths   ³³⁸| *1849*:sympathise   *1863*:sympathize   ³³⁹| *1846*:answer,
so I do—but   *1863*:do; but   *1868*:answer, "So   ³⁴¹| *1846*:action. I   *1868*:action." I
³⁴²| *1846*:only,—but   *1868*:only: but   ³⁴³⁻⁴⁴| *1846*:forms, where < > every body < >
retain   *1849*:forms of matter, where < > retain,   *1863*:everybody   ³⁴⁵| *1846*:too
my   *1849*:too, my   ³⁴⁶| *1846*:gifts . . else   *1863*:gifts; else   ³⁴⁷| *1846*:his
Archangels < > them—tho'   *1863*:His archangels < > them: though He   *1868*:his < > he
³⁴⁸| *1846*:in the   *1849*:in, the   ³⁴⁹| *1846*:and so ought to speak—I   *1863*:speak: I
1888:and, so, ought   ³⁵⁰| *1849*:all!   *1863*:all.   ³⁵²| *1846*:characteristics: what
1863:characteristics. What   ³⁵⁵| *1846*:from.—Do   *1863*:from? Do   ³⁵⁶| *1846*:there
is a   *1868*:there follows a   ³⁵⁹| *1846*:you!—That   *1868*:you! That   ³⁶⁰| *1846*:
Say—emancipated < > go! The   *1863*:Cry—emancipated   *1868*:Cry—"Emancipated

poor devil, who has been bastinadoed steadily his whole life long, finds himself let alone and able to legislate, so, begins pettishly, while he rubs his soles, "Woe be to whoever brings anything in the shape of a stick this way!"—you, rather than give up the very innocent pleasure of carrying
365 one to switch flies with,—you go away, to everybody's sorrow. Yet you were quite reconciled to staying at home while the governors used to pass, every now and then, some such edict as "Let no man indulge in owning a stick which is not thick enough to chastise our slaves, if need require!" Well, there are pre-ordained hierarchies among us, and a
370 profane vulgar subjected to a different law altogether; yet I am rather sorry you should see it so clearly: for, do you know what is to—all but save you at the Day of Judgment, all you men of genius? It is this: that, while you generally began by pulling down God, and went on to the end of your life, in one effort at setting up your own genius in his place,—
375 still, the last, bitterest concession wrung with the utmost unwillingness from the experience of the very loftiest of you, was invariably—would one think it?—that the rest of mankind, down to the lowest of the mass, stood not, nor ever could stand, just on a level and equality with yourselves. That will be a point in the favour of all such,
380 I hope and believe.

CHIAPPINO Why, men of genius are usually charged, I think, with doing just the reverse; and at once acknowledging the natural inequality of mankind, by themselves participating in the universal craving after, and deference to, the civil distinctions which represent it. You wonder
385 they pay such undue respect to titles and badges of superior rank.

OGNIBEN Not I (always on your own ground and showing, be it noted)! Who doubts that, with a weapon to brandish, a man is the more for-

---

<> go!" The   362| *1846:*so begins pettishly while   *1849:*pettishly, while   *1863:*so,
begins   363| *1846:*any thing   *1849:*anything   364| *1846:*way,"—you   *1863:*
way!"—you   365| *1846:*you, go away to every body's sorrow! Yet   *1849:*everybody's
*1863:*you go away, to <> sorrow. Yet   368| *1846:*slaves if   *1849:*slaves, if
369| *1846:*require." Well—there   *1863:*require." Well, there   *1868:*require!" Well
370| *1846:*altogether—yet   *1863:*altogether; yet   371| *1846:*clearly—for <> to . . all
*1863:*clearly: for <> to—all   372| *1846:*all you Men of Genius <> this—that,   *1863:*all
you men of genius   *1868:*this; that,   *1888:*this: that,   374| *1846:*Genius   *1863:*
genius in His   *1868:*his   376-77| *1846:*invariably . . would <> it? . . that   *1849:*
invariably—would <> it?—that   378| *1846:*mass, was not <> could be, just   *1849:*
mass, stood not <> could stand, just   379| *1846:*yourselves.—That   *1863:*yourselves.
That   380| *1846:*believe!   *1868:*believe.   382| *1846:*reverse, and   *1849:*reverse; and
383| *1846:*mankind by   *1849:*mankind, by   384| *1846:*to the   *1849:*to, the
385| *1846:*rank!   *1863:*rank.   386| *1846:*Not I! (always <> noted!)   *1868:*Not I (always

midable? Titles and badges are exercised as such a weapon, to which you and I look up wistfully. We could pin lions with it moreover, while
390 in its present owner's hands it hardly prods rats. Nay, better than a mere weapon of easy mastery and obvious use, it is a mysterious divining rod that may serve us in undreamed-of ways. Beauty, strength, intellect— men often have none of these, and yet conceive pretty accurately what kind of advantages they would bestow on the possessor. We know at
395 least what it is we make up our mind to forego, and so can apply the fittest substitute in our power. Wanting beauty, we cultivate good humour; missing wit, we get riches: but the mystic unimaginable opera- tion of that gold collar and string of Latin names which suddenly turned poor stupid little peevish Cecco of our town into natural lord of the best
400 of us—a Duke, he is now—there indeed is a virtue to be reverenced!

CHIAPPINO Ay, by the vulgar: not by Messere Stiatta the poet, who pays more assiduous court to him than anybody.

OGNIBEN What else should Stiatta pay court to? He has talent, not honour and riches: men naturally covet what they have not.

405 CHIAPPINO No, or Cecco would covet talent, which he has not, where- as he covets more riches, of which he has plenty, already.

OGNIBEN Because a purse added to a purse makes the holder twice as rich: but just such another talent as Stiatta's, added to what he now possesses, what would that profit him? Give the talent a purse indeed, to
410 do something with! But lo, how we keep the good people waiting! I only desired to do justice to the noble sentiments which animate you, and which you are too modest to duly enforce. Come, to our main business: shall we ascend the steps? I am going to propose you for Provost to the people; they know your antecedents, and will accept you with a joyful

---

§ emended to § noted)! § see Editorial Notes §   389| *1846:*wistfully.—We *1863:* wistfully. We   392| *1846:*serve you in < >ways.—Beauty, Strength, Intellect— *1863:*serve us in < >ways. Beauty, strength, intellect—   393| *1846:*these and *1863:*these, and   394| *1846:*possessor.—You know *1863:*possessor. We know
395| *1846:*is you make up your mind *1863:*is we make up our mind   396| *1846:*in your power; wanting Beauty, you cultivate Good *1863:*in our power; wanting beauty, we cultivate good *1868:*power. Wanting   397| *1846:*Humour, missing Wit, you get Riches; but *1863:*humour; missing wit, we get riches: but   399| *1846:*our own town< > Lord *1849:* our town *1865:*natural lord   400| *1846:*now! there< >Virtue *1863:*virtue *1868:* now—there   401| *1846:*vulgar—not *1863:*vulgar: not   402| *1846:*any body. *1863:* anybody.   404| *1846:*honor and riches—men *1849:*honour *1863:*riches: men
405| *1846:*No—or< >talent which *1849:*talent, which *1868:*No, or   406| *1846:* plenty already. *1868:*plenty, already.   408| *1846:*rich—but *1863:*rich:but   410|
*1846:*waiting. I *1868:*waiting! I   414| *1846:*antecedents and *1849:*antecedents, and

unanimity: whereon I confirm their choice. Rouse up! Are you nerving yourself to an effort? Beware the disaster of Messere Stiatta we were talking of! who, determining to keep an equal mind and constant face on whatever might be the fortune of his last new poem with our townsmen, heard too plainly "hiss, hiss, hiss," increase every moment.

420 Till at last the man fell senseless: not perceiving that the portentous sounds had all the while been issuing from between his own nobly clenched teeth, and nostrils narrowed by resolve.

CHIAPPINO Do you begin to throw off the mask?—to jest with me, having got me effectually into your trap?

425 OGNIBEN Where is the trap, my friend? You hear what I engage to do, for my part: you, for yours, have only to fulfil your promise made just now within doors, of professing unlimited obedience to Rome's authority in my person. And I shall authorize no more than the simple re-establish-ment of the Provostship and the conferment of its privileges upon

430 yourself: the only novel stipulation being a birth of the peculiar circum-stances of the time.

CHIAPPINO And that stipulation?

OGNIBEN Just the obvious one—that in the event of the discovery of the actual assailant of the late Provost . . .

435 CHIAPPINO Ha!

OGNIBEN Why, he shall suffer the proper penalty, of course; what did you expect?

CHIAPPINO Who heard of this?

OGNIBEN Rather, who needed to hear of this?

440 CHIAPPINO Can it be, the popular rumour never reached you . . .

OGNIBEN Many more such rumours reach me, friend, than I choose to receive; those which wait longest have best chance. Has the present one sufficiently waited? Now is its time for entry with effect. See the good people crowding about yonder palace-steps—which we may not have to

---

415| *1846:*up! you are nerving *1863:*up! are you nerving *1868:*up! Are   417| *1846:* of—who determining *1863:*of: who, determining *1868:*of! who   418| *1846:*new tragedy with *1849:*new poem with   419| *1846:*townsmen,—heard< >moment, *1863:* moment: *1868:*townsmen, heard< >moment.   420| *1846:*till< >senseless—not *1868:* Till< >senseless: not   422| *1846:*resolve! *1863:*resolve.   423| *1846:*mask? to *1863:*mask?—to   426| *1846:*part—you *1863:*part: you   428| *1846:*person—and *1849:*authorise *1863:*person. And< >authorize   430| *1846:*yourself—the only *1863:* yourself: the only   433| *1846:*OGNIBEN Oh, the obvious *1863:*OGNIBEN Just the obvious 439| *1846:*Rather who *1849:*Rather, who   440| *1849:*you . . *1863:*you . . . 442| *1846:*receive: those< >chance—has *1863:*chance. Has *1865:*receive; those   444|

ascend, after all. My good friends! (nay, two or three of you will answer every purpose)—who was it fell upon and proved nearly the death of your late Provost? His successor desires to hear, that his day of inauguration may be graced by the act of prompt bare justice we all anticipate. Who dealt the blow that night, does anybody know?

450 LUITOLFO [*coming forward.*] I!

ALL Luitolfo!

LUITOLFO I avow the deed, justify and approve it, and stand forth now, to relieve my friend of an unearned responsibility. Having taken thought, I am grown stronger: I shall shrink from nothing that awaits

455 me. Nay, Chiappino—we are friends still: I dare say there is some proof of your superior nature in this starting aside, strange as it seemed at first. So, they tell me, my horse is of the right stock, because a shadow in the path frightens him into a frenzy, makes him dash my brains out. I understand only the dull mule's way of standing stockishly, plodding

460 soberly, suffering on occasion a blow or two with due patience.

EULALIA I was determined to justify my choice, Chiappino,—to let Luitolfo's nature vindicate itself. Henceforth we are undivided, whatever be our fortune.

OGNIBEN Now, in these last ten minutes of silence, what have I been

465 doing, deem you? Putting the finishing stroke to a homily of mine, I have long taken thought to perfect, on the text, "Let whoso thinketh he standeth, take heed lest he fall." To your house, Luitolfo! Still silent, my patriotic friend? Well, that is a good sign however. And you will go aside for a time? That is better still. I understand: it would be easy for you to

470 die of remorse here on the spot and shock us all, but you mean to live

---

and grow worthy of coming back to us one day. There, I will tell every-
body; and you only do right to believe you must get better as you
get older. All men do so: they are worst in childhood, improve in
manhood, and get ready in old age for another world. Youth, with its
475 beauty and grace, would seem bestowed on us for some such reason as to
make us partly endurable till we have time for really becoming so of
ourselves, without their aid; when they leave us. The sweetest child we
all smile on for his pleasant want of the whole world to break up, or suck
in his mouth, seeing no other good in it—would be rudely handled by
480 that world's inhabitants, if he retained those angelic infantine desires
when he had grown six feet high, black and bearded. But, little by little,
he sees fit to forego claim after claim on the world, puts up with a less
and less share of its good as his proper portion; and when the octogenar-
ian asks barely a sup of gruel and a fire of dry sticks, and thanks you as
485 for his full allowance and right in the common good of life,—hoping
nobody may murder him,—he who began by asking and expecting the
whole of us to bow down in worship to him,—why, I say he is advanced,
far onward, very far, nearly out of sight like our friend Chiappino
yonder. And now—(ay, good-bye to you! He turns round the north-west
490 gate: going to Lugo again? Good-bye!)—and now give thanks to God,
the keys of the Provost's palace to me, and yourselves to profitable
meditation at home! I have known *Four*-and-twenty leaders of revolts.

---

*1863:*spot and<>you mean to live   472| *1846:*every body<>believe you will get
*1863:*everybody<>believe you must get   473| *1846:*older! All<>so,—they *1863:*
older. All *1868:*so: they   474| *1846:*world: Youth *1849:*world. Youth   475| *1846:*
Beauty and Grace, would really seem *1849:*would seem *1863:*beauty and grace
477| *1846:*aid, when *1863:*aid; when   479| *1846:*it—he would *1849:*it—would
481| *1846:*he got six<>bearded: but *1849:*he has grown six *1868:*had<>bearded.
But   483| *1846:*portion,—and *1868:*portion; and   484| *1846:*sticks, and will
thank you *1849:*sticks, and thanks you   489| *1846:*yonder! And now—(Ay, good bye
<>North-west *1863:*yonder. And<>good-bye <>north-west *1888:*now—(ay
490| *1846:*gate—going<>Good bye)!—And *1849:*bye!)—And *1863:*gate: going <>
Good-bye *1888:*Good-bye!)—and   491| *1846:*of the Provost's Palace *1865:*of the
Provost's palace   492| *1846:*home. I<>revolts!— *1863:*revolts. *1868:*home! I

42

§ The following pages reproduce the title page, B's prefatory note, and the table of contents of the 1849 collected edition of B's works. §

POEMS
BY
ROBERT BROWNING
IN TWO VOLUMES

A NEW EDITION
LONDON:
CHAPMAN & HALL, 186, STRAND
1849

Many of the pieces were out of print, the rest had been withdrawn from circulation, when the corrected edition, now submitted to the reader, was prepared. The various Poems and Dramas have received the author's most careful revision.

DECEMBER, 1848.

CONTENTS OF VOLUME I

PARACELSUS
PIPPA PASSES. A DRAMA
KING VICTOR AND KING CHARLES. A TRAGEDY
COLOMBE'S BIRTHDAY. A PLAY

CONTENTS OF VOLUME II

A BLOT IN THE 'SCUTCHEON. A TRAGEDY
THE RETURN OF THE DRUSES. A TRAGEDY
LURIA. A TRAGEDY
A SOUL'S TRAGEDY
DRAMATIC ROMANCES AND LYRICS:
CAVALIER TUNES:—
      I.—MARCHING ALONG
      II.—GIVE A ROUSE
      III.—BOOT AND SADDLE
MY LAST DUCHESS
COUNT GISMOND
INCIDENT OF THE FRENCH CAMP
SOLILOQUY OF THE SPANISH CLOISTER
IN A GONDOLA
ARTEMIS PROLOGUIZES
WARING
RUDEL TO THE LADY OF TRIPOLI
CRISTINA
 I.—MADHOUSE CELL
II.—MADHOUSE CELL
THROUGH THE METIDJA TO ABD-EL-KADR
THE PIED PIPER OF HAMELIN
"HOW THEY BROUGHT THE GOOD NEWS
    FROM GHENT TO AIX"
PICTOR IGNOTUS
THE ITALIAN IN ENGLAND
THE ENGLISHMAN IN ITALY
THE LOST LEADER
THE LOST MISTRESS
HOME-THOUGHTS, FROM ABROAD
HOME-THOUGHTS, FROM THE SEA
THE BISHOP ORDERS HIS TOMB AT
    ST. PRAXED'S CHURCH
GARDEN-FANCIES:—
      I.—THE FLOWER'S NAME
      II.—SIBRANDUS SCHAFNABURGENSIS
THE LABORATORY
THE CONFESSIONAL

47

THE FLIGHT OF THE DUCHESS
EARTH'S IMMORTALITIES
SONG
THE BOY AND THE ANGEL
MEETING AT NIGHT
PARTING AT MORNING
SAUL
TIME'S REVENGES
THE GLOVE

CHRISTMAS-EVE AND EASTER-DAY

Edited by Harry Krynicky

CHRISTMAS-EVE AND EASTER-DAY

MS: Christmas Eve and Easter Day.   1850:CHRISTMAS-EVE / AND / EASTER-DAY. / A
POEM.   1863:EASTER-DAY. / FLORENCE, 1850.   1868:CHRISTMAS-EVE AND
EASTER-DAY.   1888:EASTER-DAY. / 1850.

CHRISTMAS-EVE AND EASTER-DAY

1850

CHRISTMAS-EVE

I

Out of the little chapel I burst
    Into the fresh night-air again.
Five minutes full, I waited first
    In the doorway, to escape the rain
5   That drove in gusts down the common's centre
    At the edge of which the chapel stands,
Before I plucked up heart to enter.
Heaven knows how many sorts of hands
    Reached past me, groping for the latch
10 Of the inner door that hung on catch
More obstinate the more they fumbled,
    Till, giving way at last with a scold
Of the crazy hinge, in squeezed or tumbled
    One sheep more to the rest in fold,
15 And left me irresolute, standing sentry
In the sheepfold's lath-and-plaster entry,
Six feet long by three feet wide,
Partitioned off from the vast inside—
    I blocked up half of it at least.
20 No remedy; the rain kept driving.
    They eyed me much as some wild beast,

---

§ MS in Forster and Dyce Collection, Victoria and Albert Museum. Ed. 1850, 1863, 1865, 1868, 1888, 1889 §
Subtitle| MS:CHRISTMAS EVE   *1850:*CHRISTMAS-EVE   *1888:*CHRISTMAS EVE § emended to § CHRISTMAS-EVE § see Editorial Notes §
1| *1863:*chapel I flung, *1868:*chapel I burst, *1888:*burst   2| MS:night air *1863:* night-air   3| MS: I had waited a good five minutes first *1863:*Five minutes I waited, held my tongue *1868:*Five minutes full, I waited first   5| MS:the Common's centre, *1850:*the common's *1888:*centre   7| MS: enter: *1863:*enter.   10| MS:catch, *1865:*catch   12| MS:Till giving *1850:*Till, giving   16| MS:sheepfolds' *1850:*sheepfold's   17| MS:Four feet < > two feet DC, BrU: Six feet < > three feet *1889:*Six feet < > three feet   20| MS:driving:

That congregation, still arriving,
Some of them by the main road, white
A long way past me into the night,
25 Skirting the common, then diverging;
Not a few suddenly emerging
From the common's self thro' the paling-gaps,
—They house in the gravel-pits perhaps,
Where the road stops short with its safeguard border
30 Of lamps, as tired of such disorder;—
But the most turned in yet more abruptly
From a certain squalid knot of alleys,
Where the town's bad blood once slept corruptly,
Which now the little chapel rallies
35 And leads into day again,—its priestliness
Lending itself to hide their beastliness
So cleverly (thanks in part to the mason),
And putting so cheery a whitewashed face on
Those neophytes too much in lack of it,
40 That, where you cross the common as I did,
And meet the party thus presided,
"Mount Zion" with Love-lane at the back of it,
They front you as little disconcerted
As, bound for the hills, her fate averted,
45 And her wicked people made to mind him,
Lot might have marched with Gomorrah behind him.

II

Well, from the road, the lanes or the common,
In came the flock: the fat weary woman,
Panting and bewildered, down-clapping
50 Her umbrella with a mighty report,
Grounded it by me, wry and flapping,
A wreck of whalebones; then, with a snort,
Like a startled horse, at the interloper
(Who humbly knew himself improper,

1863:driving.   23| MS:mainroad *1863*:main road   27| MS:paling-gaps,—
1863:paling-gaps,   37| MS:cleverly, (thanks <>mason) *1850*:cleverly
(thanks <>mason),   40| MS:That, when you *1850*:That, where you
42| MS:"Mount Zion," with *1863*:"Mount Zion" with   43| MS:disconcerted,
1863:disconcerted   44| MS:averted *1863*:averted,   54| MS:Who *1863*:(Who

⁵⁵ But could not shrink up small enough)
—Round to the door, and in,—the gruff
Hinge's invariable scold
Making my very blood run cold.
Prompt in the wake of her, up-pattered
⁶⁰ On broken clogs, the many-tattered
Little old-faced peaking sister-turned-mother
Of the sickly babe she tried to smother
Somehow up, with its spotted face,
From the cold, on her breast, the one warm place;
⁶⁵ She too must stop, wring the poor ends dry
Of a draggled shawl, and add thereby
Her tribute to the door-mat, sopping
Already from my own clothes' dropping,
Which yet she seemed to grudge I should stand on:
⁷⁰   Then, stooping down to take off her pattens,
She bore them defiantly, in each hand one,
Planted together before her breast
And its babe, as good as a lance in rest.
      Close on her heels, the dingy satins
⁷⁵ Of a female something, past me flitted,
      With lips as much too white, as a streak
      Lay far too red on each hollow cheek;
And it seemed the very door-hinge pitied
All that was left of a woman once,
⁸⁰ Holding at least its tongue for the nonce.
Then a tall yellow man, like the Penitent Thief,
With his jaw bound up in a handkerchief,
And eyelids screwed together tight,
Led himself in by some inner light.
⁸⁵ And, except from him, from each that entered,
      I got the same interrogation—
"What, you, the alien, you have ventured
      To take with us, the elect, your station?

---

⁵⁵| MS:enough, *1863:*enough)   ⁵⁶| MS:Round *1863:*—Round   ⁵⁸| MS:
Making your very *1863:*Making my very   ⁶¹| MS:old-faced, peaking *1863:*old-faced,
peaking, sister-turned-mother *1868:*old-faced peaking sister-turned-mother
⁶³| MS:face; *1850:*face,   ⁶⁵| *1850:*poor suds dry *1863:*poor ends dry
⁶⁹| MS:on; *1888:*on: ⁷⁰| *1850:*Then stooping *1863:*Then,.stooping
⁷⁸| *1863:*semed *1865:*seemed   ⁸⁶| MS:I had the *1863:*I got the
⁸⁷| MS:you, the *1888:*you the § emended to § you, the § see Editorial Notes §
⁸⁸| MS:us elect your station— *1850:*us, elect, your station? *1863:*us, the elect

55

A carer for none of it, a Gallio!"—

90 Thus, plain as print, I read the glance

At a common prey, in each countenance

    As of huntsman giving his hounds the tallyho.

And, when the door's cry drowned their wonder,

    The draught, it always sent in shutting,

95 Made the flame of the single tallow candle

In the cracked square lantern I stood under,

    Shoot its blue lip at me, rebutting

As it were, the luckless cause of scandal:

I verily fancied the zealous light

100 (In the chapel's secret, too!) for spite

Would shudder itself clean off the wick,

With the airs of a Saint John's Candlestick.

There was no standing it much longer.

"Good folks," thought I, as resolve grew stronger,

105 "This way you perform the Grand-Inquisitor

When the weather sends you a chance visitor?

You are the men, and wisdom shall die with you,

And none of the old Seven Churches vie with you!

But still, despite the pretty perfection

110   To which you carry your trick of exclusiveness,

And, taking God's word under wise protection,

    Correct its tendency to diffusiveness,

And bid one reach it over hot ploughshares,—

    Still, as I say, though you've found salvation,

115 If I should choose to cry, as now, 'Shares!'—

    See if the best of you bars me my ration!

I prefer, if you please, for my expounder

Of the laws of the feast, the feast's own Founder;

Mine's the same right with your poorest and sickliest

89| MS:a Gallio?"— *1865*:a Gallio!"—   91| MS:countenance, *1863*:countenance
92| MS:tallyho: *1863*:tallyho.   93| *1868*:wonder *1888*:wonder,   96| MS:
lanthorn *1863*:lantern   97| MS:rebutting, *1865*:rebutting   99| MS:verily
thought the *1863*:verily fancied the   100| MS:spite, *1863*:spite   102| MS:
a St. John's *1863*:a Saint John's   104| MS:folks", said I *1850*:folks," said
1863:folks," thought I   105| MS:the Grand-Inquisitor, *1888*:the
Grand-Inquisitor   108| MS:the Old *1850*:the old   113| MS:Bidding *1863*:And
bid   115| MS:cry—as now—'Shares'!— *1850*:now—'Shares!'— *1863*:cry, as now,
'Shares!'—   117| MS:Because I prefer for *1863*:I prefer, if you please, for
118| MS:feasts' own Founder: *1850*:feast's *1863*:own Founder;   119| MS:sickliest,

120   Supposing I don the marriage vestiment:
      So, shut your mouth and open your Testament,
And carve me my portion at your quickliest!"
Accordingly, as a shoemaker's lad
      With wizened face in want of soap,
125   And wet apron wound round his waist like a rope,
(After stopping outside, for his cough was bad,
To get the fit over, poor gentle creature,
And so avoid disturbing the preacher)
—Passed in, I sent my elbow spikewise
130 At the shutting door, and entered likewise,
Received the hinge's accustomed greeting,
      And crossed the threshold's magic pentacle,
      And found myself in full conventicle,
—To wit, in Zion Chapel Meeting,
135 On the Christmas-Eve of 'Forty-nine,
      Which, calling its flock to their special clover,
      Found all assembled and one sheep over,
Whose lot, as the weather pleased, was mine.

III

I very soon had enough of it.
140   The hot smell and the human noises,
And my neighbour's coat, the greasy cuff of it,
      Were a pebble-stone that a child's hand poises,
Compared with the pig-of-lead-like pressure
      Of the preaching man's immense stupidity,
145 As he poured his doctrine forth, full measure,
      To meet his audience's avidity.
You needed not the wit of the Sibyl
      To guess the cause of it all, in a twinkling:
      No sooner our friend had got an inkling

---

*1888:*sickliest   ¹²⁰| MS:marriage-vestiment; *1863:*marriage-vestiment:
*1888:*marriage vestiment: ¹²¹| MS:So shut < > mouth, and *1850:*So, shut
*1863:*mouth and   ¹²⁶| MS:After *1863:*(After   ¹²⁸| MS:preacher,
*1863:*preacher)   ¹²⁹| MS:Passed *1863:*—Passed   ¹³⁰| MS:likewise,— *1863:*
likewise,   ¹³²| MS:Crossed *1863:*And crossed   ¹³⁵| MS:the Christmas Eve
*1850:*the Christmas-Eve   ¹³⁷| MS:Found them assembled *1863:*Found all
assembled   ¹⁴⁴| MS:preaching-man's *1888:*preaching man's   ¹⁴⁸| MS:
twinkling— *1863:*twinkling: ¹⁴⁹| MS:sooner had our friend an *1863:*sooner got

¹⁵⁰ Of treasure hid in the Holy Bible,
(Whene'er 'twas the thought first struck him,
How death, at unawares, might duck him
Deeper than the grave, and quench
The gin-shop's light in hell's grim drench)
¹⁵⁵ Than he handled it so, in fine irreverence,
    As to hug the book of books to pieces:
And, a patchwork of chapters and texts in severance,
    Not improved by the private dog's-ears and creases,
Having clothed his own soul with, he'd fain see equipt yours,—
¹⁶⁰ So tossed you again your Holy Scriptures.
    And you picked them up, in a sense, no doubt:
    Nay, had but a single face of my neighbours
    Appeared to suspect that the preacher's labours
Were help which the world could be saved without,
¹⁶⁵ 'Tis odds but I might have borne in quiet
A qualm or two at my spiritual diet,
Or (who can tell?) perchance even mustered
    Somewhat to urge in behalf of the sermon:
But the flock sat on, divinely flustered,
¹⁷⁰   Sniffing, methought, its dew of Hermon
With such content in every snuffle,
As the devil inside us loves to ruffle.
My old fat woman purred with pleasure,
    And thumb round thumb went twirling faster,
¹⁷⁵ While she, to his periods keeping measure,
    Maternally devoured the pastor.
The man with the handkerchief untied it,
Showed us a horrible wen inside it,
Gave his eyelids yet another screwing,
¹⁸⁰ And rocked himself as the woman was doing.
The shoemaker's lad, discreetly choking,
Kept down his cough. 'Twas too provoking!

our *1888:*sooner our friend had got an   ¹⁵¹| MS: (Whenever it was the thought
<> him *1863:*(When'er 'twas that the thought<>him, *1888:*(Whene'er 'twas
the   ¹⁵²| MS:How Death *1863:*How death   ¹⁵⁴| MS:ginshop's <>
Hell's *1850:*gin-shop's *1868:*in hell's   ¹⁵⁶| MS:the Book *1863:*the book
¹⁵⁸| MS:by the § inserted above §   ¹⁶⁰| *1863:*So, tossed *1888:*So tossed
¹⁶³| MS:labors *1850:*labours   ¹⁶⁵| MS:but I had borne *1863:*but I might have
borne   ¹⁶⁶| MS:diet; *1863:*diet,   ¹⁶⁷| MS:Or, who can tell? had even *1863:*
Or (who can tell?) perchance even   ¹⁶⁹| MS:sate *1863:*sat   ¹⁷⁷| MS:

58

My gorge rose at the nonsense and stuff of it;
  So, saying like Eve when she plucked the apple,
185   "I wanted a taste, and now there's enough of it,"
I flung out of the little chapel.

                    IV

There was a lull in the rain, a lull
  In the wind too; the moon was risen,
And would have shone out pure and full,
190   But for the ramparted cloud-prison,
Block on block built up in the West,
For what purpose the wind knows best,
Who changes his mind continually.
And the empty other half of the sky
195 Seemed in its silence as if it knew
What, any moment, might look through
A chance gap in that fortress massy:—
  Through its fissures you got hints
  Of the flying moon, by the shifting tints,
200 Now, a dull lion-colour, now, brassy
Burning to yellow, and whitest yellow,
Like furnace-smoke just ere flames bellow,
All a-simmer with intense strain
To let her through,—then blank again,
205 At the hope of her appearance failing.
Just by the chapel, a break in the railing
Shows a narrow path directly across;
'Tis ever dry walking there, on the moss—
Besides, you go gently all the way uphill.
210   I stooped under and soon felt better;
My head grew lighter, my limbs more supple,

handkerchief, untied *1888*:handkerchief untied   ¹⁸³| MS:it, *1865*:it;   ¹⁸⁴| MS:
And saying, like *1863*:So, saying, like *1865*:saying like   ¹⁹¹| MS:the
west, *1863*:the West,   ¹⁹⁷| MS:chance-gap *1865*:chance gap   ²⁰⁰| MS:lion-color
1850:lion-colour   ²⁰²| MS:ere the flames *1888*:ere flames   ²⁰⁹| MS:uphill:
1863:uphill.   ²¹⁰| MS:better: *1863*:better;   ²¹¹| MS:light *1865*:lighter

As I walked on, glad to have slipt the fetter.
My mind was full of the scene I had left,
    That placid flock, that pastor vociferant,
215   —How this outside was pure and different!
The sermon, now—what a mingled weft
Of good and ill! Were either less,
    Its fellow had coloured the whole distinctly;
But alas for the excellent earnestness,
220   And the truths, quite true if stated succinctly,
But as surely false, in their quaint presentment,
However to pastor and flock's contentment!
Say rather, such truths looked false to your eyes,
    With his provings and parallels twisted and twined,
225 Till how could you know them, grown double their size
    In the natural fog of the good man's mind,
Like yonder spots of our roadside lamps,
Haloed about with the common's damps?
Truth remains true, the fault's in the prover;
230   The zeal was good, and the aspiration;
And yet, and yet, yet, fifty times over,
    Pharaoh received no demonstration,
By his Baker's dream of Baskets Three,
Of the doctrine of the Trinity,—
235 Although, as our preacher thus embellished it,
Apparently his hearers relished it
With so unfeigned a gust—who knows if
They did not prefer our friend to Joseph?
But so it is everywhere, one way with all of them!
240   These people have really felt, no doubt,
A something, the motion they style the Call of them;
    And this is their method of bringing about,
By a mechanism of words and tones,
(So many texts in so many groans)
245 A sort of reviving and reproducing,

212| MS:fetter; *1863*:fetter.   217| MS:ill! were *1868*:ill! Were
218| MS:colored *1850*:coloured   222| MS:flocks' *1850*:flock's   223| MS:
eyes, *1888*:eyes. DC, BrU:eyes, *1889*:eyes,   225| MS:size, *1863*:size
226| MS:mind? *1863*:mind,   227| *1863*:lamps *1868*:lamps,   228| MS:damps.
1863:damps?   232| MS:demonstration *1868*:demonstration,   235| MS:Although
as *1850*:Although, as   245| MS:reviving or reproducing, *1865*:reviving

More or less perfectly, (who can tell?)
The mood itself, which strengthens by using;
And how that happens, I understand well.
A tune was born in my head last week,
250 Out of the thump-thump and shriek-shriek
Of the train, as I came by it, up from Manchester;
And when, next week, I take it back again,
My head will sing to the engine's clack again,
While it only makes my neighbour's haunches stir,
255 —Finding no dormant musical sprout
In him, as in me, to be jolted out.
'Tis the taught already that profits by teaching;
He gets no more from the railway's preaching
Than, from this preacher who does the rail's office, I:
260 Whom therefore the flock cast a jealous eye on.
Still, why paint over their door "Mount Zion,"
To which all flesh shall come, saith the prophecy?

V

But wherefore be harsh on a single case?
After how many modes, this Christmas-Eve,
265 Does the self-same weary thing take place?
The same endeavour to make you believe,
And with much the same effect, no more:
Each method abundantly convincing,
As I say, to those convinced before,
270 But scarce to be swallowed without wincing
By the not-as-yet-convinced. For me,
I have my own church equally:
And in this church my faith sprang first!
(I said, as I reached the rising ground,

---

and reproducing,   246| MS:tell?—) 1888:tell?)   247| MS:Of the <> itself, that
strengthens 1888:The <> itself, which strengthens   248| MS:how it happens
1888:how that happens   257| MS:profit 1863:profits   258| MS:preaching,
1863:preaching   259| MS:office, I, 1863:office, I 1865:office, I:
260| MS:casts 1863:cast   261| MS:door "Mount Zion", 1850:door "Mount
Zion,"   264| MS:this Christmas Eve, 1850:this Christmas-Eve,
265| MS:selfsame 1888:self-same   266| MS:endeavor 1850:endeavour
267| MS:And much with the 1863:And with much the   270| MS:wincing,
1868:wincing   272| MS:equally. 1863:equally: 273| MS:this 1868:this

275 And the wind began again, with a burst
         Of rain in my face, and a glad rebound
    From the heart beneath, as if, God speeding me,
    I entered his church-door, nature leading me)
    —In youth I looked to these very skies,
280 And probing their immensities,
    I found God there, his visible power;
         Yet felt in my heart, amid all its sense
         Of the power, an equal evidence
    That his love, there too, was the nobler dower.
285 For the loving worm within its clod,
    Were diviner than a loveless god
    Amid his worlds, I will dare to say.
         You know what I mean: God's all, man's nought:
         But also, God, whose pleasure brought
290 Man into being, stands away
         As it were a handbreadth off, to give
    Room for the newly-made to live,
    And look at him from a place apart,
    And use his gifts of brain and heart,
295 Given, indeed, but to keep for ever.
    Who speaks of man, then, must not sever
    Man's very elements from man,
    Saying, "But all is God's"—whose plan
    Was to create man and then leave him
300 Able, his own word saith, to grieve him,
    But able to glorify him too,
    As a mere machine could never do,
    That prayed or praised, all unaware
    Of its fitness for aught but praise and prayer,
305 Made perfect as a thing of course.
    Man, therefore, stands on his own stock
    Of love and power as a pin-point rock:

278| MS:entered His < >Nature *1868:*entered his < >nature   280| MS:
§ crowded between 279-281 § immensities *1850:*immensities,   281| MS:there,
His *1868:*there, his   283| MS:Of that power *1865:*Of the power
284| MS:That His *1868:*That his   291| MS:were, an *1863:*were, a *1868:*were a
293| MS:at Him *1868:*at him   294| MS:use His *1868:*use his
296| MS:of Man *1850:*of man   300| MS:Able, His < > Him, *1868:*Able, his
< > him,   301| MS:glorify Him *1868:*glorify him   307| MS:rock, *1888:*rock:

62

And, looking to God who ordained divorce
Of the rock from his boundless continent,
310 Sees, in his power made evident,
Only excess by a million-fold
O'er the power God gave man in the mould.
For, note: man's hand, first formed to carry
A few pounds' weight, when taught to marry
315 Its strength with an engine's, lifts a mountain,
—Advancing in power by one degree;
And why count steps through eternity?
But love is the ever-springing fountain:
Man may enlarge or narrow his bed
320 For the water's play, but the water-head—
How can he multiply or reduce it?
As easy create it, as cause it to cease;
He may profit by it, or abuse it,
But 'tis not a thing to bear increase
325 As power does: be love less or more
In the heart of man, he keeps it shut
Or opes it wide, as he pleases, but
Love's sum remains what it was before.
So, gazing up, in my youth, at love
330 As seen through power, ever above
All modes which make it manifest,
My soul brought all to a single test—
That he, the Eternal First and Last,
Who, in his power, had so surpassed
335 All man conceives of what is might,—
Whose wisdom, too, showed infinite,
—Would prove as infinitely good;
Would never, (my soul understood,)
With power to work all love desires,
340 Bestow e'en less than man requires;

³⁰⁹| MS:from His 1868:from his   ³¹⁰| MS:Sees in His Power 1863:Sees, in His
power 1868:in his   ³¹¹| MS:million fold 1863:million-fold   ³¹³| MS:
For, see: Man's 1863:For, note: man's   ³¹⁸| MS:But Love <> ever
springing 1863:But love <> ever-springing   ³²⁰| MS:water head—
1863:water-head—   ³²²| MS:cease: 1863:cease;   ³²³| MS:abuse it; 1863:abuse
it,   ³²⁵| MS:power will: be 1863:power does: be   ³²⁷| MS:wide as 1863:wide,
as   ³³³| MS:That He 1868:That he   ³³⁴| MS:in His 1868:in his   ³³⁸| MS:
never, my <> understood, 1863:never, (my <> understood,)   ³⁴⁰| MS:man

That he who endlessly was teaching,
Above my spirit's utmost reaching,
What love can do in the leaf or stone,
(So that to master this alone,
345 This done in the stone or leaf for me,
I must go on learning endlessly)
Would never need that I, in turn,
     Should point him out defect unheeded,
And show that God had yet to learn
350   What the meanest human creature needed,
—Not life, to wit, for a few short years,
Tracking his way through doubts and fears,
While the stupid earth on which I stay
     Suffers no change, but passive adds
355   Its myriad years to myriads,
Though I, he gave it to, decay,
Seeing death come and choose about me,
And my dearest ones depart without me.
No: love which, on earth, amid all the shows of it,
360   Has ever been seen the sole good of life in it,
The love, ever growing there, spite of the strife in it,
     Shall arise, made perfect, from death's repose of it.
And I shall behold thee, face to face,
O God, and in thy light retrace
365 How in all I loved here, still wast thou!
Whom pressing to, then, as I fain would now,
I shall find as able to satiate
     The love, thy gift, as my spirit's wonder
Thou art able to quicken and sublimate,
370   With this sky of thine, that I now walk under,
And glory in thee for, as I gaze
Thus, thus! Oh, let men keep their ways

---

§ over illegible word § requires: *1888*:requires;   341| MS:That He *1868:*That
he   348| MS:out a defect *1865:*out defect   350| MS:needed. § altered to §
needed,— *1888:*needed,   352| MS: Tracking His *1868:*Tracking his   356| MS:
Though I, He *1868:*Though I, he   359| MS:No! love *1868:*No: love   362| MS:
it! *1868:*it.   363| MS:behold Thee *1868:*behold thee   364| MS:in Thy *1868:*in
thy   365| MS:wast Thou! *1868:*wast thou!   368| MS:love, Thy< >spirits'
wonder, *1850:*spirit's wonder *1868:*love, thy   370| MS:of Thine *1868:*of thine
371| MS:in Thee as thus I gaze, *1863:*in Thee for, as I gaze *1868:*in thee   372| MS:—
Thus, thus! Oh *1850:*—Thus, thus! oh *1863:*Thus, thus! *1868:*Thus, thus! Oh

64

Of seeking thee in a narrow shrine—
Be this my way! And this is mine!

VI

375 For lo, what think you? suddenly
The rain and the wind ceased, and the sky
Received at once the full fruition
Of the moon's consummate apparition.
The black cloud-barricade was riven,
380 Ruined beneath her feet, and driven
Deep in the West; while, bare and breathless,
    North and South and East lay ready
For a glorious thing that, dauntless, deathless,
    Sprang across them and stood steady.
385 'Twas a moon-rainbow, vast and perfect,
From heaven to heaven extending, perfect
As the mother-moon's self, full in face.
It rose, distinctly at the base
    With its seven proper colours chorded,
390 Which still, in the rising, were compressed,
Until at last they coalesced,
    And supreme the spectral creature lorded
In a triumph of whitest white,—
Above which intervened the night.
395 But above night too, like only the next,
    The second of a wondrous sequence,
    Reaching in rare and rarer frequence,
Till the heaven of heavens were circumflexed,
Another rainbow rose, a mightier,
400 Fainter, flushier and flightier,—

373| MS:seeking Thee *1868:*seeking thee   374| MS:*is 1868:*is   378| MS:
moons' *1850:*moon's   381| MS:the west *1863:*the West   382| MS:and south
and east *1863:*and South and East   383| MS:glorious Thing, that *1868:*glorious
thing that   384| MS:them, and *1868:*them and   389| MS:colors *1850:*colours
391| MS:coälesced, *1850:*coälesced, *1863:*coälesced, *1888:*coalesced,   395| MS:like
the *1863:*like only the   398| MS:heavens be circumflext, *1863:*heavens were
circumflext, *1868:*circumflexed,   400| MS:flushier, and *1868:*flushier and

Rapture dying along its verge.
Oh, whose foot shall I see emerge,
Whose, from the straining topmost dark,
On to the keystone of that arc?

VII

405 This sight was shown me, there and then,—
Me, one out of a world of men,
Singled forth, as the chance might hap
To another if, in a thunderclap
Where I heard noise and you saw flame,
410 Some one man knew God called his name.
For me, I think I said, "Appear!
Good were it to be ever here.
If thou wilt, let me build to thee
Service-tabernacles three,
415 Where, forever in thy presence,
In ecstatic acquiescence,
Far alike from thriftless learning
And ignorance's undiscerning,
I may worship and remain!"
420 Thus at the show above me, gazing
With upturned eyes, I felt my brain
Glutted with the glory, blazing
Throughout its whole mass, over and under,
Until at length it burst asunder
425 And out of it bodily there streamed,
The too-much glory, as it seemed,
Passing from out me to the ground,
Then palely serpentining round
Into the dark with mazy error.

401| MS:verge! *1868:*verge.   403| MS:Whose *1850:*WHOSE *1868:*Whose
408| MS:another, if in *1868:*another if, in   409| MS:noise, and *1868:*noise and
413| MS:If Thou <> Thee *1868:*If thou <> thee   414| MS:Service-tabernacles
Three, *1863:*Service tabernacles *1865:*Service-tabernacles *1868:*Service-tabernacles
three,   415| MS:forever in Thy *1850:*for ever *1863:*forever *1868:*in thy
416| MS:extatic *1863:*ecstatic   420| MS:Thus, at *1865:*Thus at   423| *1888:*
under DC, BrU:under, *1889:*under § emended to § under, § see Editorial Notes §
424| MS:asunder, *1888:*asunder   425| MS:streamed *1868:*streamed,

VIII

430   All at once I looked up with terror.
     He was there.
     He himself with his human air.
     On the narrow pathway, just before.
     I saw the back of him, no more—
435   He had left the chapel, then, as I.
     I forgot all about the sky.
     No face: only the sight
     Of a sweepy garment, vast and white,
     With a hem that I could recognize.
440   I felt terror, no surprise;
     My mind filled with the cataract,
     At one bound of the mighty fact.
     "I remember, he did say
       Doubtless that, to this world's end,
445   Where two or three should meet and pray,
       He would be in the midst, their friend;
     Certainly he was there with them!"
       And my pulses leaped for joy
       Of the golden thought without alloy,
450   That I saw his very vesture's hem.
     Then rushed the blood back, cold and clear,
     With a fresh enhancing shiver of fear;
     And I hastened, cried out while I pressed
     To the salvation of the vest,
455   "But not so, Lord! It cannot be
     That thou, indeed, art leaving me—
     Me, that have despised thy friends!
     Did my heart make no amends?
     Thou art the love of God—above

432| MS:He Himself <> His   *1868:*He himself <> his   433| MS:before: *1863:* before.   434| MS:of Him   *1868:*of him   438| *1850:*sweepy Garment   *1863:*sweepy garment   439| MS:recognise. *1888:*recognize.   440| ' MS:surprise: *1865:* surprise;   442| MS:bound, of   *1865:*bound of   443| MS:I remembered, He *1868:*"I remember, he   444| MS:Doubtless, that   *1888:*Doubtless that   446| MS: their Friend: *1863:*their friend: *1868:*friend;   447| MS:Certainly He <>them.   *1865:* them,   *1868:*Certainly he <>them!"   450| MS:saw His   *1850:*very Vesture's *1863:*very vesture's   *1868:*saw his   451| MS:clear   *1888:*clear,   452| MS: fresh, enhancing <> fear,   *1850:*fresh enhancing   *1868:*fear;   454| *1850:*the Vest, *1863:*the vest,   456| MS:That Thou, § *Thou,* inserted above §   *1868:*That thou   457| MS:despised Thy friends.   *1868:*despised thy friends!   459| MS:the Love

460 His power, didst hear me place his love,
And that was leaving the world for thee.
Therefore thou must not turn from me
As I had chosen the other part!
Folly and pride o'ercame my heart.
465 Our best is bad, nor bears thy test;
Still, it should be our very best.
I thought it best that thou, the spirit,
Be worshipped in spirit and in truth,
And in beauty, as even we require it—
470 Not in the forms burlesque, uncouth,
I left but now, as scarcely fitted
For thee: I knew not what I pitied.
But, all I felt there, right or wrong,
What is it to thee, who curest sinning?
475 Am I not weak as thou art strong?
I have looked to thee from the beginning,
Straight up to thee through all the world
Which, like an idle scroll, lay furled
To nothingness on either side:
480 And since the time thou wast descried,
Spite of the weak heart, so have I
Lived ever, and so fain would die,
Living and dying, thee before!
But if thou leavest me——"

IX

Less or more,
485 I suppose that I spoke thus.
When,—have mercy, Lord, on us!
The whole face turned upon me full.

*1863:*the love   460| MS:His Power<>His Love,   *1863:*His power<>love,
*1868:*place his   461| MS:for Thee! *1863:*for Thee. *1868:*for thee: *1888:*thee.
462| MS:Therefore Thou *1868:*Therefore thou   463| MS:As if I <>
part. *1868:*As I *1888:*part!   465| MS:bears Thy *1868:*bears thy   466| MS:
Still it *1863:*Still, it   467| MS:that Thou, the Spirit, *1868:*that thou,
the spirit,   472| MS:For Thee <> pitied: *1863:*pitied. *1868:*For thee   474| MS:
to Thee *1868:*to thee   475| MS:as Thou *1863:*as thou   476| MS:to Thee *1868:*
to thee   477| MS:to Thee *1868:*to thee   480| MS:time Thou *1868:*time thou
483| MS: § crowded between 482-484 § dying, Thee *1868:*dying, thee   484| MS: if Thou
<> me—" § ¶ § Less *1868:*if thou *1888:*me——" § ¶ § Less   487| MS:whole Face

And I spread myself beneath it,
As when the bleacher spreads, to seethe it
490 In the cleansing sun, his wool,—
Steeps in the flood of noontide whiteness
Some defiled, discoloured web—
So lay I, saturate with brightness.
And when the flood appeared to ebb,
495 Lo, I was walking, light and swift,
With my senses settling fast and steadying,
But my body caught up in the whirl and drift
Of the vesture's amplitude, still eddying
On, just before me, still to be followed,
500 As it carried me after with its motion:
What shall I say?—as a path were hollowed
And a man went weltering through the ocean,
Sucked along in the flying wake
Of the luminous water-snake.
505 Darkness and cold were cloven, as through
I passed, upborne yet walking too.
And I turned to myself at intervals,—
"So he said, so it befalls.
God who registers the cup
510 Of mere cold water, for his sake
To a disciple rendered up,
Disdains not his own thirst to slake
At the poorest love was ever offered:
And because my heart I proffered,
515 With true love trembling at the brim,
He suffers me to follow him
For ever, my own way,—dispensed
From seeking to be influenced
By all the less immediate ways

---

*1868:*whole face   492| MS:discolored   *1850:*discoloured   498| *1850:*the Vesture's
*1863:*the vesture's   500| MS:motion,   *1850:*motion: 508| MS:"So He said, and so it
befals.   *1865:*said, so   *1868:*"So he said   *1888:*befalls.   510| MS:for His   *1868:*for
his   512| MS:not His   *1868:*not his   514| MS:because it was my   *1868:*because
my   516| MS:follow Him   *1868:*follow him   517| MS:Forever   *1850:*For ever

⁵²⁰   That earth, in worships manifold,
        Adopts to reach, by prayer and praise,
            The garment's hem, which, lo, I hold!"

                            X

        And so we crossed the world and stopped.
            For where am I, in city or plain,
⁵²⁵   Since I am 'ware of the world again?
        And what is this that rises propped
        With pillars of prodigious girth?
        Is it really on the earth,
        This miraculous Dome of God?
⁵³⁰   Has the angel's measuring-rod
        Which numbered cubits, gem from gem,
        'Twixt the gates of the New Jerusalem,
        Meted it out,—and what he meted,
        Have the sons of men completed?
⁵³⁵   —Binding, ever as he bade,
        Columns in the colonnade
        With arms wide open to embrace
        The entry of the human race
        To the breast of . . . what is it, yon building,
⁵⁴⁰   Ablaze in front, all paint and gilding,
        With marble for brick, and stones of price
        For garniture of the edifice?
        Now I see; it is no dream;
        It stands there and it does not seem:
⁵⁴⁵   For ever, in pictures, thus it looks,
        And thus I have read of it in books
        Often in England, leagues away,

---

^{522|} *1850:*The Garment's   *1863:*The garment's   ^{527|}   MS:girth— § altered to § girth?
^{530|}   MS:the Angel's   *1850:*the angel's   ^{532|}   *1863:*T'wixt   *1865:*'Twixt
^{536|}   MS:in this colonnade   *1868:*in the colonnade   ^{543|}   MS:see: it < > dream:
*1863:*see; it < > dream;   ^{544|}   MS:seem; *1863:*seem: ^{546|}   MS:books, *1863:*

And wondered how these fountains play,
Growing up eternally
550 Each to a musical water-tree,
Whose blossoms drop, a glittering boon,
Before my eyes, in the light of the moon,
To the granite lavers underneath.
Liar and dreamer in your teeth!
555 I, the sinner that speak to you,
Was in Rome this night, and stood, and knew
Both this and more. For see, for see,
The dark is rent, mine eye is free
To pierce the crust of the outer wall,
560 And I view inside, and all there, all,
As the swarming hollow of a hive,
The whole Basilica alive!
Men in the chancel, body and nave,
Men on the pillars' architrave,
565 Men on the statues, men on the tombs
With popes and kings in their porphyry wombs,
All famishing in expectation
Of the main-altar's consummation.
For see, for see, the rapturous moment
570 Approaches, and earth's best endowment
Blends with heaven's; the taper-fires
Pant up, the winding brazen spires
Heave loftier yet the baldachin;
The incense-gaspings, long kept in,
575 Suspire in clouds; the organ blatant
Holds his breath and grovels latent,
As if God's hushing finger grazed him,
(Like Behemoth when he praised him)
At the silver bell's shrill tinkling,
580 Quick cold drops of terror sprinkling
On the sudden pavement strewed
With faces of the multitude.
Earth breaks up, time drops away,
In flows heaven, with its new day

---

books   548| MS:those 1863:these   557| MS:more! For 1863:more. For
563| MS:body, and 1865:body and   571| MS:heaven's: the 1863:with Heaven's;
the 1868:with heaven's   578| MS:when He 1868:when he   584| 1863:flows

585 Of endless life, when He who trod,
Very man and very God,
This earth in weakness, shame and pain,
Dying the death whose signs remain
Up yonder on the accursed tree,—
590 Shall come again, no more to be
Of captivity the thrall,
But the one God, All in all,
King of kings, Lord of lords,
As His servant John received the words,
595 "I died, and live for evermore!"

XI

Yet I was left outside the door.
"Why sit I here on the threshold-stone
Left till He return, alone
Save for the garment's extreme fold
600 Abandoned still to bless my hold?"
My reason, to my doubt, replied,
As if a book were opened wide,
And at a certain page I traced
Every record undefaced,
605 Added by successive years,—
The harvestings of truth's stray ears
Singly gleaned, and in one sheaf
Bound together for belief.
Yes, I said—that he will go
610 And sit with these in turn, I know.
Their faith's heart beats, though her head swims
Too giddily to guide her limbs,
Disabled by their palsy-stroke
From propping mine. Though Rome's gross yoke

Heaven *1868:*flows heaven   585| *1868:*when he *1888:*when He   586| MS:Very
Man *1868:*Very man   592| MS:one God, all *1863:*one God, All   593| MS:
kings, and Lord *1863:*kings, Lord   594| *1868:*As his *1888:*As His   597| MS:
Why sate I there on the threshold-stone, *1863:*sat *1868:*"Why sit I here on *1888:*
threshold-stone   598| MS:returns *1863:*return *1868:*till he *1888:*till He
599| MS:the Garments' *1850:*Garment's *1863:*the garment's   600| MS:hold?—
*1868:*hold?"   601| MS:My Reason *1850:*My reason   606| *1868:*stray years
*1888:*stray ears   609| MS:that He *1868:*that he   614| MS:propping me. Though

615 Drops off, no more to be endured,
    Her teaching is not so obscured
    By errors and perversities,
    That no truth shines athwart the lies:
    And he, whose eye detects a spark
620 Even where, to man's, the whole seems dark,
    May well see flame where each beholder
    Acknowledges the embers smoulder.
    But I, a mere man, fear to quit
    The clue God gave me as most fit
625 To guide my footsteps through life's maze,
    Because himself discerns all ways
    Open to reach him: I, a man
    Able to mark where faith began
    To swerve aside, till from its summit
630 Judgment drops her damning plummet,
    Pronouncing such a fatal space
    Departed from the founder's base:
    He will not bid me enter too,
    But rather sit, as now I do,
635 Awaiting his return outside.
    —'Twas thus my reason straight replied
    And joyously I turned, and pressed
    The garment's skirt upon my breast,
    Until, afresh its light suffusing me,
640 My heart cried—What has been abusing me
    That I should wait here lonely and coldly,
    Instead of rising, entering boldly,
    Baring truth's face, and letting drift
    Her veils of lies as they choose to shift?
645 Do these men praise him? I will raise
    My voice up to their point of praise!

---

*1888:*propping mine. Though   618| MS: § first word illegibly crossed out § That < >
shines through § crossed out and replaced above by § athwart   619| MS:And He
*1868:*And he   626| MS:Because Himself *1868:*Because himself   627| MS:reach
Him *1868:*reach him   628| MS:He gave to *1863:*Able to   630| MS:Judgement
*1850:*Judgment   632| MS:the Founder's *1868:*the founder's   635| MS:Awaiting
His *1865:*Awaiting his   636| MS:replied, *1865:*replied   638| MS:The
Garments' *1863:*The garment's   640| MS:cried,—What *1850:*cried,—what
*1868:*cried "What *1888:*cried—What   643| MS:truths' *1850:*truth's   645| MS:

I see the error; but above
The scope of error, see the love.—
Oh, love of those first Christian days!
650 —Fanned so soon into a blaze,
From the spark preserved by the trampled sect,
That the antique sovereign Intellect
Which then sat ruling in the world,
Like a change in dreams, was hurled
655 From the throne he reigned upon:
You looked up and he was gone.
Gone, his glory of the pen!
—Love, with Greece and Rome in ken,
Bade her scribes abhor the trick
660 Of poetry and rhetoric,
And exult with hearts set free,
In blessed imbecility
Scrawled, perchance, on some torn sheet
Leaving Sallust incomplete.
665 Gone, his pride of sculptor, painter!
—Love, while able to acquaint her
With the thousand statues yet
Fresh from chisel, pictures wet
From brush, she saw on every side,
670 Chose rather with an infant's pride
To frame those portents which impart
Such unction to true Christian Art.
Gone, music too! The air was stirred
By happy wings: Terpander's bird
675 (That, when the cold came, fled away)
Would tarry not the wintry day,—
As more-enduring sculpture must,
Till filthy saints rebuked the gust

---

praise Him *1868:*praise him 653| MS:sate *1863:*sat 656| MS:—You <> up,
and <> gone! *1868:*You <> up and <> gone. 661| MS:exult, with *1868:*exult
with 663| MS:sheet, *1865:*sheet 664| MS:Leaving Livy incomplete. *1863:*
Leaving Sallust incomplete. 667| MS:With the *1868:*While the § emended to § With
the § see Editorial Notes § 670| MS:infants' *1850:*infant's 673| MS:Gone,
Music *1863:*Gone, music 678| MS:Till a filthy saint *1868:*Till filthy saints

With which they chanced to get a sight
680 Of some dear naked Aphrodite
They glanced a thought above the toes of,
By breaking zealously her nose off.
Love, surely, from that music's lingering,
Might have filched her organ-fingering,
685 Nor chosen rather to set prayings
To hog-grunts, praises to horse-neighings.
Love was the startling thing, the new:
Love was the all-sufficient too;
And seeing that, you see the rest:
690 As a babe can find its mother's breast
As well in darkness as in light,
Love shut our eyes, and all seemed right.
True, the world's eyes are open now:
—Less need for me to disallow
695 Some few that keep Love's zone unbuckled,
Peevish as ever to be suckled,
Lulled by the same old baby-prattle
With intermixture of the rattle,
When she would have them creep, stand steady
700 Upon their feet, or walk already,
Not to speak of trying to climb.
I will be wise another time,
And not desire a wall between us,
When next I see a church-roof cover
705 So many species of one genus,
All with foreheads bearing *lover*
Written above the earnest eyes of them;
All with breasts that beat for beauty,
Whether sublimed, to the surprise of them,
710 In noble daring, steadfast duty,
The heroic in passion, or in action,—
Or, lowered for sense's satisfaction,

679| MS:which he chanced *1868:*which they chanced   681| MS:He glanced
*1868:*They glanced   683| MS:lingering. *1850:*lingering,   685| MS:chose *1863:*
chosen   687| MS:new; *1888:*new: 689| MS:rest. *1863:*rest: 693| MS:
worlds' *1850:*world's   699| MS:When when § crossed out §   706| MS:with
§ followed by illegible erasure § foreheads bearing *Lover 1868:*bearing *lover*   710| MS:
stedfast *1863:*steadfast   712| MS:for the senses' *1865:*for senses' *1868:*for sense's

To the mere outside of human creatures,
Mere perfect form and faultless features.
715   What? with all Rome here, whence to levy
          Such contributions to their appetite,
With women and men in a gorgeous bevy,
          They take, as it were, a padlock, clap it tight
On their southern eyes, restrained from feeding
720   On the glories of their ancient reading,
On the beauties of their modern singing,
On the wonders of the builder's bringing,
On the majesties of Art around them,—
          And, all these loves, late struggling incessant,
725   When faith has at last united and bound them,
          They offer up to God for a present?
Why, I will, on the whole, be rather proud of it,—
          And, only taking the act in reference
To the other recipients who might have allowed it,
730   I will rejoice that God had the preference.

                    XII

So I summed up my new resolves:
Too much love there can never be.
And where the intellect devolves
          Its function on love exclusively,
735   I, a man who possesses both,
Will accept the provision, nothing loth,
—Will feast my love, then depart elsewhere,
That my intellect may find its share.
And ponder, O soul, the while thou departest,
740   And see thou applaud the great heart of the artist,

---

⁷¹⁵| MS:What! with *1863:*What? with   ⁷¹⁸| MS:padlock, and clap it *1863:*and it
*1865:*padlock, clap it   ⁷²³| MS:majesties of Art § last three words over illegible
erasure §   ⁷²⁵| MS:united § over illegible erasure §   ⁷²⁶| MS:present! *1863:*
present?   ⁷²⁹| MS:allowed of it, *1868:*allowed it, *1888:*it § emended to § it, § see
Editorial Notes §   ⁷³⁰| MS:preference! *1863:*preference. *1868:*preference." *1888:*
preference.   ⁷³²| *1868:*"Too *1888:*Too   ⁷³⁵| MS:I, as one who *1863:*I, a man

Who, examining the capabilities
    Of the block of marble he has to fashion
    Into a type of thought or passion,—
Not always, using obvious facilities,
745 Shapes it, as any artist can,
Into a perfect symmetrical man,
Complete from head to foot of the life-size,
Such as old Adam stood in his wife's eyes,—
But, now and then, bravely aspires to consummate
750 A Colossus by no means so easy to come at,
And uses the whole of his block for the bust,
    Leaving the mind of the public to finish it,
Since cut it ruefully short he must:
On the face alone he expends his devotion,
755   He rather would mar than resolve to diminish it,
—Saying, "Applaud me for this grand notion
Of what a face may be! As for completing it
    In breast and body and limbs, do that, you!"
All hail! I fancy how, happily meeting it,
760   A trunk and legs would perfect the statue,
Could man carve so as to answer volition.
    And how much nobler than petty cavils,
    Were a hope to find, in my spirit-travels,
Some artist of another ambition,
765 Who having a block to carve, no bigger,
    Has spent his power on the opposite quest,
    And believed to begin at the feet was best—
For so may I see, ere I die, the whole figure!

XIII

No sooner said than out in the night!
770 My heart beat lighter and more light:
And still, as before, I was walking swift,
    With my senses settling fast and steadying,
But my body caught up in the whirl and drift
    Of the vesture's amplitude, still eddying

---

who   ⁷⁴¹| MS:Who examining   *1850:*Who, examining   ⁷⁵²| MS:minds   *1865:*
mind   ⁷⁵⁴| MS:devotion; *1863:*devotion,   ⁷⁵⁸| MS:*that* *1868:*that,
⁷⁶³| MS:A   *1863:*Were a   ⁷⁶⁸| *1868:*figure!" *1888:*figure!   ⁷⁶⁹⁻⁷⁷⁰| MS:
night! / And still as we swept through storm and night, / My *1863:*night! / My
⁷⁷¹| MS:And, lo, as *1850:*And lo *1863:*And still, as   ⁷⁷⁴| MS:the Vesture's *1863:*

775　On just before me, still to be followed,
　　　　As it carried me after with its motion,
　　　—What shall I say?—as a path were hollowed,
　　　　And a man went weltering through the ocean,
　　　Sucked along in the flying wake
780　Of the luminous water-snake.

　　　　　　　　　XIV

　　　Alone! I am left alone once more—
　　　　(Save for the garment's extreme fold
　　　　Abandoned still to bless my hold)
　　　Alone, beside the entrance-door
785　Of a sort of temple,—perhaps a college,
　　　—Like nothing I ever saw before
　　　At home in England, to my knowledge.
　　　The tall old quaint irregular town!
　　　　It may be . . . though which, I can't affirm . . . any
790　　Of the famous middle-age towns of Germany;
　　　And this flight of stairs where I sit down,
　　　Is it Halle, Weimar, Cassel, Frankfort
　　　Or Göttingen, I have to thank for 't?
　　　It may be Göttingen,—most likely.
795　Through the open door I catch obliquely
　　　Glimpses of a lecture-hall;
　　　　And not a bad assembly neither,
　　　Ranged decent and symmetrical
　　　　On benches, waiting what's to see there;
800　Which, holding still by the vesture's hem,
　　　I also resolve to see with them,
　　　Cautious this time how I suffer to slip
　　　The chance of joining in fellowship
　　　With any that call themselves his friends;
805　　As these folk do, I have a notion.
　　　　But hist—a buzzing and emotion!

---

the vesture's　　782| MS:the Garment's　1863:the garment's　　788| MS:tall, old,
quaint, irregular　1868:tall old quaint irregular　　789| MS:be . . though *which* <>
affirm . . any　1868:which § emended to § be . . . though<>affirm . . . any § see
Editorial Notes §　　792| MS:Cassel, or Frankfort,　1868:Cassel, Frankfort,　1888:
Frankfort　　793| MS:Or Göttingen, that I　1868:or Göttingen, I　　797| MS:
neither—　1868:neither,　　800| MS:the Vesture's　1863:the vesture's　　804| MS:
themselves His friends,　1868:themselves his friends;　　805| MS:folks　1865:do I

All settle themselves, the while ascends
By the creaking rail to the lecture-desk,
Step by step, deliberate
810   Because of his cranium's over-freight,
Three parts sublime to one grotesque,
If I have proved an accurate guesser,
The hawk-nosed high-cheek-boned Professor.
I felt at once as if there ran
815 A shoot of love from my heart to the man—
That sallow virgin-minded studious
    Martyr to mild enthusiasm,
As he uttered a kind of cough-preludious
    That woke my sympathetic spasm,
820 (Beside some spitting that made me sorry)
And stood, surveying his auditory
With a wan pure look, well nigh celestial,—
    Those blue eyes had survived so much!
While, under the foot they could not smutch,
825 Lay all the fleshly and the bestial.
Over he bowed, and arranged his notes,
Till the auditory's clearing of throats
Was done with, died into a silence;
    And, when each glance was upward sent,
830   Each bearded mouth composed intent,
And a pin might be heard drop half a mile hence,—
He pushed back higher his spectacles,
Let the eyes stream out like lamps from cells,
And giving his head of hair—a hake
835   Of undressed tow, for colour and quantity—
One rapid and impatient shake,
    (As our own Young England adjusts a jaunty tie
When about to impart, on mature digestion,
Some thrilling view of the surplice-question)
840 —The Professor's grave voice, sweet though hoarse,
Broke into his Christmas-Eve discourse.

1868:do, I   *1888*:folk   ⁸¹³| MS:hawk-nosed, high-cheek-boned *1888*:hawk-nosed high-cheek-boned   ⁸¹⁶| MS:sallow, virgin-minded, studious *1868*:sallow virgin-minded studious   ⁸²³| MS:—Those *1863*:Those   ⁸²⁸| MS:into a § inserted above §   ⁸³⁴| MS:hair,—a *1850*:hair—a   ⁸³⁵| MS:color *1863*:colour *1888*:quantity DC, BrU:quantity— *1889*:quantity—   ⁸³⁷| *1850*:own young DC:own Young *1889*:own Young   ⁸⁴¹| MS:his Christmas-Eve's *1868*:his

XV

And he began it by observing
How reason dictated that men
Should rectify the natural swerving,
845   By a reversion, now and then,
To the well-heads of knowledge, few
And far away, whence rolling grew
The life-stream wide whereat we drink,
Commingled, as we needs must think,
850 With waters alien to the source;
To do which, aimed this eve's discourse;
Since, where could be a fitter time
For tracing backward to its prime
This Christianity, this lake,
855 This reservoir, whereat we slake,
From one or other bank, our thirst?
So, he proposed inquiring first
Into the various sources whence
This Myth of Christ is derivable;
860 Demanding from the evidence,
(Since plainly no such life was liveable)
How these phenomena should class?
Whether 'twere best opine Christ was,
Or never was at all, or whether
865 He was and was not, both together—
It matters little for the name,
So the idea be left the same.
Only, for practical purpose' sake,
'Twas obviously as well to take
870 The popular story,—understanding
How the ineptitude of the time,
And the penman's prejudice, expanding
Fact into fable fit for the clime,
Had, by slow and sure degrees, translated it
875   Into this myth, this Individuum,—
Which, when reason had strained and abated it

Christmas-Eve   850| MS:source: 1863:source;   851| MS:this Eve's discourse.
1863:this eve's discourse: 1865:discourse;   853| MS:prime, 1888:prime
857| MS:So he 1863:So, he   867| MS:the Idea <> same: 1863:same. 1868:

Of foreign matter, left, for residuum,
A Man!—a right true man, however,
Whose work was worthy a man's endeavour:
880 Work, that gave warrant almost sufficient
To his disciples, for rather believing
He was just omnipotent and omniscient,
As it gives to us, for as frankly receiving
His word, their tradition,—which, though it meant
885 Something entirely different
From all that those who only heard it,
In their simplicity thought and averred it,
Had yet a meaning quite as respectable:
For, among other doctrines delectable,
890 Was he not surely the first to insist on
The natural sovereignty of our race?—
Here the lecturer came to a pausing-place.
And while his cough, like a drouthy piston,
Tried to dislodge the husk that grew to him,
895 I seized the occasion of bidding adieu to him,
The vesture still within my hand.

XVI

I could interpret its command.
This time he would not bid me enter
The exhausted air-bell of the Critic.
900 Truth's atmosphere may grow mephitic
When Papist struggles with Dissenter,
Impregnating its pristine clarity,
—One, by his daily fare's vulgarity,
Its gust of broken meat and garlic;
905 —One, by his soul's too-much presuming
To turn the frankincense's fuming
And vapours of the candle starlike

---

the idea   877| MS:matter, gave, for 1868:matter, left, for   878| 1865:aright
1868:a right   879| MS:endeavour! 1863:endeavour: 887| MS:thought and
§ last two words inserted above §   890| MS:surely § over illegible word § <> on,
1863:on   895| MS:siezed 1850:seized   896| MS:The Vesture 1863:The vesture
898| MS:time He 1868:time he   905| MS:soul § altered to § soul's <> presuming,
1863:presuming 1865:presuming, 1868:presuming   906| MS:To turn § last
two words over illegible erasure § the frankincence's 1850:frankincense's

81

Into the cloud her wings she buoys on.
　　Each, that thus sets the pure air seething,
910　　May poison it for healthy breathing—
But the Critic leaves no air to poison;
Pumps out with ruthless ingenuity
Atom by atom, and leaves you—vacuity.
Thus much of Christ does he reject?
915 And what retain? His intellect?
What is it I must reverence duly?
Poor intellect for worship, truly,
Which tells me simply what was told
　　(If mere morality, bereft
920　　Of the God in Christ, be all that's left)
Elsewhere by voices manifold;
With this advantage, that the stater
　　Made nowise the important stumble
　　Of adding, he, the sage and humble,
925 Was also one with the Creator.
You urge Christ's followers' simplicity:
　　But how does shifting blame, evade it?
Have wisdom's words no more felicity?
　　The stumbling-block, his speech—who laid it?
930 How comes it that for one found able
To sift the truth of it from fable,
Millions believe it to the letter?
Christ's goodness, then—does that fare better?
Strange goodness, which upon the score
935　　Of being goodness, the mere due
Of man to fellow-man, much more

908| MS:on: *1863:*on.　　　　909| MS:And each that sets the pure § last six words
over illegible erasure § air § inserted above § *1850:*each, that *1863:*Each, that
thus sets　　　910| MS:Poisoning it § last two words over illegible erasure § *1863:*
May poison it　　　912| MS:out by a ruthless *1868:*out with ruthless
913| MS:you— § inserted above § vacuity　　　914| MS:of Christ, does *1888:*of
Christ does　　　915| MS:what, retain *1850:*what retain　　　918| MS:tells one
<> what was § inserted above § *1850:*tells me　　　920| MS:Of the § inserted above §
923| MS: § most of original line illegibly crossed out § Made nowise § last two words
in left margin § the important § inserted above §　　　929| MS:stumbling-block,
His *1865:*stumbling-block, his　　　930| MS:come § altered to § comes<>able, *1863:*
able　　　931| MS: §first word illegiby erased § to § altered to § To <> of it § last two
words inserted above §　　　935| MS:Of § next several words illegibly erased and replaced
by two words § being goodness, the mere § inserted above §　　　936| MS:Of man § last

82

To God,—should take another view
Of its possessor's privilege,
And bid him rule his race! You pledge
940　Your fealty to such rule? What, all—
From heavenly John and Attic Paul,
And that brave weather-battered Peter,
Whose stout faith only stood completer
For buffets, sinning to be pardoned,
945　As, more his hands hauled nets, they hardened,—
All, down to you, the man of men,
Professing here at Göttingen,
Compose Christ's flock! They, you and I,
Are sheep of a good man! And why?
950　The goodness,—how did he acquire it?
Was it self-gained, did God inspire it?
Choose which; then tell me, on what ground
Should its possessor dare propound
His claim to rise o'er us an inch?
955　　Were goodness all some man's invention,
　　Who arbitrarily made mention
What we should follow, and whence flinch,—
　　What qualities might take the style
　　Of right and wrong,—and had such guessing
960　　Met with as general acquiescing
As graced the alphabet erewhile,
When A got leave an Ox to be,
No Camel (quoth the Jews) like G,—
For thus inventing thing and title
965　Worship were that man's fit requital.
But if the common conscience must
Be ultimately judge, adjust
Its apt name to each quality
Already known,—I would decree

---

two words in left margin § to fellow-man, § next word illegibly erased § much
941|　MS:From Heavenly 1865:From heavenly 　　942|　MS:weather-battered Peter
1888:weather-battered Peter, 　　945|　MS:As the more 1868:As, more 　　948|　MS:
flock! So, you and I 1863:flock! They, you 1868:and I, 　　949|　MS:man! and
1868:man! And 　　957|　MS:and where flinch,— 1868:and whence flinch,—
961|　MS:the Alphabet 1868:the alphabet 　　964|　MS:For thus § last two words in left
margin § inventing § space allowed for hole in leaf § 　　965|　MS:were § over

970 Worship for such mere demonstration
    And simple work of nomenclature,
Only the day I praised, not nature,
    But Harvey, for the circulation.
I would praise such a Christ, with pride
975 And joy, that he, as none beside,
Had taught us how to keep the mind
God gave him, as God gave his kind,
Freer than they from fleshly taint:
I would call such a Christ our Saint,
980 As I declare our Poet, him
Whose insight makes all others dim:
A thousand poets pried at life,
And only one amid the strife
Rose to be Shakespeare: each shall take
985 His crown, I'd say, for the world's sake—
Though some objected—"Had we seen
The heart and head of each, what screen
Was broken there to give them light,
While in ourselves it shuts the sight,
990 We should no more admire, perchance,
That these found truth out at a glance,
Than marvel how the bat discerns
Some pitch-dark cavern's fifty turns,
Led by a finer tact, a gift
995 He boasts, which other birds must shift
Without, and grope as best they can."
No, freely I would praise the man,—
Nor one whit more, if he contended
That gift of his, from God descended.
1000 Ah friend, what gift of man's does not?
No nearer something, by a jot,

---

illegible erasure § < > man's fit § inserted above §   972| *1850:*not Nature, *1868:*not
nature,   978| MS:taint! § perhaps *taint:*§ *1863:*taint: 982| *1865:*thousand
Poets *1868:*thousand poets   984| MS:be Shakespeare! Each *1863:*be Shakespeare:
each   999| MS:from God, descended. *1888:*from God descended.   1000| MS:Ah,
friend *1865:*Ah friend   1001| MS:nearer Something *1868:*nearer something

Rise an infinity of nothings
　　　Than one: take Euclid for your teacher:
Distinguish kinds: do crownings, clothings,
1005　　　Make that creator which was creature?
Multiply gifts upon man's head,
And what, when all's done, shall be said
But—the more gifted he, I ween!
　　　That one's made Christ, this other, Pilate,
1010　And this might be all that has been,—
　　　So what is there to frown or smile at?
What is left for us, save, in growth
Of soul, to rise up, far past both,
From the gift looking to the giver,
1015　And from the cistern to the river,
And from the finite to infinity,
And from man's dust to God's divinity?

XVII

Take all in a word: the truth in God's breast
Lies trace for trace upon ours impressed:
1020　Though he is so bright and we so dim,
We are made in his image to witness him:
And were no eye in us to tell,
　　　Instructed by no inner sense,
The light of heaven from the dark of hell,
1025　　　That light would want its evidence,—
Though justice, good and truth were still
Divine, if, by some demon's will,
Hatred and wrong had been proclaimed

1002| MS:of Nothings 1868:of nothings   1005| 1850:that Creator 1868:that creator
1006| MS:upon his head, 1868:upon man's head,   1008| MS:But . . the 1863:But
—the   1009| MS:made Christ, another, Pilate, 1863:made Christ, this other,
Pilate,   1010| MS:And This <> That 1868:And this <> that   1012| MS:is
left for us, save, in growth, § last seven words over illegible erasure §
1863:growth   1013| MS:of soul, to rise § last four words over illegible
erasure §   1014| MS:the Giver, 1868:the giver,   1015| MS:the River,
1868:the river,   1016| MS:to Infinity, 1868:to infinity,   1018| MS:the
Truth 1863:the truth   1020| MS:Though He 1868:Though he   1021| MS:in
His <> Him; 1868:in his <> him: 1023| MS: § crowded between 1022-1024 §
1024| MS:of Heaven <> the § inserted above § <> Hell, 1868:of heaven
<>hell,   1026| MS:Though Justice, Good and Truth 1868:Though justice,

Law through the worlds, and right misnamed.
1030 No mere exposition of morality
Made or in part or in totality,
Should win you to give it worship, therefore:
And, if no better proof you will care for,
—Whom do you count the worst man upon earth?
1035   Be sure, he knows, in his conscience, more
Of what right is, than arrives at birth
    In the best man's acts that we bow before:
This last knows better—true, but my fact is,
'Tis one thing to know, and another to practise.
1040 And thence I conclude that the real God-function
Is to furnish a motive and injunction
For practising what we know already.
And such an injunction and such a motive
As the God in Christ, do you waive, and "heady,
1045 High-minded," hang your tablet-votive
Outside the fane on a finger-post?
Morality to the uttermost,
Supreme in Christ as we all confess,
Why need we prove would avail no jot
1050 To make him God, if God he were not?
What is the point where himself lays stress?
Does the precept run "Believe in good,
In justice, truth, now understood
For the first time"?—or, "Believe in me,
1055 Who lived and died, yet essentially
Am Lord of Life"? Whoever can take
The same to his heart and for mere love's sake
Conceive of the love,—that man obtains
A new truth; no conviction gains
1060 Of an old one only, made intense
By a fresh appeal to his faded sense.

---

good and truth   1029| MS:and Right   *1868:*and right   1036| MS:what Right
*1868:*what right   1038| MS:*knows* <>true; but   *1863:*true, but   *1868:*knows
1039| MS:practise;   *1863:*practise.   1044| MS:"heady   *1863:*"heady,   1045| MS:
High minded   *1863:*High-minded   1049| MS:*we*   *1868:*we   1050| MS:make
Him <> He   *1868:*make him <> he   1051| MS:where Himself
*1868:*where himself   1052| MS:in Good,   *1865:*in good,   1053| MS:In Justice,
Truth   *1865:*In justice, truth   1054| MS:time"?— <>Me,   *1850:*time"?— <>
ME,   *1868:*me, § emended to § time"?— § see Editorial Notes §   1056| MS:

XVIII

Can it be that he stays inside?
   Is the vesture left me to commune with?
   Could my soul find aught to sing in tune with
¹⁰⁶⁵ Even at this lecture, if she tried?
Oh, let me at lowest sympathize
With the lurking drop of blood that lies
In the desiccated brain's white roots
Without throb for Christ's attributes,
¹⁰⁷⁰ As the lecturer makes his special boast!
If love's dead there, it has left a ghost.
Admire we, how from heart to brain
   (Though to say so strike the doctors dumb)
One instinct rises and falls again,
¹⁰⁷⁵   Restoring the equilibrium.
And how when the Critic had done his best,
And the pearl of price, at reason's test,
Lay dust and ashes levigable
On the Professor's lecture-table,—
¹⁰⁸⁰ When we looked for the inference and monition
That our faith, reduced to such condition,
Be swept forthwith to its natural dust-hole,—
   He bids us, when we least expect it,
   Take back our faith,—if it be not just whole,
¹⁰⁸⁵   Yet a pearl indeed, as his tests affect it,
Which fact pays damage done rewardingly,
So, prize we our dust and ashes accordingly!
"Go home and venerate the myth
I thus have experimented with—
¹⁰⁹⁰ This man, continue to adore him

Life"? *1850:*Life?" § emended to § Life"? § see Editorial Notes §   ¹⁰⁶²| MS:
that He *1868:*"Can < > he *1888:*Can   ¹⁰⁶³| MS:the Vesture *1863:*the vesture
¹⁰⁶⁶| MS:sympathise *1863:*sympathize   ¹⁰⁶⁹| MS:Without a throb *1868:*
Without throb   ¹⁰⁷⁰| MS:the Lecturer *1868:*the lecturer   ¹⁰⁷⁷| MS:the Pearl
of Price *1868:*the pearl of price   ¹⁰⁷⁹| MS:lecture-table; *1868:*lecture-table,—
¹⁰⁸¹| MS:That our § inserted above § < > such a condition, *1868:*
such condition,   ¹⁰⁸⁴| MS:Take back § inserted above § our
faith,— §,— over illegible erasure §   ¹⁰⁸⁶| MS:pays the § inserted above § damage
*1868:*pays damage   ¹⁰⁸⁸| MS:"Go home & § last three words in erased
space § < > the Myth *1868:*the myth   ¹⁰⁹⁰| MS:This Man *1868:*This man

Rather than all who went before him,
    And all who ever followed after!"—
    Surely for this I may praise you, my brother!
Will you take the praise in tears or laughter?
1095   That's one point gained: can I compass another?
Unlearned love was safe from spurning—
Can't we respect your loveless learning?
Let us at least give learning honour!
What laurels had we showered upon her,
1100 Girding her loins up to perturb
Our theory of the Middle Verb;
Or Turk-like brandishing a scimitar
O'er anapaests in comic-trimeter;
Or curing the halt and maimed 'Iketides,'
1105 While we lounged on at our indebted ease:
Instead of which, a tricksy demon
Sets her at Titus or Philemon!
When ignorance wags his ears of leather
And hates God's word, 'tis altogether;
1110 Nor leaves he his congenial thistles
To go and browse on Paul's Epistles.
—And you, the audience, who might ravage
The world wide, enviably savage,
Nor heed the cry of the retriever,
1115 More than Herr Heine (before his fever),—
I do not tell a lie so arrant
    As say my passion's wings are furled up,
And, without plainest heavenly warrant,
    I were ready and glad to give the world up—

1092| *1889:*after!'— § emended to §   after!"— § see Editorial Notes §
1098| MS:give Learning honor! *1863:*honour! *1868:*give learning   1102| MS:Or
Turklike <> scimitar *1850:*scimetar *1863:*Or Turk-like <> scimitar
1104| MS:maimed Iketides, *1868:*maimed 'Iketides,'   1108| MS:
When Ignorance *1868:*When ignorance   1111| MS:browze *1865:*browse
1113| MS:savage *1863:*savage,   1118| MS: without the plainest Heavenly
*1865:*plainest heavenly *1868:*without plainest   1119| MS:give this world

¹¹²⁰ But still, when you rub brow meticulous,
    And ponder the profit of turning holy
    If not for God's, for your own sake solely,
—God forbid I should find you ridiculous!
Deduce from this lecture all that eases you,
¹¹²⁵ Nay, call yourselves, if the calling pleases you,
"Christians,"—abhor the deist's pravity,—
Go on, you shall no more move my gravity
Than, when I see boys ride a-cockhorse,
I find it in my heart to embarrass them
¹¹³⁰ By hinting that their stick's a mock horse,
And they really carry what they say carries them.

XIX

So sat I talking with my mind.
    I did not long to leave the door
    And find a new church, as before,
¹¹³⁵ But rather was quiet and inclined
To prolong and enjoy the gentle resting
From further tracking and trying and testing.
"This tolerance is a genial mood!"
(Said I, and a little pause ensued).
¹¹⁴⁰ "One trims the bark 'twixt shoal and shelf,
    And sees, each side, the good effects of it,
A value for religion's self,
    A carelessness about the sects of it.
Let me enjoy my own conviction,
¹¹⁴⁵   Not watch my neighbour's faith with fretfulness,
Still spying there some dereliction
    Of truth, perversity, forgetfulness!
Better a mild indifferentism,
    Teaching that both our faiths (though duller

---

*1868:*give the world   ¹¹²⁰| MS:rub the brow *1868:*rub brow   ¹¹²⁶| MS:the
Deist's *1868:*deist's   ¹¹²⁷| MS:gravity, *1868:*gravity   ¹¹²⁸| MS:a-cockhorse
*1868:*a-cockhorse,   ¹¹³¹| *1868:*them." *1888:*them.   ¹¹³²| MS:sate *1863:*sat
¹¹³⁸|MS:This <> mood! *1868:*"This <> mood!"   ¹¹³⁹| MS:ensued)
*1850:*ensued).   ¹¹⁴⁰| MS:One *1868:*"One   ¹¹⁴⁹| MS:To teach that all our

¹¹⁵⁰ His shine through a dull spirit's prism)
  Originally had one colour!
 Better pursue a pilgrimage
  Through ancient and through modern times
  To many peoples, various climes,
¹¹⁵⁵ Where I may see saint, savage, sage
 Fuse their respective creeds in one
 Before the general Father's throne!"

XX

 —'Twas the horrible storm began afresh!
 The black night caught me in his mesh,
¹¹⁶⁰ Whirled me up, and flung me prone.
 I was left on the college-step alone.
 I looked, and far there, ever fleeting
 Far, far away, the receding gesture,
 And looming of the lessening vesture!—
¹¹⁶⁵ Swept forward from my stupid hand,
 While I watched my foolish heart expand
 In the lazy glow of benevolence,
  O'er the various modes of man's belief.
 I sprang up with fear's vehemence.
¹¹⁷⁰ Needs must there be one way, our chief
 Best way of worship: let me strive
 To find it, and when found, contrive
 My fellows also take their share!
 This constitutes my earthly care:
¹¹⁷⁵ God's is above it and distinct.
 For I, a man, with men am linked
 And not a brute with brutes; no gain
 That I experience, must remain
 Unshared: but should my best endeavour

---

*1863:*Teaching that *1868:*that both our ¹¹⁵⁰ MS:shines *1863:*shine
¹¹⁵¹| MS:color— *1850:*colour— *1868:*colour! ¹¹⁵²| MS:Sending me on a *1868:*
Better pursue a ¹¹⁵³| MS: § crowded between 1152-1154; first two words illegibly
crossed out § Through ¹¹⁵⁵| MS:see Saint, Savage, Sage *1868:*see saint, savage,
sage ¹¹⁵⁷| MS:throne! *1868:*throne!" ¹¹⁵⁸| MS: . . 'Twas *1863:*—'Twas
¹¹⁵⁹| MS:mesh *1868:*mesh, ¹¹⁶⁴| MS:lessening vesture, *1850:*lessening Vesture,
*1863:*lessening vesture!— ¹¹⁷⁰| MS:—Needs *1868:*"Needs *1888:*Needs
¹¹⁷³| MS:share. *1863:*share! ¹¹⁷⁵| MS:distinct! *1863:*distinct. ¹¹⁷⁶| MS:linked,

90

1180 To share it, fail—subsisteth ever
God's care above, and I exult
That God, by God's own ways occult,
May—doth, I will believe—bring back
All wanderers to a single track.
1185 Meantime, I can but testify
God's care for me—no more, can I—
It is but for myself I know;
    The world rolls witnessing around me
    Only to leave me as it found me;
1190 Men cry there, but my ear is slow:
Their races flourish or decay
—What boots it, while yon lucid way
Loaded with stars divides the vault?
But soon my soul repairs its fault
1195 When, sharpening sense's hebetude,
She turns on my own life! So viewed,
No mere mote's-breadth but teems immense
With witnessings of providence:
And woe to me if when I look
1200 Upon that record, the sole book
Unsealed to me, I take no heed
Of any warning that I read!
Have I been sure, this Christmas-Eve,
God's own hand did the rainbow weave,
1205 Whereby the truth from heaven slid
Into my soul?—I cannot bid
The world admit he stooped to heal
My soul, as if in a thunder-peal
Where one heard noise, and one saw flame,
1210 I only knew he named my name:
But what is the world to me, for sorrow

*1888:*linked   1184| MS:track! *1863:*track.   1187| MS:myself I *Know. 1850:*myself
I *know. 1863:*know; *1868:*know;   1190| MS:slow. *1863:*slow: 1193| MS:stars,
divides *1868:*stars divides   1194| MS:How soon *1863:*But soon   1195| MS:senses'
*1863:*sense's   1198| *1863:*of Providence: *1868:*of providence: 1203| MS:this
Christmas-eve, *1850:*this Christmas-Eve,   1207| MS:admit He *1868:*admit he
1210| MS:knew He <> name. *1863:*name: *1868:*knew he   1211| MS:And what

Or joy in its censure, when to-morrow
It drops the remark, with just-turned head
Then, on again, 'That man is dead'?
1215 Yes, but for me—my name called,—drawn
As a conscript's lot from the lap's black yawn,
He has dipt into on a battle-dawn:
Bid out of life by a nod, a glance,—
Stumbling, mute-mazed, at nature's chance,—
1220 With a rapid finger circled round,
Fixed to the first poor inch of ground
To fight from, where his foot was found;
Whose ear but a minute since lay free
To the wide camp's buzz and gossipry—
1225 Summoned, a solitary man
To end his life where his life began,
From the safe glad rear, to the dreadful van!
Soul of mine, hadst thou caught and held
By the hem of the vesture!—

XXI

And I caught
1230 At the flying robe, and unrepelled
Was lapped again in its folds full-fraught
With warmth and wonder and delight,
God's mercy being infinite.
For scarce had the words escaped my tongue,
1235 When, at a passionate bound, I sprung,
Out of the wandering world of rain,
Into the little chapel again.

XXII

How else was I found there, bolt upright
On my bench, as if I had never left it?

---

*1863:*But what   1212| MS:censures *1863:*censure   1214| MS:again—That
<> dead? *1863:*again—that *1868:*again, 'That <> dead?' *1888:*dead'?
1215| MS:Yes,—but *1863:*Yes, but   1221| MS:ground, *1863:*ground   1224| MS:
camps *1850:*camp's   1225| MS:man, *1888:*man   1227| MS:safe glad rear,
§ last three words over illegible erasure § to   1229| MS:the Vesture . . . § ¶
§ And *1863:*the vesture!— § ¶ § And *1868:*vesture!—" § ¶ § And *1888:*vesture!—
§ ¶ §And   1230| MS:flying Robe *1863:*flying robe   1234| MS:And scarce
*1863:*For scarce   1235| MS:sprung *1888:*sprung,   1238| MS: § marginal note that

1240   —Never flung out on the common at night,
      Nor met the storm and wedge-like cleft it,
    Seen the raree-show of Peter's successor,
    Or the laboratory of the Professor!
    For the Vision, that was true, I wist,
1245   True as that heaven and earth exist.
    There sat my friend, the yellow and tall,
      With his neck and its wen in the selfsame place;
    Yet my nearest neighbour's cheek showed gall.
      She had slid away a contemptuous space:
1250   And the old fat woman, late so placable,
    Eyed me with symptoms, hardly mistakable,
    Of her milk of kindness turning rancid.
    In short, a spectator might have fancied
    That I had nodded, betrayed by slumber,
1255   Yet kept my seat, a warning ghastly,
    Through the heads of the sermon, nine in number,
    And woke up now at the tenth and lastly.
    But again, could such disgrace have happened?
      Each friend at my elbow had surely nudged it;
1260   And, as for the sermon, where did my nap end?
      Unless I heard it, could I have judged it?
    Could I report as I do at the close,
    First, the preacher speaks through his nose:
    Second, his gesture is too emphatic:
1265   Thirdly, to waive what's pedagogic,
      The subject-matter itself lacks logic:
    Fourthly, the English is ungrammatic.
    Great news! the preacher is found no Pascal,
    Whom, if I pleased, I might to the task call
1270   Of making square to a finite eye
    The circle of infinity,
    And find so all-but-just-succeeding!
    Great news! the sermon proves no reading
    Where bee-like in the flowers I bury me,

¶ begins § *1868:*upright. *1888:*upright   1240| MS:night *1888:*night,
1244| MS:*that 1868:*that   1245| MS:True § added in left margin § As that § next
word illegible, possibly *a* § heaven *1850:*True as that heaven   1246| MS:sate
*1863:*sat   1248| MS:gall, *1888:*gall.   1251| MS: § first word illegibly erased and
replaced by § Eyed <> mistakeable, *1863:*mistakable,   1252| MS:rancid: *1863:*
rancid.   1253| MS:short a *1868:*short, a   1254| MS:nodded betrayed by a
slumber, *1863:*by slumber, *1888:*nodded, betrayed   1257| MS:To wake *1863:*And
woke   1258| MS:such a disgrace *1868:*such disgrace   1274| MS:flowers I may

93

1275   Like Taylor's the immortal Jeremy!
        And now that I know the very worst of him,
        What was it I thought to obtain at first of him?
        Ha! Is God mocked, as he asks?
        Shall I take on me to change his tasks,
1280   And dare, despatched to a river-head
            For a simple draught of the element,
        Neglect the thing for which he sent,
            And return with another thing instead?—
        Saying, "Because the water found
1285   Welling up from underground,
        Is mingled with the taints of earth,
        While thou, I know, dost laugh at dearth,
        And couldst, at wink or word, convulse
        The world with the leap of a river-pulse,—
1290   Therefore I turned from the oozings muddy,
            And bring thee a chalice I found, instead:
        See the brave veins in the breccia ruddy!
            One would suppose that the marble bled.
        What matters the water? A hope I have nursed:
1295   The waterless cup will quench my thirst."
        —Better have knelt at the poorest stream
            That trickles in pain from the straitest rift!
            For the less or the more is all God's gift,
        Who blocks up or breaks wide the granite-seam.
1300   And here, is there water or not, to drink?
        I then, in ignorance and weakness,
        Taking God's help, have attained to think
            My heart does best to receive in meekness
        That mode of worship, as most to his mind,

---

bury *1888:*flowers I bury   1275| MS:Like Taylor's, the *1888:*Like Taylor's the
1278| MS:as He *1868:*as he   1279| MS:change His *1868:*change his
1280| *1863:*dispatched *1888:*despatched   1282| MS:which He *1868:*which he
1284| MS:Saying . . "Because *1863:*Saying, "Because   1287| MS:While Thou
*1868:*While thou   1288| MS:couldest, at a word *1868:*couldst, at wink or word
1289| MS:of its river-pulse,— *1865:*of a river-pulse,—   1291| MS:bring Thee
*1850:*bring thee *1865:*bring Thee *1868:*bring thee   1294| MS:nursed, *1888:*
nursed: 1295| MS:That the *1865:*The   1297| MS:straightest *1850:*straitest
1301| MS:I, then *1865:*I then   1303| MS:meekness §over illegible word, perhaps
weakness §   1304| MS:This mode <> His *1863:*That mode *1868:*his

1305 Where earthly aids being cast behind,
His All in All appears serene
With the thinnest human veil between,
Letting the mystic lamps, the seven,
The many motions of his spirit,
1310 Pass, as they list, to earth from heaven.
For the preacher's merit or demerit,
It were to be wished the flaws were fewer
In the earthen vessel, holding treasure
Which lies as safe in a golden ewer;
1315 But the main thing is, does it hold good measure?
Heaven soon sets right all other matters!—
Ask, else, these ruins of humanity,
This flesh worn out to rags and tatters,
This soul at struggle with insanity,
1320 Who thence take comfort—can I doubt?—
Which an empire gained, were a loss without.
May it be mine! And let us hope
That no worse blessing befall the Pope,
Turned sick at last of to-day's buffoonery,
1325 Of posturings and petticoatings,
Beside his Bourbon bully's gloatings
In the bloody orgies of drunk poltroonery!
Nor may the Professor forego its peace
At Göttingen presently, when, in the dusk
1330 Of his life, if his cough, as I fear, should increase,
Prophesied of by that horrible husk—
When thicker and thicker the darkness fills
The world through his misty spectacles,
And he gropes for something more substantial

1306| MS:serene, *1863:*serene   1308| MS:mystic Lamps, the Seven, *1868:*mystic
lamps, the seven,   1309| MS:of His *1868:*of his   1310| MS:from Heaven.
*1865:*from heaven.   1313| MS:treasure, *1888:*treasure   1314| MS:ewer, *1850:*ewer;
1316| MS:matters! *1850:*matters!—   1317| MS:of Humanity, *1850:*of humanity,
1320| MS:comfort, can I doubt, *1868:*doubt? *1888:*comfort—can I doubt?—
1323| MS:befal *1863:*befall   1324| MS:Turnd <> of the day's *1850:*Turn'd *1865:*
of to-day's *1888:*Turned   1325| MS:Of his posturings and his petticoatings,
*1863:*Of its posturings and its petticoatings, *1865:*Of posturings and petticoatings,
1326| MS:Beside the Bourbon *1863:*Beside his Bourbon   1328| MS:forgo *1850:*
forego   1329| MS:At Göttingen, presently *1865:*At Göttingen presently
1331| MS:Prophecied <> husk; *1850:*Prophesied *1865:*husk—   1332| MS:And when,
thicker and thicker, the *1863:*When, thicker *1865:*When thicker and thicker the

1335   Than a fable, myth or personification,—
       May Christ do for him what no mere man shall,
         And stand confessed as the God of salvation!
       Meantime, in the still recurring fear
         Lest myself, at unawares, be found,
1340   While attacking the choice of my neighbours round,
       With none of my own made—I choose here!
       The giving out of the hymn reclaims me;
       I have done: and if any blames me,
       Thinking that merely to touch in brevity
1345   The topics I dwell on, were unlawful,—
       Or worse, that I trench, with undue levity,
         On the bounds of the holy and the awful,—
       I praise the heart, and pity the head of him,
       And refer myself to THEE, instead of him,
1350 Who head and heart alike discernest,
         Looking below light speech we utter,
         When frothy spume and frequent sputter
       Prove that the soul's depths boil in earnest!
       May truth shine out, stand ever before us!
1355 I put up pencil and join chorus
       To Hepzibah Tune, without further apology,
         The last five verses of the third section
         Of the seventeenth hymn of Whitfield's Collection,
       To conclude with the doxology.

1335| MS:myth, or personification, _1863_:personification,— _1868_:myth or
1336| MS:him, what _1865_:him what   1337| _1865_:of Salvation! _1868_:of salvation!
1341| MS:Without my _1865_:With none of my   1343| MS:done!—And _1865_:done:
and   1346| MS:Or, worse _1865_:Or worse   1347| MS:the Holy <> awful,
_1863_:the holy <> awful,—   1349| MS:to THEE <> him, _1850_:to THEE <>
him; _1863_:to THEE <> him,   1351| _1863_:utter _1888:_
utter,   1352| MS:When the frothy _1868_:When frothy   1354| MS:May the truth
_1865_:May truth   1355| MS: § first word illegibly crossed out § I   1358| MS:hymn
in Whitfield's _1865_:hymn of Whitfield's

I

How very hard it is to be
A Christian! Hard for you and me,
—Not the mere task of making real
That duty up to its ideal,
5   Effecting thus, complete and whole,
A purpose of the human soul—
For that is always hard to do;
But hard, I mean, for me and you
To realize it, more or less,
10   With even the moderate success
Which commonly repays our strife
To carry out the aims of life.
"This aim is greater," you will say,
"And so more arduous every way."
15   —But the importance of their fruits
Still proves to man, in all pursuits,
Proportional encouragement.
"Then, what if it be God's intent
That labour to this one result
20   Should seem unduly difficult?"
Ah, that's a question in the dark—
And the sole thing that I remark
Upon the difficulty, this;
We do not see it where it is,
25   At the beginning of the race:
As we proceed, it shifts its place,
And where we looked for crowns to fall,
We find the tug's to come,—that's all.

Subtitle| MS:Easter Day *1850:*Easter-Day
9| MS:realise *1863:*realize   13| MS:you may say, *1863:*you will say,   15| MS:
of the fruits *1863:*of their fruits   20| MS:Shall seem *1863:*Should seem   21|
MS:—Ah *1863:*Ah   24| MS:*is,* *1868:*is,   27| MS:for palms to *1863:*for crowns

At first you say, "The whole, or chief
30   Of difficulties, is belief.
Could I believe once thoroughly,
The rest were simple. What? Am I
An idiot, do you think,—a beast?
Prove to me, only that the least
35   Command of God is God's indeed,
And what injunction shall I need
To pay obedience? Death so nigh,
When time must end, eternity
Begin,—and cannot I compute,
40   Weigh loss and gain together, suit
My actions to the balance drawn,
And give my body to be sawn
Asunder, hacked in pieces, tied
To horses, stoned, burned, crucified,
45   Like any martyr of the list?
How gladly!—if I make acquist,
Through the brief minute's fierce annoy,
Of God's eternity of joy."

III

—And certainly you name the point
50   Whereon all turns: for could you joint
This flexile finite life once tight
Into the fixed and infinite,
You, safe inside, would spurn what's out,
With carelessness enough, no doubt—
55   Would spurn mere life: but when time brings
To their next stage your reasonings,
Your eyes, late wide, begin to wink
Nor see the path so well, I think.

---

to   30| MS:is Belief. *1868*:is belief.   33| MS:think? A beast *1863*:think,—a
beast   34| MS:me only *1863*:me, only   37| MS:nigh *1863*:nigh,
39| MS:compute? *1863*:compute,   40| MS:together? suit *1863*:together, suit
46| MS:gladly,—if I made *1863*:gladly!—if *1868*:make   47| MS:minutes' *1863*:
minute's   48| MS:joy!" *1850*:joy."   55| MS:but where § perhaps *when* § time
1850:but where time *1863*:but when time   58| MS:the way § erased and replaced

IV

⁶⁰

You say, "Faith may be, one agrees,
A touchstone for God's purposes,
Even as ourselves conceive of them.
Could he acquit us or condemn
For holding what no hand can loose,
Rejecting when we can't but choose?
As well award the victor's wreath
To whosoever should take breath
Duly each minute while he lived—
Grant heaven, because a man contrived
To see its sunlight every day
He walked forth on the public way.
You must mix some uncertainty
With faith, if you would have faith be.
Why, what but faith, do we abhor
And idolize each other for—
Faith in our evil or our good,
Which is or is not understood
Aright by those we love or those
We hate, thence called our friends or foes?
Your mistress saw your spirit's grace,
When, turning from the ugly face,
I found belief in it too hard;
And she and I have our reward.
—Yet here a doubt peeps: well for us
Weak beings, to go using thus
A touchstone for our little ends,
Trying with faith the foes and friends;
—But God, bethink you! I would fain
Conceive of the Creator's reign
As based upon exacter laws
Than creatures build by with applause.
In all God's acts—(as Plato cries
He doth)—he should geometrize.
Whence, I desiderate . . ."

by § path   ⁶⁰| MS:Gods' *1850*:God's   ⁶²| MS:Could He *1868*:Could he
⁶⁸| MS:Grant Heaven *1863*:Grant heaven   ⁶⁹| MS:see the sunlight *1863*:see its
sunlight   ⁷²|MS:*be.* *1868*:be.   ⁷⁵| MS:—Faith <> evil, or *1863*:Faith
1868:evil or   ⁷⁹| MS:spirits' *1850*:spirit's   ⁸²| MS:And both of us have
1863:And she and I have   ⁸⁶| MS:And try *1863*:Trying   ⁹²| MS:doth)—He

V

I see!
You would grow as a natural tree,
95   Stand as a rock, soar up like fire.
The world's so perfect and entire,
Quite above faith, so right and fit!
Go there, walk up and down in it!
No. The creation travails, groans—
100 Contrive your music from its moans,
Without or let or hindrance, friend!
That's an old story, and its end
As old—you come back (be sincere)
With every question you put here
105 (Here where there once was, and is still,
We think, a living oracle,
Whose answers you stand carping at)
This time flung back unanswered flat,—
Beside, perhaps, as many more
110 As those that drove you out before,
Now added, where was little need.
Questions impossible, indeed,
To us who sat still, all and each
Persuaded that our earth had speech,
115 Of God's, writ down, no matter if
In cursive type or hieroglyph,—
Which one fact freed us from the yoke
Of guessing why He never spoke.
You come back in no better plight
120 Than when you left us,—am I right?

---

should geometrise. *1863:*geometrize. *1868:*doth)—he should ⁹⁴| MS:grow
smoothly as a tree, *1863:*grow as a natural tree, ⁹⁵| MS:Soar heavenward, straightly
§ over illegible erasure, perhaps *straight* § up <> fire— *1863:*Stand as a rock, soar up
<> fire. ⁹⁶| MS:God bless you—there's your world entire *1863:*The world's so
perfect and entire, ⁹⁷| MS:Needing no faith, if you think fit; *1863:*Quite above
faith, so right and fit! ⁹⁹| MS:The whole creation *1863:*No. The creation
¹⁰⁷| MS:stood *1863:*stand ¹⁰⁹| MS:Besides, perhaps § last two words over illegible
erasure § *1865:*Beside ¹¹¹| MS:need! *1868:*need. ¹¹³| MS:sate *1863:*sat
¹¹⁴| MS:speech *1868:*speech, ¹¹⁷| MS:frees *1863:*freed ¹¹⁸| *1868:*why he

VI

So, the old process, I conclude,
Goes on, the reasoning's pursued
Further. You own, "'Tis well averred,
A scientific faith's absurd,
125 —Frustrates the very end 'twas meant
To serve. So, I would rest content
With a mere probability,
But, probable; the chance must lie
Clear on one side,—lie all in rough,
130 So long as there be just enough
To pin my faith to, though it hap
Only at points: from gap to gap
One hangs up a huge curtain so,
Grandly, nor seeks to have it go
135 Foldless and flat along the wall.
What care I if some interval
Of life less plainly may depend
On God? I'd hang there to the end;
And thus I should not find it hard
140 To be a Christian and debarred
From trailing on the earth, till furled
Away by death.—Renounce the world!
Were that a mighty hardship? Plan
A pleasant life, and straight some man
145 Beside you, with, if he thought fit,
Abundant means to compass it,
Shall turn deliberate aside
To try and live as, if you tried
You clearly might, yet most despise.
150 One friend of mine wears out his eyes,
Slighting the stupid joys of sense,
In patient hope that, ten years hence,
'Somewhat completer,' he may say,
'My list of *coleoptera!*'

---

*1888:*why He   121| MS:So the *1863:*So, the   123| MS:own, "Tis *1863:*own,
" 'Tis   126| MS:serve: so I *1863:*serve. So, I   130| MS:there is just *1863:*there be
just   135| MS:wall: *1863:*wall.   136| MS:—What care I that some *1863:*care
I if some *1868:*What   137| MS:might *1863:*may   142| MS:death!—Renounce
the world? *1863:*death.—Renounce the world!   153| MS:Somewhat completer he may
see *1863:*'Somewhat completer,' he may say,   154| MS:His list of *lepidopterae:* *1863:*

101

155 While just the other who most laughs
At him, above all epitaphs
Aspires to have his tomb describe
Himself as sole among the tribe
Of snuffbox-fanciers, who possessed
160 A Grignon with the Regent's crest.
So that, subduing, as you want,
Whatever stands predominant
Among my earthly appetites
For tastes and smells and sounds and sights,
165 I shall be doing that alone,
To gain a palm-branch and a throne,
Which fifty people undertake
To do, and gladly, for the sake
Of giving a Semitic guess,
170 Or playing pawns at blindfold chess."

VII

Good: and the next thing is,—look round
For evidence enough! 'Tis found,
No doubt: as is your sort of mind,
So is your sort of search: you'll find
175 What you desire, and that's to be
A Christian. What says history?
How comforting a point it were
To find some mummy-scrap declare
There lived a Moses! Better still,
180 Prove Jonah's whale translatable
Into some quicksand of the seas,
Isle, cavern, rock, or what you please,
That faith might flap her wings and crow
From such an eminence! Or, no—

'My list of *coleoptera!*' 157| MS:have his tomb § last three words over illegible erasure § 158| MS:as Sole § possibly originally *rare* altered to *Sole* § *1868:*as sole 160| MS:the Regent's Crest. *1850:*the Regent's crest. 161| MS:subduing as *1863:* subduing, as 164| MS:tastes, and smells, and sounds, and *1868:*tastes and smells and sounds and 166| MS:throne, *1888:*throne. § emended to § throne, § see Editorial Notes § 169| MS:a Semitic § over illegible erasure § 170| MS:pawns at § last two words over illegible erasure § 171| MS:Good! and *1868:*Good: and 172| MS:enough. 'Tis *1868:*enough! 'Tis 174| MS:search—you'll *1868:*search: you'll 176| MS:A Christian: what<>History? *1863:*A Christian. What<> history? 183| MS:That Faith might clap *1863:*That faith *1888:*might flap

102

185　The human heart's best; you prefer
　　　Making that prove the minister
　　　To truth; you probe its wants and needs,
　　　And hopes and fears, then try what creeds
　　　Meet these most aptly,—resolute
190　That faith plucks such substantial fruit
　　　Wherever these two correspond,
　　　She little needs to look beyond,
　　　And puzzle out who Orpheus was,
　　　Or Dionysius Zagrias.
195　You'll find sufficient, as I say,
　　　To satisfy you either way;
　　　You wanted to believe; your pains
　　　Are crowned—you do: and what remains?
　　　"Renounce the world!"—Ah, were it done
200　By merely cutting one by one
　　　Your limbs off, with your wise head last,
　　　How easy were it!—how soon past,
　　　If once in the believing mood!
　　　"Such is man's usual gratitude,
205　Such thanks to God do we return,
　　　For not exacting that we spurn
　　　A single gift of life, forego
　　　One real gain,—only taste them so
　　　With gravity and temperance,

185| MS:The Human Heart's *1863:*The human heart's   187| MS:needs *1863:*needs,
190| MS:That Faith *1863:*That faith   192| MS: § first word illegibly erased and
replaced by § She <> needs § next word illegibly crossed out, making hole in paper;
replaced above by § to   193| MS:To puzzle out what Orpheus *1863:*And puzzle
out who Orpheus   196| MS:way. *1863:*way;   199| MS:Renouce the world!—
Ah *1863:*"Renounce the world!"—Ah   204| MS:Such is Man's *1850:*is man's

103

210   That those mild virtues may enhance
     Such pleasures, rather than abstract—
     Last spice of which, will be the fact
     Of love discerned in every gift;
     While, when the scene of life shall shift,
215   And the gay heart be taught to ache,
     As sorrows and privations take
     The place of joy,—the thing that seems
     Mere misery, under human schemes,
     Becomes, regarded by the light
220   Of love, as very near, or quite
     As good a gift as joy before.
     So plain is it that, all the more
     A dispensation's merciful,
     More pettishly we try and cull
225   Briers, thistles, from our private plot,
     To mar God's ground where thorns are not!"

VIII

     Do you say this, or I?—Oh, you!
     Then, what, my friend?—(thus I pursue
     Our parley)—you indeed opine
230   That the Eternal and Divine
     Did, eighteen centuries ago,
     In very truth . . . Enough! you know
     The all-stupendous tale,—that Birth,
     That Life, that Death! And all, the earth
235   Shuddered at,—all, the heavens grew black
     Rather than see; all, nature's rack
     And throe at dissolution's brink
     Attested,—all took place, you think,
     Only to give our joys a zest,

1863:"Such   210| MS:those § over illegible word §   220| MS:Of Love *1863:*Of love   222| MS:that all *1863:*that, all   223| MS:God's dispensation's *1888:*A dispensation's   225| MS:Briars *1888:*Briers   226| MS:not! *1863:*not!" 228| MS:friend,—(so I *1863:*friend,—(thus I *1868:*friend?—(thus I   232| MS:Enough! You *1850:*Enough! you   236| MS:see,—all, Nature's *1850:*see; all *1868:*all, nature's 238| MS:Attested, § over illegible erasure §—it § next word illegibly crossed out § took *1863:*Attested,—all took

104

240 And prove our sorrows for the best?
We differ, then! Were I, still pale
And heartstruck at the dreadful tale,
Waiting to hear God's voice declare
What horror followed for my share,
245 As implicated in the deed,
Apart from other sins,—concede
That if He blacked out in a blot
My brief life's pleasantness, 'twere not
So very disproportionate!
250 Or there might be another fate—
I certainly could understand
(If fancies were the thing in hand)
How God might save, at that day's price,
The impure in their impurities,
255 Give licence formal and complete
To choose the fair and pick the sweet.
But there be certain words, broad, plain,
Uttered again and yet again,
Hard to mistake or overgloss—
260 Announcing this world's gain for loss,
And bidding us reject the same:
The whole world lieth (they proclaim)
In wickedness,—come out of it!
Turn a deaf ear, if you think fit,
265 But I who thrill through every nerve

245| MS:in that § altered to § the   247| *1868*:if he *1888*:if He   253| MS:that
Day's *1868*:that day's   255| MS:Leave formal licence and *1863*:Give formal
1888:Give licence formal and   256| MS:fair, and *1863*:fair and   259| MS:
mistake, to overgloss— *1863*:mistake, or overgloss— *1865*:mistake or   261| MS:us
reject § last two words over illegible erasure §   263| MS:it!— *1863*:it!

At thought of what deaf ears deserve—
How do you counsel in the case?

IX

"I'd take, by all means, in your place,
The safe side, since it so appears:
270 Deny myself, a few brief years,
The natural pleasure, leave the fruit
Or cut the plant up by the root.
Remember what a martyr said
On the rude tablet overhead!
275 'I was born sickly, poor and mean,
A slave: no misery could screen
The holders of the pearl of price
From Caesar's envy; therefore twice
I fought with beasts, and three times saw
280 My children suffer by his law;
At last my own release was earned:
I was some time in being burned,
But at the close a Hand came through
The fire above my head, and drew
285 My soul to Christ, whom now I see.
Sergius, a brother, writes for me
This testimony on the wall—
For me, I have forgot it all.'
You say right; this were not so hard!
290 And since one nowise is debarred
From this, why not escape some sins
By such a method?"

X

Then begins
To the old point revulsion new—
(For 'tis just this I bring you to)

266| MS:deserve,— 1888:deserve— 274| MS:overhead— 1863:overhead!
280| MS:law— 1863:law; 283| MS:the § next word illegibly crossed
out and replaced above by § close 292| MS:method?" §¶§—Then 1863:method?"
§¶§ Then 293| MS:point, revulsion 1888:point revulsion 294| MS:this, I

295 If after all we should mistake,
And so renounce life for the sake
Of death and nothing else? You hear
Each friend we jeered at, send the jeer
Back to ourselves with good effect—
300 "There were my beetles to collect!
My box—a trifle, I confess,
But here I hold it, ne'ertheless!"
Poor idiots, (let us pluck up heart
And answer) we, the better part
305 Have chosen, though 'twere only hope,—
Nor envy moles like you that grope
Amid your veritable muck,
More than the grasshoppers would truck,
For yours, their passionate life away,
310 That spends itself in leaps all day
To reach the sun, you want the eyes
To see, as they the wings to rise
And match the noble hearts of them!
Thus the contemner we contemn,—
315 And, when doubt strikes us, thus we ward
Its stroke off, caught upon our guard,
—Not struck enough to overturn
Our faith, but shake it—make us learn
What I began with, and, I wis,
320 End, having proved,—how hard it is
To be a Christian!

XI

"Proved, or not,
Howe'er you wis, small thanks, I wot,
You get of mine, for taking pains
To make it hard to me. Who gains
325 By that, I wonder? Here I live
In trusting ease; and here you drive
At causing me to lose what most
Yourself would mourn for had you lost!"

---

*1888:*this I   ²⁹⁸ MS:Our friends *1888:*Each friend   ³⁰⁰ MS:"There
were my *1868:*"There were my   ³¹⁴ MS:So, the *1863:*Thus the   ³¹⁵ MS:us,
so, we *1863:*us, thus we   ³²⁶ MS:and do you *1863:*and here you
³²⁸ MS:would mourn § last two words over illegible erasure § for § inserted

107

But, do you see, my friend, that thus
330 You leave Saint Paul for Æschylus?
—Who made his Titan's arch-device
The giving men *blind hopes* to spice
The meal of life with, else devoured
In bitter haste, while lo, death loured
335 Before them at the platter's edge!
If faith should be, as I allege,
Quite other than a condiment
To heighten flavours with, or meant
(Like that brave curry of his Grace)
340 To take at need the victuals' place?
If, having dined, you would digest
Besides, and turning to your rest
Should find instead . . .

XIII

Now, you shall see
And judge if a mere foppery
345 Pricks on my speaking! I resolve
To utter—yes, it shall devolve
On you to hear as solemn, strange
And dread a thing as in the range
Of facts,—or fancies, if God will—
350 E'er happened to our kind! I still
Stand in the cloud and, while it wraps
My face, ought not to speak perhaps;
Seeing that if I carry through
My purpose, if my words in you
355 Find a live actual listener,
My story, reason must aver

---

above § when 'twas lost?" *1863:*for had you lost!"   ³³⁰| MS:leave St. < > for
Æschylus?— *1863:*for Æschylus? *1888:*leave Saint   ³³⁴| MS:lo! Death *1863:*lo!
death *1868:*lo, death   ³³⁶| MS:as we allege, *1863:*as I allege,   ³³⁸| MS:
flavors *1863:*flavours   ³⁴¹| MS:If having dined you *1863:*If, having dined, you
³⁴⁶| MS:utter . . yes *1868:*utter—yes   ³⁵¹| MS:cloud, and while *1865:*cloud
and, while   ³⁵²| MS:speak, perhaps; *1865:*speak perhaps;   ³⁵³| MS:that
if § incompletely erased and replaced by § as I *1863:*that if I   ³⁵⁴| MS:if my
§ last two words over illegible erasure §   ³⁵⁵| MS:Find veritable listeners, *1863:*
Find a live actual listener,   ³⁵⁶| MS:reason's self avers *1863:*reason must aver

False after all—the happy chance!
While, if each human countenance
I meet in London day by day,
360 Be what I fear,—my warnings fray
No one, and no one they convert,
And no one helps me to assert
How hard it is to really be
A Christian, and in vacancy
365 I pour this story!

XIV

I commence
By trying to inform you, whence
It comes that every Easter-night
As now, I sit up, watch, till light,
Upon those chimney-stacks and roofs,
370 Give, through my window-pane, grey proofs
That Easter-day is breaking slow.
On such a night three years ago,
It chanced that I had cause to cross
The common, where the chapel was,
375 Our friend spoke of, the other day—
You've not forgotten, I dare say.
I fell to musing of the time
So close, the blessed matin-prime
All hearts leap up at, in some guise—
380 One could not well do otherwise.
Insensibly my thoughts were bent
Toward the main point; I overwent
Much the same ground of reasoning

357| MS:Must needs be false—the 1863:False after all—the   359| MS:in
London streets all day, 1863:in London day by day,   364| MS:A Christian;
§ altered to § A Christian, and in vacancy § last three words over erased space in
hand not Browning's, possibly EBB's §   364-365| MS: § between the two lines, an
obliterated partial line, possibly *Hearing inquire Time* §   367| MS:every
Easter night 1850:every Easter-night   368| MS:As now § last two words over
illegible erasure § <> watch till light 1850:watch, till 1863:light,
369| MS:Shall break, those <> roofs 1863:Upon those <> roofs,
372| MS:night, three 1888:night three   383| MS:reasoning, 1850:reasoning

As you and I just now. One thing
385 Remained, however—one that tasked
My soul to answer; and I asked,
Fairly and frankly, what might be
That History, that Faith, to me
—Me there—not me in some domain
390 Built up and peopled by my brain,
Weighing its merits as one weighs
Mere theories for blame or praise,
—The kingcraft of the Lucumons,
Or Fourier's scheme, its pros and cons,—
395 But my faith there, or none at all.
"How were my case, now, did I fall
Dead here, this minute—should I lie
Faithful or faithless?" Note that I
Inclined thus ever!—little prone
400 For instance, when I lay alone
In childhood, to go calm to sleep
And leave a closet where might keep
His watch perdue some murderer
Waiting till twelve o'clock to stir,
405 As good authentic legends tell:
"He might: but how improbable!
How little likely to deserve
The pains and trial to the nerve
Of thrusting head into the dark!"—
410 Urged my old nurse, and bade me mark
Beside, that, should the dreadful scout
Really lie hid there, and leap out

384| MS:now: one *1863*:now. One   388| MS:me— *1863*:me   389| MS:—Me,
there <> me, in *1850*:—Me there *1863*:not me in   393| MS:—The Kingcraft
1863:—The kingcraft   395| MS:But as *my* faith, or *1863*:But *my* faith *there*,
or *1868*:my <> there   396| MS:now, should I *1863*:now, did I   397| MS:
minute—do I *1863*:minute—should I   398| MS:faithless?"—Note *1888*:faithless?"
Note   399| MS:Inclined thus ever!— § last three words, possibly in hand of
EBB, and !— over illegible erasure §   400| MS:when I slept alone *1863*:when I
lay alone   405| MS:good, authentic <> tell *1863*:tell: *1868*:good authentic
406| MS:He *might* § altered to § might—"But how *1850*:He might *1863*:"He might:
but how   409| MS:dark,—" *1850*:dark,"— *1863*:dark!"—   410| MS:
§ first word illegibly erased § Urged my old § inserted above §   411| MS:Besides
1863:Beside   412| MS:hid § over illegible erasure, may have been *hiding*; next
word illegibly crossed out § there, to § inserted above § leap *1863*:there, and leap

110

At first turn of the rusty key,
Mine were small gain that she could see,
415 Killed not in bed but on the floor,
And losing one night's sleep the more.
I tell you, I would always burst
The door ope, know my fate at first.
This time, indeed, the closet penned
420 No such assassin: but a friend
Rather, peeped out to guard me, fit
For counsel, Common Sense, to wit,
Who said a good deal that might pass,—
Heartening, impartial too, it was,
425 Judge else: "For, soberly now,—who
Should be a Christian if not you?"
(Hear how he smoothed me down.) "One takes
A whole life, sees what course it makes
Mainly, and not by fits and starts—
430 In spite of stoppage which imparts
Fresh value to the general speed.
A life, with none, would fly indeed:
Your progressing is slower—right!
We deal with progress and not flight.
435 Through baffling senses passionate,
Fancies as restless,—with a freight
Of knowledge cumbersome enough
To sink your ship when waves grow rough,
Though meant for ballast in the hold,—
440 I find, 'mid dangers manifold,
The good bark answers to the helm
Where faith sits, easier to o'erwhelm
Than some stout peasant's heavenly guide,
Whose hard head could not, if it tried,

---

⁴¹⁴| MS:It were <> see *1863*:Mine were <> see,   ⁴¹⁵| MS:In being killed
upon the floor *1863*:Killed not in bed but on the floor,   ⁴¹⁸| MS:first.—
1863:first.   ⁴²²| MS:For counsel § last two words over illegible erasure §<>
to-wit, *1863*:to wit,   ⁴²⁴| MS:too it *1850*:too, it   ⁴²⁵| MS:else: "For
§ over illegible erasure §   ⁴²⁷| MS:down) "One *1850*:down). "One *1863*:down.) "One
⁴³¹| MS:speed: *1863*:speed.   ⁴³⁴| MS:with progressing, not *1863*:with progress
and not   ⁴³⁹| MS:Not serve as ballast <> hold, *1863*:Though meant for ballast <>
hold,—   ⁴⁴⁰| MS:mid *1850*:'mid   ⁴⁴²| MS:Where Faith *1863*:Where faith

445 Conceive a doubt, nor understand
How senses hornier than his hand
Should 'tice the Christian off his guard.
More happy! But shall we award
Less honour to the hull which, dogged
450 By storms, a mere wreck, waterlogged,
Masts by the board, her bulwarks gone
And stanchions going, yet bears on,—
Than to mere life-boats, built to save,
And triumph o'er the breaking wave?
455 Make perfect your good ship as these,
And what were her performances!"
I added—"Would the ship reach home!
I wish indeed 'God's kingdom come—'
The day when I shall see appear
460 His bidding, as my duty, clear
From doubt! And it shall dawn, that day,
Some future season; Easter may
Prove, not impossibly, the time—
Yes, that were striking—fates would chime
465 So aptly! Easter-morn, to bring
The Judgment!—deeper in the spring
Than now, however, when there's snow
Capping the hills; for earth must show
All signs of meaning to pursue
470 Her tasks as she was wont to do
—The skylark, taken by surprise
As we ourselves, shall recognize
Sudden the end. For suddenly
It comes; the dreadfulness must be

445| MS:doubt, nor§altered to§or understand 1863:doubt, nor understand   447| MS:
guard— 1863:guard.   448| MS:shall we § last two words over illegible erasure §
449| MS:honor <> hull, which 1863:honour <> hull which   451| MS:board,
and bulwarks gone, 1863:board, her bulwarks 1868:gone   456| MS:performances!"—
1850:performances!"   457| MS: § first word illegibly crossed out and replaced above
by§ I added— <>reached 1863:reach   458| MS:§first word illegibly crossed out and
replaced above by § I wish<>come'— 1850:come—" 1868:come—'   466| MS:
the Spring 1865:the spring   470| MS:do— 1863:do   471| MS:—The lark,
as taken 1863:—The skylark, taken   472| MS:recognise 1863:recognize
473| MS:end: for 1863:end. For   474| MS:comes—the 1863:comes; the

⁴⁷⁵ In that; all warrants the belief—
'At night it cometh like a thief.'
I fancy why the trumpet blows;
—Plainly, to wake one. From repose
We shall start up, at last awake
⁴⁸⁰ From life, that insane dream we take
For waking now, because it seems.
And as, when now we wake from dreams,
We laugh, while we recall them, 'Fool,
To let the chance slip, linger cool
⁴⁸⁵ When such adventure offered! Just
A bridge to cross, a dwarf to thrust
Aside, a wicked mage to stab—
And, lo ye, I had kissed Queen Mab!'
So shall we marvel why we grudged
⁴⁹⁰ Our labour here, and idly judged
Of heaven, we might have gained, but lose!
Lose? Talk of loss, and I refuse
To plead at all! You speak no worse
Nor better than my ancient nurse
⁴⁹⁵ When she would tell me in my youth
I well deserved that shapes uncouth
Frighted and teased me in my sleep:
Why could I not in memory keep
Her precept for the evil's cure?
⁵⁰⁰ 'Pinch your own arm, boy, and be sure
You'll wake forthwith!' "

xv

And as I said
This nonsense, throwing back my head
With light complacent laugh, I found
Suddenly all the midnight round

---

⁴⁷⁵| MS:that—all < > that § altered to § the   *1863:*that; all   ⁴⁸⁰| MS:dream,
we   *1850:*dream we   ⁴⁸³| MS:We say while   *1850:*say, while   *1863:*We laugh,
while   ⁴⁸⁸| MS:kissed Queen Mab,'—   *1863:*kissed Queen Mab!'—   *1868:*
kissed Queen Mab!'   ⁴⁹⁰| MS:labours here; and   *1850:*here, and   *1863:*labour
⁴⁹¹| MS:Of Heaven   *1868:*Of heaven   ⁴⁹³| MS:all! You § erased and replaced by §
I speak   *1863:*all! You speak   ⁴⁹⁷| MS:Should fright and tease < > sleep—   *1863:*
Frighted and teased   *1868:*sleep: ⁴⁹⁸| MS:Why did I   *1863:*Why could I

505   One fire. The dome of heaven had stood
       As made up of a multitude
       Of handbreadth cloudlets, one vast rack
       Of ripples infinite and black,
       From sky to sky. Sudden there went,
510   Like horror and astonishment,
       A fierce vindictive scribble of red
       Quick flame across, as if one said
       (The angry scribe of Judgment) "There—
       Burn it!" And straight I was aware
515   That the whole ribwork round, minute
       Cloud touching cloud beyond compute,
       Was tinted, each with its own spot
       Of burning at the core, till clot
       Jammed against clot, and spilt its fire
520   Over all heaven, which 'gan suspire
       As fanned to measure equable,—
       Just so great conflagrations kill
       Night overhead, and rise and sink,
       Reflected. Now the fire would shrink
525   And wither off the blasted face
       Of heaven, and I distinct might trace
       The sharp black ridgy outlines left
       Unburned like network—then, each cleft
       The fire had been sucked back into,
530   Regorged, and out it surging flew
       Furiously, and night writhed inflamed,
       Till, tolerating to be tamed
       No longer, certain rays world-wide
       Shot downwardly. On every side

505| MS:of Heaven had § inserted above § *1863:*of heaven   513| MS:of judgment
*1850:*of Judgment   514| MS:straight I § last two words over illegible erasure §
517| MS:tinted each *1863:*tinted, each   522| MS: § first words illegibly erased
and replaced by § As when great *1868:*Just so great   524| MS:Now the fire
§ last three words over illegible erasure § would §next word illegibly erased § shrink
526| MS:and I distinct §last three words over illegible erasure; next word illegibly
crossed out § could trace *1863:*distinct might trace   530| MS: §first word illegibly
erased and replaced by § Regorged < > it surging §last two words over illegible
erasure§   534| MS:downwardly, § *wardly,* over illegible erasure § on

⁵³⁵   Caught past escape, the earth was lit;
    As if a dragon's nostril split
    And all his famished ire o'erflowed;
    Then, as he winced at his lord's goad,
    Back he inhaled: whereat I found
⁵⁴⁰   The clouds into vast pillars bound,
    Based on the corners of the earth,
    Propping the skies at top: a dearth
    Of fire i' the violet intervals,
    Leaving exposed the utmost walls
⁵⁴⁵   Of time, about to tumble in
    And end the world.

XVI

              I felt begin
    The Judgment-Day: to retrocede
    Was too late now. "In very deed,"
    (I uttered to myself) "that Day!"
⁵⁵⁰   The intuition burned away
    All darkness from my spirit too:
    There, stood I, found and fixed, I knew,
    Choosing the world. The choice was made;
    And naked and disguiseless stayed,
⁵⁵⁵   And unevadable, the fact.
    My brain held all the same compact
    Its senses, nor my heart declined
    Its office; rather, both combined
    To help me in this juncture. I
⁵⁶⁰   Lost not a second,—agony
    Gave boldness: since my life had end
    And my choice with it—best defend,

---

*1863:*downwardly. On   ⁵³⁵| MS:escape; the earth was lit; §last three words over illegible erasure § *1863:*escape, the   ⁵³⁸| MS:his Lord's *1863:*his lord's *1868:* Then as DC, BrU:Then, as *1889:*Then, as   ⁵³⁹| MS:whereat I §last two words over illegible erasure §   ⁵⁴⁷| MS:The Judgment Day *1850:*The Judgment-Day
⁵⁴⁸| MS:now.—"In very deed, *1863:*now. "In very deed,"   ⁵⁵¹| MS:too— *1863:*too:
⁵⁵³| MS:*Choosing the world* <> made— *1863:*made; *1868:*Choosing the world
⁵⁵⁵| MS:unevadeable *1863:*unevadable   ⁵⁵⁶| MS:held ne'ertheless compact *1888:*held all the same compact   ⁵⁵⁸| MS:office—rather *1863:*office; rather
⁵⁵⁹| MS:juncture—I *1863:*juncture. I   ⁵⁶¹| MS:boldness: there, my *1863:*boldness:

Applaud both! I resolved to say,
"So was I framed by thee, such way
565   I put to use thy senses here!
It was so beautiful, so near,
Thy world,—what could I then but choose
My part there? Nor did I refuse
To look above the transient boon
570   Of time; but it was hard so soon
As in a short life, to give up
Such beauty: I could put the cup
Undrained of half its fulness, by;
But, to renounce it utterly,
575   —That was too hard! Nor did the cry
Which bade renounce it, touch my brain
Authentically deep and plain
Enough to make my lips let go.
But Thou, who knowest all, dost know
580   Whether I was not. life's brief while,
Endeavouring to reconcile
Those lips (too tardily, alas!)
To letting the dear remnant pass,
One day,—some drops of earthly good
585   Untasted! Is it for this mood,
That Thou, whose earth delights so well,
Hast made its complement a hell?"

XVII

A final belch of fire like blood,
Overbroke all heaven in one flood
590   Of doom. Then fire was sky, and sky
Fire, and both, one brief ecstasy,

---

since my   563| MS:Applaud them! I   *1863:*Applaud both! I   564| MS:by Thee,
this way *1863:*by Thee, such way *1868:*by thee   565| MS:use Thy *1868:*use thy
567| MS:could I do but *1863:*could I then but   570| MS:In time—but *1863:*Of
time; but   572| MS:beauty: I had put *1863:*beauty: I could put   575| MS:the
Cry *1863:*the cry   578| MS:Enough, to *1863:*Enough to *1865:*go, *1888:*go.
579| *1868:*But thou *1888:*But Thou   582| MS:lips—too < > alas! *1863:*lips (too
< > alas!)   586| *1868:*That thou *1888:*That Thou   587| MS:its § next word
illegibly crossed out and erased and replaced above by § complement a Hell?"
*1863:*a hell?"   589| MS:§ first word illegibly crossed out and replaced above by §
Overbroke all, next, in *1863:*all heaven in   591| MS:Was fire, and both, § last

116

Then ashes. But I heard no noise
(Whatever was) because a voice
Beside me spoke thus, "Life is done,
595   Time ends, Eternity's begun,
And thou art judged for evermore."

XVIII

I looked up; all seemed as before;
Of that cloud-Tophet overhead
No trace was left: I saw instead
600   The common round me, and the sky
Above, stretched drear and emptily
Of life. 'Twas the last watch of night,
Except what brings the morning quite;
When the armed angel, conscience-clear,
605   His task nigh done, leans o'er his spear
And gazes on the earth he guards,
Safe one night more through all its wards,
Till God relieve him at his post.
"A dream—a waking dream at most!"
610   (I spoke out quick, that I might shake
The horrid nightmare off, and wake.)
"The world gone, yet the world is here?
Are not all things as they appear?
Is Judgment past for me alone?
615   —And where had place the great white throne?
The rising of the quick and dead?
Where stood they, small and great? Who read
The sentence from the opened book?"

---

four words over illegible erasure; in hand not B's, perhaps EBB's § one extacy,
*1863:*Fire, and both, one brief ecstasy,   593| MS:(Whatever was) § last two words
over illegible erasure §   *1850:*a Voice   *1868:*a voice   594| MS:thus, "All is *1863:*thus,
"Life is   596| MS:evermore"! *1850:*evermore!" *1863:*evermore."
597| MS:all was as *1863:*all seemed as   598| MS:overhead, *1888:*overhead
602| MS:life: 'twas *1863:*life. 'Twas   603| MS:§ first word illegibly erased and replaced
by § Except < > quite, *1863:*quite;   604| MS:§ first words illegibly erased and
replaced by four words § When the armed angel, conscience-clear *1863:*conscience-clear,
608| MS: § first words illegibly erased and replaced by four words § Till God relieve him
610| MS:quick that *1863:*quick, that   612| MS:world's gone, *1863:*world gone
615| MS:the Great White Throne? *1863:*the great white throne?   616| MS:the Quick
and Dead? *1863:*the quick and dead?   618| MS:the Opened Book?" *1863:*the

So, by degrees, the blood forsook
620   My heart, and let it beat afresh;
I knew I should break through the mesh
Of horror, and breathe presently:
When, lo, again, the voice by me!

XIX

I saw . . . Oh brother, 'mid far sands
625   The palm-tree-cinctured city stands,
Bright-white beneath, as heaven, bright-blue,
Leans o'er it, while the years pursue
Their course, unable to abate
Its paradisal laugh at fate!
630   One morn,—the Arab staggers blind
O'er a new tract of death, calcined
To ashes, silence, nothingness,—
And strives, with dizzy wits, to guess
Whence fell the glow. What if, 'twixt skies
635   And prostrate earth, he should surprise
The imaged vapour, head to foot,
Surveying, motionless and mute,
Its work, ere, in a whirlwind rapt
It vanish up again?—So hapt
640   My chance. HE stood there. Like the smoke
Pillared o'er Sodom, when day broke,—
I saw Him. One magnific pall
Mantled in massive fold and fall
His dread, and coiled in snaky swathes
645   About His feet: night's black, that bathes
All else, broke, grizzled with despair,
Against the soul of blackness there.

opened book?''   620| MS:afresh: 1863:afresh;   622| MS:presently—   1863:
presently: 623| 1850:the Voice   1868:the voice   624| MS:saw . . . Oh,
brother   1868:saw . . . Oh brother   625| MS:stands,—   1863:stands,
626| MS:as Heaven   1863:as heaven   627| MS:Above it   1863:Leans o'er it
629| MS:fate: 1863:fate!   631| MS:O'er the § erased and replaced by § a
633| MS:Striving   1863:And strives   634| MS:blow: what   1863:blow. What
636| MS:imaged Vapour   1863:imaged vapour   638| MS:rapt,   1865:rapt
640| MS:smoke § below Like the §   642| 1868:saw him   1888:saw Him
644| MS:His Dread, and   1863:His dread   645| 1868:About his

A gesture told the mood within—
That wrapped right hand which based the chin,
650 That intense meditation fixed
On His procedure,—pity mixed
With the fulfilment of decree.
Motionless, thus, He spoke to me,
Who fell before His feet, a mass,
655 No man now.

xx

"All is come to pass.
Such shows are over for each soul
They had respect to. In the roll
Of Judgment which convinced mankind
Of sin, stood many, bold and blind,
660 Terror must burn the truth into:
Their fate for them!—thou hadst to do
With absolute omnipotence,
Able its judgments to dispense
To the whole race, as every one
665 Were its sole object. Judgment done,
God is, thou art,—the rest is hurled
To nothingness for thee. This world,
This finite life, thou hast preferred,
In disbelief of God's plain word,
670 To heaven and to infinity.
Here the probation was for thee,
To show thy soul the earthly mixed
With heavenly, it must choose betwixt.
The earthly joys lay palpable,—
675 A taint, in each, distinct as well;
The heavenly flitted, faint and rare,

1888:About His   648| MS:The § erased and replaced by § A   649| MS:chin,—
§ below *based the* §   1863:chin,   651| 1868:On his   1888:On His
653| 1868:thus, he   1888:thus, He   654| MS:before his   1850:before His   1868:before
his   1888:before His   661| MS:had'st   1863:hadst   665| MS:object: that is
done: 1863:object. Judgment done,   667| MS:world   1850:world,
669| MS:of God's own word,   1888:of God's plain word,   670| MS:To
Heaven < > Infinity.   1868:To heaven < > infinity.   671| MS:Here, the   1863:
Here the   673| MS:With Heavenly   1863:With heavenly   676| MS:The Heavenly

Above them, but as truly were
Taintless, so, in their nature, best.
Thy choice was earth: thou didst attest
680 'Twas fitter spirit should subserve
The flesh, than flesh refine to nerve
Beneath the spirit's play. Advance
No claim to their inheritance
Who chose the spirit's fugitive
685 Brief gleams, and yearned, 'This were to live
Indeed, if rays, completely pure
From flesh that dulls them, could endure,—
Not shoot in meteor-light athwart
Our earth, to show how cold and swart
690 It lies beneath their fire, but stand
As stars do, destined to expand,
Prove veritable worlds, our home!'
Thou saidst,—'Let spirit star the dome
Of sky, that flesh may miss no peak,
695 No nook of earth,—I shall not seek
Its service further!' Thou art shut
Out of the heaven of spirit; glut
Thy sense upon the world: 'tis thine
For ever—take it!''

XXI

"How? Is mine,
700 The world?'' (I cried, while my soul broke
Out in a transport.) "Hast Thou spoke
Plainly in that? Earth's exquisite

---

*1863:*The heavenly   678| MS:so in   *1863:*so, in   680| MS:Twas
1850:'Twas   685| MS:and thought,—'This   *1863:*and yearned, 'This
686| MS:if gleams § crossed out and replaced above by § rays   687| MS: § first
word illegibly crossed out and replaced above by § From < > them, should endure,—
*1863:*them, could endure,—   691| MS:stars should, destined   *1863:*stars do,
destined   693| MS: § first words illegibly erased and replaced above by two words §
'Thou said'st,—Let Spirit   *1863:*saidst,—'Let spirit   694| MS:peak   *1850:*peak,
697| MS:the Heaven of Spirit   *1863:*the heaven of spirit   700| MS:world''?
*1850:*world?''   701| MS:transport) "Hast Thou   *1863:*transport,) "Hast
*1868:*transport.) "Hast thou   *1888:*"Hast Thou   702| MS:exquisite § over illegible

Treasures of wonder and delight,
For me?"

XXII

The austere voice returned,—
705 "So soon made happy? Hadst thou learned
What God accounteth happiness,
Thou wouldst not find it hard to guess
What hell may be his punishment
For those who doubt if God invent
710 Better than they. Let such men rest
Content with what they judged the best.
Let the unjust usurp at will:
The filthy shall be filthy still:
Miser, there waits the gold for thee!
715 Hater, indulge thine enmity!
And thou, whose heaven self-ordained
Was, to enjoy earth unrestrained,
Do it! Take all the ancient show!
The woods shall wave, the rivers flow,
720 And men apparently pursue
Their works, as they were wont to do,
While living in probation yet.
I promise not thou shalt forget
The past, now gone to its account;
725 But leave thee with the old amount
Of faculties, nor less nor more,
Unvisited, as heretofore,
By God's free spirit, that makes an end.
So, once more, take thy world! Expend

---

erasure §   704| MS:austere Voice *1868:*austere voice   708| MS:What § over
illegible word § Hell < > His *1863:*What hell *1868:*be his   712| MS:the
Unjust *1863:*the unjust   713| MS:The Filthy *1863:*The filthy
716| MS:heaven, self-ordained, *1863:*heaven self-ordained   717| MS:Was to *1863:*
Was, to   720| MS: § first word illegibly erased and replaced by two words § And men
722| MS:yet: *1863:*yet.   724| MS:account, *1863:*The Past   account; *1868:*The
past   728| MS:end. § above *an* §   729| MS:world; expend *1863:*world! expend

⁷³⁰ Eternity upon its shows,
Flung thee as freely as one rose
Out of a summer's opulence,
Over the Eden-barrier whence
Thou art excluded. Knock in vain!"

XXIII

⁷³⁵ I sat up. All was still again.
I breathed free: to my heart, back fled
The warmth. "But, all the world!"—I said.
I stooped and picked a leaf of fern,
And recollected I might learn
⁷⁴⁰ From books, how many myriad sorts
Of fern exist, to trust reports,
Each as distinct and beautiful
As this, the very first I cull.
Think, from the first leaf to the last!
⁷⁴⁵ Conceive, then, earth's resources! Vast
Exhaustless beauty, endless change
Of wonder! And this foot shall range
Alps, Andes,—and this eye devour
The bee-bird and the aloe-flower?

XXIV

⁷⁵⁰ Then the voice, "Welcome so to rate
The arras-folds that variegate
The earth, God's antechamber, well!
The wise, who waited there, could tell
By these, what royalties in store
⁷⁵⁵ Lay one step past the entrance-door.
For whom, was reckoned, not too much,

---

*1868:*world! Expend   ⁷³⁰| MS:shows,— *1865:*shows,   ⁷³⁵| MS:sate
*1863:*sat   ⁷³⁷| MS:world!" (I said) *1868:*world!"—I said.   ⁷⁴¹| MS:Exist,
if one may § last two words over illegible erasure § trust   *1863:*Of fern exist, to
trust   ⁷⁴²| MS:Each § over illegible word §   ⁷⁴⁷| MS:wonder! and
*1868:*wonder! And   ⁷⁵⁰| MS:And the Voice *1863:*Then the *1868:*the voice
⁷⁵¹| MS:that § next word illegibly crossed out and replaced above by § variegate

This life's munificence? For such
As thou,—a race, whereof scarce one
Was able, in a million,
760 To feel that any marvel lay
In objects round his feet all day;
Scarce one, in many millions more,
Willing, if able, to explore
The secreter, minuter charm!
765 —Brave souls, a fern-leaf could disarm
Of power to cope with God's intent,—
Or scared if the south firmament
With north-fire did its wings refledge!
All partial beauty was a pledge
770 Of beauty in its plenitude:
But since the pledge sufficed thy mood,
Retain it! plenitude be theirs
Who looked above!"

XXV

Though sharp despairs
Shot though me, I held up, bore on.
775 "What matter though my trust were gone
From natural things? Henceforth my part
Be less with nature than with art!
For art supplants, gives mainly worth
To nature; 'tis man stamps the earth—

758| MS:whereof not one *1863:*whereof scarce one   762| MS:Nor one *1863:*Scarce
one   767–768| MS:scared § over illegible erasure § if the South Firmament /
§there follow six or eight lines apparently first crossed out and then cut—save for
fragmentary endings of three lines—from the MS. B has indicated in margin that the
MS continues unbroken with the first line following the hole in the MS§ With North-fire
*1863:*the south firmament / With north-fire   772| MS:it—plenitude *1863:*it! plenitude
774| MS:I held up, bore on. § last five words over illegible erasure §   775| MS:
'What is it though my trust § last six words over illegible erasure § is gone
1863:'What matter though my trust were gone   777| MS: § entire line over illegible
erasure § with Nature < > Art! *1868:*with nature < > art!   778| MS:For Art
supplants, gives § last four words over illegible erasure § *1868:*For art
779| MS:To Nature § two words over illegible erasure §; 'tis Man *1868:*To nature; 'tis

⁷⁸⁰ And I will seek his impress, seek
The statuary of the Greek,
Italy's painting—there my choice
Shall fix!"

XXVI

"Obtain it!" said the voice,
"—The one form with its single act,
⁷⁸⁵ Which sculptors laboured to abstract,
The one face, painters tried to draw,
With its one look, from throngs they saw.
And that perfection in their soul,
These only hinted at? The whole,
⁷⁹⁰ They were but parts of? What each laid
His claim to glory on?—afraid
His fellow-men should give him rank
By mere tentatives which he shrank
Smitten at heart from, all the more,
⁷⁹⁵ That gazers pressed in to adore!
'Shall I be judged by only these?'
If such his soul's capacities,
Even while he trod the earth,—think, now,
What pomp in Buonarroti's brow,
⁸⁰⁰ With its new palace-brain where dwells
Superb the soul, unvexed by cells
That crumbled with the transient clay!
What visions will his right hand's sway
Still turn to forms, as still they burst

man ⁷⁸³| MS:it" said the Voice. *1850*:it," said *1863*:it!" said
1865:the Voice, *1868*:the voice, ⁷⁸⁴| MS:"The *1863*:"—The ⁷⁸⁵| MS:labored
1863:laboured ⁷⁸⁷| MS:saw! *1863*:saw. ⁷⁹⁰| MS:They § over *These* §
⁷⁹¹| MS:His his § crossed out § ⁷⁹³| MS:By the poor tentatives he
1888:By mere tentatives which he ⁷⁹⁸| MS:now *1868*:now, ⁷⁹⁹| MS:in
Buonarotti's *1863*:in Buonarroti's ⁸⁰³| MS:will § next word, perhaps *man's*,
erased, crossed out, and replaced above by § his ⁸⁰⁴| MS:form *1888*:forms

⁸⁰⁵ Upon him? How will he quench thirst,
Titanically infantine,
Laid at the breast of the Divine?
Does it confound thee,—this first page
Emblazoning man's heritage?—
⁸¹⁰ Can this alone absorb thy sight,
As pages were not infinite,—
Like the omnipotence which tasks
Itself to furnish all that asks
The soul it means to satiate?
⁸¹⁵ What was the world, the starry state
Of the broad skies,—what, all displays
Of power and beauty intermixed,
Which now thy soul is chained betwixt,—
What else than needful furniture
⁸²⁰ For life's first stage? God's work, be sure,
No more spreads wasted, than falls scant!
He filled, did not exceed, man's want
Of beauty in this life. But through
Life pierce,—and what has earth to do,
⁸²⁵ Its utmost beauty's appanage,
With the requirement of next stage?
Did God pronounce earth 'very good'?
Needs must it be, while understood
For man's preparatory state;
⁸³⁰ Nought here to heighten nor abate;
Transfer the same completeness here,
To serve a new state's use,—and drear
Deficiency gapes every side!
The good, tried once, were bad, retried.

---

^{808|} MS: § first word, possibly *Dos't,* erased and replaced by §—Does it < > thee, with
§ *with* crossed out and replaced above by § —this   ^{810|} MS: § first word
illegibly erased and replaced above by § Can < > sight;   *1850:*sight,
^{811|} MS:As if they were   *1863:*As pages were   ^{813|} MS:Itself, to   *1888:*Itself to
^{819|} MS:What, else § over illegible erasure §, than   *1863:*What else than
^{821|} MS:scant: *1868:*scant!   ^{822|} MS:exceed Man's   *1850:*exceed, Man's   *1865:*exceed,
man's   ^{823|} MS:life. And pass   *1863:*life. But through   ^{824|} MS:Life's
line,—and   *1863:*Life pierce,—and   ^{826|} MS:requirements   *1863:*requirement
^{830|} MS:Nothing to heighten § over illegible erasure § nor abate: *1888:*Nought
here to < > abate;   ^{831|} MS:But transfer the completeness   *1863:*Transfer the same

⁸³⁵ See the enwrapping rocky niche,
Sufficient for the sleep in which
The lizard breathes for ages safe:
Split the mould—and as light would chafe
The creature's new world-widened sense,
⁸⁴⁰ Dazzled to death at evidence
Of all the sounds and sights that broke
Innumerous at the chisel's stroke,—
So, in God's eye, the earth's first stuff
Was, neither more nor less, enough
⁸⁴⁵ To house man's soul, man's need fulfil.
Man reckoned it immeasurable?
So thinks the lizard of his vault!
Could God be taken in default,
Short of contrivances, by you,—
⁸⁵⁰ Or reached, ere ready to pursue
His progress through eternity?
That chambered rock, the lizard's world,
Your easy mallet's blow has hurled
To nothingness for ever; so,
⁸⁵⁵ Has God abolished at a blow
This world, wherein his saints were pent,—
Who, though found grateful and content,
With the provision there, as thou,
Yet knew he would not disallow
⁸⁶⁰ Their spirit's hunger, felt as well,—
Unsated,—not unsatable,

---

completeness   ⁸³⁶ MS:sleep, in   <i>1888:</i>sleep in   ⁸³⁷ MS:breathes
§ over illegible word §   ⁸³⁸ MS: § first word illegibly erased and replaced by §
Split < > as this would   <i>1888:</i>as light would   ⁸⁴⁰ MS:One minute after you
dispense   <i>1863:</i>after day dispense   <i>1888:</i>Dazzled to death at evidence
⁸⁴¹ MS:The thousand sounds   1888:Of all the sounds   ⁸⁴² MS:In, on him, at
1865:In on him at   1888:Innumerous at   ⁸⁴³ MS:eyes   1863:eye
⁸⁴⁶ MS:You reckoned § over illegible erasure; next word, possibly immeasurable, crossed
out § it immeasurable: <i>1863:</i>Man reckoned it immeasurable?   ⁸⁵⁷ MS:though,
found   <i>1863:</i>though found   ⁸⁵⁸ MS:With § next several words erased, crossed out,
and replaced above by three words § the provision there,   ⁸⁵⁹ MS:knew
He   <i>1868:</i>knew he   ⁸⁶⁰ MS:spirits'   <i>1863:</i>spirit's   ⁸⁶¹ MS:not § altered from

As paradise gives proof. Deride
Their choice now, thou who sit'st outside!"

XXVII

I cried in anguish, "Mind, the mind,
865 So miserably cast behind,
To gain what had been wisely lost!
Oh, let me strive to make the most
Of the poor stinted soul, I nipped
Of budding wings, else now equipped
870 For voyage from summer isle to isle!
And though she needs must reconcile
Ambition to the life on ground,
Still, I can profit by late found
But precious knowledge. Mind is best—
875 I will seize mind, forego the rest,
And try how far my tethered strength
May crawl in this poor breadth and length.
Let me, since I can fly no more,
At least spin dervish-like about
880 (Till giddy rapture almost doubt
I fly) through circling sciences,
Philosophies and histories!
Should the whirl slacken there, then verse,
Fining to music, shall asperse
885 Fresh and fresh fire-dew, till I strain
Intoxicate, half-break my chain!
Not joyless, though more favoured feet
Stand calm, where I want wings to beat
The floor. At least earth's bond is broke!"

---

illegible word, perhaps *nor* §   862| MS:As Paradise   *1865:*As paradise
863| MS:sitst   *1850:*sit'st   869| MS:else well equipt   *1863:*else now equipt   *1868:*
equipped   874| *1865:*Mine   *1868:*Mind   875| *1850:*rest   *1863:*rest,
878| MS:—Let <> fly § next word illegibly crossed out §   *1863:*Let   881| MS: § first
word illegibly erased and replaced by two words § I fly) through   883| MS:whirl
slacken there, § last three words in erased space § then Verse,   *1863:*then verse,
887| MS:Not joyless, § last two words in left margin; original words excised from MS §
though   889| MS:floor? At <> broke!"   *1863:*floor. At

127

XXVIII

890   Then, (sickening even while I spoke)
        "Let me alone! No answer, pray,
        To this! I know what Thou wilt say!
        All still is earth's,—to know, as much
        As feel its truths, which if we touch
895   With sense, or apprehend in soul,
        What matter? I have reached the goal—
        'Whereto does knowledge serve!' will burn
        My eyes, too sure, at every turn!
        I cannot look back now, nor stake
900   Bliss on the race, for running's sake.
        The goal's a ruin like the rest!"—
        "And so much worse thy latter quest,"
        (Added the voice) "that even on earth—
        Whenever, in man's soul, had birth
905   Those intuitions, grasps of guess,
        Which pull the more into the less,
        Making the finite comprehend
        Infinity,—the bard would spend
        Such praise alone, upon his craft,
910   As, when wind-lyres obey the waft,
        Goes to the craftsman who arranged
        The seven strings, changed them and rechanged—
        Knowing it was the South that harped.
        He felt his song, in singing, warped;
915   Distinguished his and God's part: whence
        A world of spirit as of sense
        Was plain to him, yet not too plain,

---

*1888:*broke! § emended to § broke!" § see Editorial Notes §   892| *1868:*what thou
*1888:*what Thou   893| MS:earths',—to Know *1850:*earth's,— *1868:*to know
894| MS:As Feel *1868:*As feel   895| MS:sense or *1863:*sense, or
897| MS:does Knowledge serve?' will *1850:*serve!' will *1868:*does knowledge
901| MS:rest!"— *1868:*rest!— § emended to § rest!"— § see Editorial Notes §
902| MS:"—And < > quest, *1850:*—"And *1865:*"And *1868:*quest,"   903| MS:the
Voice § in erased space §   earth *1863:*earth— *1868:*the voice   904| MS:mans'
*1850:*man's   906| MS:That pull *1888:*Which pull   908| MS:Infinity, the
*1863:*Infinity,—the   909| MS: § first word illegibly erased and replaced by § Such
911| MS: § first words illegibly erased § Goes to § last two words above § the § in
erased space § craftsman, who *1850:*craftsman who   914| MS:warped, *1863:*warped;

Which he could traverse, not remain
A guest in:—else were permanent
920   Heaven on the earth its gleams were meant
To sting with hunger for full light,—
Made visible in verse, despite
The veiling weakness,—truth by means
Of fable, showing while it screens,—
925   Since highest truth, man e'er supplied,
Was ever fable on outside.
Such gleams made bright the earth an age;
Now the whole sun's his heritage!
Take up thy world, it is allowed,
930   Thou who hast entered in the cloud!"

XXIX

Then I—"Behold, my spirit bleeds,
Catches no more at broken reeds,—
But lilies flower those reeds above:
I let the world go, and take love!
935   Love survives in me, albeit those
I love be henceforth masks and shows,
Not living men and women: still
I mind how love repaired all ill,
Cured wrong, soothed grief, made earth amends
940   With parents, brothers, children, friends!
Some semblance of a woman yet
With eyes to help me to forget,
Shall look on me; and I will match
Departed love with love, attach

920| MS:Heaven on the § last two words erased and replaced by § upon earth, its
*1863:*Heaven on earth, which its   *1868:*earth which   *1888:*on the earth its
921| MS:for the light,—   *1863:*for full light,—   922| MS:in Verse   *1863:*in verse
928| MS:Now, the <> his § over illegible word §   *1888:*Now the   931| MS:Then
I,—"Behold   *1850:*Then I—"Behold   932-933| MS:reeds,— / § next two lines
illegibly crossed out, perhaps *Able to wound it if not sustain / But let me not choose
all in vain!* § But <> above—   *1863:*reeds,— / <> above: 935| MS:survives
in me, albeit § last four words over illegible erasure §   936| MS:I loved § over illegible
erasure § are § inserted above § henceforth   *1863:*I love be henceforth
937| MS:Not loving men   *1888:*Not living men   943| MS:Shall live with me; and
§ over illegible erasure §   *1888:*Shall look on me   944| MS:Departed § over

129

⁹⁴⁵ Old memories to new dreams, nor scorn
The poorest of the grains of corn
I save from shipwreck on this isle,
Trusting its barrenness may smile
With happy foodful green one day,
⁹⁵⁰ More precious for the pains. I pray,—
Leave to love, only!"

xxx

At the word,
The form, I looked to have been stirred
With pity and approval, rose
O'er me, as when the headsman throws
⁹⁵⁵ Axe over shoulder to make end—
I fell prone, letting Him expend
His wrath, while thus the inflicting voice
Smote me. "Is this thy final choice?
Love is the best? 'Tis somewhat late!
⁹⁶⁰ And all thou dost enumerate
Of power and beauty in the world,
The mightiness of love was curled
Inextricably round about.
Love lay within it and without,
⁹⁶⁵ To clasp thee,—but in vain! Thy soul
Still shrunk from Him who made the whole,
Still set deliberate aside
His love!—Now take love! Well betide
Thy tardy conscience! Haste to take
⁹⁷⁰ The show of love for the name's sake,
Remembering every moment Who,

---

illegible erasure §   ⁹⁴⁵| MS:Its fragments to my whole, nor   *1888:*Old memories to
new dreams, nor   ⁹⁵⁰| MS:pray,   *1888:*pray,—   ⁹⁵¹| MS:For love, then,
only   *1888:*Leave to love, only   ⁹⁵²| MS:The Form   *1868:*The form
⁹⁵⁶| *1868:*letting him   *1888:*letting Him   ⁹⁵⁷| MS:while, thus, the inflicting Voice
*1865:*while thus the inflicting Voice   *1868:*inflicting voice   ⁹⁶⁶| *1868:*from him
*1888:*from Him   ⁹⁷⁰| MS:The show of love for the name's § last
seven words over illegible erasure §   ⁹⁷¹| MS:moment Who   *1888:*moment Who,

130

Beside creating thee unto
These ends, and these for thee, was said
To undergo death in thy stead
975 In flesh like thine: so ran the tale.
What doubt in thee could countervail
Belief in it? Upon the ground
'That in the story had been found
Too much love! How could God love so?'
980 He who in all his works below
Adapted to the needs of man,
Made love the basis of the plan,—
Did love, as was demonstrated:
While man, who was so fit instead
985 To hate, as every day gave proof,—
Man thought man, for his kind's behoof,
Both could and did invent that scheme
Of perfect love: 'twould well beseem
Cain's nature thou wast wont to praise,
990 Not tally with God's usual ways!''

XXXI

And I cowered deprecatingly—
"Thou Love of God! Or let me die,
Or grant what shall seem heaven almost!
Let me not know that all is lost,
995 Though lost it be—leave me not tied
To this despair, this corpse-like bride!
Let that old life seem mine—no more—
With limitation as before,
With darkness, hunger, toil, distress:

976| MS:doubt in thee § last three words over illegible erasure §   977| MS:it? upon the
ground § last three words over illegible erasure §   *1850*:it? Upon   978| MS:in
the story had been § last five words over illegible erasure §   979| MS:*so?*'
1850:love? How < > *so? 1863*:love! How < > *so? 1868*:so?'   980| *1863*:all His
1868:all his   983| MS:*Did* < > as was demonstrated § last three words over
illegible erasure §:   *1868*:Did   984| MS:who was so fit instead, § last five words
over illegible erasure §   *1863*:instead   985| MS:To hate, as every day gave
§ last six words over illegible erasure §   986| MS:You thought man, for his kind
§ last six words over illegible erasure §   *1863*:Man thought   987| MS:and
would invent   *1863*:and did invent   988| MS:love—'twould   *1868*:love: 'twould
993| MS:seem Heaven   *1868*:seem heaven   999| MS:With darkness § last two words

131

1000   Be all the earth a wilderness!
Only let me go on, go on,
Still hoping ever and anon
To reach one eve the Better Land!''

XXXII

Then did the form expand, expand—
1005   I knew Him through the dread disguise
As the whole God within His eyes
Embraced me.

XXXIII

When I lived again,
The day was breaking,—the grey plain
I rose from, silvered thick with dew.
1010   Was this a vision? False or true?
Since then, three varied years are spent,
And commonly my mind is bent
To think it was a dream—be sure
A mere dream and distemperature—
1015   The last day's watching: then the night,—
The shock of that strange Northern Light
Set my head swimming, bred in me
A dream. And so I live, you see,
Go through the world, try, prove, reject,
1020   Prefer, still struggling to effect
My warfare; happy that I can
Be crossed and thwarted as a man,
Not left in God's contempt apart,
With ghastly smooth life, dead at heart,
1025   Tame in earth's paddock as her prize.
Thank God, she still each method tries
To catch me, who may yet escape,
She knows,—the fiend in angel's shape!

---

over illegible erasure §   1000| MS:wilderness; *1850:*wilderness!   1001| MS:—Only
*1850:*Only   1003| *1888:*the Better Land!' § emended to § the Better Land!'' see Editorial
Notes §   1004| MS:the Form *1868:*the form   1005| MS:disguise, *1868:*knew
him *1888:*knew Him <> disguise   1006| *1850:*within his *1865:*within
His *1868:*within his *1888:*within His   1021| MS:warfare § over illegible erasure §
1026| MS: Thank God she *1863:*Thank God, she   1028| MS:knows, the

132

Thank God, no paradise stands barred
1030 To entry, and I find it hard
To be a Christian, as I said!
Still every now and then my head
Raised glad, sinks mournful—all grows drear
Spite of the sunshine, while I fear
1035 And think, "How dreadful to be grudged
No ease henceforth, as one that's judged,
Condemned to earth for ever, shut
From heaven!"
　　　　　　　But Easter-Day breaks! But
Christ rises! Mercy every way
1040 Is infinite,—and who can say?

*1888:*knows,—the　　1035| MS:And think, "How dreadful to § last five words over
illegible erasure § be § added above §　　1038| MS:From Heaven" . . §¶§ But Easter-day
*1850:*From Heaven" . . §¶§ But Easter-Day　*1863:*From Heaven!" §¶§ But　*1868:*heaven

ESSAY ON SHELLEY

Edited by Donald Smalley

ESSAY ON SHELLEY

1852

An opportunity having presented itself for the acquisition of a series of unedited letters by Shelley, all more or less directly supplementary to and illustrative of the collection already published by Mr. Moxon, that gentleman has decided on securing them. They will prove an acceptable addition to a body of correspondence, the value of which towards a right understanding of its author's purpose and work, may be said to exceed that of any similar contribution exhibiting the worldly relations of a poet whose genius has operated by a different law.

Doubtless we accept gladly the biography of an objective poet, as the phrase now goes; one whose endeavour has been to reproduce things external (whether the phenomena of the scenic universe, or the manifested action of the human heart and brain) with an immediate reference, in every case, to the common eye and apprehension of his fellow men, assumed capable of receiving and profiting by this reproduction. It has been obtained through the poet's double faculty of seeing external objects more clearly, widely, and deeply, than is possible to the average mind, at the same time that he is so acquainted and in sympathy with its narrower comprehension as to be careful to supply it with no other materials than it can combine into an intelligible whole. The auditory of such a poet will include, not only the intelligences which, save for such assistance, would have missed the deeper meaning and enjoyment of the original objects, but also the spirits of a like endowment with his own, who, by means of his abstract, can forthwith pass to the reality it was made from, and either corroborate their impressions of things known already, or supply themselves with new from whatever shows in the inexhaustible variety of existence may have hitherto escaped their knowledge. Such a poet is properly the ποιητης, the fashioner; and the thing fashioned, his poetry, will of necessity be substantive, projected from himself and distinct. We are ignorant what the inventor of "Othello" conceived of that fact as he beheld it in completeness, how he accounted for it, under what known law he registered its nature, or to what unknown law he traced its coincidence. We learn only what he intended we should learn by that particular exercise of his power,—the fact itself,—which, with its infinite significances, each of us receives for the first time as a creation, and is hereafter left to deal with, as, in proportion to his own intelligence, he best may. We are ignorant, and would fain be otherwise.

Doubtless, with respect to such a poet, we covet his biography. We desire to look back upon the process of gathering together in a lifetime, the materials of the work we behold entire; of elaborating, perhaps under difficulty and with hindrance, all that is familiar to our admiration in the apparent facility of success. And the inner impulse of this effort and operation, what induced it? Did a soul's delight in its own extended sphere of vision set it, for the gratification of an insuppressible power, on labour, as other men are set on rest? Or did a sense of duty or of love lead it to communicate its own sensations to mankind? Did an irresistible sympathy with men compel it to bring down and suit its own provision of knowledge and beauty to their narrow scope? Did the personality of such an one stand like an open watch-tower in the midst of the territory it is erected to gaze on, and were the storms and calms, the stars and meteors, its watchman was wont to report of, the habitual variegation of his every-day life, as they glanced across its open roof or lay reflected on its four-square parapet? Or did some sunken and darkened chamber of imagery witness, in the artificial illumination of every storied compartment we are permitted to contemplate, how rare and precious were the outlooks through here and there an embrasure upon a world beyond, and how blankly would have pressed on the artificer the boundary of his daily life, except for the amorous diligence with which he had rendered permanent by art whatever came to diversify the gloom? Still, fraught with instruction and interest as such details undoubtedly are, we can, if needs be, dispense with them. The man passes, the work remains. The work speaks for itself, as we say: and the biography of the worker is no more necessary to an understanding or enjoyment of it, than is a model or anatomy of some tropical tree, to the right tasting of the fruit we are familiar with on the market-stall,—or a geologist's map and stratification, to the prompt recognition of the hill-top, our land-mark of every day.

We turn with stronger needs to the genius of an opposite tendency—the subjective poet of modern classification. He, gifted like the objective poet with the fuller perception of nature and man, is impelled to embody the thing he perceives, not so much with reference to the many below as to the one above him, the supreme Intelligence which apprehends all things in their absolute truth,—an ultimate view ever aspired to, if but partially attained, by the poet's own soul. Not what man sees, but what God sees—the *Ideas* of Plato, seeds of creation lying burningly on the Divine Hand—it is toward these that he strug-

gles. Not with the combination of humanity in action, but with the
primal elements of humanity he has to do; and he digs where he
stands,—preferring to seek them in his own soul as the nearest reflex of
that absolute Mind, according to the intuitions of which he desires to
perceive and speak. Such a poet does not deal habitually with the
picturesque groupings and tempestuous tossings of the forest-trees, but
with their roots and fibres naked to the chalk and stone. He does not
paint pictures and hang them on the walls, but rather carries them on
the retina of his own eyes: we must look deep into his human eyes, to see
those pictures on them. He is rather a seer, accordingly, than a fash-
ioner, and what he produces will be less a work than an effluence. That
effluence cannot be easily considered in abstraction from his personality,
—being indeed the very radiance and aroma of his personality, pro-
jected from it but not separated. Therefore, in our approach to the
poetry, we necessarily approach the personality of the poet; in appre-
hending it we apprehend him, and certainly we cannot love it without
loving him. Both for love's and for understanding's sake we desire to
know him, and as readers of his poetry must be readers of his biography
also.

I shall observe, in passing, that it seems not so much from any
essential distinction in the faculty of the two poets or in the nature of the
objects contemplated by either, as in the more immediate adaptability
of these objects to the distinct purpose of each, that the objective poet, in
his appeal to the aggregate human mind, chooses to deal with the
doings of men, (the result of which dealing, in its pure form, when even
description, as suggesting a describer, is dispensed with, is what we call
dramatic poetry), while the subjective poet, whose study has been him-
self, appealing through himself to the absolute Divine mind, prefers to
dwell upon those external scenic appearances which strike out most
abundantly and uninterruptedly his inner light and power, selects that
silence of the earth and sea in which he can best hear the beating of his
individual heart, and leaves the noisy, complex, yet imperfect exhibi-
tions of nature in the manifold experience of man around him, which
serve only to distract and suppress the working of his brain. These
opposite tendencies of genius will be more readily descried in their
artistic effect than in their moral spring and cause. Pushed to an ex-
treme and manifested as a deformity, they will be seen plainest of all
in the fault of either artist, when subsidiarily to the human interest of
his work his occasional illustrations from scenic nature are introduced
as in the earlier works of the originative painters—men and women
filling the foreground with consummate mastery, while mountain,

grove and rivulet show like an anticipatory revenge on that succeeding race of landscape-painters whose "figures" disturb the perfection of their earth and sky. It would be idle to inquire, of these two kinds of poetic faculty in operation, which is the higher or even rarer endowment. If the subjective might seem to be the ultimate requirement of every age, the objective, in the strictest state, must still retain its original value. For it is with this world, as starting point and basis alike, that we shall always have to concern ourselves: the world is not to be learned and thrown aside, but reverted to and relearned. The spiritual comprehension may be infinitely subtilised, but the raw material it operates upon, must remain. There may be no end of the poets who communicate to us what they see in an object with reference to their own individuality; what it was before they saw it, in reference to the aggregate human mind, will be as desirable to know as ever. Nor is there any reason why these two modes of poetic faculty may not issue hereafter from the same poet in successive perfect works, examples of which, according to what are now considered the exigences of art, we have hitherto possessed in distinct individuals only. A mere running-in of the one faculty upon the other, is, of course, the ordinary circumstance. Far more rarely it happens that either is found so decidedly prominent and superior, as to be pronounced comparatively pure: while of the perfect shield, with the gold and the silver side set up for all comers to challenge, there has yet been no instance. Either faculty in its eminent state is doubtless conceded by Providence as a best gift to men, according to their especial want. There is a time when the general eye has, so to speak, absorbed its fill of the phenomena around it, whether spiritual or material, and desires rather to learn the exacter significance of what it possesses, than to receive any augmentation of what is possessed. Then is the opportunity for the poet of loftier vision, to lift his fellows, with their half-apprehensions, up to his own sphere, by intensifying the import of details and rounding the universal meaning. The influence of such an achievement will not soon die out. A tribe of successors (Homerides) working more or less in the same spirit, dwell on his discoveries and reinforce his doctrine; till, at unawares, the world is found to be subsisting wholly on the shadow of a reality, on sentiments diluted from passions, on the tradition of a fact, the convention of a moral, the straw of last year's harvest. Then is the imperative call for the appearance of another sort of poet, who shall at once replace this intellectual rumination of food swallowed long ago, by a supply of the fresh and living swathe; getting at new substance by breaking up the assumed wholes into parts of independent and unclassed value, careless of the unknown laws for recombining them (it

will be the business of yet another poet to suggest those hereafter),
prodigal of objects for men's outer and not inner sight, shaping for their
uses a new and different creation from the last, which it displaces by the
right of life over death,—to endure until, in the inevitable process, its
very sufficiency to itself shall require, at length, an exposition of its
affinity to something higher,—when the positive yet conflicting facts
shall again precipitate themselves under a harmonising law, and one
more degree will be apparent for a poet to climb in that mighty ladder,
of which, however cloud-involved and undefined may glimmer the
topmost step, the world dares no longer doubt that its gradations
ascend.

Such being the two kinds of artists, it is naturally, as I have shown,
with the biography of the subjective poet that we have the deeper
concern. Apart from his recorded life altogether, we might fail to deter-
mine with satisfactory precision to what class his productions belong,
and what amount of praise is assignable to the producer. Certainly, in
the face of any conspicuous achievement of genius, philosophy, no less
than sympathetic instinct, warrants our belief in a great moral purpose
having mainly inspired even where it does not visibly look out of the
same. Greatness in a work suggests an adequate instrumentality; and
none of the lower incitements, however they may avail to initiate or even
effect many considerable displays of power, simulating the nobler inspi-
ration to which they are mistakenly referred, have been found able,
under the ordinary conditions of humanity, to task themselves to the
end of so exacting a performance as a poet's complete work. As soon will
the galvanism that provokes to violent action the muscles of a corpse,
induce it to cross the chamber steadily: sooner. The love of displaying
power for the display's sake, the love of riches, of distinction, of notori-
ety,—the desire of a triumph over rivals, and the vanity in the applause
of friends,—each and all of such whetted appetites grow intenser by
exercise and increasingly sagacious as to the best and readiest means of
self-appeasement,—while for any of their ends, whether the money or
the pointed finger of the crowd, or the flattery and hate to heart's
content, there are cheaper prices to pay, they will all find soon enough,
than the bestowment of a life upon a labour, hard, slow, and not sure.
Also, assuming the proper moral aim to have produced a work, there are
many and various states of an aim: it may be more intense than clear-
sighted, or too easily satisfied with a lower field of activity than a
steadier aspiration would reach. All the bad poetry in the world (ac-
counted poetry, that is, by its affinities) will be found to result from some
one of the infinite degrees of discrepancy between the attributes of the

141

²⁰⁰ poet's soul, occasioning a want of correspondency between his work and the verities of nature,—issuing in poetry, false under whatever form, which shows a thing not as it is to mankind generally, nor as it is to the particular describer, but as it is supposed to be for some unreal neutral mood, midway between both and of value to neither, and living its brief
²⁰⁵ minute simply through the indolence of whoever accepts it or his incapacity to denounce a cheat. Although of such depths of failure there can be no question here we must in every case betake ourselves to the review of a poet's life ere we determine some of the nicer questions concerning his poetry,—more especially if the performance we seek to estimate
²¹⁰ aright, has been obstructed and cut short of completion by circumstances,—a disastrous youth or a premature death. We may learn from the biography whether his spirit invariably saw and spoke from the last height to which it had attained. An absolute vision is not for this world, but we are permitted a continual approximation to it, every
²¹⁵ degree of which in the individual, provided it exceed the attainment of the masses, must procure him a clear advantage. Did the poet ever attain to a higher platform than where he rested and exhibited a result? Did he know more than he spoke of?

I concede however, in respect to the subject of our study as well as
²²⁰ some few other illustrious examples, that the unmistakeable quality of the verse would be evidence enough, under usual circumstances, not only of the kind and degree of the intellectual but of the moral constitution of Shelley: the whole personality of the poet shining forward from the poems, without much need of going further to seek it. The "Re-
²²⁵ mains"—produced within a period of ten years, and at a season of life when other men of at all comparable genius have hardly done more than prepare the eye for future sight and the tongue for speech—present us with the complete enginery of a poet, as signal in the excellence of its several adaptitudes as transcendent in the combination of effects,—
²³⁰ examples, in fact, of the whole poet's function of beholding with an understanding keenness the universe, nature and man, in their actual state of perfection in imperfection,—of the whole poet's virtue of being untempted by the manifold partial developments of beauty and good on every side, into leaving them the ultimates he found them,—
²³⁵ induced by the facility of the gratification of his own sense of those qualities, or by the pleasure of acquiescence in the short-comings of his predecessors in art, and the pain of disturbing their conventionalisms,—the whole poet's virtue, I repeat, of looking higher than any manifestation yet made of both beauty and good, in order to suggest
²⁴⁰ from the utmost actual realisation of the one a corresponding capability

in the other, and out of the calm, purity and energy of nature, to reconstitute and store up for the forthcoming stage of man's being, a gift in repayment of that former gift, in which man's own thought and passion had been lavished by the poet on the else-incompleted magni-
245 ficence of the sunrise, the else-uninterpreted mystery of the lake,—so drawing out, lifting up, and assimilating this ideal of a future man, thus descried as possible, to the present reality of the poet's soul already arrived at the higher state of development, and still aspirant to elevate and extend itself in conformity with its still-improving perceptions of,
250 no longer the eventual Human, but the actual Divine. In conjunction with which noble and rare powers, came the subordinate power of delivering these attained results to the world in an embodiment of verse more closely answering to and indicative of the process of the informing spirit, (failing as it occasionally does, in art, only to succeed in highest
255 art),—with a diction more adequate to the task in its natural and acquired richness, its material colour and spiritual transparency,—the whole being moved by and suffused with a music at once of the soul and the sense, expressive both of an external might of sincere passion and an internal fitness and consonancy,—than can be attributed to any other
260 writer whose record is among us. Such was the spheric poetical faculty of Shelley, as its own self-sufficing central light, radiating equally through immaturity and accomplishment, through many fragments and occa- sional completion, reveals it to a competent judgment.

But the acceptance of this truth by the public, has been retarded by
265 certain objections which cast us back on the evidence of biography, even with Shelley's poetry in our hands. Except for the particular character of these objections, indeed, the non-appreciation of his contemporaries would simply class, now that it is over, with a series of experiences which have necessarily happened and needlessly been wondered at, ever
270 since the world began, and concerning which any present anger may well be moderated, no less in justice to our forerunners than in policy to ourselves. For the misapprehensiveness of his age is exactly what a poet is sent to remedy; and the interval between his operation and the generally perceptible effect of it, is no greater, less indeed, than in many
275 other departments of the great human effort. The "E pur si muove" of the astronomer was as bitter a word as any uttered before or since by a poet over his rejected living work, in that depth of conviction which is so like despair.

But in this respect was the experience of Shelley peculiarly unfortu-
280 nate—that the disbelief in him as a man, even preceded the disbelief in him as a writer; the misconstruction of his moral nature preparing the

way for the misappreciation of his intellectual labours. There existed
from the beginning,—simultaneous with, indeed anterior to his earliest
noticeable works, and not brought forward to counteract any impres-
sion they had succeeded in making,—certain charges against his private
character and life, which, if substantiated to their whole breadth, would
materially disturb, I do not attempt to deny, our reception and enjoy-
ment of his works, however wonderful the artistic qualities of these. For
we are not sufficiently supplied with instances of genius of his order, to
be able to pronounce certainly how many of its constituent parts have
been tasked and strained to the production of a given lie, and how high
and pure a mood of the creative mind may be dramatically simulated as
the poet's habitual and exclusive one. The doubts, therefore, arising
from such a question, required to be set at rest, as they were effectually,
by those early authentic notices of Shelley's career and the corroborative
accompaniment of his letters, in which not only the main tenor and
principal result of his life, but the purity and beauty of many of the
processes which had conduced to them, were made apparent enough for
the general reader's purpose,—whoever lightly condemned Shelley first,
on the evidence of reviews and gossip, as lightly acquitting him now, on
that of memoirs and correspondence. Still, it is advisable to lose no
opportunity of strengthening and completing the chain of biographical
testimony; much more, of course, for the sake of the poet's original
lovers, whose volunteered sacrifice of particular principle in favour of
absorbing sympathy we might desire to dispense with, than for the sake
of his foolish haters, who have long since diverted upon other objects
their obtuseness or malignancy. A full life of Shelley should be written at
once, while the materials for it continue in reach; not to minister to the
curiosity of the public, but to obliterate the last stain of that false life
which was forced on the public's attention before it had any curiosity on
the matter,—a biography, composed in harmony with the present gen-
eral disposition to have faith in him, yet not shrinking from a candid
statement of all ambiguous passages, through a reasonable confidence
that the most doubtful of them will be found consistent with a belief in
the eventual perfection of his character, according to the poor limits of
our humanity. Nor will men persist in confounding, any more than God
confounds, with genuine infidelity and an atheism of the heart, those
passionate, impatient struggles of a boy towards distant truth and love,
made in the dark, and ended by one sweep of the natural seas before the
full moral sunrise could shine out on him. Crude convictions of boy-
hood, conveyed in imperfect and inapt forms of speech,—for such things
all boys have been pardoned. There are growing-pains, accompanied by

temporary distortion, of the soul also. And it would be hard indeed upon this young Titan of genius, murmuring in divine music his human ignorances, through his very thirst for knowledge, and his rebellion, in mere aspiration to law, if the melody itself substantiated the error, and the tragic cutting short of life perpetuated into sins, such faults as, under happier circumstances, would have been left behind by the consent of the most arrogant moralist, forgotten on the lowest steps of youth.

The responsibility of presenting to the public a biography of Shelley, does not, however lie with me: I have only to make it a little easier by arranging these few supplementary letters, with a recognition of the value of the whole collection. This value I take to consist in a most truthful conformity of the Correspondence, in its limited degree, with the moral and intellectual character of the writer as displayed in the highest manifestations of his genius. Letters and poems are obviously an act of the same mind, produced by the same law, only differing in the application to the individual or collective understanding. Letters and poems may be used indifferently as the basement of our opinion upon the writer's character; the finished expression of a sentiment in the poems, giving light and significance to the rudiments of the same in the letters, and these, again, in their incipiency and unripeness, authenticating the exalted mood and reattaching it to the personality of the writer. The musician speaks on the note he sings with; there is no change in the scale, as he diminishes the volume into familiar intercourse. There is nothing of that jarring between the man and the author, which has been found so amusing or so melancholy; no dropping of the tragic mask, as the crowd melts away; no mean discovery of the real motives of a life's achievement, often, in other lives, laid bare as pitifully as when, at the close of a holiday, we catch sight of the internal lead-pipes and wood-valves, to which, and not to the ostensible conch and dominant Triton of the fountain, we have owed our admired waterwork. No breaking out, in household privacy, of hatred anger and scorn, incongruous with the higher mood and suppressed artistically in the book: no brutal return to self-delighting, when the audience of philanthropic schemes is out of hearing: no indecent stripping off the grander feeling and rule of life as too costly and cumbrous for every-day wear. Whatever Shelley was, he was with an admirable sincerity. It was not always truth that he thought and spoke; but in the purity of truth he spoke and thought always. Everywhere is apparent his belief in the existence of Good, to which Evil is an accident; his faithful holding by what he assumed to be the former, going everywhere in company with the tenderest pity for

145

those acting or suffering on the opposite hypothesis. For he was tender, though tenderness is not always the characteristic of very sincere natures; he was eminently both tender and sincere. And not only do the same affection and yearning after the well-being of his kind, appear in the letters as in the poems, but they express themselves by the same theories and plans, however crude and unsound. There is no reservation of a subtler, less costly, more serviceable remedy for his own ill, than he has proposed for the general one; nor does he ever contemplate an object on his own account, from a less elevation than he uses in exhibiting it to the world. How shall we help believing Shelley to have been, in his ultimate attainment, the splendid spirit of his own best poetry, when we find even his carnal speech to agree faithfully, at faintest as at strongest, with the tone and rhythm of his most oracular utterances?

For the rest, these new letters are not offered as presenting any new feature of the poet's character. Regarded in themselves, and as the substantive productions of a man, their importance would be slight. But they possess interest beyond their limits, in confirming the evidence just dwelt on, of the poetical mood of Shelley being only the intensification of his habitual mood; the same tongue only speaking, for want of the special excitement to sing. The very first letter, as one instance for all, strikes the key-note of the predominating sentiment of Shelley throughout his whole life—his sympathy with the oppressed. And when we see him at so early an age, casting out, under the influence of such a sympathy, letters and pamphlets on every side, we accept it as the simple exemplification of the sincerity, with which, at the close of his life, he spoke of himself, as—

> "One whose heart a stranger's tear might wear
> As water-drops the sandy fountain stone;
> Who loved and pitied all things, and could moan
> For woes which others hear not, and could see
> The absent with the glass of phantasy,
> And near the poor and trampled sit and weep,
> Following the captive to his dungeon deep—
> One who was as a nerve o'er which do creep
> The else-unfelt oppressions of this earth."

Such sympathy with his kind was evidently developed in him to an extraordinary and even morbid degree, at a period when the general intellectual powers it was impatient to put in motion, were immature or deficient.

I conjecture, from a review of the various publications of Shelley's youth, that one of the causes of his failure at the outset, was the peculiar

⁴⁰⁵ *practicalness* of his mind, which was not without a determinate effect on his progress in theorising. An ordinary youth, who turns his attention to similar subjects, discovers falsities, incongruities, and various points for amendment, and, in the natural advance of the purely critical spirit unchecked by considerations of remedy, keeps up before his young eyes
⁴¹⁰ so many instances of the same error and wrong, that he finds himself unawares arrived at the startling conclusion, that all must be changed— or nothing: in the face of which plainly impossible achievement, he is apt (looking perhaps a little more serious by the time he touches at the decisive issue), to feel, either carelessly or considerately, that
⁴¹⁵ his own attempting a single piece of service would be worse than use- less even, and to refer the whole task to another age and person—safe in proportion to his incapacity. Wanting words to speak, he has never made a fool of himself by speaking. But, in Shelley's case, the early fer- vour and power to *see*, was accompanied by as precocious a fertility to
⁴²⁰ *contrive*: he endeavoured to realise as he went on idealising; every wrong had simultaneously its remedy, and, out of the strength of his hatred for the former, he took the strength of his confidence in the latter—till suddenly he stood pledged to the defence of a set of miserable little expedients, just as if they represented great principles, and to an
⁴²⁵ attack upon various great principles, really so, without leaving himself time to examine whether, because they were antagonistical to the reme- dy he had suggested, they must therefore be identical or even essentially connected with the wrong he sought to cure,—playing with blind pas- sion into the hands of his enemies, and dashing at whatever red cloak
⁴³⁰ was held forth to him, as the cause of the fireball he had last been stung with—mistaking Churchdom for Christianity, and for marriage, "the sale of love" and the law of sexual oppression.

Gradually, however, he was leaving behind him this low practical dexterity, unable to keep up with his widening intellectual perception;
⁴³⁵ and, in exact proportion as he did so, his true power strengthened and proved itself. Gradually he was raised above the contemplation of spots and the attempt at effacing them, to the great Abstract Light, and, through the discrepancy of the creation, to the sufficiency of the First Cause. Gradually he was learning that the best way of removing abuses
⁴⁴⁰ is to stand fast by truth. Truth is one, as they are manifold; and in- numerable negative effects are produced by the upholding of one positive principle. I shall say what I think,—had Shelley lived he would have finally ranged himself with the Christians; his very instinct for helping the weaker side (if numbers make strength), his very "hate of
⁴⁴⁵ hate," which at first mistranslated itself into delirious Queen Mab notes

147

and the like, would have got clearer-sighted by exercise. The prelimi-
nary step to following Christ, is the leaving the dead to bury their
dead—not clamouring on His doctrine for an especial solution of dif-
ficulties which are referable to the general problem of the universe.
450 Already he had attained to a profession of "a worship to the Spirit of
good within, which requires (before it sends that inspiration forth,
which impresses its likeness upon all it creates) devoted and disinter-
ested homage, *as Coleridge says*,"—and Paul likewise. And we find in
one of his last exquisite fragments, avowedly a record of one of his own
455 mornings and its experience, as it dawned on him at his soul and body's
best in his boat on the Serchio—that as surely as

> "The stars burnt out in the pale blue air,
> And the thin white moon lay withering there—
> Day had kindled the dewy woods,
460 And the rocks above, and the stream below,
> And the vapours in their multitudes,
> And the Apennine's shroud of summer snow—
> Day had awakened all things that be;"

just so surely, he tells us (stepping forward from this delicious dance-
465 music, choragus-like, into the grander measure befitting the final enun-
ciation),

> "All rose to do the task He set to each,
> Who shaped us to his ends and not our own;
470 The million rose to learn, and One to teach
> What none yet ever knew or can be known."

No more difference than this, from David's pregnant conclusion so
long ago!

Meantime, as I call Shelley a moral man, because he was true,
475 simple-hearted, and brave, and because what he acted corresponded to
what he knew, so I call him a man of religious mind, because every
audacious negative cast up by him against the Divine, was interpene-
trated with a mood of reverence and adoration,—and because I find him
everywhere taking for granted some of the capital dogmas of Christian-
480 ity, while most vehemently denying their historical basement. There is
such a thing as an efficacious knowledge of and belief in the politics of
Junius, or the poetry of Rowley, though a man should at the same time
dispute the title of Chatterton to the one, and consider the author of the

other, as Byron wittily did, "really, truly, nobody at all." * There is even
such a thing, we come to learn wonderingly in these very letters, as a
profound sensibility and adaptitude for art, while the science of the
percipient is so little advanced as to admit of his stronger admiration for
Guido (and Carlo Dolce!) than for Michael Angelo. A Divine Being has
Himself said, that "a word against the Son of man shall be forgiven to a
man," while "a word against the Spirit of God" (implying a general
deliberate preference of perceived evil to perceived good) "shall not be
forgiven to a man." Also, in religion, one earnest and unextorted asser-
tion of belief should outweigh, as a matter of testimony, many assertions
of unbelief. The fact that there is a gold-region is established by the
finding of one lump, though you miss the vein never so often.

He died before his youth ended. In taking the measure of him as a
man, he must be considered on the whole and at his ultimate spiritual
stature, and not be judged of at the immaturity and by the mistakes of
ten years before: that, indeed, would be to judge of the author of "Julian
and Maddalo" by "Zastrozzi." Let the whole truth be told of his worst
mistake. I believe, for my own part, that if anything could now shame or
grieve Shelley, it would be an attempt to vindicate him at the expense of
another.

In forming a judgment, I would, however, press on the reader the
simple justice of considering tenderly his constitution of body as well as
mind, and how unfavourable it was to the steady symmetries of conven-
tional life; the body, in the torture of incurable disease, refusing to give
repose to the bewildered soul, tossing in its hot fever of the fancy,—and
the laudanum-bottle making but a perilous and pitiful truce between
these two. He was constantly subject to "that state of mind" (I quote his
own note to "Hellas") "in which ideas may be supposed to assume the
force of sensation, through the confusion of thought with the objects of
thought, and excess of passion animating the creations of the imagina-
tion:" in other words, he was liable to remarkable delusions and halluci-
nations. The nocturnal attack in Wales, for instance, was assuredly a

---

* Or, to take our illustrations from the writings of Shelley himself, there is such a thing
as admirably appreciating a work by Andrea Verocchio,—and fancifully characterising
the Pisan Torre Guelfa by the Ponte a Mare, black against the sunsets,—and consum-
mately painting the islet of San Clemente with its penitentiary for rebellious priests, to
the west between Venice and the Lido—while you believe the first to be a fragment of an
antique sarcophagus,—the second, Ugolino's Tower of Famine (the vestiges of which
should be sought for in the Piazza de'Cavalieri)—and the third (as I convinced myself
last summer at Venice), San Servolo with its madhouse—which, far from being "window-
less," is as full of windows as a barrack.

delusion; and I venture to express my own conviction, derived from a little attention to the circumstances of either story, that the idea of the enamoured lady following him to Naples, and of the "man in the cloak" who struck him at the Pisan post-office, were equally illusory,—the mere projection, in fact, from himself, of the image of his own love and hate.

> "To thirst and find no fill—to wail and wander
> With short unsteady steps—to pause and ponder—
> To feel the blood run through the veins and tingle
> When busy thought and blind sensation mingle,—
> To nurse the image of *unfelt caresses*
> Till dim imagination just possesses
> The half-created shadow"—

of unfelt caresses,—and of unfelt blows as well: to such conditions was his genius subject. It was not at Rome only (where he heard a mystic voice exclaiming, "Cenci, Cenci," in reference to the tragic theme which occupied him at the time),—it was not at Rome only that he mistook the cry of "old rags." The habit of somnambulism is said to have extended to the very last days of his life.

Let me conclude with a thought of Shelley as a poet. In the hierarchy of creative minds, it is the presence of the highest faculty that gives first rank, in virtue of its kind, not degree; no pretension of a lower nature, whatever the completeness of development or variety of effect, impeding the precedency of the rarer endowment though only in the germ. The contrary is sometimes maintained; it is attempted to make the lower gifts (which are potentially included in the higher faculty) of independent value, and equal to some exercise of the special function. For instance, should not a poet possess common sense? Then the possession of abundant common sense implies a step towards becoming a poet. Yes; such a step as the lapidary's, when, strong in the fact of carbon entering largely into the composition of the diamond, he heaps up a sack of charcoal in order to compete with the Koh-i-noor. I pass at once, therefore, from Shelley's minor excellencies to his noblest and predominating characteristic.

This I call his simultaneous perception of Power and Love in the absolute, and of Beauty and Good in the concrete, while he throws, from his poet's station between both, swifter, subtler, and more numerous films for the connexion of each with each, than have been thrown by any modern artificer of whom I have knowledge; proving how, as he says,

> "The spirit of the worm within the sod,
> In love and worship blends itself with God."

I would rather consider Shelley's poetry as a sublime fragmentary
essay towards a presentment of the correspondency of the universe to
Deity, of the natural to the spiritual, and of the actual to the ideal, than
I would isolate and separately appraise the worth of many detachable
portions which might be acknowledged as utterly perfect in a lower
moral point of view, under the mere conditions of art. It would be easy
to take my stand on successful instances of objectivity in Shelley: there is
the unrivalled "Cenci;" there is the "Julian and Maddalo" too; there is
the magnificent "Ode to Naples:" why not regard, it may be said, the less
organised matter as the radiant elemental foam and solution, out of
which would have been evolved, eventually, creations as perfect even as
those? But I prefer to look for the highest attainment, not simply the
high,—and, seeing it, I hold by it. There is surely enough of the work
"Shelley" to be known enduringly among men, and, I believe, to be
accepted of God, as human work may; and around the imperfect pro-
portions of such, the most elaborated productions of ordinary art must
arrange themselves as inferior illustrations.

It is because I have long held these opinions in assurance and
gratitude, that I catch at the opportunity offered to me of expressing
them here; knowing that the alacrity to fulfil an humble office conveys
more love than the acceptance of the honour of a higher one, and that
better, therefore, than the signal service it was the dream of my boyhood
to render to his fame and memory, may be the saying of a few, inade-
quate words upon these scarcely more important supplementary letters
of SHELLEY.

PARIS, *Dec. 4th, 1851.*

MEN AND WOMEN. Volume I

Edited by Allan C. Dooley

§ In this section, the poems of *Men and Women*, Volume I, are presented in the order in which they appeared in the first edition of 1855. In his collected editions, B rearranged his shorter poems; the following is a brief account of the altered groupings.

Dramatic Lyrics (Bells and Pomegranates III, 1842) contained 16 poems; *Dramatic Romances and Lyrics (Bells and Pomegranates* VII, 1845) contained 21 poems. With one omission ("Claret and Tokay," from the 1845 publication) and one addition ("Home-Thoughts, from the Sea," added after "Home-Thoughts, from Abroad") the contents of these two publications were reproduced in volume 2 of B's two-volume *Poems* (1849), under the heading "Dramatic Romances and Lyrics." The poems were arranged in the same order as in 1842 and 1845, although "Night and Morning" (of 1845) was separated into "Meeting at Night" and "Parting at Morning."

Men and Women (1855) contained 51 poems, 27 in Volume I and 24 in Volume II.

For the *Poetical Works* of 1863, B arranged these three original collections of poems under the three headings, "Lyrics" (50 poems), "Romances" (26 poems), and "Men, and Women" (12 poems). This made up volume 1 of the three-volume 1863 edition. "In a Balcony," originally in Volume II of *Men and Women* (1855), was placed in volume 2 of the 1863 edition under the heading "Tragedies and Other Plays."

The tables of contents provided below demonstrate the rearrangements of the poems and the alterations of titles. Additional minor changes in titles and groupings of the poems were made between 1863 and the 1888-1889 edition, where the three groups are entitled "Men and Women" (volume 4 of 1888-1889; 13 poems), "Dramatic Romances" (volume 5; 25 poems), and "Dramatic Lyrics" (volume 6; 49 poems). §

DRAMATIC LYRICS (1842)

CAVALIER TUNES
    I.—MARCHING ALONG
    II.—GIVE A ROUSE
    III.—MY WIFE GERTRUDE
ITALY AND FRANCE
    I.—ITALY
    II.—FRANCE
CAMP AND CLOISTER
    I.—CAMP (*French*)
    II.—CLOISTER (*Spanish*)
IN A GONDOLA
ARTEMIS PROLOGUIZES
WARING
QUEEN-WORSHIP
    I.—RUDEL AND THE LADY OF TRIPOLI
    II.—CRISTINA
MADHOUSE CELLS
    I.
    II.
THROUGH THE METIDJA TO ABD-EL-KADR.—1842
THE PIED PIPER OF HAMELIN; A CHILD'S STORY
    (*Written for, and inscribed to, W. M. the Younger.*)

DRAMATIC ROMANCES AND LYRICS (1845)

"HOW THEY BROUGHT THE GOOD NEWS
    FROM GHENT TO AIX"
PICTOR IGNOTUS
ITALY IN ENGLAND
ENGLAND IN ITALY
THE LOST LEADER
THE LOST MISTRESS
HOME THOUGHTS FROM ABROAD
THE TOMB AT ST. PRAXED'S
GARDEN FANCIES
    I.—THE FLOWER'S NAME
    II.—SIBRANDUS SCHAFNABURGENSIS
FRANCE AND SPAIN
    I.—THE LABORATORY
    II.—THE CONFESSIONAL
THE FLIGHT OF THE DUCHESS
EARTH'S IMMORTALITIES
SONG
THE BOY AND THE ANGEL
NIGHT AND MORNING

155

CLARET AND TOKAY
SAUL
TIME'S REVENGES
THE GLOVE

DRAMATIC ROMANCES AND LYRICS (1849)

CAVALIER TUNES:—
      I.—MARCHING ALONG
      II.—GIVE A ROUSE
      III.—BOOT AND SADDLE
MY LAST DUCHESS
COUNT GISMOND
INCIDENT OF THE FRENCH CAMP
SOLILOQUY OF THE SPANISH CLOISTER
IN A GONDOLA
ARTEMIS PROLOGUIZES
WARING
RUDEL TO THE LADY OF TRIPOLI
CRISTINA
 I. MADHOUSE CELL
II. MADHOUSE CELL
THROUGH THE METIDJA TO ABD-EL-KADR
THE PIED PIPER OF HAMELIN
"HOW THEY BROUGHT THE GOOD NEWS
   FROM GHENT TO AIX"
PICTOR IGNOTUS
THE ITALIAN IN ENGLAND
THE ENGLISHMAN IN ITALY
THE LOST LEADER
THE LOST MISTRESS
HOME-THOUGHTS, FROM ABROAD
HOME-THOUGHTS, FROM THE SEA
THE BISHOP ORDERS HIS TOMB AT
   ST. PRAXED'S CHURCH
GARDEN-FANCIES:—
      I.   THE FLOWER'S NAME
      II.   SIBRANDUS SCHAFNABURGENSIS
THE LABORATORY
THE CONFESSIONAL
THE FLIGHT OF THE DUCHESS
EARTH'S IMMORTALITIES
SONG
THE BOY AND THE ANGEL
MEETING AT NIGHT
PARTING AT MORNING
SAUL

TIME'S REVENGES
THE GLOVE

MEN AND WOMEN (1855)

VOLUME I

LOVE AMONG THE RUINS
A LOVER'S QUARREL
EVELYN HOPE
UP AT A VILLA—DOWN IN THE CITY
    (As Distinguished By an Italian Person of Quality)
A WOMAN'S LAST WORD
FRA LIPPO LIPPI
A TOCCATA OF GALUPPI'S
BY THE FIRE-SIDE
ANY WIFE TO ANY HUSBAND
AN EPISTLE CONTAINING THE STRANGE MEDICAL
    EXPERIENCE OF KARSHISH
    THE ARAB PHYSICIAN
MESMERISM
A SERENADE AT THE VILLA
MY STAR
INSTANS TYRANNUS
A PRETTY WOMAN
"CHILDE ROLAND TO THE DARK TOWER CAME"
RESPECTABILITY
A LIGHT WOMAN
THE STATUE AND THE BUST
LOVE IN A LIFE
LIFE IN A LOVE
HOW IT STRIKES A CONTEMPORARY
THE LAST RIDE TOGETHER
THE PATRIOT—AN OLD STORY
MASTER HUGUES OF SAXE-GOTHA
BISHOP BLOUGRAM'S APOLOGY
MEMORABILIA

VOLUME II

ANDREA DEL SARTO (Called "The Faultless Painter")
BEFORE
AFTER
IN THREE DAYS
IN A YEAR
OLD PICTURES IN FLORENCE

IN A BALCONY—FIRST PART
                SECOND PART
                THIRD PART
SAUL
"DE GUSTIBUS—"
WOMEN AND ROSES
PROTUS
HOLY-CROSS DAY (On which the Jews were Forced to Attend
    an Annual Christian Sermon in Rome.)
THE GUARDIAN-ANGEL: A PICTURE AT FANO
CLEON
THE TWINS
POPULARITY
THE HERETIC'S TRAGEDY (A Middle-Age Interlude.)
TWO IN THE CAMPAGNA
A GRAMMARIAN'S FUNERAL
ONE WAY OF LOVE
ANOTHER WAY OF LOVE
"TRANSCENDENTALISM:" A POEM IN TWELVE BOOKS
MISCONCEPTIONS
ONE WORD MORE. TO E. B. B.

LYRICS, ROMANCES, MEN, AND WOMEN (1863)

LYRICS

CAVALIER TUNES
        I.—MARCHING ALONG
        II.—GIVE A ROUSE
        III.—BOOT AND SADDLE
THE LOST LEADER
"HOW THEY BROUGHT THE GOOD NEWS
    FROM GHENT TO AIX"
THROUGH THE METIDJA TO ABD-EL-KADR
NATIONALITY IN DRINKS
GARDEN FANCIES
        I.   THE FLOWER'S NAME
        II.   SIBRANDUS SCHAFNABURGENSIS
THE LABORATORY
THE CONFESSIONAL
CRISTINA
THE LOST MISTRESS
EARTH'S IMMORTALITIES
MEETING AT NIGHT
PARTING AT MORNING
SONG

A WOMAN'S LAST WORD
EVELYN HOPE
LOVE AMONG THE RUINS
A LOVERS' QUARREL
UP AT A VILLA—DOWN IN THE CITY
A TOCCATA OF GALUPPI'S
OLD PICTURES IN FLORENCE
"DE GUSTIBUS—"
HOME-THOUGHTS, FROM ABROAD
HOME-THOUGHTS, FROM THE SEA
SAUL
MY STAR
BY THE FIRE-SIDE
ANY WIFE TO ANY HUSBAND
TWO IN THE CAMPAGNA
MISCONCEPTIONS
A SERENADE AT THE VILLA
ONE WAY OF LOVE
ANOTHER WAY OF LOVE
A PRETTY WOMAN
RESPECTABILITY
LOVE IN A LIFE
LIFE IN A LOVE
IN THREE DAYS
IN A YEAR
WOMEN AND ROSES
BEFORE
AFTER
THE GUARDIAN-ANGEL—A PICTURE AT FANO
MEMORABILIA
POPULARITY
MASTER HUGUES OF SAXE-GOTHA

ROMANCES

INCIDENT OF THE FRENCH CAMP
THE PATRIOT.—AN OLD STORY
MY LAST DUCHESS.—FERRARA
COUNT GISMOND.—AIX IN PROVENCE
THE BOY AND THE ANGEL
INSTANS TYRANNUS
MESMERISM
THE GLOVE
TIME'S REVENGES
THE ITALIAN IN ENGLAND
THE ENGLISHMAN IN ITALY.—PIANO DI SORRENTO

IN A GONDOLA
WARING
THE TWINS
A LIGHT WOMAN
THE LAST RIDE TOGETHER
THE PIED PIPER OF HAMELIN; A CHILD'S STORY
THE FLIGHT OF THE DUCHESS
A GRAMMARIAN'S FUNERAL
JOHANNES AGRICOLA IN MEDITATION
THE HERETIC'S TRAGEDY.—A MIDDLE AGE INTERLUDE
HOLY-CROSS DAY
PROTUS
THE STATUE AND THE BUST
PORPHYRIA'S LOVER
"CHILDE ROLAND TO THE DARK TOWER CAME"

MEN, AND WOMEN

'TRANSCENDENTALISM:' A POEM IN TWELVE BOOKS
HOW IT STRIKES A CONTEMPORARY
ARTEMIS PROLOGIZES
AN EPISTLE CONTAINING THE STRANGE MEDICAL
    EXPERIENCE OF KARSHISH,
    THE ARAB PHYSICIAN
PICTOR IGNOTUS
FRA LIPPO LIPPI
ANDREA DEL SARTO
THE BISHOP ORDERS HIS TOMB AT
    SAINT PRAXED'S CHURCH
BISHOP BLOUGRAM'S APOLOGY
CLEON
RUDEL TO THE LADY OF TRIPOLI
ONE WORD MORE

MEN AND WOMEN
Volume I

§ Dates added by B for MEN AND WOMEN sections of 1868 and 1888-1889 §   *1868*:Florence, 185—. *1888*:184—, 185—.

1855

LOVE AMONG THE RUINS

I

Where the quiet-coloured end of evening smiles,
    Miles and miles
On the solitary pastures where our sheep
    Half-asleep
5 Tinkle homeward thro' the twilight, stray or stop
    As they crop—
Was the site once of a city great and gay,
    (So they say)
Of our country's very capital, its prince
10   Ages since
Held his court in, gathered councils, wielding far
    Peace or war.

II

Now,—the country does not even boast a tree,
    As you see,
15 To distinguish slopes of verdure, certain rills
    From the hills

---

§ P: Proof of 1855. Ed. 1855, 1863, 1865, 1868, 1888, 1889. No full MS known to be extant. For discussion of MSS of individual poems, see Editorial Notes. §
LOVE AMONG THE RUINS § MS in Houghton Library, Harvard University.
Subsequent placement: *1863*:DL. MS:7 stanzas of 12 lines P:14 stanzas of 6 lines
1868:7 stanzas of 12 lines § *Title*| MS:*SICILIAN PASTORAL* P:*LOVE AMONG THE RUINS* ¹| MS:quiet-colored < > even P:quiet-coloured < > evening < > smiles *1888*:smiles, ²| MS:and miles, P:and miles ⁷| MS:a City P:a city ⁸| MS:So< >say; P:(So< >say) ⁹| MS:Was our< >its § over perhaps *the* § P:Of our ¹¹| MS:in, had his councils, sent afar P:in, gathered councils, wielding far ¹³| MS:Now—the *1888*:Now,—the < > tree DC, BrU:tree. *1889*:tree,

Intersect and give a name to, (else they run
        Into one)
Where the domed and daring palace shot its spires
20   Up like fires
O'er the hundred-gated circuit of a wall
        Bounding all,
Made of marble, men might march on nor be pressed,
        Twelve abreast.

                            III

25 And such plenty and perfection, see, of grass
        Never was!
Such a carpet as, this summer-time, o'erspreads
        And embeds
Every vestige of the city, guessed alone,
30   Stock or stone—
Where a multitude of men breathed joy and woe
        Long ago;
Lust of glory pricked their hearts up, dread of shame
        Struck them tame;
35 And that glory and that shame alike, the gold
        Bought and sold.

                            IV

Now,—the single little turret that remains
        On the plains,
By the caper overrooted, by the gourd
40   Overscored,
While the patching houseleek's head of blossom winks
        Through the chinks—
Marks the basement whence a tower in ancient time
        Sprang sublime,

---

¹⁷| MS:to, else *1855*:to, (else   ¹⁸| MS:one— *1855*:one)   ²³| MS:marble men
<> prest P:marble, men <> prest, *1868*:pressed, *1888*:pressed DC,BrU:pressed,
1889:pressed,   ²⁶| MS:was, P:was!   ²⁷| MS:summer time P:summer-time
³⁴| MS:Stopt § crossed out and replaced in L margin by § Struck<>tame,
1855:tame;   ³⁹| MS:Which the caper roots a-top of, by P:By the caper overrooted,
by   ⁴⁰| MS:Oversoared, P:Overscored.   ⁴¹| MS:While § crossed out and replaced
in L margin by § When P:While the   ⁴³| MS:Was the P:Marks the

45   And a burning ring, all round, the chariots traced
            As they raced,
      And the monarch and his minions and his dames
            Viewed the games.

                                    V

      And I know, while thus the quiet-coloured eve
50   Smiles to leave
      To their folding, all our many-tinkling fleece
            In such peace,
      And the slopes and rills in undistinguished grey
            Melt away—
55   That a girl with eager eyes and yellow hair
            Waits me there
      In the turret whence the charioteers caught soul
            For the goal,
      When the king looked, where she looks now, breathless, dumb
60   Till I come.

                                    VI

      But he looked upon the city, every side,
            Far and wide,
      All the mountains topped with temples, all the glades'
            Colonnades,
65   All the causeys, bridges, aqueducts,—and then,
            All the men!
      When I do come, she will speak not, she will stand,
            Either hand
      On my shoulder, give her eyes the first embrace
70   Of my face,
      Ere we rush, ere we extinguish sight and speech
            Each on each.

45| MS:ring all round the   1855:round, the   1863:ring, all   46| MS:raced P:raced,
47| MS:While the monarch, and his minions   P:And the monarch and his minions
49| MS:quiet-colored P:quiet-coloured   51| MS:folding all   1855:folding, all
56| MS:there, P:there   57| 1855:turret, whence   1863:turret whence
59| MS:dumb, P:dumb   61| MS:But the city he looked out on, every P:But
he looked upon the city every   1855:city, every   72| MS:on each! P:on each.

In one year they sent a million fighters forth
    South and North,
75 And they built their gods a brazen pillar high
    As the sky,
Yet reserved a thousand chariots in full force—
    Gold, of course.
Oh heart! oh blood that freezes, blood that burns!
80   Earth's returns
For whole centuries of folly, noise and sin!
    Shut them in,
With their triumphs and their glories and the rest!
    Love is best.

73| MS:year, they *1855:*year they   74| MS:and north, P:and North, *1855:*and
north, *1863:*and North,   77| MS:And yet mustered five-score chariots
<>force P:And reserved a thousand chariots <>force— *1855:*Yet reserved
78| MS:—Gold P:Gold   79| MS:Oh, heart! Oh, blood that freezes § last word crossed
out and replaced above by § tingles § crossed out, restoring § freezes P:heart! oh <>that
freezes, blood *1868:*Oh heart! oh blood   83| MS:their grandeurs and their
<>rest— P:their triumphs and their *1855:*rest. *1868:*rest!   84| MS:*This* is best!
P:This *1855:*Love is *1868:*best.

A LOVERS' QUARREL

I

Oh, what a dawn of day!
How the March sun feels like May!
    All is blue again
    After last night's rain,
And the South dries the hawthorn-spray.
    Only, my Love's away!
I'd as lief that the blue were grey.

II

Runnels, which rillets swell,
Must be dancing down the dell,
    With a foaming head
    On the beryl bed
Paven smooth as a hermit's cell;
    Each with a tale to tell,
Could my Love but attend as well.

III

Dearest, three months ago!
When we lived blocked-up with snow,—
    When the wind would edge
    In and in his wedge,
In, as far as the point could go—
    Not to our ingle, though,
Where we loved each the other so!

IV

Laughs with so little cause!
We devised games out of straws.
    We would try and trace
    One another's face

5

10

15

20

25

A LOVERS' QUARREL § Subsequent placement: *1863:*DL §   2| *1868:*like
May   *1888:*like May!   5| P:hawthorn spray. *1855:*hawthorn-spray.
6| P:Only my *1855:*Only, my   9| P:dell *1868:*dell,   10| P:foamy
*1868:*foaming   11| P:O'er each beryl *1855:*On the beryl   13| P:tell *1855:*tell,
15| P:ago *1855:*ago!   16| P:snow, *1855:*snow,—   17| P:the cold would

In the ash, as an artist draws;
    Free on each other's flaws,
How we chattered like two church daws!

V

What's in the "Times"?—a scold
At the Emperor deep and cold;
    He has taken a bride
    To his gruesome side,
That's as fair as himself is bold:
    There they sit ermine-stoled,
And she powders her hair with gold.

VI

Fancy the Pampas' sheen!
Miles and miles of gold and green
    Where the sunflowers blow
    In a solid glow,
And—to break now and then the screen—
    Black neck and eyeballs keen,
Up a wild horse leaps between!

VII

Try, will our table turn?
Lay your hands there light, and yearn
    Till the yearning slips
    Thro' the finger-tips
In a fire which a few discern,
    And a very few feel burn,
And the rest, they may live and learn!

VIII

Then we would up and pace,
For a change, about the place,

30

35

40

45

50

1855:the wind would   ²⁹| P:the "Times?"—a *1863*:the "Times"?—a   ³⁰| P:the
emperor *1863*:the Emperor   ³⁶| P:sheen, *1855*:sheen!   ³⁸| P:sun-flowers
1863:sunflowers   ⁴⁰| P:And to break once a while the *1855*:break now and then the
1888:And—to   ⁴⁶| P:finger tips *1863*:finger-tips   ⁵¹| *1865*:ahout *1868*:about

Each with arm o'er neck:
'Tis our quarter-deck,
We are seamen in woeful case.
55   Help in the ocean-space!
Or, if no help, we'll embrace.

IX

See, how she looks now, dressed
In a sledging-cap and vest!
'Tis a huge fur cloak—
60   Like a reindeer's yoke
Falls the lappet along the breast:
Sleeves for her arms to rest,
Or to hang, as my Love likes best.

X

Teach me to flirt a fan
65   As the Spanish ladies can,
Or I tint your lip
With a burnt stick's tip
And you turn into such a man!
Just the two spots that span
70   Half the bill of the young male swan.

XI

Dearest, three months ago
When the mesmerizer Snow
With his hand's first sweep
Put the earth to sleep:

52| P:neck. *1863*:neck: 54| P:case. *1855*:case.   56| P:embrace!
1855:embrace.   57| P:drest *1868*:dressed   58| P:vest; *1855*:vest. *1863*:vest!
72| P:mesmeriser *1863*:mesmerizer   74| P:sleep, *1863*:sleep! *1888*:sleep:

75   'Twas a time when the heart could show
       All—how was earth to know,
       'Neath the mute hand's to-and-fro?

XII

       Dearest, three months ago
       When we loved each other so,
80   Lived and loved the same
            Till an evening came
       When a shaft from the devil's bow
          Pierced to our ingle-glow,
       And the friends were friend and foe!

XIII

85   Not from the heart beneath—
       'Twas a bubble born of breath,
          Neither sneer nor vaunt,
          Nor reproach nor taunt.
       See a word, how it severeth!
90   Oh, power of life and death
       In the tongue, as the Preacher saith!

XIV

       Woman, and will you cast
       For a word, quite off at last
          Me, your own, your You,—
95   Since, as truth is true,
       I was You all the happy past—
       Me do you leave aghast
       With the memories We amassed?

---

⁷⁷| P:to-and-fro! *1863*:to-and-fro?   ⁸²| P:the Devil's *1868*:the devil's
⁹³| P:word quite off, at last, *1855*:word, quite off at *1863*:last   ⁹⁴| P:own, your
you,— *1863*:own, your You,—   ⁹⁵| P:as Truth *1863*:as truth   ⁹⁶| P:was
you *1863*:was You <> happy Past— *1868*:happy past—   ⁹⁸| P:
memories you amassed? *1855*:memories we amassed? *1863*:memories We

Love, if you knew the light
100 That your soul casts in my sight,
How I look to you
For the pure and true
And the beauteous and the right,—
Bear with a moment's spite
105 When a mere mote threats the white!

What of a hasty word?
Is the fleshly heart not stirred
By a worm's pin-prick
Where its roots are quick?
110 See the eye, by a fly's foot blurred—
Ear, when a straw is heard
Scratch the brain's coat of curd!

Foul be the world or fair
More or less, how can I care?
115 'Tis the world the same
For my praise or blame,
And endurance is easy there.
Wrong in the one thing rare—
Oh, it is hard to bear!

120 Here's the spring back or close,
When the almond-blossom blows:
We shall have the word
In a minor third

102| P:true, DC,BrU:true *1889*:true   110| P:fly's-foot *1888*:fly's foot
113| P:fair, *1863*:fair   121| P:almond blossom blows; *1855*:almond-blossom
1888:blows: 122| *1863:* § some copies omit line; see Editorial Notes §   123|P:In

There is none but the cuckoo knows:
125   Heaps of the guelder-rose!
I must bear with it, I suppose.

                    XIX

Could but November come,
Were the noisy birds struck dumb
        At the warning slash
130   Of his driver's-lash—
I would laugh like the valiant Thumb
    Facing the castle glum
And the giant's fee-faw-fum!

                    XX

Then, were the world well stripped
135 Of the gear wherein equipped
        We can stand apart,
        Heart dispense with heart
In the sun, with the flowers unnipped,—
    Oh, the world's hangings ripped,
140 We were both in a bare-walled crypt!

                    XXI

Each in the crypt would cry
"But one freezes here! and why?
        When a heart, as chill,
        At my own would thrill
145 Back to life, and its fires out-fly?
    Heart, shall we live or die?
The rest, . . . settle by-and-by!"

that minor *1868:*In a minor   124| P:knows— *1863:*knows: 125| P:guelder
rose! *1855:*guelder-rose!   134| P:stript *1868:*stripped   143| P:heart as chill
*1865:*heart, as chill,   147| P:settle it by and by!" *1888:*settle by-and-by!"

XXII

So, she'd efface the score,
And forgive me as before.
150   It is twelve o'clock:
          I shall hear her knock
In the worst of a storm's uproar,
          I shall pull her through the door,
I shall have her for evermore!

148| P:So she'll efface *1855*:So, she'd efface   150| P:Just at twelve o'clock *1863*:It is twelve o'clock: 152| P:uproar— *1863*:uproar,   153| P:door— *1863*:door,

EVELYN HOPE

I

Beautiful Evelyn Hope is dead!
    Sit and watch by her side an hour.
That is her book-shelf, this her bed;
    She plucked that piece of geranium-flower,
5 Beginning to die too, in the glass;
    Little has yet been changed, I think:
The shutters are shut, no light may pass
    Save two long rays thro' the hinge's chink.

II

Sixteen years old when she died!
10   Perhaps she had scarcely heard my name;
It was not her time to love; beside,
    Her life had many a hope and aim,
Duties enough and little cares,
    And now was quiet, now astir,
15 Till God's hand beckoned unawares,—
    And the sweet white brow is all of her.

III

Is it too late then, Evelyn Hope?
    What, your soul was pure and true,
The good stars met in your horoscope,
20   Made you of spirit, fire and dew—
And, just because I was thrice as old
    And our paths in the world diverged so wide,
Each was nought to each, must I be told?
    We were fellow mortals, nought beside?

EVELYN HOPE § Subsequent placement: 1863:DL §   1| *1855*:dead *1863*:dead!
4| P:geranium flower, *1855*:geranium-flower,   5| *1855*:glass. *1863*:glass;
6| P:think— *1863*:think: 7| P:shut, nor light *1855*:shut, no light
10| P:name— *1863*:name;   11| P:love, beside: *1855*:love: beside, *1863*:love; beside,
14| P:astir— *1863*:astir,   15| P:unawares, *1863*:unawares,—   21| P:And just

174

25 No, indeed! for God above
    Is great to grant, as mighty to make,
And creates the love to reward the love:
    I claim you still, for my own love's sake!
Delayed it may be for more lives yet,
30   Through worlds I shall traverse, not a few:
Much is to learn, much to forget
    Ere the time be come for taking you.

V

But the time will come,—at last it will,
    When, Evelyn Hope, what meant (I shall say)
35 In the lower earth, in the years long still,
    That body and soul so pure and gay?
Why your hair was amber, I shall divine,
    And your mouth of your own geranium's red—
And what you would do with me, in fine,
40   In the new life come in the old one's stead.

VI

I have lived (I shall say) so much since then,
    Given up myself so many times,
Gained me the gains of various men,
    Ransacked the ages, spoiled the climes;
45 Yet one thing, one, in my soul's full scope,
    Either I missed or itself missed me:
And I want and find you, Evelyn Hope!
    What is the issue? let us see!

VII

I loved you, Evelyn, all the while.
50   My heart seemed full as it could hold?

<> old, *1863*:And, just <> old   ²⁷| P:reward the love,— *1863*:reward
the love: ³⁰| P:few— *1863*:few: ³¹| P:learn and much *1888*:learn, much
³⁴| P:meant, I shall say, *1865*:meant (I shall say)   ⁴¹| P:lived, I shall say, so
1865:lived (I shall say) so   ⁴⁶| P:me— *1863*:me: ⁴⁹| P:while
1855:while; *1863*:while! *1888*:while DC,BrU:while. *1889*:while.   ⁵⁰| P:hold—

There was place and to spare for the frank young smile,
    And the red young mouth, and the hair's young gold.
So, hush,—I will give you this leaf to keep:
    See, I shut it inside the sweet cold hand!
55 There, that is our secret: go to sleep!
    You will wake, and remember, and understand.

*1888:*hold?   51| P:smile *1868:*smile,   52| P:mouth and   *1868:*mouth, and
53| P:So hush < > keep— *1855:*So, hush *1868:*keep: 54| P:hand— *1855:*hand.
*1868:*hand!   55| P:secret! go to sleep; *1868:*secret: go to sleep!

UP AT A VILLA—DOWN IN THE CITY

(AS DISTINGUISHED BY AN ITALIAN PERSON OF QUALITY)

I

Had I but plenty of money, money enough and to spare,
The house for me, no doubt, were a house in the city-square;
Ah, such a life, such a life, as one leads at the window there!

II

Something to see, by Bacchus, something to hear, at least!
5   There, the whole day long, one's life is a perfect feast;
While up at a villa one lives, I maintain it, no more than a beast.

III

Well now, look at our villa! stuck like the horn of a bull
Just on a mountain-edge as bare as the creature's skull,
Save a mere shag of a bush with hardly a leaf to pull!
10   —I scratch my own, sometimes, to see if the hair's turned wool.

IV

But the city, oh the city—the square with the houses! Why?
They are stone-faced, white as a curd, there's something to take the
    eye!

UP AT A VILLA—DOWN IN THE CITY § Subsequent placement: 1863:DL §
²│ P:city-square. *1863*:city-square;   ³│ P:such a life, such a life as
1855:such a life, such a life, as   ⁸│ P:mountain's edge *1888*:mountain-edge

Houses in four straight lines, not a single front awry;
You watch who crosses and gossips, who saunters, who hurries by;
15 Green blinds, as a matter of course, to draw when the sun gets high;
And the shops with fanciful signs which are painted properly.

V

What of a villa? Though winter be over in March by rights,
'Tis May perhaps ere the snow shall have withered well off the heights:
You've the brown ploughed land before, where the oxen steam and wheeze,
20 And the hills over-smoked behind by the faint grey olive-trees.

VI

Is it better in May, I ask you? You've summer all at once;
In a day he leaps complete with a few strong April suns.
'Mid the sharp short emerald wheat, scarce risen three fingers well,
The wild tulip, at end of its tube, blows out its great red bell
25 Like a thin clear bubble of blood, for the children to pick and sell.

VII

Is it ever hot in the square? There's a fountain to spout and splash!
In the shade it sings and springs; in the shine such foam-bows flash
On the horses with curling fish-tails, that prance and paddle and pash
Round the lady atop in her conch—fifty gazers do not abash,
30 Though all that she wears is some weeds round her waist in a sort of sash.

13| P:awry! 1868:awry;   14| P:by: 1863:by;   20| P:olive trees.
1863:olive-trees.   21| P:you? you've 1868:you? You've   22| P:suns!
1868:suns.   24| P:bell, 1863:bell   27| 1888:foam bows DC,BrU:foam-bows
1889:foam-bows   29| P:in the conch 1888:in her conch   30| P:sash!

All the year long at the villa, nothing to see though you linger,
Except yon cypress that points like death's lean lifted forefinger.
Some think fireflies pretty, when they mix i' the corn and mingle,
Or thrid the stinking hemp till the stalks of it seem a-tingle.
35 Late August or early September, the stunning cicala is shrill,
And the bees keep their tiresome whine round the resinous firs on
    the hill.
Enough of the seasons,—I spare you the months of the fever and
    chill.

IX

Ere you open your eyes in the city, the blessed church-bells begin:
No sooner the bells leave off than the diligence rattles in:
40 You get the pick of the news, and it costs you never a pin.
By-and-by there's the travelling doctor gives pills, lets blood, draws
    teeth;
Or the Pulcinello-trumpet breaks up the market beneath.
At the post-office such a scene-picture—the new play, piping hot!
And a notice how, only this morning, three liberal thieves were
    shot.
45 Above it, behold the Archbishop's most fatherly of rebukes,
And beneath, with his crown and his lion, some little new law of
    the Duke's!
Or a sonnet with flowery marge, to the Reverend Don So-and-so
Who is Dante, Boccaccio, Petrarca, Saint Jerome and Cicero,
"And moreover," (the sonnet goes rhyming,) "the skirts of Saint
    Paul has reached,
50 Having preached us those six Lent-lectures more unctuous than
    ever he preached."

1868:sash. ³¹| P:nothing's *1888*:nothing ³²| P:like Death's *1868*:like death's
³³|P:in *1888*:i' ³⁵| P:cicala blows shrill, *1855*:cicala is shrill, ³⁸| P:Ere
opening your *1888*:Ere you open your ³⁹| *1855*:off, than *1888*:off than
⁴¹| P:By and by *1888*:By-and-by ⁴²| P:the Pulcinello's trumpet < > beneath!
1855:the Pulcinello-trumpet < > beneath. ⁴³| P:a huge picture
1855:a scene-picture ⁴⁴| P:shot! *1855*:shot. ⁴⁵| P:the archbishop's
1888:the Archbishop's ⁴⁸| P:is < > Jerome, and *1888*:is < > Jerome and
⁴⁹| P:of St. *1863*:of Saint ⁵⁰| P:us six Lenten lectures *1855*:us those six

Noon strikes,—here sweeps the procession! our Lady borne smiling
and smart
With a pink gauze gown all spangles, and seven swords stuck in
her heart!
Bang-whang-whang goes the drum, *tootle-te-tootle* the fife;
No keeping one's haunches still: it's the greatest pleasure in life.

x

55   But bless you, it's dear—it's dear! fowls, wine, at double the rate.
They have clapped a new tax upon salt, and what oil pays passing
the gate
It's a horror to think of. And so, the villa for me, not the city!
Beggars can scarcely be choosers: but still—ah, the pity, the pity!
Look, two and two go the priests, then the monks with cowls and
sandals,
60   And the penitents dressed in white shirts, a-holding the yellow
candles;
One, he carries a flag up straight, and another a cross with handles,
And the Duke's guard brings up the rear, for the better prevention
of scandals:
Bang-whang-whang goes the drum, *tootle-te-tootle* the fife.
Oh, a day in the city-square, there is no such pleasure in life!

Lent-lectures   53| P:*Bang, whang, whang,* goes *1863:whang, whang* goes   *1868:*
Bang-whang-whang   54| P:still—it's <> life! *1855:*still:it's <> life.
55| P:rate! *1855:*rate.   56| P:new impost on salt *1855:*new tax upon salt
57| P:of! and *1855:*of. And   58| P:choosers—but *1863:*choosers: but
60| P:candles. *1863:*candles;   61| P:handles, *1888:*handles. DC,BrU:handles,
*1889:*handles § emended to § handles, § to conform to DC and BrU §   62| P:scandals.
*1863:*scandals: 63| P:*Bang, whang, whang,* goes <> fife,—   *1855:*fife.
1863:whang, whang goes *1868:Bang-whang-whang*

A WOMAN'S LAST WORD

I

Let's contend no more, Love,
    Strive nor weep:
All be as before, Love,
    —Only sleep!

II

5   What so wild as words are?
    I and thou
In debate, as birds are,
    Hawk on bough!

III

See the creature stalking
10   While we speak!
Hush and hide the talking,
    Cheek on cheek!

IV

What so false as truth is,
    False to thee?
15 Where the serpent's tooth is
    Shun the tree—

A WOMAN'S LAST WORD § Subsequent placement: 1863:DL §   ²│ P:weep—
1863:weep: ⁶│ P:—I *1863*:I   ¹⁰│ P:speak— *1863*:speak!   ¹⁵│ P:is,

V

Where the apple reddens
    Never pry—
Lest we lose our Edens,
20   Eve and I.

VI

Be a god and hold me
    With a charm!
Be a man and fold me
    With thine arm!

VII

25 Teach me, only teach, Love!
        As I ought
I will speak thy speech, Love,
    Think thy thought—

VIII

Meet, if thou require it,
30   Both demands,
Laying flesh and spirit
    In thy hands.

IX

That shall be to-morrow
    Not to-night:
35 I must bury sorrow
    Out of sight:

X

—Must a little weep, Love,
    (Foolish me!)
And so fall asleep, Love,
40   Loved by thee.

1863:is 1865:is, 1888:is   20| P:I! 1865:I 1868:I.   22| P:charm—
1863:charm!   24| 1888:arm DC,BrU:arm! 1889:arm!   26| P:ought,
1855:ought   32| P:hands! 1863:hands. 36| P:sight. 1863:sight:
38| P:—Foolish me! 1863:(Foolish me!)   40| P:thee! 1855:thee.

182

FRA LIPPO LIPPI

I am poor brother Lippo, by your leave!
You need not clap your torches to my face.
Zooks, what's to blame? you think you see a monk!
What, 'tis past midnight, and you go the rounds,
5   And here you catch me at an alley's end
Where sportive ladies leave their doors ajar?
The Carmine's my cloister: hunt it up,
Do,—harry out, if you must show your zeal,
Whatever rat, there, haps on his wrong hole,
10   And nip each softling of a wee white mouse,
Weke, weke, that's crept to keep him company!
Aha, you know your betters! Then, you'll take
Your hand away that's fiddling on my throat,
And please to know me likewise. Who am I?
15   Why, one, sir, who is lodging with a friend
Three streets off—he's a certain . . . how d'ye call?
Master—a . . . Cosimo of the Medici,
I' the house that caps the corner. Boh! you were best!
Remember and tell me, the day you're hanged,
20   How you affected such a gullet's-gripe!
But you, sir, it concerns you that your knaves
Pick up a manner nor discredit you:
Zooks, are we pilchards, that they sweep the streets
And count fair prize what comes into their net?
25   He's Judas to a tittle, that man is!
Just such a face! Why, sir, you make amends.
Lord, I'm not angry! Bid your hangdogs go
Drink out this quarter-florin to the health
Of the munificent House that harbours me
30   (And many more beside, lads! more beside!)
And all's come square again. I'd like his face—
His, elbowing on his comrade in the door

FRA LIPPO LIPPI § Subsequent placement: 1863:MW §   4| P:What, it's past
<>rounds? *1855*:rounds, *1868*:What, 'tis past   6| P::ajar! *1855*:ajar. *1863*:ajar?
9| P:rat there haps *1855*:rat, there, haps   11| P:Weke, weke *1863:Weke, weke*
12| P:betters? Then *1888*:betters! Then   13| P:away, that's *1855*:away that's
18| P:In *1888*:I'   22| P:you! *1855*:you. *1868*:you: 26| P:face! why *1868*:face!
Why   27| P:angry! Have your *1855*:angry! Bid your   29| P:munificent

183

With the pike and lantern,—for the slave that holds
John Baptist's head a-dangle by the hair
35 With one hand ("Look you, now," as who should say)
And his weapon in the other, yet unwiped!
It's not your chance to have a bit of chalk,
A wood-coal or the like? or you should see!
Yes, I'm the painter, since you style me so.
40 What, brother Lippo's doings, up and down,
You know them and they take you? like enough!
I saw the proper twinkle in your eye—
'Tell you, I liked your looks at very first.
Let's sit and set things straight now, hip to haunch.
45 Here's spring come, and the nights one makes up bands
To roam the town and sing out carnival,
And I've been three weeks shut within my mew,
A-painting for the great man, saints and saints
And saints again. I could not paint all night—
50 Ouf! I leaned out of window for fresh air.
There came a hurry of feet and little feet,
A sweep of lute-strings, laughs, and whifts of song,—
Flower o' the broom,
Take away love, and our earth is a tomb!
55 *Flower o' the quince,*
I let Lisa go, and what good in life since?
Flower o' the thyme—and so on. Round they went.
Scarce had they turned the corner when a titter
Like the skipping of rabbits by moonlight,—three slim
        shapes,
60 And a face that looked up . . . zooks, sir, flesh and blood,
That's all I'm made of! Into shreds it went,
Curtain and counterpane and coverlet,

---

house *1855:*munificent House 35| P:hand, "look <> say, *1855:*hand ("look
<> say) *1868:*hand ("Look 38| P:like? and you *1855:*like? or you
40| P:What, works about the city, up *1855:*What, brother Lippo's doings, up
43| P:you I *1863:*you, I 46| P:sing at carnival, *1855:*sing out carnival,
50| P:air; *1855:*air. 54| P:*love and 1855:love, and* 56| P:*go and what good's
in 1855:go, and 1868:what good in* 57| P:*the Thyme 1855:the thyme*
58| P:titter, *1863:*titter 59| P:shapes— *1868:*shapes, 60| P:up
. . . zooks *1888:*up . . zooks § emended to § up . . . zooks § see Editorial
Notes § 62| P:Curtain, and counterpane *1855:*Curtain and counterpane

184

All the bed-furniture—a dozen knots,
There was a ladder! Down I let myself,
⁶⁵ Hands and feet, scrambling somehow, and so dropped,
And after them. I came up with the fun
Hard by Saint Laurence, hail fellow, well met,—
Flower o' the rose,
If I've been merry, what matter who knows?
⁷⁰ And so as I was stealing back again
To get to bed and have a bit of sleep
Ere I rise up to-morrow and go work
On Jerome knocking at his poor old breast
With his great round stone to subdue the flesh,
⁷⁵ You snap me of the sudden. Ah, I see!
Though your eye twinkles still, you shake your head—
Mine's shaved—a monk, you say—the sting's in that!
If Master Cosimo announced himself,
Mum's the word naturally; but a monk!
⁸⁰ Come, what am I a beast for? tell us, now!
I was a baby when my mother died
And father died and left me in the street.
I starved there, God knows how, a year or two
On fig-skins, melon-parings, rinds and shucks,
⁸⁵ Refuse and rubbish. One fine frosty day,
My stomach being empty as your hat,
The wind doubled me up and down I went.
Old Aunt Lapaccia trussed me with one hand,
(Its fellow was a stinger as I knew)
⁹⁰ And so along the wall, over the bridge,
By the straight cut to the convent. Six words there,
While I stood munching my first bread that month:
"So, boy, you're minded," quoth the good fat father
Wiping his own mouth, 'twas refection-time,—
⁹⁵ "To quit this very miserable world?
Will you renounce" . . . "the mouthful of bread?" thought I;

---

⁶³| P:bed furniture *1863:*bed-furniture   ⁶⁴| P:ladder! down *1868:*ladder! Down
⁶⁷| P:by St. *1863:*by Saint   ⁷⁷| P:shaved,—a *1865:*shaved—a
⁷⁹| P:naturally: but *1855:*naturally; but   ⁸⁰| P:for? Tell *1855:*for? tell
⁸²| P:died, and *1855:*died and   ⁸⁵| P:day *1868:*day,   ⁸⁹| P:Its < > knew,
1855:(Its < > knew)   ⁹⁰| P:bridge *1855:*bridge,   ⁹¹| P:words, there, *1865:*words
there,   ⁹³| P:father, *1855:*father   ⁹⁶| P:renounce" . . . the < > bread?
thought *1855:*renounce" . . . The mouthful *1865:*renounce" . . . the

185

By no means! Brief, they made a monk of me;
I did renounce the world, its pride and greed,
Palace, farm, villa, shop and banking-house,
100   Trash, such as these poor devils of Medici
Have given their hearts to—all at eight years old.
Well, sir, I found in time, you may be sure,
'Twas not for nothing—the good bellyful,
The warm serge and the rope that goes all round,
105   And day-long blessed idleness beside!
"Let's see what the urchin's fit for"—that came next.
Not overmuch their way, I must confess.
Such a to-do! They tried me with their books:
Lord, they'd have taught me Latin in pure waste!
110   *Flower o' the clove,*
All the Latin I construe is, "amo" I love!
But, mind you, when a boy starves in the streets
Eight years together, as my fortune was,
Watching folk's faces to know who will fling
115   The bit of half-stripped grape-bunch he desires,
And who will curse or kick him for his pains,—
Which gentleman processional and fine,
Holding a candle to the Sacrament,
Will wink and let him lift a plate and catch
120   The droppings of the wax to sell again,
Or holla for the Eight and have him whipped,—
How say I?—nay, which dog bites, which lets drop
His bone from the heap of offal in the street,—

---

mouthful *1868:*renounce" . . . "the <> bread?" thought   ¹⁰⁰| P:such poor devils
as these Medici *1855:*such as these poor devils of Medici   ¹⁰¹| P:Give
their <> to—and all *1855:*Have given their <> to—all   ¹⁰³| P:nothing, the
*1855:*nothing—the   ¹⁰⁷ P:over much *1855:*overmuch   ¹⁰⁸| P:to-do! they <>
books. *1868:*to-do! They <> books: ¹⁰⁹| P:Lord, Latin they'd <> me in pure
waste. *1855:*Lord, they'd <> me Latin in pure waste!   ¹¹¹| P:*is "amo*
1855:is, "amo   ¹¹²| P:But mind *1855:*But, mind   ¹¹³| P:together as
*1855:*together, as *1868:*together as *1888:*together, as   ¹¹⁵| P:grape-bunch that he
eyes, *1855:*grape-bunch he desires,   ¹¹⁶| P:pains— *1868:*pains,—
¹¹⁷| P:What gentleman processioning *1855:*Which gentleman processional
¹¹⁸| P:the Sacrament *1888:*the Sacrament,   ¹²⁰| P:again,— *1855:*again,
¹²¹| P:whipped;— *1855:*whipped,—   ¹²³| P:street, *1855:*street! *1863:*street,—

186

Why, soul and sense of him grow sharp alike,

125   He learns the look of things, and none the less
For admonition from the hunger-pinch.
I had a store of such remarks, be sure,
Which, after I found leisure, turned to use.
I drew men's faces on my copy-books,
130   Scrawled them within the antiphonary's marge,
Joined legs and arms to the long music-notes,
Found eyes and nose and chin for A's and B's,
And made a string of pictures of the world
Betwixt the ins and outs of verb and noun,
135   On the wall, the bench, the door. The monks looked black.
"Nay," quoth the Prior, "turn him out, d'ye say?
In no wise. Lose a crow and catch a lark.
What if at last we get our man of parts,
We Carmelites, like those Camaldolese
140   And Preaching Friars, to do our church up fine
And put the front on it that ought to be!"
And hereupon he bade me daub away.
Thank you! my head being crammed, the walls a blank,
Never was such prompt disemburdening.
145   First, every sort of monk, the black and white,
I drew them, fat and lean: then, folk at church,
From good old gossips waiting to confess
Their cribs of barrel-droppings, candle-ends,—
To the breathless fellow at the altar-foot,
150   Fresh from his murder, safe and sitting there
With the little children round him in a row
Of admiration, half for his beard and half

---

¹²⁴| P:—The soul   *1863:*Why, soul   ¹²⁶| P:admonitions < > hunger pinch.   *1855:*
hunger-pinch.   *1865:*admonition   ¹²⁸| P:Which, now that I < > use: *1855:*Which,
after I   *1888:*use.   ¹²⁹| P:copy books,   *1855:*copy-books,   ¹³⁰| P:them
on the   *1855:*them within the   ¹³²| P:Found nose and eyes and chin for A.s and
B.s,   *1868:*Found eyes and nose and chin   *1888:*for A's and B's,   ¹³⁵| P:monks were
mazed.   *1855:*monks looked black.   ¹⁴⁰| P:And Preaching Friars, shall do
*1855:*And Preaching Friars, to do   ¹⁴¹| P:be!   *1855:*be!"   ¹⁴²| P:hereupon they
bade < > away,   *1855:*away.   *1868:*hereupon he bade   ¹⁴³| P:head was crammed,
their walls   *1855:*head being crammed   *1868:*crammed, the walls   ¹⁴⁴| P:
disemburdening!   *1855:*disemburdening.   ¹⁴⁶| P:them, good and bad: then, folks
*1855:*them, fat and lean: then   *1888:*folk   ¹⁵¹| P:a ring   *1855:*a row

187

For that white anger of his victim's son
Shaking a fist at him with one fierce arm,
155 Signing himself with the other because of Christ
(Whose sad face on the cross sees only this
After the passion of a thousand years)
Till some poor girl, her apron o'er her head,
(Which the intense eyes looked through) came at eve
160 On tiptoe, said a word, dropped in a loaf,
Her pair of earrings and a bunch of flowers
(The brute took growling), prayed, and so was gone.
I painted all, then cried " 'Tis ask and have;
Choose, for more's ready!"—laid the ladder flat,
165 And showed my covered bit of cloister-wall.
The monks closed in a circle and praised loud
Till checked, taught what to see and not to see,
Being simple bodies,—"That's the very man!
Look at the boy who stoops to pat the dog!
170 That woman's like the Prior's niece who comes
To care about his asthma: it's the life!"
But there my triumph's straw-fire flared and funked;
Their betters took their turn to see and say:
The Prior and the learned pulled a face
175 And stopped all that in no time. "How? what's here?
Quite from the mark of painting, bless us all!
Faces, arms, legs and bodies like the true
As much as pea and pea! it's devil's-game!
Your business is not to catch men with show,

156| P:only that 1855:only this   158| P:head 1865:head,   159| P:Which
<> through, came 1868:(Which <> through) came   160| P:tip-toe <> word,
threw in 1855:word, dropped in 1888:tiptoe   161| P:ear-rings
1888:earrings   162| P:The <> growling, prayed and then was 1855:prayed, and
1865:and so was 1868:(The <> growling) prayed 1888:growling), prayed
163| P:I got all ready, cried " 'tis <> have— 1855:I painted all, then cried
1868:cried " 'Tis <> have;   164| P:for my head's full!"—laid 1855:for more's
ready!"—laid   165| 1888:cloister-wall DC,BrU:cloister-wall. 1889:
cloister-wall.   166| P:loud, 1855:loud   167| 1855:checked, (taught
1863:checked,—taught 1868:checked, taught   168| P:bodies: "that's 1855:bodies)
"that's 1863:bodies,—"that's 1868:bodies,—"That's   172| P:straw fire <> funked,
1855:straw-fire <> funked— 1868:funked;   173| P:betters had to see and say
instead: 1855:betters took their turn to see and say: 178| 1865:devil's
game! 1888:devil's-game!   179| P:to maze men 1855:to catch men

180 With homage to the perishable clay,
But lift them over it, ignore it all,
Make them forget there's such a thing as flesh.
Your business is to paint the souls of men—
Man's soul, and it's a fire, smoke . . . no, it's not . . .

185 It's vapour done up like a new-born babe—
(In that shape when you die it leaves your mouth)
It's . . . well, what matters talking, it's the soul!
Give us no more of body than shows soul!
Here's Giotto, with his Saint a-praising God,

190 That sets us praising,—why not stop with him?
Why put all thoughts of praise out of our head
With wonder at lines, colours, and what not?
Paint the soul, never mind the legs and arms!
Rub all out, try at it a second time.

195 Oh, that white smallish female with the breasts,
She's just my niece . . . Herodias, I would say,—
Who went and danced and got men's heads cut off!
Have it all out!" Now, is this sense, I ask?
A fine way to paint soul, by painting body

200 So ill, the eye can't stop there, must go further
And can't fare worse! Thus, yellow does for white
When what you put for yellow's simply black,
And any sort of meaning looks intense
When all beside itself means and looks nought.

205 Why can't a painter lift each foot in turn,
Left foot and right foot, go a double step,
Make his flesh liker and his soul more like,
Both in their order? Take the prettiest face,
The Prior's niece . . . patron-saint—is it so pretty

210 You can't discover if it means hope, fear,
Sorrow or joy? won't beauty go with these?

180| P:Mere homage *1855:*With homage   184| P:a vapour . . no it's not . .
*1855:*a fire, smoke . . no *1868:*no, it's *1888:*smoke . . . no <> not . . .
186| P:In <> when they die it leaves their mouth, *1855:*(In <> when you die it
leaves your mouth)   187| P:It's . . well *1888:*It's . . . well   188| P:shows
that. *1855:*shows soul. *1863:*soul!   189| P:a-praising there, *1855:*a-praising God!
*1863:*a-praising God,   190| P:sets you praising *1865:*sets us praising
191| P:heads *1865:*head   193| P:arms, *1855:*arms!   197| P:off— *1868:*off!
198| P:is that sense *1855:*is this sense   199| P:soul by *1855:*soul, by   201| P:
worse! Thus yellow *1855:*worse! Thus, yellow   211| P:joy? Won't *1855:*joy? won't

Suppose I've made her eyes all right and blue,
Can't I take breath and try to add life's flash,
And then add soul and heighten them threefold?
215 Or say there's beauty with no soul at all—
(I never saw it—put the case the same—)
If you get simple beauty and nought else,
You get about the best thing God invents:
That's somewhat: and you'll find the soul you have missed,
220 Within yourself, when you return him thanks.
"Rub all out!" Well, well, there's my life, in short,
And so the thing has gone on ever since.
I'm grown a man no doubt, I've broken bounds:
You should not take a fellow eight years old
225 And make him swear to never kiss the girls.
I'm my own master, paint now as I please—
Having a friend, you see, in the Corner-house!
Lord, it's fast holding by the rings in front—
Those great rings serve more purposes than just
230 To plant a flag in, or tie up a horse!
And yet the old schooling sticks, the old grave eyes
Are peeping o'er my shoulder as I work,
The heads shake still—"It's art's decline, my son!
You're not of the true painters, great and old;
235 Brother Angelico's the man, you'll find;
Brother Lorenzo stands his single peer:
Fag on at flesh, you'll never make the third!"
Flower o' the pine,
You keep your mistr . . . manners, and I'll stick to mine!

---

²¹⁶| P:I <> saw that—put the case, the same— *1855:*(I <> saw it—put the case the same—) ²¹⁷| P:else *1855:*else, ²¹⁸| P:invents,— *1868:*invents: ²¹⁹| P:Is not that somewhat? And the *1855:*That's somewhat. And you'll find the *1868:*somewhat: and ²²⁰| P:Find in yourself when <> thanks! *1855:* Within yourself <> return Him *1863:*thanks, *1865:*yourself, when <> thanks. *1868:*return him ²²¹| P:out!" well, well <> short: *1855:*short, *1863:*out!" Well, well <> short. *1865:*short, *1868:*short *1888:*short, ²²²| P:That way the *1855:*And so the ²²³| P:bounds— *1868:*bounds: ²²⁵| P:girls— *1863:*girls. ²²⁷| P:see—the Corner-house— *1855:* see, in the Corner-house! *1868:*see in *1888:*see, in ²²⁹| P:than one, *1855:*than just ²³¹| P:sticks—the *1863:*sticks, the ²³²| P:Still peeping *1855:*Are peeping ²³³| P:The shaking heads—'It's Art's *1855:*The heads shake still—"It's *1868:*still—"It's art's ²³⁴| P:old: *1863:*old; ²³⁵| P:find: *1863:*find; ²³⁶| P:Brother Lorenzo, that's his <>peer,

240 I'm not the third, then: bless us, they must know!
Don't you think they're the likeliest to know,
They with their Latin? So, I swallow my rage,
Clench my teeth, suck my lips in tight, and paint
To please them—sometimes do and sometimes don't;
245 For, doing most, there's pretty sure to come
A turn, some warm eve finds me at my saints—
A laugh, a cry, the business of the world—
(*Flower o' the peach,*
Death for us all, and his own life for each!)
250 And my whole soul revolves, the cup runs over,
The world and life's too big to pass for a dream,
And I do these wild things in sheer despite,
And play the fooleries you catch me at,
In pure rage! The old mill-horse, out at grass
255 After hard years, throws up his stiff heels so,
Although the miller does not preach to him
The only good of grass is to make chaff.
What would men have? Do they like grass or no—
May they or mayn't they? all I want's the thing
260 Settled for ever one way. As it is,
You tell too many lies and hurt yourself:
You don't like what you only like too much,
You do like what, if given you at your word,
You find abundantly detestable.
265 For me, I think I speak as I was taught;
I always see the garden and God there
A-making man's wife: and, my lesson learned,
The value and significance of flesh,
I can't unlearn ten minutes afterwards.

---

*1855:*Brother Lorenzo stands his <> peer. *1863:*peer: 242| P:They, with
<> Latin? so I   *1863:*They with <> so, I   *1868:*their Latin? So   244| P:do,
and <> don't,   *1868:*don't;   *1888:*do and   245| P:For doing most—there's
*1855:*For, doing most, there's   246| P:turn—some   *1863:*turn, some
248| P:*Flower*   *1855:*(*Flower*   249| P:*all and* <> *each!*   *1855:*all, and <>
each!)   250| P:over— *1855:*o'er, *1863:*over,   254| P:rage: the   *1855:*rage!
the   *1868:*rage! The   260| P:way: as *1868:*way. As   261| P:tell so many<>
yourself.   *1855:*tell too many *1868:*yourself: 262| P:like, what
*1855:*like what   263| P:like, what *1855:*like what   264| P:Is found
abundantly   *1855:* You find abundantly   265| P:taught— *1865:*taught;
266| P:the Garden *1868:*the garden   267| P:man his wife—my   *1855:*man's
wife—and, my *1865:*wife: and   269| P:afterward. *1863:*afterwards.   *1888:*

191

²⁷⁰   You understand me: I'm a beast, I know.
But see, now—why, I see as certainly
As that the morning-star's about to shine,
What will hap some day. We've a youngster here
Comes to our convent, studies what I do,
²⁷⁵   Slouches and stares and lets no atom drop:
His name is Guidi—he'll not mind the monks—
They call him Hulking Tom, he lets them talk—
He picks my practice up—he'll paint apace,
I hope so—though I never live so long,
²⁸⁰   I know what's sure to follow. You be judge!
You speak no Latin more than I, belike;
However, you're my man, you've seen the world
—The beauty and the wonder and the power,
The shapes of things, their colours, lights and shades,
²⁸⁵   Changes, surprises,—and God made it all!
—For what? Do you feel thankful, ay or no,
For this fair town's face, yonder river's line,
The mountain round it and the sky above,
Much more the figures of man, woman, child,
²⁹⁰   These are the frame to? What's it all about?
To be passed over, despised? or dwelt upon,
Wondered at? oh, this last of course!—you say.
But why not do as well as say,—paint these
Just as they are, careless what comes of it?
²⁹⁵   God's works—paint anyone, and count it crime
To let a truth slip. Don't object, "His works
Are here already; nature is complete:
Suppose you reproduce her—(which you can't)
There's no advantage! you must beat her, then."

---

afterwards, § emended to § afterwards. § see Editorial Notes §   ²⁷¹| P:why,
I know as *1855*:why, I see as   ²⁷²| P:morning star's <> shine
1855:morning-star's <> shine,   ²⁷³| P:day. There's a *1855*:day. We've a
²⁷⁵| P:drop— *1865*:drop: ²⁷⁹| P:live to see, *1855*:live so long,   ²⁸¹| P:belike—
1865:belike;   ²⁸²| P:You've seen the world however, you're my man.
1855:However, you're my man, you've seen the world   ²⁸⁴| *1868*:light *1888*:
lights   ²⁸⁶| P:what? do *1868*:what? Do   ²⁹¹| *1855*:o'er *1863*:over
²⁹²| P:course, you *1863*:course!—you   ²⁹³| P:say? Paint *1855*:say,—paint
²⁹⁴| P:it, *1855*:it?   ²⁹⁵| P:anyone and *1855*:anyone, and   ²⁹⁷| P:
already—nature *1865*:already; nature   ²⁹⁸| P:reproduced *1855*:

300 For, don't you mark? we're made so that we love
First when we see them painted, things we have passed
Perhaps a hundred times nor cared to see;
And so they are better, painted—better to us,
Which is the same thing. Art was given for that;
305 God uses us to help each other so,
Lending our minds out. Have you noticed, now,
Your cullion's hanging face? A bit of chalk,
And trust me but you should, though! How much
      more,
If I drew higher things with the same truth!
310 That were to take the Prior's pulpit-place,
Interpret God to all of you! Oh, oh,
It makes me mad to see what men shall do
And we in our graves! This world's no blot for us,
Nor blank; it means intensely, and means good:
315 To find its meaning is my meat and drink.
"Ay, but you don't so instigate to prayer!"
Strikes in the Prior: "when your meaning's plain
It does not say to folk—remember matins,
Or, mind you fast next Friday!" Why, for this
320 What need of art at all? A skull and bones,
Two bits of stick nailed crosswise, or, what's best,
A bell to chime the hour with, does as well.
I painted a Saint Laurence six months since
At Prato, splashed the fresco in fine style:
325 "How looks my painting, now the scaffold's down?"
I ask a brother: "Hugely," he returns—
"Already not one phiz of your three slaves
Who turn the Deacon off his toasted side,

---

reproduce   300| P:mark, we're 1888:mark? we're   301| P:First, when 1855:First
when   302| P:see, 1855:see;   304| P:that— 1865:that;   311| P:you!
oh, oh, 1868:you! Oh, oh,   312| P:men will do 1855:men shall do
313| P:no trap for 1855:no blot for   314| P:blank—it 1865:blank; it   316| P:
"Ay but < > prayer" 1855:"Ay, but 1863:prayer!"   317| P:when a
meaning's 1855:the Prior! "when your meaning's 1863:the Prior: "when
318| P:folks—remember Matins— 1855:remember matins— 1863:matins, 1888:
folk   319| P:next Friday." Why, for this, 1855:this 1865:next Friday!"
Why   321| P:cross-wise 1888:crosswise   322| P:a St. 1863:a Saint
324| P:style. 1863:style: 325| P:painting now 1855:painting, now   328| P:

But's scratched and prodded to our heart's content,
330 The pious people have so eased their own
With coming to say prayers there in a rage:
We get on fast to see the bricks beneath.
Expect another job this time next year,
For pity and religion grow i' the crowd—
335 Your painting serves its purpose!" Hang the fools!

—That is—you'll not mistake an idle word
Spoke in a huff by a poor monk, God wot,
Tasting the air this spicy night which turns
The unaccustomed head like Chianti wine!
340 Oh, the church knows! don't misreport me, now!
It's natural a poor monk out of bounds
Should have his apt word to excuse himself:
And hearken how I plot to make amends.
I have bethought me: I shall paint a piece
345 . . . There's for you! Give me six months, then go, see
Something in Sant' Ambrogio's! Bless the nuns!
They want a cast o' my office. I shall paint
God in the midst, Madonna and her babe,
Ringed by a bowery flowery angel-brood,
350 Lilies and vestments and white faces, sweet
As puff on puff of grated orris-root
When ladies crowd to Church at midsummer.
And then i' the front, of course a saint or two—
Saint John, because he saves the Florentines,
355 Saint Ambrose, who puts down in black and white
The convent's friends and gives them a long day,
And Job, I must have him there past mistake,

That turned *1855:*That turn *1865:*Who turn   329| P:content— *1855:*
content,   330| P:own, *1855:*own   331| P:When coming < > rage, *1855:*rage.
*1863:*rage: *1865:*With coming   332| P:beneath: *1855:*beneath.
333| P:year! *1855:*year,   334| P:So pity *1855:*For pity   337| P:monk,
God wot, *1865:*monk, Got wot, § emended to § God § see Editorial Notes §
338| P:night, which *1855:*night which   340| P:knows! Don't *1855:*knows! don't
343| P:But hearken *1855:*And hearken   346| P:in Sant' Ambrogio's: bless
*1855:*in Sant' Ambrogio's . . . (bless *1863:*in Sant' Ambrogio's! Bless
347| P:of *1855:*office) I *1863:*office. I *1888:*o'   348| P:God, in *1855:*God in
349| P:bowery, flowery *1888:*bowery flowery   352| P:to church *1868:*to
Church   353| P:in *1888:*i'   354| P:the Florentines. *1855:*the
Florentines,   355| P:Sant' *1855:*Saint   357| P:And Job, I mean to set there

The man of Uz (and Us without the z,
Painters who need his patience). Well, all these
360   Secured at their devotion, up shall come
Out of a corner when you least expect,
As one by a dark stair into a great light,
Music and talking, who but Lippo! I!—
Mazed, motionless and moonstruck—I'm the man!
365   Back I shrink—what is this I see and hear?
I, caught up with my monk's-things by mistake,
My old serge gown and rope that goes all round,
I, in this presence, this pure company!
Where's a hole, where's a corner for escape?
370   Then steps a sweet angelic slip of a thing
Forward, puts out a soft palm—"Not so fast!"
—Addresses the celestial presence, "nay—
He made you and devised you, after all,
Though he's none of you! Could Saint John there draw—
375   His camel-hair make up a painting-brush?
We come to brother Lippo for all that,
Iste perfecit opus!" So, all smile—
I shuffle sideways with my blushing face
Under the cover of a hundred wings
380   Thrown like a spread of kirtles when you're gay
And play hot cockles, all the doors being shut,
Till, wholly unexpected, in there pops
The hothead husband! Thus I scuttle off
To some safe bench behind, not letting go
385   The palm of her, the little lily thing
That spoke the good word for me in the nick,

---

*1855:*And Job, I must have him there   358| P:of Uz and   *1855:*of Uz, (and
*1863:*of Uz, (an Us   *1865:*of Uz, (and Us   *1888:*of Uz (and   359| P:Who need his
patience—I at least. Well, these   *1855:*Painters who need his patience.) Well, all
these   *1888:*patience). Well   360| P:devotions, up there comes   *1855:*up shall
come *1865:*devotion   362| *1855:*light   *1863:*light,   364| P:moon struck. I'm
*1855:*moon-struck—I'm   *1888:*moonstruck   366| P:monk's things   *1888:*
monk's-things   368| P:company?   *1855:*company!   374| P:there, draw?   *1855:*draw—
*1888:*there draw—   375| P:camel hair <> painting brush?   *1855:*camel-hair
<> painting-brush?   377| P:*opus!*" so   *1855:*opus!*" So   379| P:And under
cover   *1855:*Under the cover   382| P:Till wholly unexpected in   *1855:*
Till, wholly unexpected, in   383| P:husband—So I   *1855:*husband!
Thus I   386| P:That said the good <> i'   *1855:*That spoke the good <>

Like the Prior's niece . . . Saint Lucy, I would say.
And so all's saved for me, and for the church
A pretty picture gained. Go, six months hence!
390 Your hand, sir, and good-bye: no lights, no lights!
The street's hushed, and I know my own way back,
Don't fear me! There's the grey beginning. Zooks!

in   387| P:niece . . . Saint   1888:niece . . Saint § emended to § niece . . .
Saint § see Editorial Notes §   390| P:good bye   1888:good-bye   391| P:
hushed and < > back—   1855:hushed, and   1863:back,

A TOCCATA OF GALUPPI'S

I

Oh Galuppi, Baldassaro, this is very sad to find!
I can hardly misconceive you; it would prove me deaf and blind;
But although I take your meaning, 'tis with such a heavy mind!

II

Here you come with your old music, and here's all the good it brings.
5   What, they lived once thus at Venice where the merchants were the
       kings,
Where Saint Mark's is, where the Doges used to wed the sea with rings?

III

Ay, because the sea's the street there; and 'tis arched by . . . what you
    call
. . . Shylock's bridge with houses on it, where they kept the carnival:
I was never out of England—it's as if I saw it all.

IV

10   Did young people take their pleasure when the sea was warm in May?
Balls and masks begun at midnight, burning ever to mid-day,
When they made up fresh adventures for the morrow, do you say?

V

Was a lady such a lady, cheeks so round and lips so red,—
On her neck the small face buoyant, like a bell-flower on its bed,
15   O'er the breast's superb abundance where a man might base his head?

A TOCCATA OF GALUPPI'S § Subsequent placement: *1863*:DL §   ¹| P:Oh!
Galuppi *1855*:Oh, Galuppi *1868*:Oh Galuppi   ²| P:you; that would *1855*:you;
it would   ³| P:But if I must give you credit, 'tis *1855*:But although I give *1863:*
although I take your meaning, 'tis   ⁵| P:at Venice, where *1863*:at Venice where
⁶| P:Where St. *1888*:Where Saint   ⁸| *1855*:carnival! *1863*:carnival: ⁹| P:
all! *1868*:all.   ¹¹| P:began <> mid-day; *1855*:begun <> mid-day, *1863*:mid-day
1888:mid-day,   ¹²| P:Then they *1855*:When they   ¹³| P:red; *1855*:red,—

197

Well, and it was graceful of them—they'd break talk off and afford
—She, to bite her mask's black velvet—he, to finger on his sword,
While you sat and played Toccatas, stately at the clavichord?

What? Those lesser thirds so plaintive, sixths diminished, sigh on sigh,
20 Told them something? Those suspensions, those solutions—"Must
we die?"
Those commiserating sevenths—"Life might last! we can but try!"

"Were you happy?"—"Yes."—"And are you still as happy?"—"Yes.
And you?"
—"Then, more kisses!"—"Did *I* stop them, when a million seemed
so few?"
Hark, the dominant's persistence till it must be answered to!

25 So, an octave struck the answer. Oh, they praised you, I dare say!
"Brave Galuppi! that was music! good alike at grave and gay!
I can always leave off talking when I hear a master play!"

---

¹⁶| P:them; they'd *1855:*Well (and it < > them) they'd *1863:*Well, (and it *1868:*Well,
and it < > them—they'd   ¹⁷| P:velvet, he to   *1863:*he, to   *1888:*velvet—he
¹⁸| P:clavichord.   *1855:*clavichord?   ¹⁹| *1868:*diminished sigh on   *1888:*
diminished, sigh on   ²¹| P:last we   *1855:*last! we   ²²| P:are you happy?"—
"Yes—And *1855:*are you still as happy   *1863:*as happy?"—"Yes. And   ²³| P:—
"Then more kisses"—"Did I < > them when   *1855:*kisses"—"Did *I* < > them, when
1863:—"Then, more kisses!"—"Did   ²⁴| P:Hark—the < > persistance   *1855:*
persistence, till   *1863:*Hark! the   *1868:*Hark, the   *1888:*persistence till   ²⁵| P:So an
*1865:*So, an   ²⁶| P:music, good *1855:*music! good   ²⁷| P:play." *1855:*talking,

198

Then they left you for their pleasure: till in due time, one by one,
Some with lives that came to nothing, some with deeds as well undone,
30 Death stepped tacitly and took them where they never see the sun.

XI

But when I sit down to reason, think to take my stand nor swerve,
While I triumph o'er a secret wrung from nature's close reserve,
In you come with your cold music till I creep thro' every nerve.

XII

Yes, you, like a ghostly cricket, creaking where a house was burned:
35 "Dust and ashes, dead and done with, Venice spent what Venice earned.
The soul, doubtless, is immortal—where a soul can be discerned.

XIII

"Yours for instance: you know physics, something of geology,
Mathematics are your pastime; souls shall rise in their degree;
Butterflies may dread extinction,—you'll not die, it cannot be!

XIV

40 "As for Venice and her people, merely born to bloom and drop,
Here on earth they bore their fruitage, mirth and folly were the crop:
What of soul was left, I wonder, when the kissing had to stop?

XV

"Dust and ashes!" So you creak it, and I want the heart to scold.
Dear dead women, with such hair, too—what's become of all the gold
45 Used to hang and brush their bosoms? I feel chilly and grown old.

---

when   *1888:*talking when < > play!"   28| P:Thus they   *1855:*Then they
30| P:Death came tacitly   *1865:*Death stepped tacitly   31| P:reason,—say I'll take
*1855:*reason,—think to take < > swerve   *1863:*reason, think < > swerve,   32| P:When
I   *1855:*Till I   *1863:*While I   33| *1855:*music, till   *1888:*music till   34| *1855:*
burned—   *1868:*burned: 35| P:earned,   *1855:*earned!   *1868:*earned.   36| P:
immortal—if a   *1855:*immortal—where   37| P:instance, you   *1888:*instance: you
40| P:and its people < > to blow and   *1855:*to bloom and   *1865:*and her people
41| P:crop,   *1855:*crop.   *1863:*crop:

BY THE FIRE-SIDE

I

How well I know what I mean to do
    When the long dark autumn-evenings come;
And where, my soul, is thy pleasant hue?
    With the music of all thy voices, dumb
5 In life's November too!

II

I shall be found by the fire, suppose,
    O'er a great wise book as beseemeth age,
While the shutters flap as the cross-wind blows
    And I turn the page, and I turn the page,
10 Not verse now, only prose!

III

Till the young ones whisper, finger on lip,
    "There he is at it, deep in Greek:
Now then, or never, out we slip
    To cut from the hazels by the creek
15 A mainmast for our ship!"

IV

I shall be at it indeed, my friends:
    Greek puts already on either side
Such a branch-work forth as soon extends
    To a vista opening far and wide,
20 And I pass out where it ends.

BY THE FIRE-SIDE § Subsequent placement: *1863:*DL §   2| P:dark Autumn
evenings come, *1865:*dark autumn <> come; *1888:*autumn-evenings *1889:*
§ punctuation at end of line decayed; emended to § come; § see Editorial Notes §
4| P:of thy *1855:*of all thy   7| P:age; *1855:*age,   8| P:How the shutters
<> blows, *1855:*While the shutters *1888:*blows   12| P:There <> Greek—
1855:"There *1863:*in Greek: 13| P:then or *1855:*Now or never, then, out *1863:*
Now, then, or never, out *1865:*Now then   15| P:ship. *1855:*ship." *1863:*ship!"
16| P:friends; *1855:*friends! *1888:*friends DC, BrU:friends: *1889:*friends: 18| *1855:*

The outside-frame, like your hazel-trees:
    But the inside-archway widens fast,
And a rarer sort succeeds to these,
    And we slope to Italy at last
25 And youth, by green degrees.

VI

I follow wherever I am led,
    Knowing so well the leader's hand:
Oh woman-country, wooed not wed,
    Loved all the more by earth's male-lands,
30 Laid to their hearts instead!

VII

Look at the ruined chapel again
    Half-way up in the Alpine gorge!
Is that a tower, I point you plain,
    Or is it a mill, or an iron-forge
35 Breaks solitude in vain?

VIII

A turn, and we stand in the heart of things;
    The woods are round us, heaped and dim;
From slab to slab how it slips and springs,
    The thread of water single and slim,
40 Through the ravage some torrent brings!

forth, as *1863*:forth as   ²¹⎪ P:outside-frame like < > hazel-trees— *1863*:outside-frame, like *1888*:hazel-trees: ²²⎪ P:inside-archway narrows fast, *1865*:inside-archway widens fast,   ²⁷⎪ P:hand— *1863*:hand: ²⁸⎪ P:Oh, woman-country, wooed, not *1863*:wooed not *1865*:Oh woman-country   ³²⎪ P:Half way < > gorge: *1855*:gorge. *1863*:Half-way *1868*:gorge!   ³³⎪ P:tower which I *1855*:tower, I   ³⁴⎪ P:mill or an iron forge *1863*:mill, or *1888*:iron-forge   ³⁸⎪ P:springs *1855:* springs, *1863*:springs— *1865*:springs,   ³⁹⎪ P:slim *1855*:slim,   ⁴⁰⎪ P:Thro'

Does it feed the little lake below?
 That speck of white just on its marge
Is Pella; see, in the evening-glow,
 How sharp the silver spear-heads charge
45 When Alp meets heaven in snow!

On our other side is the straight-up rock;
 And a path is kept 'twixt the gorge and it
By boulder-stones where lichens mock
 The marks on a moth, and small ferns fit
50 Their teeth to the polished block.

Oh the sense of the yellow mountain-flowers,
 And thorny balls, each three in one,
The chestnuts throw on our path in showers!
 For the drop of the woodland fruit's begun,
55 These early November hours,

That crimson the creeper's leaf across
 Like a splash of blood, intense, abrupt,
O'er a shield else gold from rim to boss,
 And lay it for show on the fairy-cupped
60 Elf-needled mat of moss,

---

*1863:*Through ⁴²| P:And the speck *1855:*That speck ⁴³| P:evening glow
*1863:*evening-glow, ⁴⁵| P:meets Heaven in snow. *1868:*meets heaven in snow!
⁴⁹| P:moth, while small *1855:*moth, and small ⁵¹| P:Oh, the < > mountain
flowers, *1863:*mountain-flowers, *1868:*Oh the ⁵²| P:And the thorny *1865:*And
thorny ⁵³| P:throw in this path of ours, *1855:*throw on our path in showers,
*1863:*showers! ⁵⁴| *1855:*begun *1863:*—For < > begun, *1868:*For ⁵⁵| P:
hours— *1863:*hours, ⁵⁶| P:across, *1855:*across ⁵⁸| P:shield, else
*1863:*shield else ⁵⁹| P:it to show *1855:*it for show ⁶⁰| P:moss— *1855:*moss,

By the rose-flesh mushrooms, undivulged
    Last evening—nay, in to-day's first dew
Yon sudden coral nipple bulged,
    Where a freaked fawn-coloured flaky crew
65 Of toadstools peep indulged.

And yonder, at foot of the fronting ridge
    That takes the turn to a range beyond,
Is the chapel reached by the one-arched bridge
    Where the water is stopped in a stagnant pond
70 Danced over by the midge.

The chapel and bridge are of stone alike,
    Blackish-grey and mostly wet;
Cut hemp-stalks steep in the narrow dyke.
    See here again, how the lichens fret
75 And the roots of the ivy strike!

Poor little place, where its one priest comes
    On a festa-day, if he comes at all,
To the dozen folk from their scattered homes,
    Gathered within that precinct small
80 By the dozen ways one roams—

To drop from the charcoal-burners' huts,
    Or climb from the hemp-dressers' low shed,
Leave the grange where the woodman stores his nuts,
    Or the wattled cote where the fowlers spread
85 Their gear on the rock's bare juts.

63| P:bulged *1865*:bulged,　　64| P:freaked, fawn-coloured, flaky *1868*:freaked
fawn-coloured flaky　　65| P:toad-stools *1888*:toadstools　　72| P:Blackish
grey *1863*:Blackish-grey　　80| *1855*:roams *1863*:roams—　　81| P:Who drops
1855:To drop　　82| P:climbs *1855*:climb　　83| P:Or the grange *1855*:Leave

It has some pretension too, this front,
　　With its bit of fresco half-moon-wise
Set over the porch, Art's early wont:
　　'Tis John in the Desert, I surmise,
90　But has borne the weather's brunt—

Not from the fault of the builder, though,
　　For a pent-house properly projects
Where three carved beams make a certain show,
　　Dating—good thought of our architect's—
95　'Five, six, nine, he lets you know.

And all day long a bird sings there,
　　And a stray sheep drinks at the pond at times;
The place is silent and aware;
　　It has had its scenes, its joys and crimes,
100　But that is its own affair.

My perfect wife, my Leonor,
　　Oh heart, my own, oh eyes, mine too,
Whom else could I dare look backward for,
　　With whom beside should I dare pursue
105　The path grey heads abhor?

For it leads to a crag's sheer edge with them;
　　Youth, flowery all the way, there stops—

---

the grange　　86| P:front;　1855:front,　　88| P:o'er the porch, art's <> wont—
1855:over　1863:porch, Art's <> wont:　　91| P:though—　1855:though,
94| P:our Architect's—　1855:our architect's—　　95| P:Five　1855:'Five
97|P:times:　1863:times;　　99| P:scenes, and joys　1855:scenes, its joys　　102| P:Oh,
heart my own, oh eyes　1865:Oh heart, my own, oh eyes　　103| P:could I look
1855:could I dare look　　105| P:grey-heads　1855:grey heads　　106| P:them—

Not they; age threatens and they contemn,
　　Till they reach the gulf wherein youth drops,
110　One inch from life's safe hem!

XXIII

With me, youth led . . . I will speak now,
　　No longer watch you as you sit
Reading by fire-light, that great brow
　　And the spirit-small hand propping it,
115　Mutely, my heart knows how—

XXIV

When, if I think but deep enough,
　　You are wont to answer, prompt as rhyme;
And you, too, find without rebuff
　　Response your soul seeks many a time
120　Piercing its fine flesh-stuff.

XXV

My own, confirm me! If I tread
　　This path back, is it not in pride
To think how little I dreamed it led
　　To an age so blest that, by its side,
125　Youth seems the waste instead?

XXVI

My own, see where the years conduct!
　　At first, 'twas something our two souls
Should mix as mists do; each is sucked
　　In each now: on, the new stream rolls,
130　Whatever rocks obstruct.

---

*1855:*them; 　　 109| P:drops *1855:*drops, 　　 110| P:from our life's *1888:*from
life's 　　 111| P:led—I *1863:*led . . . I 　　 114| P:it *1863:*it, 　　 115| P:Mutely—
my *1863:*Mutely, my 　　 118| P:without a rebuff *1865:*without rebuff 　　 119| P:
The response your *1868:*Response your 　　 120| P:flesh stuff— *1855:*flesh-stuff—
*1863:*flesh-stuff. 　　 123| P:how blind I was, it *1855:*how little I dreamed it
124| P:that by its side *1865:*that, by its side, 　　 125| P:instead! *1863:*instead?
128| P:do—each *1855:*do: each *1863:*do; each 　　 129| P:Into each now, on the

XXVII

Think, when our one soul understands
　　The great Word which makes all things new,
When earth breaks up and heaven expands,
　　How will the change strike me and you
135　In the house not made with hands?

XXVIII

Oh I must feel your brain prompt mine,
　　Your heart anticipate my heart,
You must be just before, in fine,
　　See and make me see, for your part,
140　New depths of the divine!

XXIX

But who could have expected this
　　When we two drew together first
Just for the obvious human bliss,
　　To satisfy life's daily thirst
145　With a thing men seldom miss?

XXX

Come back with me to the first of all,
　　Let us lean and love it over again,
Let us now forget and now recall,
　　Break the rosary in a pearly rain,
150　And gather what we let fall!

---

*1855:*now; on, the　*1863:*now: on　*1865:*In each　　¹³²|　P:great word <> new—
*1855:*great Word　*1865:*new,　　¹³³|　P:and Heaven expands—　*1865:*expands,
*1868:*and heaven　　¹³⁵|　P:the House　*1868:*the house　　¹³⁶|　P:Oh, I
*1865:*Oh I　　¹⁴⁰|　P:the Divine!　*1868:*the divine!　　¹⁴¹|　P:And who <> this,
*1855:*But who　*1865:*this　　¹⁴⁷|　P:again—　*1865:*again,　　¹⁴⁸|　P:and then
recall,　*1863:*and now recall,　　¹⁵⁰|　P:And pick up what　*1855:*And gather what

206

XXXI

What did I say?—that a small bird sings
    All day long, save when a brown pair
Of hawks from the wood float with wide wings
    Strained to a bell: 'gainst noon-day glare
¹⁵⁵ You count the streaks and rings.

XXXII

But at afternoon or almost eve
    'Tis better; then the silence grows
To that degree, you half believe
    It must get rid of what it knows,
¹⁶⁰ Its bosom does so heave.

XXXIII

Hither we walked then, side by side,
    Arm in arm and cheek to cheek,
And still I questioned or replied,
    While my heart, convulsed to really speak,
¹⁶⁵ Lay choking in its pride.

XXXIV

Silent the crumbling bridge we cross,
    And pity and praise the chapel sweet,
And care about the fresco's loss,
    And wish for our souls a like retreat,
¹⁷⁰ And wonder at the moss.

XXXV

Stoop and kneel on the settle under,
    Look through the window's grated square:
Nothing to see! For fear of plunder,
    The cross is down and the altar bare,
¹⁷⁵ As if thieves don't fear thunder.

---

¹⁵⁴| P:bell—'gainst the noon-day *1855:*bell: 'gainst *1863:*bell; 'gainst *1865:*bell:
'gainst *1868:*'gainst noon-day   ¹⁵⁶| P:afternoon, or *1855:*afternoon or
¹⁶¹| P:walked, then *1865:*walked then   ¹⁶⁴| P:heart convulsed *1855:*heart,
convulsed *1868:*heart convulsed *1888:*heart, convulsed   ¹⁷¹| P:under—
*1865:*under,   ¹⁷²| P:windows *1855:*window's   ¹⁷³| P:see! for *1868:*see!

XXXVI

We stoop and look in through the grate,
    See the little porch and rustic door,
Read duly the dead builder's date;
    Then cross the bridge that we crossed before,
180 Take the path again—but wait!

XXXVII

Oh moment, one and infinite!
    The water slips o'er stock and stone;
The West is tender, hardly bright:
    How grey at once is the evening grown—
185 One star, its chrysolite!

XXXVIII

We two stood there with never a third,
    But each by each, as each knew well:
The sights we saw and the sounds we heard,
    The lights and the shades made up a spell
190 Till the trouble grew and stirred.

XXXIX

Oh, the little more, and how much it is!
    And the little less, and what worlds away!
How a sound shall quicken content to bliss,
    Or a breath suspend the blood's best play,
195 And life be a proof of this!

For   176| P:grate— *1855:*grate,   178| P:date— *1855:*date, *1865:*date;
179| P:bridge we *1888:*bridge that we   181| P:Oh, moment *1855:*Oh moment
183| P:bright— *1855:*The west <> bright. *1863:*The West <> bright:
185| P:star, the chrysolite! *1888:*star, its chrysolite!   187| *1855:*well. *1863:*well:
191| P:more and *1855:*more, and   192| P:less and *1855:*less, and   194| P:

XL

Had she willed it, still had stood the screen
   So slight, so sure, 'twixt my love and her:
I could fix her face with a guard between,
   And find her soul as when friends confer,
200   Friends—lovers that might have been.

XLI

For my heart had a touch of the woodland-time,
   Wanting to sleep now over its best.
Shake the whole tree in the summer-prime,
   But bring to the last leaf no such test!
205   "Hold the last fast!" runs the rhyme.

XLII

For a chance to make your little much,
   To gain a lover and lose a friend,
Venture the tree and a myriad such,
   When nothing you mar but the year can mend:
210   But a last leaf—fear to touch!

XLIII

Yet should it unfasten itself and fall
   Eddying down till it find your face
At some slight wind—best chance of all!
   Be your heart henceforth its dwelling-place
215   You trembled to forestall!

---

play *1855:*play, *1865:*play. *1868:*play,   196| P:willed so, still <> screen,
*1855:*willed it, still <> screen   197| P:her— *1855:*her. *1863:*her: 200| P:
been— *1855:*been.   201| P:woodland time, *1863:*woodland-time,   202| P:
best: *1855:*best.   203| P:summer prime, *1855:*summer-prime,   204| P:bring
the <> leaf to no <> test, *1855:*bring to the <> leaf no <> test. *1863:*test: *1868:*
test!   205| P:fast!" says the *1863:*fast!" runs the   206| *1865:*much. *1868:*much,
207| P:friend *1855:*friend,   208| P:Tug though you venture a <> such;
*1855:*Venture the tree and a <> such,   209| P:Nothing you *1855:*When nothing
you <> mend! *1865:*mend: 210| *1855:*touch. *1863:*touch!   212| P:Eddying
it down *1855:*Eddying down   213| *1855:*wind—(best <> all!) *1863:*all) *1865:*
wind—best <> all!   214| P:dwelling place *1855:*dwelling-place   215| P:

XLIV

Worth how well, those dark grey eyes,
    That hair so dark and dear, how worth
That a man should strive and agonize,
    And taste a veriest hell on earth
220 For the hope of such a prize!

XLV

You might have turned and tried a man,
    Set him a space to weary and wear,
And prove which suited more your plan,
    His best of hope or his worst despair,
225 Yet end as he began.

XLVI

But you spared me this, like the heart you are,
    And filled my empty heart at a word.
If two lives join, there is oft a scar,
    They are one and one, with a shadowy third;
230 One near one is too far.

XLVII

A moment after, and hands unseen
    Were hanging the night around us fast;

---

forestal! *1868:*forestall! ²¹⁷| P:—That <> so brown and *1855:*so dark and
*1865:*That ²¹⁸| P:agonise, *1888:*agonize, ²¹⁹| P:very *1888:*veriest
²²¹| P:Oh, you might *1865:*Oh you *1868:*You might ²²²| P:him such a *1855:*him
a *1863:*wear *1868:*wear, ²²⁴| P:despair,— *1855:*despair, ²²⁵| P:And end
*1855:*Yet end ²²⁷| P:filled up my <> word: *1855:*filled my <> word.
²²⁸| P:If you join two lives, there *1865:*If two lives join, there ²²⁹| P:third—
*1855:*third; ²³⁰| P:One beside one *1855:*One near one ²³²| P:fast: *1855:*fast.

But we knew that a bar was broken between
    Life and life: we were mixed at last
²³⁵ In spite of the mortal screen.

XLVIII

The forests had done it; there they stood;
    We caught for a moment the powers at play:
They had mingled us so, for once and good,
    Their work was done—we might go or stay,
²⁴⁰ They relapsed to their ancient mood.

XLIX

How the world is made for each of us!
    How all we perceive and know in it
Tends to some moment's product thus,
    When a soul declares itself—to wit,
²⁴⁵ By its fruit, the thing it does!

L

Be hate that fruit or love that fruit,
    It forwards the general deed of man,
And each of the Many helps to recruit
    The life of the race by a general plan;
²⁵⁰ Each living his own, to boot.

---

*1863:*fast;   ²³⁴| P:and life; we *1863:*and life: we   ²³⁶| P:stood— *1863:*stood;
²³⁷| P:a second the *1865:*a moment the   ²³⁸| P:us here for once and for good,
*1855:*us so, for once *1868:*and good,   ²⁴²| P:we see and *1855:*we perceive and
²⁴⁵| P:fruit—the *1865:*fruit, the   ²⁴⁶| P:Be Hate < > or Love *1868:*Be hate < >
or love   ²⁴⁷| P:It goes to the General Deed of Man, *1855:*It forwards the
*1868:*the general deed of man,   ²⁴⁸| P:the millions helps recruit *1855:*the Many
helps to recruit   ²⁴⁹| P:plan, *1863:*plan;   ²⁵⁰| P:Each man with his

LI

I am named and known by that moment's feat;
    There took my station and degree;
So grew my own small life complete,
    As nature obtained her best of me—
255   One born to love you, sweet!

LII

And to watch you sink by the fire-side now
    Back again, as you mutely sit
Musing by fire-light, that great brow
    And the spirit-small hand propping it,
260   Yonder, my heart knows how!

LIII

So, earth has gained by one man the more,
    And the gain of earth must be heaven's gain too;
And the whole is well worth thinking o'er
    When autumn comes: which I mean to do
265   One day, as I said before.

---

*1855:*Each living his   251| P:that hour's feat, *1863:*feat; *1865:*that moment's
feat;   252| P:So took *1855:*There took<> degree. *1863:*degree: *1865:*degree
*1868:*degree;   253| P:There grew <> complete *1855:*So grew *1868:*complete,
255| *1863:*you, Sweet! *1868:*you, sweet!   258| P:fire light <> brow, *1855:*fire-light
<> brow   259| *1855:*it *1868:*it,   261| P:So the earth <> man more, *1863:*So,
the *1888:*So, earth <> man the more,   262| P:be Heaven's <> too, *1868:*too;
*1888:*be heaven's   264| P:When the autumn *1865:*When autumn

I

My love, this is the bitterest, that thou—
Who art all truth, and who dost love me now
    As thine eyes say, as thy voice breaks to say—
Shouldst love so truly, and couldst love me still
5   A whole long life through, had but love its will,
    Would death that leads me from thee brook delay.

II

I have but to be by thee, and thy hand
Will never let mine go, nor heart withstand
    The beating of my heart to reach its place.
10   When shall I look for thee and feel thee gone?
When cry for the old comfort and find none?
    Never, I know! Thy soul is in thy face.

III

Oh, I should fade—'tis willed so! Might I save,
Gladly I would, whatever beauty gave
15   Joy to thy sense, for that was precious too.
It is not to be granted. But the soul
Whence the love comes, all ravage leaves that whole;
    Vainly the flesh fades; soul makes all things new.

IV

It would not be because my eye grew dim
20 Thou couldst not find the love there, thanks to Him
    Who never is dishonoured in the spark

ANY WIFE TO ANY HUSBAND § Subsequent placement: *1863*:DL §   1| P:thou
1865:thou—   2| *1855*:truth and *1865*:truth, and   4| P:Should'st < > could'st
1855:truly and *1863*:Shouldst < > couldst *1865*:truly, and   6| P:And death < >
brooked delay! *1855*:Would death < > brook *1868*:delay.   8| P:Would never < >
go, thy heart *1863*:go, nor heart *1865*:Will never   9| P:place: *1855*:place.
10| P:When should I < > gone, *1855*:gone? *1865*:When shall I   13| P:should
change—'tis < > so! could I *1855*:should fade—'tis < > so! might I *1868*:so!
Might   18| P:fades—soul *1863*:fades; soul   19| *1855*:And 'twould not
1868:It would not   20| P:could'st *1863*:couldst   21| P:Who will not be

He gave us from his fire of fires, and bade
Remember whence it sprang, nor be afraid
    While that burns on, though all the rest grow dark.

V

25 So, how thou wouldst be perfect, white and clean
Outside as inside, soul and soul's demesne
    Alike, this body given to show it by!
Oh, three-parts through the worst of life's abyss,
What plaudits from the next world after this,
30   Couldst thou repeat a stroke and gain the sky!

VI

And is it not the bitterer to think
That, disengage our hands and thou wilt sink
    Although thy love was love in very deed?
I know that nature! Pass a festive day,
35 Thou dost not throw its relic-flower away
    Nor bid its music's loitering echo speed.

VII

Thou let'st the stranger's glove lie where it fell;
If old things remain old things all is well,
    For thou art grateful as becomes man best:
40 And hadst thou only heard me play one tune,
Or viewed me from a window, not so soon
    With thee would such things fade as with the rest.

dishonoured *1855:*Who never is dishonoured   22| *1863:*from His *1868:*from his
23| P:sprung *1855:*sprang nor *1868:*sprang, nor   24| P:grew *1855:*grow
25| P:would'st *1863:*wouldst   30| P:Could'st *1863:*Couldst   32| *1868:*That
disengage *1888:*That, disengage   33| P:Because thy *1855:*Although thy
34| P:day *1865:*day, *1888:*day DC, BrU:day, *1889:*day,   36| P:Or bid *1855:*
Nor bid   37| P:fell, *1855:*fell;   38| P:things keep but old *1855:*things

VIII

I seem to see! We meet and part; 'tis brief;
The book I opened keeps a folded leaf,
45   The very chair I sat on, breaks the rank;
That is a portrait of me on the wall—
Three lines, my face comes at so slight a call:
      And for all this, one little hour to thank!

IX

But now, because the hour through years was fixed,
50 Because our inmost beings met and mixed,
      Because thou once hast loved me—wilt thou dare
Say to thy soul and Who may list beside,
"Therefore she is immortally my bride;
      Chance cannot change my love, nor time impair.

X

55 "So, what if in the dusk of life that's left,
I, a tired traveller of my sun bereft,
      Look from my path when, mimicking the same,
The fire-fly glimpses past me, come and gone?
—Where was it till the sunset? where anon
60   It will be at the sunrise! What's to blame?"

XI

Is it so helpful to thee? Canst thou take
The mimic up, nor, for the true thing's sake,
      Put gently by such efforts at a beam?
Is the remainder of the way so long,

remain old   ⁴³| P:part 'tis brief: *1855*:see! we *1863*:part; 'tis brief; *1868*:see! We
⁴⁷| P:call; *1863*:call: ⁴⁸| P:this one <> hour's to thank: *1855*:this, one <>
thank. *1865*:hour to thank!   ⁵²| P:soul, and who *1855*:soul and Who
⁵³| P:bride, *1865*:bride;   ⁵⁴| P:change that love nor Time impair— *1855*:love,
nor time impair. *1863*:change my love   ⁵⁶| P:A foot-sore traveller of his sun
bereft *1855*:I, a tired traveller, of my sun bereft, *1865*:traveller of   ⁵⁷| P:from his
path *1855*:from my path   ⁵⁸| P:past him, come and gone— *1855*:past me, come
and gone?   ⁵⁹| P:Where *1855*:—Where   ⁶⁰| P:sunrise: what's *1855*:sunrise!
what's *1868*:sunrise! What's   ⁶¹| P:thee? canst *1868*:thee? Canst   ⁶⁴| P:long

65   Thou need'st the little solace, thou the strong?
       Watch out thy watch, let weak ones doze and dream!

XII

—Ah, but the fresher faces! "Is it true,"
Thou'lt ask, "some eyes are beautiful and new?
       Some hair,—how can one choose but grasp such wealth?
70 And if a man would press his lips to lips
Fresh as the wilding hedge-rose-cup there slips
       The dew-drop out of, must it be by stealth?

XIII

"It cannot change the love still kept for Her,
More than if such a picture I prefer
75   Passing a day with, to a room's bare side:
The painted form takes nothing she possessed,
Yet, while the Titian's Venus lies at rest,
       A man looks. Once more, what is there to chide?"

XIV

So must I see, from where I sit and watch,
80 My own self sell myself, my hand attach
       Its warrant to the very thefts from me—
Thy singleness of soul that made me proud,
Thy purity of heart I loved aloud,
       Thy man's-truth I was bold to bid God see!

---

*1888:*long,   65| P:need'st their little   *1855:*need'st the little   67| P:"—Ah <>
faces! Is it true,   *1855:*true,"   *1868:*—Ah <> faces! "Is   68| P:Or not, some
*1855:*Thou'lt ask, "some   71| P:hedge-cup-rose   *1855:*hedge-rose-cup
73| P:"As if it changed the love kept still for her,   *1855:*"It cannot change the <> for
Her,   *1863:*love still kept for   74| P:Much more than such a picture to prefer   *1855:*
than, such   *1865:*More than if such a picture I prefer   75| P:side;   *1855:*side.
*1863:*side: 77| P:Yet while <> rest   *1863:*Yet, while <> rest,   78| P:I gaze—
and, once   *1855:*A man looks. Once   82| P:proud,   *1888:*proud. § emended to §
proud, § see Editorial Notes §   84| P:man's truth, I   *1855:*truth I   *1863:*man's-truth

XV

⁸⁵ Love so, then, if thou wilt! Give all thou canst
Away to the new faces—disentranced,
(Say it and think it) obdurate no more:
Re-issue looks and words from the old mint,
Pass them afresh, no matter whose the print
⁹⁰ Image and superscription once they bore!

XVI

Re-coin thyself and give it them to spend,—
It all comes to the same thing at the end,
Since mine thou wast, mine art and mine shalt be,
Faithful or faithless, sealing up the sum
⁹⁵ Or lavish of my treasure, thou must come
Back to the heart's place here I keep for thee!

XVII

Only, why should it be with stain at all?
Why must I, 'twixt the leaves of coronal,
Put any kiss of pardon on thy brow?
¹⁰⁰ Why need the other women know so much,
And talk together, "Such the look and such
The smile he used to love with, then as now!"

XVIII

Might I die last and show thee! Should I find
Such hardship in the few years left behind,
¹⁰⁵ If free to take and light my lamp, and go

---

⁸⁵| P:Love them, then *1855*:Love so, then   ⁸⁶| P:disentranced— *1863:*
disentranced,   ⁸⁷| P:(Say so and think so) obdurate no more, *1855*:(Say it and think
it) obdurate *1888*:more: ⁸⁸| P:mint— *1863*:mint,   ⁸⁹| P:print, *1855*:print
⁹³| P:art, and *1863*:art and   ⁹⁵| P:my hoard,—at last shalt come *1855*:my
treasure, thou must come   ⁹⁶| P:here, I *1855*:here I   ¹⁰⁰| *1855*:much
1863:much,   ¹⁰¹| P:together "such *1855*:together, "Such   ¹⁰³| P:shew thee!
should *1855*:thee! Should *1863*:show   ¹⁰⁵| P:lamp and *1855*:lamp, and

217

Into thy tomb, and shut the door and sit,
Seeing thy face on those four sides of it
        The better that they are so blank, I know!

XIX

Why, time was what I wanted, to turn o'er
110 Within my mind each look, get more and more
        By heart each word, too much to learn at first;
And join thee all the fitter for the pause
'Neath the low doorway's lintel. That were cause
        For lingering, though thou calledst, if I durst!

XX

115 And yet thou art the nobler of us two:
What dare I dream of, that thou canst not do,
        Outstripping my ten small steps with one stride?
I'll say then, here's a trial and a task—
Is it to bear?—if easy, I'll not ask:
120   Though love fail, I can trust on in thy pride.

XXI

Pride?—when those eyes forestall the life behind
The death I have to go through!—when I find,
        Now that I want thy help most, all of thee!
What did I fear? Thy love shall hold me fast
125 Until the little minute's sleep is past
        And I wake saved.—And yet it will not be!

106| P:tomb and <> sit *1855*:tomb, and *1865*:sit,   109| P:Why, Time *1855:*
Why, time   110| P:look, yet more and *1855*:look, get more and   111| P:word
too <> first: *1855*:word, too <> first, *1863*:first;   112| P:To join *1855*:And
join   113| P:door-way's lintel—that *1855*:lintel. That *1888*:doorway's
114| P:thou call me, if *1855*:thou calledst, if   115| P:two; *1855*:two. *1863*:two:
116| P:do— *1855*:do,   119| P:ask— *1863*:ask: 120| P:can hold on by thy
1855:can trust on in thy   121| P:forestal *1868*:forestall   122| P:through—when
I find *1855*:through!—when I find,   123| P:Now, when I *1855*:Now that I
126| P:saved!—And *1855*:saved.—And yet, it *1863*:yet it

CONTAINING THE STRANGE MEDICAL EXPERIENCE OF KARSHISH,
THE ARAB PHYSICIAN

Karshish, the picker-up of learning's crumbs,
The not-incurious in God's handiwork
(This man's-flesh he hath admirably made,
Blown like a bubble, kneaded like a paste,
5 To coop up and keep down on earth a space
That puff of vapour from his mouth, man's soul)
—To Abib, all-sagacious in our art,
Breeder in me of what poor skill I boast,
Like me inquisitive how pricks and cracks
10 Befall the flesh through too much stress and strain,
Whereby the wily vapour fain would slip
Back and rejoin its source before the term,—
And aptest in contrivance (under God)
To baffle it by deftly stopping such:—
15 The vagrant Scholar to his Sage at home
Sends greeting (health and knowledge, fame with peace)
Three samples of true snakestone—rarer still,
One of the other sort, the melon-shaped,
(But fitter, pounded fine, for charms than drugs)
20 And writeth now the twenty-second time.

My journeyings were brought to Jericho:
Thus I resume. Who studious in our art
Shall count a little labour unrepaid?
I have shed sweat enough, left flesh and bone
25 On many a flinty furlong of this land.
Also, the country-side is all on fire

---

*AN EPISTLE CONTAINING THE STRANGE MEDICAL EXPERIENCE OF
KARSHISH, THE ARAB PHYSICIAN* § Subsequent placement: *1863:*MW §
Title P:*THE MEDICAL<>OF BEN KARSHISH 1855:THE STRANGE
MEDICAL<>OF KARSHISH*   ³| P:This<>made— *1855:*(This man's-flesh
He <>made, *1868:*man's-flesh he   ⁶| P:from His <>soul— *1855:*soul)
*1868:*from his   ¹⁰| P:flesh, through *1855:*flesh through   ¹²| P:term, *1855:*
term,—   ¹³| P:contrivance, under God, *1868:*contrivance (under God)   ¹⁴| P:
it, by *1855:*it by   ¹⁵| P:home, *1855:*home   ¹⁶| P:greeting, health <>
peace, *1855:*greeting (health <> peace)   ¹⁷| P:snake-stone *1888:*snakestone
¹⁹| P:But <> drugs,— *1855:*(But <> drugs)   ²¹| P:to Jericho, *1863:*to Jericho:
²²| P:resume. Who, studious <> art, *1855:*resume. Who studious <> art   ²⁶| P:

With rumours of a marching hitherward:
Some say Vespasian cometh, some, his son.
A black lynx snarled and pricked a tufted ear;
30   Lust of my blood inflamed his yellow balls:
I cried and threw my staff and he was gone.
Twice have the robbers stripped and beaten me,
And once a town declared me for a spy;
But at the end, I reach Jerusalem,
35   Since this poor covert where I pass the night,
This Bethany, lies scarce the distance thence
A man with plague-sores at the third degree
Runs till he drops down dead. Thou laughest here!
'Sooth, it elates me, thus reposed and safe,
40   To void the stuffing of my travel-scrip
And share with thee whatever Jewry yields.
A viscid choler is observable
In tertians, I was nearly bold to say;
And falling-sickness hath a happier cure
45   Than our school wots of: there's a spider here
Weaves no web, watches on the ledge of tombs,
Sprinkled with mottles on an ash-grey back;
Take five and drop them . . . but who knows his mind,
The Syrian runagate I trust this to?
50   His service payeth me a sublimate
Blown up his nose to help the ailing eye.
Best wait: I reach Jerusalem at morn,
There set in order my experiences,
Gather what most deserves, and give thee all—
55   Or I might add, Judæa's gum-tragacanth
Scales off in purer flakes, shines clearer-grained,
Cracks 'twixt the pestle and the porphyry,
In fine exceeds our produce. Scalp-disease
Confounds me, crossing so with leprosy—

Also the *1863:*Also, the   27| P:hitherward— *1863:*hitherward: 28| P:son—
*1855:*son.   29| P:ear, *1855:*ear;   30| P:balls. *1855:*balls: 32| P:me
*1855:*me,   33| P:spy. *1855:*spy, *1865:*spy;   43| P:say, *1865:*say;
47| P:ash grey *1855:*ash-grey   48| P:them . . . but *1888:*them . . but § emended
to § them . . . but § see Editorial Notes §   49| P:run-a-gate *1888:*runagate
51| P:eye: *1855:*eye.   54| P:deserves and *1863:*deserves, and   55| P:add,
Judea's *1863:*add, Judæa's   57| P:twixt *1855:'*twixt   58| P:produce. Scalp

60 Thou hadst admired one sort I gained at Zoar—
But zeal outruns discretion. Here I end.

Yet stay: my Syrian blinketh gratefully,
Protesteth his devotion is my price—
Suppose I write what harms not, though he steal?
65 I half resolve to tell thee, yet I blush,
What set me off a-writing first of all.
An itch I had, a sting to write, a tang!
For, be it this town's barrenness—or else
The Man had something in the look of him—
70 His case has struck me far more than 'tis worth.
So, pardon if—(lest presently I lose
In the great press of novelty at hand
The care and pains this somehow stole from me)
I bid thee take the thing while fresh in mind,
75 Almost in sight—for, wilt thou have the truth?
The very man is gone from me but now,
Whose ailment is the subject of discourse.
Thus then, and let thy better wit help all!

'Tis but a case of mania—subinduced
80 By epilepsy, at the turning-point
Of trance prolonged unduly some three days:
When, by the exhibition of some drug
Or spell, exorcization, stroke of art
Unknown to me and which 'twere well to know,
85 The evil thing out-breaking all at once
Left the man whole and sound of body indeed,—
But, flinging (so to speak) life's gates too wide,
Making a clear house of it too suddenly,

---

disease *1855:*produce. Scalp-disease   62| P:gratefully; *1855:*gratefully,
65| P:thee, though I   *1855:*thee, yet I   67| *1863:*tang   *1865:*tang!   70| P:it's
1855:'tis   76| P:now   *1855:*now,   78| P:all.   *1868:*all!   81| P:trance,
prolonged <> days, *1855:*trance prolonged   *1865:*days;   *1888:*days: 82| P:When
by *1863:*When, by   83| P:exorcisation   *1863:*exorcization   84| P:which
were fit to *1855:*which 'twere well to   *1888:*know   DC, BrU:know,   *1889:*know,
86| P:indeed,   *1855:*indeed,—   87| P:But flinging, so to speak, life's   *1855:*But,
flinging *1868:*flinging (so to speak) life's   *1888:*wide   DC, BrU:wide,   *1889:*wide,

The first conceit that entered might inscribe
90 Whatever it was minded on the wall
So plainly at that vantage, as it were,
(First come, first served) that nothing subsequent
Attaineth to erase those fancy-scrawls
The just-returned and new-established soul
95 Hath gotten now so thoroughly by heart
That henceforth she will read or these or none.
And first—the man's own firm conviction rests
That he was dead (in fact they buried him)
—That he was dead and then restored to life
100 By a Nazarene physician of his tribe:
—'Sayeth, the same bade "Rise," and he did rise.
"Such cases are diurnal," thou wilt cry.
Not so this figment!—not, that such a fume,
Instead of giving way to time and health,
105 Should eat itself into the life of life,
As saffron tingeth flesh, blood, bones and all!
For see, how he takes up the after-life.
The man—it is one Lazarus a Jew,
Sanguine, proportioned, fifty years of age,
110 The body's habit wholly laudable,
As much, indeed, beyond the common health
As he were made and put aside to show.
Think, could we penetrate by any drug
And bathe the wearied soul and worried flesh,
115 And bring it clear and fair, by three days' sleep!
Whence has the man the balm that brightens all?
This grown man eyes the world now like a child.
Some elders of his tribe, I should premise,
Led in their friend, obedient as a sheep,
120 To bear my inquisition. While they spoke,

⁸⁹| P:entered pleased to write *1863:*entered might inscribe   ⁹¹| *1888:*were
DC, BrU: were, *1889:* were,   ⁹³| P:erase her fancy-scrawls; *1855:*erase the
fancy-scrawls *1863:*erase those fancy-scrawls   ⁹⁴| P:And the returned and *1855:*
Which the *1863:*The just-returned and   ⁹⁵| P:Hath got them now *1855:*Hath
gotten now   ⁹⁹| P:That *1863:*—That   ¹⁰⁰| P:a Nazarite *1855:*a Nazarene
¹⁰²| P:cry— *1855:*cry.   ¹⁰³| P:fume *1855:*fume,   ¹⁰⁴| P:health *1855:*
health,   ¹¹²| P:shew. *1863:*show.   ¹¹⁵| P:days *1863:*days'   ¹²⁰| P:

Now sharply, now with sorrow,—told the case,—
He listened not except I spoke to him,
But folded his two hands and let them talk,
Watching the flies that buzzed: and yet no fool.
125 And that's a sample how his years must go.
Look, if a beggar, in fixed middle-life,
Should find a treasure,—can he use the same
With straitened habits and with tastes starved small,
And take at once to his impoverished brain
130 The sudden element that changes things,
That sets the undreamed-of rapture at his hand
And puts the cheap old joy in the scorned dust?
Is he not such an one as moves to mirth—
Warily parsimonious, when no need,
135 Wasteful as drunkenness at undue times?
All prudent counsel as to what befits
The golden mean, is lost on such an one:
The man's fantastic will is the man's law.
So here—we call the treasure knowledge, say,
140 Increased beyond the fleshly faculty—
Heaven opened to a soul while yet on earth,
Earth forced on a soul's use while seeing heaven:
The man is witless of the size, the sum,
The value in proportion of all things,
145 Or whether it be little or be much.
Discourse to him of prodigious armaments
Assembled to besiege his city now,
And of the passing of a mule with gourds—
'Tis one! Then take it on the other side,
150 Speak of some trifling fact,—he will gaze rapt
With stupor at its very littleness,

---

inquisition—while *1855*:inquisition. While   ¹²²| P:him *1855*:him,   ¹²⁶| P:
Look if *1888*:Look, if   ¹²⁷| P:treasure, can *1868*:treasure,—can   ¹²⁸| P:
straightened *1863*:straitened   ¹³⁰| P:things? *1855*:things,   ¹³¹| P:—That
< > hand, *1863*:That *1888*:hand   ¹³⁴| P:when's no need; *1855*:need, *1863*:
when   ¹³⁷| P:mean is < > one, *1855*:mean, is< > one. *1863*:one: ¹³⁸| P:law,
1855:law.   ¹³⁹| P:we'll < > say— *1863*:say, *1865*:we   ¹⁴⁰| P:faculty,
1855:faculty—   ¹⁴²| P:seeing Heaven: *1855*:seeing Heaven. *1865*:seeing Heaven:
1868:seeing heaven: ¹⁴⁴| P:things *1855*:things,   ¹⁵⁰| P:fact—he < > rapt,
1855:rapt *1868*:fact,—he   ¹⁵¹| P:stupor from its < > littleness *1855*:stupor at

(Far as I see) as if in that indeed
He caught prodigious import, whole results;
And so will turn to us the bystanders
155 In ever the same stupor (note this point)
That we too see not with his opened eyes.
Wonder and doubt come wrongly into play,
Preposterously, at cross purposes.
Should his child sicken unto death,—why, look
160 For scarce abatement of his cheerfulness,
Or pretermission of the daily craft!
While a word, gesture, glance from that same child
At play or in the school or laid asleep,
Will startle him to an agony of fear,
165 Exasperation, just as like. Demand
The reason why—" 'tis but a word," object—
"A gesture"—he regards thee as our lord
Who lived there in the pyramid alone,
Looked at us (dost thou mind?) when, being young,
170 We both would unadvisedly recite
Some charm's beginning, from that book of his,
Able to bid the sun throb wide and burst
All into stars, as suns grown old are wont.
Thou and the child have each a veil alike
175 Thrown o'er your heads, from under which ye both
Stretch your blind hands and trifle with a match
Over a mine of Greek fire, did ye know!
He holds on firmly to some thread of life—
(It is the life to lead perforcedly)

its <> littleness— *1863*:littleness, ¹⁵²| *1863*:see)—as *1868*:see) as ¹⁵³| P:
results— *1855*:results; ¹⁵⁶| P:eyes— *1855*:eyes! *1863*:eyes. ¹⁵⁷| P:doubt
brought wrongly *1855*:doubt come wrongly ¹⁶¹| P:Nor <> craft— *1855*:Or <>
of his daily *1865*:of the daily *1868*:craft! ¹⁶²| P:glance, from *1865*:glance from
¹⁶³| P:asleep *1855*:asleep, ¹⁶⁴| P:Will start him *1863*:Will startle him
¹⁶⁵| P:like: demand *1855*:like! demand *1868*:like. Demand ¹⁶⁶| P:why—'tis but
"a *1855*:why—" 'tis but a ¹⁶⁷| P:our Lord *1855*:our lord ¹⁶⁸| P:the
Pyramid alone *1855*:the pyramid alone, ¹⁶⁹| P:us, dost <> mind, when being
young *1863*:mind?—when *1868*:us (dost <> mind?) when, being young, ¹⁷¹| P:
beginning in that <> his *1855*:beginning, from that <> his, ¹⁷³| P:wont—
1855:wont. ¹⁷⁴| P:and this man's child have a *1855*:and the child have each a
¹⁷⁵| P:heads from *1863*:heads, from ¹⁷⁹| P:(Perforcedly it is <> lead) *1855*:

180   Which runs across some vast distracting orb
       Of glory on either side that meagre thread,
       Which, conscious of, he must not enter yet—
       The spiritual life around the earthly life:
       The law of that is known to him as this,
185   His heart and brain move there, his feet stay here.
       So is the man perplext with impulses
       Sudden to start off crosswise, not straight on,
       Proclaiming what is right and wrong across,
       And not along, this black thread through the blaze—
190   "It should be" baulked by "here it cannot be."
       And oft the man's soul springs into his face
       As if he saw again and heard again
       His sage that bade him "Rise" and he did rise.
       Something, a word, a tick o' the blood within
195   Admonishes: then back he sinks at once
       To ashes, who was very fire before,
       In sedulous recurrence to his trade
       Whereby he earneth him the daily bread;
       And studiously the humbler for that pride,
200   Professedly the faultier that he knows
       God's secret, while he holds the thread of life.
       Indeed the especial marking of the man
       Is prone submission to the heavenly will—
       Seeing it, what it is, and why it is.
205   'Sayeth, he will wait patient to the last
       For that same death which must restore his being
       To equilibrium, body loosening soul
       Divorced even now by premature full growth:
       He will live, nay, it pleaseth him to live

(It is <> lead perforcedly)   182| P:yet: 1855:yet—   183| P:The universal
life, the <> life, 1855:The spiritual life around the <> life! 1865:earthly life:
184| P:this— 1868:this, 185| P:here: 1855:here. 186| P:impulses. 1855:
impulses 188| P:is Right and Wrong across— 1863:across, 1868:is right and
wrong 189| P:along—this 1863:along, this 190| P:balked <> be:" 1855:
be." 1865:baulked 193| P:did rise— 1855:did rise. 194| P:Something—a
word <> of 1863:Something, a word 1888:o' 195| P:Admonishes—then
1868:Admonishes: then 196| P:ashes, that was 1865:ashes, who was 198| P:
bread— 1863:bread; 199| P:Most studiously 1855:And studiously 203| P:
the Heavenly 1868:the heavenly 206| P:which will restore 1863:which must

²¹⁰ So long as God please, and just how God please.
He even seeketh not to please God more
(Which meaneth, otherwise) than as God please.
Hence, I perceive not he affects to preach
The doctrine of his sect whate'er it be,
²¹⁵ Make proselytes as madmen thirst to do:
How can he give his neighbour the real ground,
His own conviction? Ardent as he is—
Call his great truth a lie, why, still the old
"Be it as God please" reassureth him.
²²⁰ I probed the sore as thy disciple should:
"How, beast," said I, "this stolid carelessness
Sufficeth thee, when Rome is on her march
To stamp out like a little spark thy town,
Thy tribe, thy crazy tale and thee at once?"
²²⁵ He merely looked with his large eyes on me.
The man is apathetic, you deduce?
Contrariwise, he loves both old and young,
Able and weak, affects the very brutes
And birds—how say I? flowers of the field—
²³⁰ As a wise workman recognizes tools
In a master's workshop, loving what they make.
Thus is the man as harmless as a lamb:
Only impatient, let him do his best,
At ignorance and carelessness and sin—
²³⁵ An indignation which is promptly curbed:
As when in certain travel I have feigned
To be an ignoramus in our art
According to some preconceived design,
And happed to hear the land's practitioners

restore   ²¹¹| P:more, *1855*:more   ²¹²| P:Which meaneth otherwise, than
1855:(Which meaneth, otherwise) than   ²¹³| P:Hence I *1865*:Hence, I   ²¹⁴| P:
be— *1863*:be,   ²¹⁵| P:do— *1855*:do. *1863*:do: ²¹⁷| P:conviction? ardent
1868:conviction? Ardent   ²¹⁸| P:why still *1863*:why, still   ²²⁰| P:should—
1865:should: ²²⁷| P:Contrariwise he *1865*:Contrariwise, he   ²²⁸| P:weak—
affects the very beasts *1855*:very brutes *1865*:weak, affects   ²³⁰| P:recognises
1888:recognizes   ²³¹| P:make— *1855*:make.   ²³⁵| P:is curbed by
fear; *1855*:is promptly curbed. *1863*:curbed: ²³⁶| P:travels *1865*:travel

²⁴⁰ Steeped in conceit sublimed by ignorance,
Prattle fantastically on disease,
Its cause and cure—and I must hold my peace!

Thou wilt object—Why have I not ere this
Sought out the sage himself, the Nazarene
²⁴⁵ Who wrought this cure, inquiring at the source,
Conferring with the frankness that befits?
Alas! it grieveth me, the learned leech
Perished in a tumult many years ago,
Accused,—our learning's fate,—of wizardry,
²⁵⁰ Rebellion, to the setting up a rule
And creed prodigious as described to me.
His death, which happened when the earthquake fell
(Prefiguring, as soon appeared, the loss
To occult learning in our lord the sage
²⁵⁵ Who lived there in the pyramid alone)
Was wrought by the mad people—that's their wont!
On vain recourse, as I conjecture it,
To his tried virtue, for miraculous help—
How could he stop the earthquake? That's their way!
²⁶⁰ The other imputations must be lies:
But take one, though I loathe to give it thee,
In mere respect for any good man's fame.
(And after all, our patient Lazarus
Is stark mad; should we count on what he says?

---

^{243|} P:object—why <> ere thus *1855:*ere this *1868:*object—Why   ^{245|} P:
enquiring *1863:*inquiring   ^{249|} P:wizardry— *1855:*wizardry,   ^{250|} P:a crown,
*1855:*a rule   ^{252|} P:death which *1865:*death, which   ^{255|} P:That lived *1863:*
Who lived   ^{256|} P:wont— *1865:*wont!   ^{259|} *1865:*earthquake? hat's
*1868:*earthquake? That's   ^{261|} P:Take but this one—though *1855:*But take one
*1868:*one, though   ^{262|} P:respect to any <> fame, *1855:*fame! *1865:*respect for
any <> fame.   ^{263|} P:And <> all our *1855:*(And *1863:*all, our   ^{264|} P:mad—

265 Perhaps not: though in writing to a leech
     'Tis well to keep back nothing of a case.)
     This man so cured regards the curer, then,
     As—God forgive me! who but God himself,
     Creator and sustainer of the world,
270 That came and dwelt in flesh on it awhile!
     —'Sayeth that such an one was born and lived,
     Taught, healed the sick, broke bread at his own house,
     Then died, with Lazarus by, for aught I know,
     And yet was . . . what I said nor choose repeat,
275 And must have so avouched himself, in fact,
     In hearing of this very Lazarus
     Who saith—but why all this of what he saith?
     Why write of trivial matters, things of price
     Calling at every moment for remark?
280 I noticed on the margin of a pool
     Blue-flowering borage, the Aleppo sort,
     Aboundeth, very nitrous. It is strange!

        Thy pardon for this long and tedious case,
     Which, now that I review it, needs must seem
285 Unduly dwelt on, prolixly set forth!
     Nor I myself discern in what is writ
     Good cause for the peculiar interest
     And awe indeed this man has touched me with.
     Perhaps the journey's end, the weariness
290 Had wrought upon me first. I met him thus:
     I crossed a ridge of short sharp broken hills
     Like an old lion's cheek teeth. Out there came

should *1863*:mad; should   265| P:not—yet in *1855*:not—though in *1863*:not:
though   266| P:case. *1855*:case.)   267| P:curer then, *1868*:curer, then,
268| P:me—who *1868*:me! who   269| P:and Sustainer < > world *1855*:world,
1865:and sustainer   271| *1855*:an One *1868*:an one   276| P:very
Lazarus. *1855*:very Lazarus   277| P:He saith—but *1855*:Who saith—but
279| P:for record! *1855*:for remark?   280| P:a lake *1855*:a pool   285| P:forth.
1863:forth!   286| P:Nor I discern myself in *1855*:Nor I myself discern in   290| P:
thus— *1863*:thus: 292| P:cheek-teeth: out *1855*:cheek-teeth. Out *1865*:cheek

A moon made like a face with certain spots
Multiform, manifold and menacing:
295 Then a wind rose behind me. So we met
In this old sleepy town at unaware,
The man and I. I send thee what is writ.
Regard it as a chance, a matter risked
To this ambiguous Syrian—he may lose,
300 Or steal, or give it thee with equal good.
Jerusalem's repose shall make amends
For time this letter wastes, thy time and mine;
Till when, once more thy pardon and farewell!

The very God! think, Abib; dost thou think?
305 So, the All-Great, were the All-Loving too—
So, through the thunder comes a human voice
Saying, "O heart I made, a heart beats here!
Face, my hands fashioned, see it in myself!
Thou hast no power nor mayst conceive of mine,
310 But love I gave thee, with myself to love,
And thou must love me who have died for thee!"
The madman saith He said so: it is strange.

---

teeth   294| P:manifold, and   *1863:*manifold and   296| P:unaware   *1855:*
unaware,   302| P:mine: *1855:*mine,   *1863:*mine;   303| P:Till then, once
*1855:*Till when, once   3, 5| P:came   *1855:*comes   307| P:Saying, "Oh, heart
I <> here—   *1855:*Saying, "O heart I <> here!   308| P:myself.   *1863:*Face, My
<> in Myself.   *1868:*Face, my <> in myself,   *1888:*myself!   309| P:may'st
*1863:*of Mine,   *1868:*of mine,   *1888:*mayst   310| P:But Love   *1855:*But love <>
with Myself   *1868:*with myself   *1888:*to love   DC, BrU:to love,   *1889:*to love,
311| P:thee!   *1855:*thee!"   *1863:*love Me   *1868:*love me

MESMERISM

I

All I believed is true!
   I am able yet
   All I want, to get
By a method as strange as new:
⁵   Dare I trust the same to you?

II

If at night, when doors are shut,
   And the wood-worm picks,
   And the death-watch ticks,
And the bar has a flag of smut,
¹⁰   And a cat's in the water-butt—

III

And the socket floats and flares,
   And the house-beams groan,
   And a foot unknown
Is surmised on the garret-stairs,
¹⁵   And the locks slip unawares—

MESMERISM § Subsequent placement: *1863*:DR §   ¹| P:true; *1855*:true!
²| P:yet, *1855*:yet   ³| *1855*:want to *1865*:want, to   ⁴| *1888*:new DC, BrU:

And the spider, to serve his ends,
    By a sudden thread,
    Arms and legs outspread,
On the table's midst descends,
20 Comes to find, God knows what friends!—

V

If since eve drew in, I say,
    I have sat and brought
    (So to speak) my thought
To bear on the woman away,
25 Till I felt my hair turn grey—

VI

Till I seemed to have and hold,
    In the vacancy
    'Twixt the wall and me,
From the hair-plait's chestnut gold
30 To the foot in its muslin fold—

new: *1889:*new: 20| P:find God   *1855:*find, God   21| P:since Eve
*1855:*since eve   22| P:sate *1863:*sat   23| P:(Thus to   *1855:*(So to   24| P:So
to bear <> away   *1855:*To bear <> away,   25| P:That I   *1855:*Till I   26| P:
hold *1863:*hold,   28| P:me *1855:*me, *1868:*me *1888:*me,   29| P:chestnut-

Have and hold, then and there,
   Her, from head to foot,
   Breathing and mute,
Passive and yet aware,
35   In the grasp of my steady stare—

Hold and have, there and then,
   All her body and soul
   That completes my whole,
All that women add to men,
40   In the clutch of my steady ken—

Having and holding, till
   I imprint her fast
   On the void at last
As the sun does whom he will
45   By the calotypist's skill—

Then,—if my heart's strength serve,
   And through all and each
   Of the veils I reach
To her soul and never swerve,
50   Knitting an iron nerve—

Command her soul to advance
   And inform the shape
   Which has made escape
And before my countenance
55   Answers me glance for glance—

---

gold *1888:*chestnut gold   ³⁴| P:aware *1855:*aware,   ³⁸| P:my Whole
*1855:*my Whole, *1868:*my whole,   ⁴⁵| *1863:*skill *1865:*skill—   ⁵¹| P:

I, still with a gesture fit
   Of my hands that best
   Do my soul's behest,
Pointing the power from it,
60   While myself do steadfast sit—

XIII

Steadfast and still the same
   On my object bent,
   While the hands give vent
To my ardour and my aim
65   And break into very flame—

XIV

Then I reach, I must believe,
   Not her soul in vain,
   For to me again
It reaches, and past retrieve
70   Is wound in the toils I weave;

XV

And must follow as I require,
   As befits a thrall,
   Bringing flesh and all,
Essence and earth-attire,
75   To the source of the tractile fire:

XVI

Till the house called hers, not mine,
   With a growing weight
   Seems to suffocate
If she break not its leaden line
80   And escape from its close confine.

Commanding that to *1865:*Command her soul to   59| P:it *1855:*it,   62| P:
bent *1863:*bent,   66| P:Then, I reach *1865:*Then I reach   70| P:weave—
*1868:*weave;   75| P:fire— *1868:*fire: 80| P:confine— *1868:*confine.

XVII

Out of doors into the night!
　　On to the maze
　　Of the wild wood-ways,
Not turning to left nor right
85　From the pathway, blind with sight—

XVIII

Making thro' rain and wind
　　O'er the broken shrubs,
　　'Twixt the stems and stubs,
With a still, composed, strong mind,
90　Nor a care for the world behind—

XIX

Swifter and still more swift,
　　As the crowding peace
　　Doth to joy increase
In the wide blind eyes uplift
95　Thro' the darkness and the drift!

XX

While I—to the shape, I too
　　Feel my soul dilate
　　Nor a whit abate,
And relax not a gesture due,
100　As I see my belief come true.

---

⁸¹| P:night *1855:*night!　　⁸³| P:wood ways *1855:*wood-ways,　　⁸⁴| P:left
or right *1863:*left nor right　　⁸⁵| P:the path, too blind *1855:*the pathway, blind
⁸⁶| P:Making, thro' *1855:*Making thro'　　⁸⁷| P:shrubs *1855:*shrubs,　　⁸⁸| P:
stubs *1855:*stubs,　　⁸⁹| P:still composed strong *1863:*still, composed, strong
⁹⁰| P:Not a *1865:*Nor a　　⁹¹| P:swift *1855:*swift,　　⁹⁴| P:wide level eyes
*1855:*wide blind eyes uplift, *1868:*uplift　　⁹⁵| P:drift,— *1855:*drift!　　⁹⁸| P:
abate *1863:*Not a *1865:*Nor a <> abate,　　⁹⁹| P:due *1863:*due,　　¹⁰⁰| P:true—

XXI

For, there! have I drawn or no
   Life to that lip?
   Do my fingers dip
In a flame which again they throw
105 On the cheek that breaks a-glow?

XXII

Ha! was the hair so first?
   What, unfilleted,
   Made alive, and spread
Through the void with a rich outburst,
110 Chestnut gold-interspersed?

XXIII

Like the doors of a casket-shrine,
   See, on either side,
   Her two arms divide
Till the heart betwixt makes sign,
115 Take me, for I am thine!

XXIV

"Now—now"—the door is heard!
   Hark, the stairs! and near—
   Nearer—and here—
"Now!" and at call the third
120 She enters without a word.

---

*1863:*true.   101| P:For there   *1863:*For, there   102| P:lip!   *1855:*lip?
107| P:What unfilleted,   *1855:*What, unfilleted,   108| P:alive and   *1855:*alive,
and   109| P:outburst   *1855:*outburst,   110| P:gold-interspersed!   *1863:*gold-
interspersed?   115| P:thine—   *1855:*thine!   116| P:Now—now—the <> heard
1863:"Now—now"—the <> heard!   117| P:Hark! the stairs and   *1863:*Hark, the
stairs! and   119| P:Now! and   *1863:*"Now!" and   120| P:word—   *1855:*

XXV

On doth she march and on
    To the fancied shape;
    It is, past escape,
Herself, now: the dream is done
125   And the shadow and she are one.

XXVI

First I will pray. Do Thou
    That ownest the soul,
    Yet wilt grant control
To another, nor disallow
130   For a time, restrain me now!

XXVII

I admonish me while I may,
    Not to squander guilt,
    Since require Thou wilt
At my hand its price one day!
135   What the price is, who can say?

word. *1888:*word DC, BrU:word. *1889:*word. ¹²²⌐ P:shape— *1863:*shape;
¹²³⌐ P:is past escape *1863:*is, past escape, ¹²⁴⌐ P:now—the *1863:*now:the
¹²⁶⌐ P:pray: do *1855:*pray. Do ¹²⁷⌐ P:soul *1855:*soul, ¹²⁸⌐ P:controul
*1863:*control ¹²⁹⌐ P:another nor *1863:*another, nor ¹³⁴⌐ P:day— *1855:*day!

A SERENADE AT THE VILLA

I

That was I, you heard last night,
    When there rose no moon at all,
Nor, to pierce the strained and tight
    Tent of heaven, a planet small:
5 Life was dead and so was light.

II

Not a twinkle from the fly,
    Not a glimmer from the worm;
When the crickets stopped their cry,
    When the owls forbore a term,
10 You heard music; that was I.

III

Earth turned in her sleep with pain,
    Sultrily suspired for proof:
In at heaven and out again,
    Lightning!—where it broke the roof,
15 Bloodlike, some few drops of rain.

IV

What they could my words expressed,
    O my love, my all, my one!
Singing helped the verses best,
    And when singing's best was done,
20 To my lute I left the rest.

A SERENADE AT THE VILLA § Subsequent placement: *1863:*DL §   ¹| P:was I
you <> night *1855:*was I, you *1888:*night,   ⁴| P:small— *1855:*small:
⁵| P:dead, and *1865:*dead and   ⁷| *1855:*worm. *1888:*worm;   ¹⁷| *1863:*my
Love, my All, my One! *1865:*my Love, my all, my one! *1868:*my love, my all

So wore night; the East was gray,
White the broad-faced hemlock-flowers:
There would be another day;
Ere its first of heavy hours
25 Found me, I had passed away.

What became of all the hopes,
Words and song and lute as well?
Say, this struck you—"When life gropes
Feebly for the path where fell
30 Light last on the evening slopes,

"One friend in that path shall be,
To secure my step from wrong;
One to count night day for me,
Patient through the watches long,
35 Serving most with none to see."

Never say—as something bodes—
"So, the worst has yet a worse!
When life halts 'neath double loads,
Better the taskmaster's curse
40 Than such music on the roads!

---

²¹| P:grey, *1855:*the east *1863:*the East was gray, ²²| P:hemlock flowers, *1855:*
flowers; *1863:*hemlock-flowers; *1888:*hemlock-flowers: ²³| P:Soon would come
another *1863:*There would be another ²⁵| P:past *1868:*passed ²⁶| P:hopes?
*1855:*hopes, ²⁸| P:you—"when *1855:*you—"When ³⁰| P:slopes— *1855:*
slopes, ³¹| P:be *1865:*be, ³²| P:steps <> wrong, *1855:*wrong; *1868:*step
³⁷| P:So the <> worse *1855:*worse! *1863:*So, the ³⁹| P:task-master's *1888:*

"When no moon succeeds the sun,
　　Nor can pierce the midnight's tent
Any star, the smallest one,
　　While some drops, where lightning rent,
45　Show the final storm begun—

X

"When the fire-fly hides its spot,
　　When the garden-voices fail
In the darkness thick and hot,—
　　Shall another voice avail,
50　That shape be where these are not?

XI

"Has some plague a longer lease,
　　Proffering its help uncouth?
Can't one even die in peace?
　　As one shuts one's eyes on youth,
55　Is that face the last one sees?"

XII

Oh how dark your villa was,
　　Windows fast and obdurate!
How the garden grudged me grass
　　Where I stood—the iron gate
60　Ground its teeth to let me pass!

---

taskmaster's　　44| P:lightning went, *1865*:lightning rent,　　48| P:hot,
1855:hot,—　　50| *1855*:those *1863*:these　　51| P:lease *1865*:lease,
52| P:Proffering this help *1855*:Proffering its help　　54| P:youth *1855*:youth,
56| P:Oh, how *1865*:Oh how　　57| P:obdurate— *1855*:obdurate!

MY STAR

All that I know
  Of a certain star
Is, it can throw
  (Like the angled spar)
5 Now a dart of red,
  Now a dart of blue;
Till my friends have said
  They would fain see, too,
My star that dartles the red and the blue!
10 Then it stops like a bird; like a flower, hangs furled:
  They must solace themselves with the Saturn above it.
What matter to me if their star is a world?
  Mine has opened its soul to me; therefore I love it.

MY STAR § Subsequent placement: *1863*:DL §   2| P:star, *1865*:star   4| P:
Like <> spar *1855*:(Like <> spar)   6| P:blue, *1865*:blue;   9| P:blue:
1855:blue!   10| P:bird,—like <> furled; *1863*:bird; like <> furled:

INSTANS TYRANNUS

I

Of the million or two, more or less,
I rule and possess,
One man, for some cause undefined,
Was least to my mind.

II

5   I struck him, he grovelled of course—
For, what was his force?
I pinned him to earth with my weight
And persistence of hate:
And he lay, would not moan, would not curse,
10   As his lot might be worse.

III

"Were the object less mean, would he stand
At the swing of my hand!
For obscurity helps him and blots
The hole where he squats."
15   So, I set my five wits on the stretch
To inveigle the wretch.
All in vain! Gold and jewels I threw,
Still he couched there perdue;
I tempted his blood and his flesh,
20   Hid in roses my mesh,
Choicest cates and the flagon's best spilth:
Still he kept to his filth.

INSTANS TYRANNUS § Subsequent placement: *1863*:DR §   3| P:man for < >
undefined *1855*:man, for < > undefined,   6| P:For what *1855*:For, what
8| P:hate— *1863*:hate: 10| P:As if lots might *1863*:As his lot might
15| P:So I *1865*:So, I   17| P:vain! gold *1868*:vain! Gold   18| P:perdue—
1855:perdue. *1865*:perdue;   21| P:spilth— *1863*:spilth: 22| P:filth! *1868:*

IV

Had he kith now or kin, were access
To his heart, did I press:
25   Just a son or a mother to seize!
No such booty as these.
Were it simply a friend to pursue
'Mid my million or two,
Who could pay me in person or pelf
30   What he owes me himself!
No: I could not but smile through my chafe:
For the fellow lay safe
As his mates do, the midge and the nit,
—Through minuteness, to wit.

V

35   Then a humour more great took its place
At the thought of his face,
The droop, the low cares of the mouth,
The trouble uncouth
'Twixt the brows, all that air one is fain
40   To put out of its pain.
And, "no!" I admonished myself,
"Is one mocked by an elf,
Is one baffled by toad or by rat?
The gravamen's in that!
45   How the lion, who crouches to suit
His back to my foot,
Would admire that I stand in debate!
But the small turns the great
If it vexes you,—that is the thing!

---

filth.   23| P:kin, some access 1855:kin, were access   24| P:heart, if I press—
1863:heart, did I 1888:press: 25| P:But a < > seize— 1855:Just a 1863:seize!
26| P:these! 1868:these.   30| P:himself. 1868:himself!   31| P:No! I < >
chafe— 1863:chafe: 1868:No: I   35| P:humor 1863:humour   39| P:'Twixt
1888:Twixt § emended to § 'Twixt § see Editorial Notes §   40| P:pain— 1865:pain.
41| P:And, no, I 1863:And, "no!" I   42| P:Is once mocked 1855:"Is one mocked
43| P:rat,— 1855:rat?   45| P:lion who 1855:lion, who   46| P:foot 1855:
foot,   48| P:the Small is the Great 1863:the Small turns the 1868:the small < >

50   Toad or rat vex the king?

Though I waste half my realm to unearth
Toad or rat, 'tis well worth!"

VI

So, I soberly laid my last plan
To extinguish the man.
55   Round his creep-hole, with never a break
Ran my fires for his sake;
Over-head, did my thunder combine
With my underground mine:
Till I looked from my labour content
60   To enjoy the event.

VII

When sudden . . . how think ye, the end?
Did I say "without friend"?
Say rather, from marge to blue marge
The whole sky grew his targe
65   With the sun's self for visible boss,
While an Arm ran across
Which the earth heaved beneath like a breast
Where the wretch was safe prest!
Do you see? Just my vengeance complete,
70   The man sprang to his feet,
Stood erect, caught at God's skirts, and prayed!
—So, *I* was afraid!

---

the great   ⁵⁰| P:the King? *1868:*the king?   ⁵²| P:worth! *1855:*worth!"
⁵³| P:So I *1863:*So, I   ⁵⁵| P:creep-hole,—with *1863:*creep-hole, with   ⁵⁷| P:
thunders *1863:*thunder   ⁵⁸| P:under-ground mine *1855:*mine: *1888:*underground
⁵⁹| P:labor *1868:*labour   ⁶²| P:friend?" *1888:*friend"?   ⁶⁷| P:beneath, like
*1855:*beneath like   ⁶⁹| P:see? just *1868:*see? Just   ⁷²| P:—So, I *1855:*—So, *I*

A PRETTY WOMAN

I

That fawn-skin-dappled hair of hers,
    And the blue eye
    Dear and dewy,
And that infantine fresh air of hers!

II

5   To think men cannot take you, Sweet,
    And enfold you,
    Ay, and hold you,
And so keep you what they make you, Sweet!

III

You like us for a glance, you know—
10   For a word's sake
    Or a sword's sake,
All's the same, whate'er the chance, you know.

IV

And in turn we make you ours, we say—
    You and youth too,
15   Eyes and mouth too,
All the face composed of flowers, we say.

V

All's our own, to make the most of, Sweet—
    Sing and say for,
    Watch and pray for,
20   Keep a secret or go boast of, Sweet!

A PRETTY WOMAN § Subsequent placement: *1863:*DL §   5| *1868:*you, sweet,
*1888:*you, Sweet,   8| *1868:*you, sweet! *1888:*you, Sweet!   10| P:sake, *1865:*
sake   11| P:sword's ache, *1855:*sword's sake,   15| P:too *1855:*too,
17| *1868:*of, sweet— *1888:*of, Sweet—   20| *1855:*of, Sweet. *1863:*of, Sweet!

But for loving, why, you would not, Sweet,
          Though we prayed you,
          Paid you, brayed you
In a mortar—for you could not, Sweet!

25 So, we leave the sweet face fondly there:
          Be its beauty
          Its sole duty!
Let all hope of grace beyond, lie there!

And while the face lies quiet there,
30   Who shall wonder
          That I ponder
A conclusion? I will try it there.

As,—why must one, for the love foregone,
          Scout mere liking?
35   Thunder-striking
Earth,—the heaven, we looked above for, gone!

Why, with beauty, needs there money be,
          Love with liking?
          Crush the fly-king

1868:of, sweet! 1888:of, Sweet!   21| P:not, Sweet,— 1855:not, Sweet, 1868:not,
sweet, 1888:not, Sweet,   24| 1855:not, Sweet. 1863:not, Sweet! 1868:not,
sweet! 1888:not, Sweet!   25| P:there— 1863:there: 27| P:All its duty,
1855:Its sole duty!   30| P:Do you wonder 1855:Who shall wonder   33| P:one
for < > forgone 1855:one, for < > forgone, 1868:foregone,   34| P:Despise
liking? 1855:Scout mere liking?   35| P:Thunder—striking 1855:Thunder-striking
1868:Thunder striking 1888:Thunder-striking   36| P:Earth,—heaven 1855:
Earth,—the heaven 1863:the Heaven 1868:the heaven   37| P:Why with 1855:

⁴⁰   In his gauze, because no honey-bee?

XI

May not liking be so simple-sweet,
    If love grew there
    'Twould undo there
All that breaks the cheek to dimples sweet?

XII

⁴⁵   Is the creature too imperfect, say?
    Would you mend it
    And so end it?
Since not all addition perfects aye!

XIII

Or is it of its kind, perhaps,
⁵⁰   Just perfection—
    Whence, rejection
Of a grace not to its mind, perhaps?

---

be— *1865:*Why, with <> be,   ⁴⁰| P:honey bee? *1863:*honey-bee?   ⁴⁷| P:it,
*1855:*it?   ⁴⁸| *1889:* § punctuation at end of line decayed; emended to § aye! § see

XIV

Shall we burn up, tread that face at once
      Into tinder,
55   And so hinder
Sparks from kindling all the place at once?

XV

Or else kiss away one's soul on her?
      Your love-fancies!
      —A sick man sees
60 Truer, when his hot eyes roll on her!

XVI

Thus the craftsman thinks to grace the rose,—
      Plucks a mould-flower
      For his gold flower,
Uses fine things that efface the rose:

XVII

65 Rosy rubies make its cup more rose,
      Precious metals
      Ape the petals,—
Last, some old king locks it up, morose!

XVIII

Then how grace a rose? I know a way!
70   Leave it, rather.
      Must you gather?
Smell, kiss, wear it—at last, throw away!

Editorial Notes §   54| P:tinder *1855*:tinder,   58| P:love-fancies— *1855*: love-fancies!— *1863*:love-fancies!   59| P:A *1863*:—A   61| P:There's the craftsman <> rose, *1855*:Thus the craftsman <> rose,—   64| P:rose— *1855*: rose. *1863*:rose: 65| P:Red rubies *1855*:Rosy rubies   67| P:petals, *1855*:petals,—   69| P:How grace *1855*:Then, how grace *1865*:Then how <> way *1868*:way!   70| P:it rather! *1855*:rather. *1863*:it, rather.

247

"CHILDE ROLAND TO THE DARK TOWER CAME"

(See Edgar's song in "Lear")

I

My first thought was, he lied in every word,
That hoary cripple, with malicious eye
Askance to watch the working of his lie
On mine, and mouth scarce able to afford
5   Suppression of the glee, that pursed and scored
    Its edge, at one more victim gained thereby.

II

What else should he be set for, with his staff?
What, save to waylay with his lies, ensnare
All travellers who might find him posted there,
10   And ask the road? I guessed what skull-like laugh
Would break, what crutch 'gin write my epitaph
    For pastime in the dusty thoroughfare,

III

If at his counsel I should turn aside
Into that ominous tract which, all agree,
15   Hides the Dark Tower. Yet acquiescingly
I did turn as he pointed: neither pride
Nor hope rekindling at the end descried,
    So much as gladness that some end might be.

"CHILDE ROLAND TO THE DARK TOWER CAME" § Subsequent placement: *1863:*
DR § *Subtitle*| P:(See the Fool's Song *1855:*(See Edgar's Song ¹| P:word
*1855:*word, ³| P:the lurking of *1855:*the working of ⁵| P:glee that
*1865:*glee, that ⁶| P:edge at *1865:*edge, at ⁷| P:he bet set for, on his *1855:*he
be set for, with his ⁹| P:travellers that might *1865:*travellers who might
¹¹| P:break, whose crutch *1855:*break, what crutch ¹²| P:thoroughfare— *1855:*
thoroughfare, ¹³| P:council *1855:*counsel ¹⁵| P:the Dark Tower; yet
*1855:*the Dark Tower. Yet ¹⁶| *1855:*pointed; neither *1868:*pointed: neither
¹⁸| P:end should be. *1863:*end might be. *1888:*be DC, BrU:be. *1889:*be.

For, what with my whole world-wide wandering,
²⁰   What with my search drawn out thro' years, my hope
    Dwindled into a ghost not fit to cope
With that obstreperous joy success would bring,—
I hardly tried now to rebuke the spring
    My heart made, finding failure in its scope.

V

²⁵ As when a sick man very near to death
    Seems dead indeed, and feels begin and end
    The tears and takes the farewell of each friend,
And hears one bid the other go, draw breath
Freelier outside, ("since all is o'er," he saith,
³⁰   "And the blow fallen no grieving can amend;")

VI

While some discuss if near the other graves
    Be room enough for this, and when a day
    Suits best for carrying the corpse away,
With care about the banners, scarves and staves:
³⁵ And still the man hears all, and only craves
    He may not shame such tender love and stay.

VII

Thus, I had so long suffered in this quest,
    Heard failure prophesied so oft, been writ
    So many times among "The Band"—to wit,
⁴⁰ The knights who to the Dark Tower's search addressed

---

²³| P: now, to *1855*:now to ²⁵| P:death, *1855*:death ²⁶| P:indeed; and feels
1855:indeed, and feels ²⁹| P:outside, "since <> o'er" he *1855*:outside, ("since
<> o'er," he ³⁰| P:fall'n <> amend"— *1855*:amend") *1863*:fallen <> amend;")
³¹| P:graves, *1855*:graves ³³| P:away; *1855*:away, ³⁴| *1855*:staves,—
1868:staves: ³⁵| P:all and *1855*:all, and ⁴⁰| P:Of those who *1855*:The

Their steps—that just to fail as they, seemed best,
　　And all the doubt was now—should I be fit?

VIII

So, quiet as despair, I turned from him,
　　That hateful cripple, out of his highway
45　　　Into the path he pointed. All the day
Had been a dreary one at best, and dim
Was settling to its close, yet shot one grim
　　Red leer to see the plain catch its estray.

IX

For mark! no sooner was I fairly found
50　　Pledged to the plain, after a pace or two,
　　Than, pausing to throw backward a last view
O'er the safe road, 'twas gone; grey plain all round:
Nothing but plain to the horizon's bound.
　　I might go on; nought else remained to do.

X

55　So, on I went. I think I never saw
　　Such starved ignoble nature; nothing throve:
　　For flowers—as well expect a cedar grove!
But cockle, spurge, according to their law
Might propagate their kind, with none to awe,
60　　You'd think; a burr had been a treasure-trove.

---

knights who　　42| P:fit. *1865:*fit?　　45| P:;pointed: all　*1855:*pointed. All
51| P:Than pausing　*1863:*Than, pausing　　52| P:To the <> gone! grey <>
round;　*1855:*round!　*1863:*gone; grey <> round:　*1865:*O'er the　　54| P:on, nought
*1855:*on; nought　　55| P:So on　*1863:*So, on　　60| P:think: a burr　*1863:*

XI

No! penury, inertness and grimace,
    In some strange sort, were the land's portion. "See
    Or shut your eyes," said Nature peevishly,
"It nothing skills: I cannot help my case:
65   'Tis the Last Judgment's fire must cure this place,
    Calcine its clods and set my prisoners free."

XII

If there pushed any ragged thistle-stalk
    Above its mates, the head was chopped; the bents
    Were jealous else. What made those holes and rents
70   In the dock's harsh swarth leaves, bruised as to baulk
All hope of greenness? 'tis a brute must walk
    Pashing their life out, with a brute's intents.

XIII

As for the grass, it grew as scant as hair
    In leprosy; thin dry blades pricked the mud
75   Which underneath looked kneaded up with blood.
One stiff blind horse, his every bone a-stare,
Stood stupefied, however he came there:
    Thrust out past service from the devil's stud!

XIV

Alive? he might be dead for aught I know,
80   With that red gaunt and colloped neck a-strain,
    And shut eyes underneath the rusty mane;

---

think; a burr   61| P:inertness, and *1863*:inertness and   62| P:portion. See *1855*:portion. "See   63| P:eyes—said <> peevishly— *1855*:eyes"—said *1863*:eyes," said <> peevishly,   64| P:It *1855*:"It   65| P:The Judgment's fire alone can cure *1863*:'Tis the Last Judgment's fire must cure   66| P:free. *1855*:free." 68| P:chopped—the *1865*:chopped; the   69| P:else! what *1855*:else. What 70| P:leaves?—bruised *1855*:leaves—bruised *1865*:leaves, bruised   71| P: greenness—'tis *1855*:greenness? 'tis   74| P:leprosy—thin *1863*:leprosy; thin 77| P:stupified <> there— *1863*:there: *1868*:stupefied   79| P:for all I know *1855*:know, *1863*:for aught I   80| *1863*:red, gaunt *1868*:red gaunt   81| P:

Seldom went such grotesqueness with such woe;
    I never saw a brute I hated so;
        He must be wicked to deserve such pain.

XV

85   I shut my eyes and turned them on my heart.
    As a man calls for wine before he fights,
        I asked one draught of earlier, happier sights,
    Ere fitly I could hope to play my part.
    Think first, fight afterwards—the soldier's art:
90   One taste of the old time sets all to rights.

XVI

Not it! I fancied Cuthbert's reddening face
    Beneath its garniture of curly gold,
    Dear fellow, till I almost felt him fold
An arm in mine to fix me to the place,
95   That way he used. Alas, one night's disgrace!
    Out went my heart's new fire and left it cold.

XVII

Giles then, the soul of honour—there he stands
    Frank as ten years ago when knighted first.
    What honest man should dare (he said) he durst.
100   Good—but the scene shifts—faugh! what hangman-hands
Pin to his breast a parchment? His own bands
    Read it. Poor traitor, spit upon and curst!

XVIII

Better this present than a past like that;
    Back therefore to my darkening path again!

---

mane— *1855*:mane. *1863*:mane;   ⁸²| P:woe— *1855*:woe: *1863*:woe;
⁸³| P:so— *1863*:so;   ⁸⁵| P:heart; *1855*:heart.   ⁸⁷| P:sights *1863*:sights,
⁸⁸| P:part— *1855*:part.   ⁹⁰| P: times< >rights! *1863*:time *1865*:rights.
⁹⁵| P:used. Alas! one *1863*:used. Alas, one   ⁹⁷| P:Giles, then *1865*:Giles then
⁹⁸| P:first: *1855*:first.   ⁹⁹| P:men *1888*:man   ¹⁰⁰| P:hangman's hands
1868:hangman *1888*:hangman-hands   ¹⁰¹| P:parchment? his *1868*:parchment?
His   ¹⁰²| P:it: poor *1855*:it. Poor   ¹⁰³| P:that— *1863*:this Present < >
a Past < > that; *1868*:this present < > a past   ¹⁰⁴| P:again. *1868*:again!

¹⁰⁵ No sound, no sight as far as eye could strain.
　　Will the night send a howlet or a bat?
　　I asked: when something on the dismal flat
　　　　Came to arrest my thoughts and change their train.

XIX

　　A sudden little river crossed my path
¹¹⁰　　As unexpected as a serpent comes.
　　No sluggish tide congenial to the glooms;
　　This, as it frothed by, might have been a bath
　　For the fiend's glowing hoof—to see the wrath
　　　　Of its black eddy bespate with flakes and spumes.

XX

¹¹⁵ So petty yet so spiteful! All along,
　　Low scrubby alders kneeled down over it;
　　Drenched willows flung them headlong in a fit
　　Of mute despair, a suicidal throng:
　　The river which had done them all the wrong,
¹²⁰　　Whate'er that was, rolled by, deterred no whit.

XXI

　　Which, while I forded,—good saints, how I feared
　　To set my foot upon a dead man's cheek,
　　Each step, or feel the spear I thrust to seek
　　For hollows, tangled in his hair or beard!
¹²⁵ —It may have been a water-rat I speared,
　　But, ugh! it sounded like a baby's shriek.

XXII

　　Glad was I when I reached the other bank.
　　Now for a better country. Vain presage!
　　Who were the strugglers, what war did they wage,

---

¹¹¹| P:glooms— *1865*:glooms;　　¹¹³| P:hoof, to *1855*:hoof—to　　¹¹⁵| P:
spiteful! all along *1855*:along, *1868*:spiteful! All　　¹¹⁶| P:it, *1855*:it;
¹²⁰| P:whit— *1855*:whit.　　¹²¹| P:Which while <> good Saints *1855*:Which, while
<> good saints　　¹²⁴| P:beard. *1855*:beard!　　¹²⁷| P:bank— *1855*:bank.
¹²⁸| P:country! vain *1855*:country. Vain　　¹²⁹| *1855*:wage *1888*:wage,

253

¹³⁰ Whose savage trample thus could pad the dank
  Soil to a plash? Toads in a poisoned tank,
    Or wild cats in a red-hot iron cage—

XXIII

The fight must so have seemed in that fell cirque.
  What penned them there, with all the plain to choose?
¹³⁵   No foot-print leading to that horrid mews,
None out of it. Mad brewage set to work
Their brains, no doubt, like galley-slaves the Turk
    Pits for his pastime, Christians against Jews.

XXIV

And more than that—a furlong on—why, there!
¹⁴⁰   What bad use was that engine for, that wheel,
  Or brake, not wheel—that harrow fit to reel
Men's bodies out like silk? with all the air
Of Tophet's tool, on earth left unaware,
    Or brought to sharpen its rusty teeth of steel.

XXV

¹⁴⁵ Then came a bit of stubbed ground, once a wood,
  Next a marsh, it would seem, and now mere earth
  Desperate and done with; (so a fool finds mirth,
Makes a thing and then mars it, till his mood
Changes and off he goes!) within a rood—
¹⁵⁰   Bog, clay and rubble, sand and stark black dearth.

XXVI

Now blotches rankling, coloured gay and grim,
  Now patches where some leanness of the soil's
  Broke into moss or substances like boils;
Then came some palsied oak, a cleft in him
¹⁵⁵ Like a distorted mouth that splits its rim
    Gaping at death, and dies while it recoils.

---

^{131|} P:plash? toads *1868:*plash? Toads ^{132|} P:red hot *1855:*red-hot ^{134|} P:
What kept them there with *1855:*there, with *1863:*What penned them ^{136|} P:it:
mad *1863:*it. Mad ^{137|} P:galley slaves *1855:*galley-slaves ^{139|} P:why there!
*1855:*why, there! ^{141|} P:wheel, that *1855:*wheel—that ^{147|} P:with; so
*1855:*with; (so ^{149|} P:goes: within a rood *1855:*goes!) within *1863:*rood—
^{150|} P:rubble stones and *1855:*rubble, sand and ^{156|} P:death and *1855:*death, and

XXVII

And just as far as ever from the end!
    Nought in the distance but the evening, nought
    To point my footstep further! At the thought,
160   A great black bird, Apollyon's bosom-friend,
Sailed past, nor beat his wide wing dragon-penned
    That brushed my cap—perchance the guide I sought.

XXVIII

For, looking up, aware I somehow grew,
    'Spite of the dusk, the plain had given place
165   All round to mountains—with such name to grace
Mere ugly heights and heaps now stolen in view.
    How thus they had surprised me,—solve it, you!
    How to get from them was no clearer case.

XXIX

Yet half I seemed to recognize some trick
170   Of mischief happened to me, God knows when—
    In a bad dream perhaps. Here ended, then,
Progress this way. When, in the very nick
Of giving up, one time more, came a click
    As when a trap shuts—you're inside the den!

XXX

175   Burningly it came on me all at once,
    This was the place! those two hills on the right,
    Crouched like two bulls locked horn in horn in fight;
While to the left, a tall scalped mountain . . . Dunce,
Dotard, a-dozing at the very nonce,
180   After a life spent training for the sight!

157| P:end, *1855*:end!   159| P:further! at the thought *1855*:further! At the thought,
160| P:bosom friend, *1855*:bosom-friend,   161| P:dragon-penned, *1855*:dragon-
penned   163| P:For looking up aware *1855*:up, aware *1863*:For, looking
164| P:Spite *1855*:'Spite   166| P:view: *1855*:stol'n in view. *1863*:stolen
167| P:me, tell who knew, *1855*:me,—solve it, you!   168| P:get through them was
no plainer case. *1855*:get from them *1863*:no clearer case.   169| P:recognise
1888:recognize   175| P:once *1855*:once,   176| P:right *1863*:right,
177| P:fight— *1863*:fight;   178| P:mountain . . . dunce, *1855*:mountain . . .
Dunce,   179| P:Fool, to be caught blind at *1855*:be dozing at *1865*:Dotard, a-dozing
at   180| P:With my life spent in training *1855*:After a life spent training

What in the midst lay but the Tower itself?
    The round squat turret, blind as the fool's heart,
    Built of brown stone, without a counterpart
In the whole world. The tempest's mocking elf
185   Points to the shipman thus the unseen shelf
    He strikes on, only when the timbers start.

Not see? because of night perhaps?—why, day
    Came back again for that! before it left,
    The dying sunset kindled through a cleft:
190   The hills, like giants at a hunting, lay,
    Chin upon hand, to see the game at bay,—
    "Now stab and end the creature—to the heft!"

Not hear? when noise was everywhere! it tolled
    Increasing like a bell. Names in my ears
195   Of all the lost adventurers my peers,—
    How such a one was strong, and such was bold,
And such was fortunate, yet each of old
    Lost, lost! one moment knelled the woe of years.

There they stood, ranged along the hill-sides, met
200   To view the last of me, a living frame
    For one more picture! in a sheet of flame
I saw them and I knew them all. And yet
Dauntless the slug-horn to my lips I set,
    And blew. *"Childe Roland to the Dark Tower came."*

187| P:perhaps—why *1855*:perhaps?—Why *1865*:perhaps?—why   188| P:that,
before *1855*:that! before   190| P:hills like <> lay *1855*:hills, like <> lay—
1863:lay,   191| P:—Chin <> bay *1855*:Chin <> bay,—   192| P:heft!"
1888:heft! § emended to § heft!" § see Editorial Notes §   193| P:everywhere: it
1855:everywhere? it *1863*:everywhere! it   194| P:ears, *1888*:ears
195| P:peers, *1855*:peers,—   196| P:such an one was strong and <> bold
1855:such a one was strong, and <> bold,   199| P:stood ranged <> hill-sides—met
1855:stood, ranged *1863*:hill-sides, met   201| P:picture: in *1855*:picture! in
203| P:slug-horn, to <> set *1855*:slug-horn to *1863*:set,   204| P:*the dark 1855:*
the Dark 1865:blew *"Childe 1888*:blew. *"Childe*

RESPECTABILITY

I

Dear, had the world in its caprice
    Deigned to proclaim "I know you both,
    Have recognized your plighted troth,
Am sponsor for you: live in peace!"—
5 How many precious months and years
    Of youth had passed, that speed so fast,
    Before we found it out at last,
The world, and what it fears?

II

How much of priceless life were spent
10   With men that every virtue decks,
    And women models of their sex,
Society's true ornament,—
Ere we dared wander, nights like this,
    Thro' wind and rain, and watch the Seine,
15   And feel the Boulevart break again
To warmth and light and bliss?

III

I know! the world proscribes not love;
    Allows my finger to caress
    Your lips' contour and downiness,
20 Provided it supply a glove.
The world's good word!—the Institute!
    Guizot receives Montalembert!
    Eh? Down the court three lampions flare:
Put forward your best foot!

RESPECTABILITY § Subsequent placement: *1863*:DL §   ³| P:recognised
1863:recognized   ⁴| P:you—live in peace!" *1855*:peace!"— *1863*:you: live
¹⁰| P:deck *1855*:decks,   ¹²| P:ornament, *1855*:ornament,—   ¹⁵| P:And
bid the *1855*:And feel the   ¹⁷| P:love, *1855*:love;   ¹⁹| P:lip's contour, and
downiness *1855*:contour and downiness, *1868*:lips'   ²¹| P:And then, rewards—
the *1855*:The world's good word!—the   ²³| P:Eh? down < > flare— *1865:*
flare: *1868*:Eh? Down

257

A LIGHT WOMAN

I

So far as our story approaches the end,
　　Which do you pity the most of us three?—
My friend, or the mistress of my friend
　　With her wanton eyes, or me?

II

5　My friend was already too good to lose,
　　And seemed in the way of improvement yet,
When she crossed his path with her hunting-noose
　　And over him drew her net.

III

When I saw him tangled in her toils,
10　　A shame, said I, if she adds just him
To her nine-and-ninety other spoils,
　　The hundredth for a whim!

IV

And before my friend be wholly hers,
　　How easy to prove to him, I said,
15　An eagle's the game her pride prefers,
　　Though she snaps at a wren instead!

V

So, I gave her eyes my own eyes to take,
　　My hand sought hers as in earnest need,
And round she turned for my noble sake,
20　　And gave me herself indeed.

A LIGHT WOMAN § Subsequent placement: *1863:*DR §　　2| P:three?
*1855:*three?—　　5| P:lose *1855:*lose,　　11| P:To the nine-and-ninety *1855:*
To her nine-and-ninety　　12| P:Her hundreth, for　*1855:*The hundredth *1865:*
hundredth for　　14| P:to show the fool (I said)　*1855:*to prove to him, I said,
15| P:prefers *1855:*prefers,　　16| P:at the wren *1865:*at a wren　　17| P:So I<>

The eagle am I, with my fame in the world,
  The wren is he, with his maiden face.
—You look away and your lip is curled?
  Patience, a moment's space!

25 For see, my friend goes shaking and white;
  He eyes me as the basilisk:
I have turned, it appears, his day to night,
  Eclipsing his sun's disk.

And I did it, he thinks, as a very thief:
30 "Though I love her—that, he comprehends—
One should master one's passions, (love, in chief)
  And be loyal to one's friends!"

And she,—she lies in my hand as tame
  As a pear late basking over a wall;
35 Just a touch to try and off it came;
  'Tis mine,—can I let it fall?

With no mind to eat it, that's the worst!
  Were it thrown in the road, would the case assist?
'Twas quenching a dozen blue-flies' thirst
40 When I gave its stalk a twist.

---

take *1855*:take, *1863*:So, I   22| P:face: *1855*:face.   23| P:You *1855*:—You
24| P:But, patience *1855*:Patience   25| P:see—my < > white, *1855*:white;
1865:see, my   28| *1855*:disc. *1863*:disk.   30| P:her—and that he
1855:her—that *1868*:that, he   31| P:passions, love, in chief, *1855*:passions,
(love, in chief)   34| P:pear that hung basking *1855*:pear hung basking *1863*:
pear late basking   36| P:mine, can *1855*:mine,—can   38| P:road would

And I,—what I seem to my friend, you see:
What I soon shall seem to his love, you guess:
What I seem to myself, do you ask of me?
No hero, I confess.

XII

45 'Tis an awkward thing to play with souls,
And matter enough to save one's own:
Yet think of my friend, and the burning coals
He played with for bits of stone!

XIII

One likes to show the truth for the truth;
50 That the woman was light is very true:
But suppose she says,—Never mind that youth!
What wrong have I done to you?

XIV

Well, any how, here the story stays,
So far at least as I understand;
55 And, Robert Browning, you writer of plays,
Here's a subject made to your hand!

1855:road, would   41| P:see— 1865:see; 1888:see: 42| P:guess;
1855:guess. 1865:guess: 46| 1855:own. 1865:own: 47| P:friend and 1855:
friend, and   49| P:Then one likes 1855:One likes   51| P:says,—never <>
youth— 1863:says,—Never 1865:youth!   54| P:understand: 1855:understand;
55| P:So, Robert 1855:And, Robert

THE STATUE AND THE BUST

There's a palace in Florence, the world knows well,
And a statue watches it from the square,
And this story of both do our townsmen tell.

Ages ago, a lady there,
₅ At the farthest window facing the East
Asked, "Who rides by with the royal air?"

The bridesmaids' prattle around her ceased;
She leaned forth, one on either hand;
They saw how the blush of the bride increased—

₁₀ They felt by its beats her heart expand—
As one at each ear and both in a breath
Whispered, "The Great-Duke Ferdinand."

That self-same instant, underneath,
The Duke rode past in his idle way,
₁₅ Empty and fine like a swordless sheath.

Gay he rode, with a friend as gay,
Till he threw his head back—"Who is she?"
—"A bride the Riccardi brings home to-day."

Hair in heaps lay heavily
₂₀ Over a pale brow spirit-pure—
Carved like the heart of the coal-black tree,

Crisped like a war-steed's encolure—
And vainly sought to dissemble her eyes
Of the blackest black our eyes endure.

THE STATUE AND THE BUST § Subsequent placement: *1863*:DR §   2| P:a
Statue <> the Square; *1855*:a statue <> the square,   3| P:do the townsmen
1863:do our townsmen   4| P:ago a *1855*:ago, a   5| *1855*:the east
1863:the East   7| P:brides-maids' *1865*:bridesmaids'   8| P:forth one
1855:forth, one   13| P:selfsame <> underneath *1855*:underneath,
1888:self-same   16| P:rode with *1855*:rode, with   17| P:back "Who *1855*:
back—"Who   18| P:—"A Bride *1868*:—"A bride   19| P:laid
1863:lay   22| P:warsteed's *1855*:war-steed's   23| P:It vainly *1855*:Which

261

²⁵ And lo, a blade for a knight's emprise
Filled the fine empty sheath of a man,—
The Duke grew straightway brave and wise.

He looked at her, as a lover can;
She looked at him, as one who awakes:
³⁰ The past was a sleep, and her life began.

Now, love so ordered for both their sakes,
A feast was held that selfsame night
In the pile which the mighty shadow makes.

(For Via Larga is three-parts light,
³⁵ But the palace overshadows one,
Because of a crime which may God requite!

To Florence and God the wrong was done,
Through the first republic's murder there
By Cosimo and his cursed son.)

⁴⁰ The Duke (with the statue's face in the square)
Turned in the midst of his multitude
At the bright approach of the bridal pair.

Face to face the lovers stood
A single minute and no more,
⁴⁵ While the bridegroom bent as a man subdued—

vainly *1863:*And vainly   ²⁶| P:man, *1855:*man,—   ²⁸| P:can, *1855:*can;
²⁹| P:him as <> awakes, *1855:*him, as <> awakes,— *1865:*awakes: ³⁰| P:
sleep and *1855:*sleep, and *1863:*The Past *1868:*The past   ³¹| P:As love
<> sakes *1855:*sakes, *1863:*Now, love   ³³| P:pile that the *1855:*pile which the
³⁴| P:light *1855:*light,   ³⁵| P:the Palace *1868:*the palace   ³⁷| P:done
*1855:*done,   ⁴⁰| P:The Duke, with the Statue's <> the Square *1855:*The Duke
(with the statue's <> the square)   ⁴¹| P:multitude, *1855:*multitude

Bowed till his bonnet brushed the floor—
For the Duke on the lady a kiss conferred,
As the courtly custom was of yore.

In a minute can lovers exchange a word?
50   If a word did pass, which I do not think,
Only one out of the thousand heard.

That was the bridegroom. At day's brink
He and his bride were alone at last
In a bedchamber by a taper's blink.

55   Calmly he said that her lot was cast,
That the door she had passed was shut on her
Till the final catafalk repassed.

The world meanwhile, its noise and stir,
Through a certain window facing the East,
60   She could watch like a convent's chronicler.

Since passing the door might lead to a feast,
And a feast might lead to so much beside,
He, of many evils, chose the least.

"Freely I choose too," said the bride—
65   "Your window and its world suffice,"
Replied the tongue, while the heart replied—

"If I spend the night with that devil twice,
May his window serve as my loop of hell
Whence a damned soul looks on paradise!

47| P:conferred *1855*:conferred,   51| P:thousands *1855*:thousand
52| P:the Bridegroom *1855*:the bridegroom   53| P:his Bride *1855*:his bride
54| P:bed-chamber *1888*:bedchamber   55| P:cast *1855*:cast,   56| P:And the
< > passed through, shut *1855*:That the < > passed was shut   57| P:catafalque
1855:catafalk   59| P:the East *1855*:the east *1863*:the East DC,BrU:the East,
1889:the East,   60| P:She might watch *1863*:She could watch   61| P:a
Feast *1855*:a feast,   62| P:a Feast *1855*:a feast   64| P:the Bride—
1855:the bride—   65| P:suffice"— *1855*:suffice." *1863*:suffice,"   66| P:So
spoke the tongue; while *1855*:So replied the tongue, while *1863*:Replied
68| P:of Hell *1855*:of hell   69| P:on Paradise! *1868*:on paradise!

<blockquote>
⁷⁰   "I fly to the Duke who loves me well,
        Sit by his side and laugh at sorrow
        Ere I count another ave-bell.

        " 'Tis only the coat of a page to borrow,
        And tie my hair in a horse-boy's trim,
⁷⁵   And I save my soul—but not to-morrow"—

        (She checked herself and her eye grew dim)
        "My father tarries to bless my state:
        I must keep it one day more for him.

        "Is one day more so long to wait?
⁸⁰   Moreover the Duke rides past, I know;
        We shall see each other, sure as fate."

        She turned on her side and slept. Just so!
        So we resolve on a thing and sleep:
        So did the lady, ages ago.

⁸⁵   That night the Duke said, "Dear or cheap
        As the cost of this cup of bliss may prove
        To body or soul, I will drain it deep."

        And on the morrow, bold with love,
        He beckoned the bridegroom (close on call,
⁹⁰   As his duty bade, by the Duke's alcove)

        And smiled " 'Twas a very funeral,
        Your lady will think, this feast of ours,—
        A shame to efface, whate'er befall!
</blockquote>

---

⁷²| P:another Ave-bell. *1855*:another ave-bell.   ⁷⁶| P:dim)— *1865*:dim)
⁸⁰| P:know— *1863*:know;   ⁸³| P:sleep; *1855*:sleep. *1863*:sleep: ⁸⁴| P:the
Lady ages *1855*:the lady, ages   ⁸⁵| P:said "Dear *1855*:said, "Dear
⁸⁷| P:soul, I drain *1855*:soul, I will drain   ⁹⁰| P:bade by *1855*:bade, by
⁹¹| P:funeral— *1855*:funeral *1863*:funeral,   ⁹²| P:think this <> ours,
1855:think, this <> ours,—   ⁹³| P:efface whate'er *1855*:efface, whate'er

"What if we break from the Arno bowers,
And try if Petraja, cool and green,
Cure last night's fault with this morning's flowers?"

The bridegroom, not a thought to be seen
On his steady brow and quiet mouth,
Said, "Too much favour for me so mean!

"But, alas! my lady leaves the South;
Each wind that comes from the Apennine
Is a menace to her tender youth:

"Nor a way exists, the wise opine,
If she quits her palace twice this year,
To avert the flower of life's decline."

Quoth the Duke, "A sage and a kindly fear.
Moreover Petraja is cold this spring:
Be our feast to-night as usual here!"

And then to himself—"Which night shall bring
Thy bride to her lover's embraces, fool—
Or I am the fool, and thou art the king!

"Yet my passion must wait a night, nor cool—
For to-night the Envoy arrives from France
Whose heart I unlock with thyself, my tool.

"I need thee still and might miss perchance.
To-day is not wholly lost, beside,
With its hope of my lady's countenance:

95

100

105

110

115

94| P:bowers 1855:bowers,   95| P:And let Petraja 1863:And try if Petraja
99| P:Said "Too 1855:Said, "Too   100| P:"Alas! my 1855:the south. 1863:"But,
alas! my <> the South;   102| P:a canker to her rose of youth. 1855:a
menace to her tender youth. 1863:youth: 103| P:"No way 1863:"Nor a way
107| P:spring— 1863:spring: 111| P:art his king! 1863:art the
king!   113| P:from France, 1888:from France   117| P:countenance—

"For I ride—what should I do but ride?
And passing her palace, if I list,
120 May glance at its window—well betide!"

So said, so done: nor the lady missed
One ray that broke from the ardent brow,
Nor a curl of the lips where the spirit kissed.

Be sure that each renewed the vow,
125 No morrow's sun should arise and set
And leave them then as it left them now.

But next day passed, and next day yet,
With still fresh cause to wait one day more
Ere each leaped over the parapet.

130 And still, as love's brief morning wore,
With a gentle start, half smile, half sigh,
They found love not as it seemed before.

They thought it would work infallibly,
But not in despite of heaven and earth:
135 The rose would blow when the storm passed by.

Meantime they could profit in winter's dearth
By store of fruits that supplant the rose:
The world and its ways have a certain worth:

And to press a point while these oppose
140 Were simple policy; better wait:
We lose no friends and we gain no foes.

*1863:*countenance: ¹¹⁸| P:but ride! *1855:*but ride? ¹¹⁹| P:list *1855:*list,
¹²²| P:brow *1855:*brow, ¹²⁷| P:passed and <> yet *1855:*passed, and <> yet,
¹²⁸| P:one more *1863:*one day more ¹³⁰| P:They found, as *1855:*And
still, as ¹³²| P:Their love not all it had been before. *1855:*They found love not as it
seemed before. ¹³³| P:infallibly *1855:*infallibly, ¹³⁴| P:of Heaven and earth—
*1855:*of heaven *1865:*earth: ¹³⁵| P:by— *1855:*by. ¹³⁶| P:could
gather in *1855:*could profit in ¹³⁷| P:Winter's fruits <> rose, *1855:*By winter's
fruits <> rose: *1865:*By store of fruits ¹³⁸| P:worth— *1855:*worth! *1865:*worth:
¹⁴⁰| P:Were a simple policy—best wait *1855:*wait, *1863:*policy; better wait:
*1865:*Were simple ¹⁴¹| P:And lose <> and gain *1863:*We lose <> and we

Meantime, worse fates than a lover's fate,
Who daily may ride and pass and look
Where his lady watches behind the grate!

145   And she—she watched the square like a book
Holding one picture and only one,
Which daily to find she undertook:

When the picture was reached the book was done,
And she turned from the picture at night to scheme
150   Of tearing it out for herself next sun.

So weeks grew months, years; gleam by gleam
The glory dropped from their youth and love,
And both perceived they had dreamed a dream;

Which hovered as dreams do, still above:
155   But who can take a dream for a truth?
Oh, hide our eyes from the next remove!

One day as the lady saw her youth
Depart, and the silver thread that streaked
Her hair, and, worn by the serpent's tooth,

160   The brow so puckered, the chin so peaked,—
And wondered who the woman was,
Hollow-eyed and haggard-cheeked,

---

gain   142| P:Meanwhile, worse <> fate 1855:fate, 1863:Meantime,
worse   143| P:and lean and 1863:and pass and   144| P:grate. 1855:grate!
146| P:That holds one <> one 1855:Holding one <> one,   147| P:undertook.
1863:undertook: 148| P:picture came the <> done 1855:picture was reached the
<> done,   149| P:from it all night 1863:from the picture at night
151| P:But weeks <> months, and gleam by 1855:Weeks <> months, years—
gleam by 1863:So weeks 1865:years; gleam by   152| P:from youth and love
1855:love, 1863:from their youth   153| P:dream. 1855:dream,
1863:dream;   154| P:It hovered <> do still above, 1855:Which hovered <> do,
still above,— 1865:above: 155| P:for truth? 1863:for a truth?   157| P:the
Lady saw 1855:the lady saw   158| P:Depart and 1855:Depart, and
159| P:and, traced by 1855:and, worn by   160| P:peaked, 1855:peaked,—
162| P:The hollow-eyed and the haggard-cheeked, 1855:So hollow-eyed and

267

Fronting her silent in the glass—
"Summon here," she suddenly said,
165   "Before the rest of my old self pass,

"Him, the Carver, a hand to aid,
Who fashions the clay no love will change,
And fixes a beauty never to fade.

"Let Robbia's craft so apt and strange
170   Arrest the remains of young and fair,
And rivet them while the seasons range.

"Make me a face on the window there,
Waiting as ever, mute the while,
My love to pass below in the square!

175   "And let me think that it may beguile
Dreary days which the dead must spend
Down in their darkness under the aisle,

"To say, 'What matters it at the end?
I did no more while my heart was warm
180   Than does that image, my pale-faced friend.'

"Where is the use of the lip's red charm,
The heaven of hair, the pride of the brow,
And the blood that blues the inside arm—

"Unless we turn, as the soul knows how,
185   The earthly gift to an end divine?
A lady of clay is as good, I trow."

---

haggard-cheeked, *1863:*Hollow-eyed and   ¹⁶⁴| P:"Call him here
1855:"Summon here   ¹⁶⁵| P:pass! *1855:*pass,   ¹⁶⁶| P:"Him the Carver, I call
in aid, *1855:*"Him, the Carver, a hand to aid,   ¹⁶⁷| P:Who moulds the clay our
touch would change, *1855:*clay no love will change, *1863:*Who fashions the
¹⁶⁹| P:so true and *1855:*so apt and   ¹⁷⁰| P:fair *1855:*fair,   ¹⁷²| P:there
*1863:*there,   ¹⁷⁴| P:square; *1855:*square!   ¹⁷⁵| P:Let me <> beguile,
*1855:*And let me <> beguile   ¹⁷⁷| P:aisle— *1863:*aisle,   ¹⁷⁸| P:say,
what matters at *1855:*say,—'What matters *1863:*say, 'What matters it at
¹⁷⁹| *1855:*warm, *1863:*warm   ¹⁸⁰| P:friend. *1855:*friend.'   ¹⁸⁴| P:Unless
<> how *1855:*how, *1863:*"Unless *1888:*Unless § emended to § "Unless § see Editorial

But long ere Robbia's cornice, fine,
With flowers and fruits which leaves enlace,
Was set where now is the empty shrine—

190 (And, leaning out of a bright blue space,
As a ghost might lean from a chink of sky,
The passionate pale lady's face—

Eyeing ever, with earnest eye
And quick-turned neck at its breathless stretch,
195 Some one who ever is passing by—)

The Duke had sighed like the simplest wretch
In Florence, "Youth—my dream escapes!
Will its record stay?" And he bade them fetch

Some subtle moulder of brazen shapes—
200 "Can the soul, the will, die out of a man
Ere his body find the grave that gapes?

"John of Douay shall effect my plan,
Set me on horseback here aloft,
Alive, as the crafty sculptor can,

205 "In the very square I have crossed so oft:
That men may admire, when future suns
Shall touch the eyes to a purpose soft,

Notes §   187| P:fine 1888:fine,   189| P:set, where 1855:set where
190| P:And 1855:(With, leaning 1863:(And, leaning   191| P:might from
1863:might lean from   193| P:Eying ever with 1855:Eyeing 1865:ever, with
194| P:quick turned <> stretch 1855:quick-turned <> stretch,   195| P:ever passes
by— 1855:by—) 1863:ever is passing by—)   196| P:The Duke sighed
1863:The Duke had sighed   197| P:In Florence "And so my 1855:In Florence,
"So, my 1863:In Florence, "Youth—my   198| P:stay?" and 1855:stay?"
And   199| P:Some subte fashioner of shapes— 1855:subtle 1863:subtle moulder
of brazen shapes—   200| P:will die 1855:will, die   202| P:shall work my
1863:shall effect my   203| P:Make me 1855:Mould me 1863:Set me
204| P:Alive—the subtle artisan! 1855:Alive—(the <> artisan!) 1863:Alive, as the
crafty sculptor can,   205| P:square I crossed so oft 1855:cross so oft! 1863:square I
have crossed 1868:oft: 206| P:admire when other suns 1855:admire, when

"While the mouth and the brow stay brave in bronze—
Admire and say, 'When he was alive
210   How he would take his pleasure once!'

"And it shall go hard but I contrive
To listen the while, and laugh in my tomb
At idleness which aspires to strive."

———————

So! While these wait the trump of doom,
215   How do their spirits pass, I wonder,
Nights and days in the narrow room?

Still, I suppose, they sit and ponder
What a gift life was, ages ago,
Six steps out of the chapel yonder.

220   Only they see not God, I know,
Nor all that chivalry of his,
The soldier-saints who, row on row,

Burn upward each to his point of bliss—
Since, the end of life being manifest,
225   He had burned his way thro' the world to this.

I hear you reproach, "But delay was best,
For their end was a crime."—Oh, a crime will do
As well, I reply, to serve for a test,

future suns   ²⁰⁸| P:brow are brave 1863:brow stay brave   ²⁰⁹| P:alive,
1868:alive   ²¹²|P:listen meanwhile and 1863:listen the while and
1865:while, and   ²¹³| P:At the idleness 1855:At indolence which 1863:At
idleness which   ²¹³⁻¹⁴| P: § no rule § 1855: § rule added §   ²¹⁴| P:So! while
1865:So! While   ²¹⁸| P:was ages 1855:was, ages   ²²⁰| P:Surely they
see not God, I trow 1855:not God, I know 1863:Only they   ²²¹| P:And all
<>of His, 1855:Nor all 1868:of his,   ²²²| P:who row on 1855:who,
row on   ²²³| P:to a point of bliss 1855:to his point of bliss—   ²²⁴| P:For
the <>life made manifest, 1855:Since, the <>life being manifest,
²²⁵| P:They had cut their way 1855:He had cut his way 1863:had burned his
²²⁶| P:your reproach—"but Delay 1855:reproach—"But delay 1863:you
reproach, "But   ²²⁷| P:Since their <>crime!"—And a 1855:For their <>

As a virtue golden through and through,
230 Sufficient to vindicate itself
And prove its worth at a moment's view!

Must a game be played for the sake of pelf?
Where a button goes, 'twere an epigram
To offer the stamp of the very Guelph.

235 The true has no value beyond the sham:
As well the counter as coin, I submit,
When your table's a hat, and your prize a dram.

Stake your counter as boldly every whit,
Venture as warily, use the same skill,
240 Do your best, whether winning or losing it,

If you choose to play!—is my principle.
Let a man contend to the uttermost
For his life's set prize, be it what it will!

The counter our lovers staked was lost
245 As surely as if it were lawful coin:
And the sin I impute to each frustrate ghost

Is—the unlit lamp and the ungirt loin,
Though the end in sight was a vice, I say.
You of the virtue (we issue join)
250 How strive you? *De te, fabula.*

---

crime!"—Oh, a *1863:*crime."—Oh   ²²⁹| P:virtue, golden   *1855:*virtue golden
²³¹| P:view. *1863:*view!   ²³⁴| P:very Guelph—   *1855:*very Guelph.
²³⁵| P:The real has <>sham,   *1855:*The true has <> sham.   *1863:*sham:
²³⁶| P:The coin than the counter, I submit.   *1855:*As well the counter as coin, I
submit,   ²³⁷| P:prize, a dram,   *1855:*dram.   *1888:*prize a   ²³⁹| P:as truly, use
*1865:*as warily, use   ²⁴¹| P:play—is my principle,   *1855:*principle!   *1863:*play!—is my
principle.   ²⁴⁵| P:coin—   *1855:*coin: ²⁴⁶| P:sin we impute   *1855:*sin I impute
²⁴⁷| P:Was, the unlit <> loin—   *1855:*loin,   *1863:*Is, the unlit   *1888:*Is—the unlit
²⁴⁸| P:a crime, we say.   *1855:*crime, I say.   *1863:*a vice, I   ²⁴⁹| P:You with
the   *1855:*You of the virtue, (we   *1868:*virtue (we   ²⁵⁰| P:*fabula!*
1888:fabula   DC,BrU:*fabula.*   *1889:fabula.*

271

LOVE IN A LIFE

I

Room after room,
I hunt the house through
We inhabit together.
Heart, fear nothing, for, heart, thou shalt find her—
5   Next time, herself!—not the trouble behind her
Left in the curtain, the couch's perfume!
As she brushed it, the cornice-wreath blossomed anew:
Yon looking-glass gleamed at the wave of her feather.

II

Yet the day wears,
10   And door succeeds door;
I try the fresh fortune—
Range the wide house from the wing to the centre.
Still the same chance! she goes out as I enter.
Spend my whole day in the quest,—who cares?
15   But 'tis twilight, you see,—with such suites to explore,
Such closets to search, such alcoves to importune!

LOVE IN A LIFE § Subsequent placement: 1863:DL §   1| P:after room;
1855:after room,   4| P:her!— 1855:her, 1865:her—   5| P:herself—not
1855:herself!—not   6| P:couche's perfume: 1855:couch's perfume!
7| P:anew, 1855:anew,— 1863:anew: 12| P:centre: 1855:centre.

Escape me?
Never—
Beloved!
While I am I, and you are you,
5   So long as the world contains us both,
          Me the loving and you the loth,
While the one eludes, must the other pursue.
My life is a fault at last, I fear:
          It seems too much like a fate, indeed!
10   Though I do my best I shall scarce succeed.
But what if I fail of my purpose here?
It is but to keep the nerves at strain,
          To dry one's eyes and laugh at a fall,
And, baffled, get up and begin again,—
15   So the chace takes up one's life, that's all.
While, look but once from your farthest bound
          At me so deep in the dust and dark,
No sooner the old hope goes to ground
          Than a new one, straight to the self-same mark,
20 I shape me—
Ever
Removed!

LIFE IN A LOVE § Subsequent placement: 1863:DL §   ¹⁻³| P: § double-indented §
1868 § not indented §   ⁸| P:fear— *1863*:fear: ⁹| P:fate indeed, *1855*:fate,
indeed!   ¹⁰| P:succeed— *1863*:succeed.   ¹⁴| P:And baffled, get up to
begin again, *1855*:again,— *1863*:up and begin *1888*:And, baffled
¹⁶| P:bound; *1855*:bound, *1863*:bound   ¹⁸| P:hope drops to *1865*:hope
goes to   ²⁰⁻²²| P: § double-indented § *1868*: § not indented §

I only knew one poet in my life:
And this, or something like it, was his way.

You saw go up and down Valladolid,
A man of mark, to know next time you saw.
5 His very serviceable suit of black
Was courtly once and conscientious still,
And many might have worn it, though none did:
The cloak, that somewhat shone and showed the threads,
Had purpose, and the ruff, significance.
10 He walked and tapped the pavement with his cane,
Scenting the world, looking it full in face,
An old dog, bald and blindish, at his heels.
They turned up, now, the alley by the church,
That leads nowhither; now, they breathed themselves
15 On the main promenade just at the wrong time:
You'd come upon his scrutinizing hat,
Making a peaked shade blacker than itself
Against the single window spared some house
Intact yet with its mouldered Moorish work,—
20 Or else surprise the ferrel of his stick
Trying the mortar's temper 'tween the chinks
Of some new shop a-building, French and fine.
He stood and watched the cobbler at his trade,
The man who slices lemons into drink,
25 The coffee-roaster's brazier, and the boys
That volunteer to help him turn its winch.
He glanced o'er books on stalls with half an eye,
And fly-leaf ballads on the vendor's string,
And broad-edge bold-print posters by the wall.
30 He took such cognizance of men and things,

HOW IT STRIKES A CONTEMPORARY § Subsequent placement: 1863:MW §
8| P:cloak that <> shewed the threads *1863*:cloak, that <> showed the threads,
1865:threads *1868*:threads, 14| P:no whither *1888*:nowhither 15| P:time.
1863:time: 16| P:scrutinising hat *1855*:hat, *1863*:scrutinizing
19| P:work: *1855*:work,— 20| *1863*:ferule *1865*:ferrel 22|P:a-building
French *1855*:a-building, French 25| *1863*:brasier *1888*:brazier
26| P:turn his winch. *1855*:turn its winch. 27| P:He took in books
1855:He glanced o'er books 28| P:The fly-leaf *1855*:And fly-leaf
29| P:bold print *1855*:bold-print 30| P:cognisance *1888*:cognizance

If any beat a horse, you felt he saw;
If any cursed a woman, he took note;
Yet stared at nobody,—you stared at him,
And found, less to your pleasure than surprise,
He seemed to know you and expect as much.
So, next time that a neighbour's tongue was loosed,
It marked the shameful and notorious fact,
We had among us, not so much a spy,
As a recording chief-inquisitor,
The town's true master if the town but knew!
We merely kept a governor for form,
While this man walked about and took account
Of all thought, said and acted, then went home,
And wrote it fully to our Lord the King
Who has an itch to know things, he knows why,
And reads them in his bedroom of a night.
Oh, you might smile! there wanted not a touch,
A tang of . . . well, it was not wholly ease
As back into your mind the man's look came.
Stricken in years a little,—such a brow
His eyes had to live under!—clear as flint
On either side the formidable nose
Curved, cut and coloured like an eagle's claw.
Had he to do with A.'s surprising fate?
When altogether old B. disappeared
And young C. got his mistress,—was't our friend,
His letter to the King, that did it all?
What paid the bloodless man for so much pains?
Our Lord the King has favourites manifold,

³³| P:Yet looked at nobody, they looked at   *1855:*Yet stared at nobody,—they stared at
*1868:*nobody,—you stared   ³⁴| P:to their pleasure   *1868:*to your pleasure
³⁵| P:know them and < > much: *1855:*much.   *1868:*know you and   ³⁶| P:loosed
*1855:*loosed,   ³⁹| P:chief-inquisitor   *1855:*chief-inquisitor,   ⁴⁰| P:knew,
*1855:*knew!   ⁴¹| P:Which merely < > a Governor   *1855:*We merely
*1865:*a governor   ⁴³| P:said, and   *1863:*said and   ⁴⁵| P:things, He
*1868:*things, he   ⁴⁶| P:bed-room   *1855:*in His   *1868:*in his < > night,   *1888:*
bedroom < > night.   ⁴⁸| P:well, 'twas not of easiness   *1855:*well, it was not wholly
ease   ⁴⁹| P:came—   *1888:*came.   ⁵³| P:cut, and coloured, like   *1863:*cut and
coloured like   ⁵⁶| P:friend   *1855:*friend,   ⁵⁷| P:the King that
*1855:*the King, that   ⁵⁸| P:for all his pains?   *1855:*for so much pains?

⁶⁰ And shifts his ministry some once a month;
Our city gets new governors at whiles,—
But never word or sign, that I could hear,
Notified to this man about the streets
The King's approval of those letters conned
⁶⁵ The last thing duly at the dead of night.
Did the man love his office? Frowned our Lord,
Exhorting when none heard—"Beseech me not!
Too far above my people,—beneath me!
I set the watch,—how should the people know?
⁷⁰ Forget them, keep me all the more in mind!"
Was some such understanding 'twixt the two?

I found no truth in one report at least—
That if you tracked him to his home, down lanes
Beyond the Jewry, and as clean to pace,
⁷⁵ You found he ate his supper in a room
Blazing with lights, four Titians on the wall,
And twenty naked girls to change his plate!
Poor man, he lived another kind of life
In that new stuccoed third house by the bridge,
⁸⁰ Fresh-painted, rather smart than otherwise!
The whole street might o'erlook him as he sat,
Leg crossing leg, one foot on the dog's back,
Playing a decent cribbage with his maid
(Jacynth, you're sure her name was) o'er the cheese
⁸⁵ And fruit, three red halves of starved winter-pears,
Or treat of radishes in April. Nine,
Ten, struck the church clock, straight to bed went he.

My father, like the man of sense he was,
Would point him out to me a dozen times;
90 " 'St—'St," he'd whisper, "the Corregidor!"
I had been used to think that personage
Was one with lacquered breeches, lustrous belt,
And feathers like a forest in his hat,
Who blew a trumpet and proclaimed the news,
95 Announced the bull-fights, gave each church its turn,
And memorized the miracle in vogue!
He had a great observance from us boys;
We were in error; that was not the man.

I'd like now, yet had haply been afraid,
100 To have just looked, when this man came to die,
And seen who lined the clean gay garret-sides
And stood about the neat low truckle-bed,
With the heavenly manner of relieving guard.
Here had been, mark, the general-in-chief,
105 Thro' a whole campaign of the world's life and death,
Doing the King's work all the dim day long,
In his old coat and up to knees in mud,
Smoked like a herring, dining on a crust,—
And, now the day was won, relieved at once!
110 No further show or need for that old coat,
You are sure, for one thing! Bless us, all the while
How sprucely we are dressed out, you and I!
A second, and the angels alter that.
Well, I could never write a verse,—could you?
115 Let's to the Prado and make the most of time.

*1855:*Ten, struck < > clock, straight to   90| P:"St—St" he'd *1855:*"St—St,"
he'd *1888:*" 'St—'St   95| P:turn *1855:*turn,   97| P:boys— *1863:*boys;
98| P:I was in *1863:*We were in   100| P:when that man *1855:*when this man
101| P:garret's sides *1868:*garret sides *1888:*garret-sides   102| P:truckle
bed, *1855:*truckle-bed,   105| P:A *1855:*Thro' a   107| P:to his knees *1855:*coat,
and *1863:*coat and *1868:*to knees   108| P:crust, *1855:*crust,—
109| P:And now the day's won, he's relieved at once. *1855:*the day was won,
relieved at once! *1863:*And, now   115| P:time! *1855:*time.

THE LAST RIDE TOGETHER

I

I said—Then, dearest, since 'tis so,
Since now at length my fate I know,
Since nothing all my love avails,
Since all, my life seemed meant for, fails,
5   Since this was written and needs must be—
My whole heart rises up to bless
Your name in pride and thankfulness!
Take back the hope you gave,—I claim
Only a memory of the same,
10   —And this beside, if you will not blame,
      Your leave for one more last ride with me.

II

My mistress bent that brow of hers;
Those deep dark eyes where pride demurs
When pity would be softening through,
15   Fixed me a breathing-while or two
      With life or death in the balance: right!
The blood replenished me again;
My last thought was at least not vain:
I and my mistress, side by side
20   Shall be together, breathe and ride,
So, one day more am I deified.
      Who knows but the world may end to-night?

III

Hush! if you saw some western cloud
All billowy-bosomed, over-bowed
25   By many benedictions—sun's

THE LAST RIDE TOGETHER § Subsequent placement: *1863:*DR §   ¹| P:said
then *1855:*said—Then *1863:*said—Then, Dearest *1868:*said—Then, dearest
⁴| P:And all *1855:*Since all my *1863:*all, my   ¹⁰| P:—Or this *1855:*—And this
¹²| P:hers, *1863:*hers;   ¹⁴| P:through *1855:*through,   ¹⁶| P:or Death < >
balance—Right! *1855:*or death *1863:*balance: right!   ¹⁷| P:again: *1863:*again;
¹⁸| P:vain, *1855:*vain. *1863:*vain: ²¹| P:So one < > deified *1855:*deified. *1863:*
deified— *1865:*So, one < > deified.   ²²| *1863:*to-night. *1865:*to-night?   ²⁵| P:

And moon's and evening-star's at once—
    And so, you, looking and loving best,
Conscious grew, your passion drew
Cloud, sunset, moonrise, star-shine too,
30 Down on you, near and yet more near,
Till flesh must fade for heaven was here!—
Thus leant she and lingered—joy and fear!
    Thus lay she a moment on my breast.

IV

    Then we began to ride. My soul
35 Smoothed itself out, a long-cramped scroll
Freshening and fluttering in the wind.
Past hopes already lay behind.
    What need to strive with a life awry?
Had I said that, had I done this,
40 So might I gain, so might I miss.
Might she have loved me? just as well
She might have hated, who can tell!
Where had I been now if the worst befell?
    And here we are riding, she and I.

V

45 Fail I alone, in words and deeds?
Why, all men strive and who succeeds?
We rode; it seemed my spirit flew,
Saw other regions, cities new,
    As the world rushed by on either side.
50 I thought,—All labour, yet no less

---

sun's, *1855*:sun's   26| P:evening star's *1855*:evening-star's   27| P:you
looking *1855*:you, looking   28| P:Conscious you grew   *1855*:Conscious grew
29| P:star-shine, too, *1855*:star-shine too *1863*:too,   31| P:here! *1855*:
here!—   32| P:fear— *1855*:fear!   33| P:breast! *1855*:breast. *1888*:
breast § emended to § breast. § see Editorial Notes §   35| P:long cramped *1855*:
long-cramped *1863*:out—a *1865*:out, a   38| P:life away? *1855*:life awry?
40| P:miss: *1855*:miss.   42| P:tell? *1855*:hated,—who *1865*:hated, who *1868*:
tell!   43| P:Where were I now *1855*:Where had I been now   45| P:Fail I,
alone *1855*:Fail I alone   49| P:side: *1855*:side.   50| P:thought, All *1863*:

Bear up beneath their unsuccess.
Look at the end of work, contrast
The petty done, the undone vast,
This present of theirs with the hopeful past!
55   I hoped she would love me; here we ride.

VI

What hand and brain went ever paired?
What heart alike conceived and dared?
What act proved all its thought had been?
What will but felt the fleshly screen?
60   We ride and I see her bosom heave.
There's many a crown for who can reach.
Ten lines, a statesman's life in each!
The flag stuck on a heap of bones,
A soldier's doing! what atones?
65   They scratch his name on the Abbey-stones.
        My riding is better, by their leave.

VII

What does it all mean, poet? Well,
Your brains beat into rhythm, you tell
What we felt only; you expressed
70   You hold things beautiful the best,
        And pace them in rhyme so, side by side.
'Tis something, nay 'tis much: but then,
Have you yourself what's best for men?

---

thought,—All   51| P:unsuccess: *1855:*unsuccess.   53| P:petty Done and
Undone *1855:*petty Done the Undone *1863:*petty Done, the *1868:*petty done, the
undone   54| P:This Present <> hopeful Past! *1855:*This present <> hopeful
past! *1863:*This Present <> hopeful Past! *1868:*This present <> hopeful past!
55| P:me. Here *1863:*me: here *1865:*me; here   59| *1888:*fleshy DC, BrU:fleshly
*1889:*fleshly   60| P:heave— *1855:*heave.   61| P:There is the Poet's crown of
years, *1855:*There's many a crown for who can reach.   62| P:That page, the
statesman life appears; *1855:*Ten lines, a statesman's life in each!   63| P:A flag
*1855:*The flag   64| P:The soldier's *1855:*A soldier's   66| P:The riding
*1855:*My riding   67| P:mean, Poet? well, *1855:*mean, poet? *1868:*poet? Well,
68| P:The brain's <> rhythm—you *1855:*Your brain's *1863:*brains *1865:*rhythm, you
69| P:expressed, *1855:*expressed   71| P:by side— *1855:*by side.   72| P:much—

Are you—poor, sick, old ere your time—
75 Nearer one whit your own sublime
Than we who never have turned a rhyme?
    Sing, riding's a joy! For me, I ride.

VIII

And you, great sculptor—so, you gave
A score of years to Art, her slave,
80 And that's your Venus, whence we turn
To yonder girl that fords the burn!
    You acquiesce, and shall I repine?
What, man of music, you grown grey
With notes and nothing else to say,
85 Is this your sole praise from a friend,
"Greatly his opera's strains intend,
But in music we know how fashions end!"
    I gave my youth; but we ride, in fine.

IX

Who knows what's fit for us? Had fate
90 Proposed bliss here should sublimate
My being—had I signed the bond—
Still one must lead some life beyond,
    Have a bliss to die with, dim-descried.
This foot once planted on the goal,
95 This glory-garland round my soul,
Could I descry such? Try and test!

---

but *1865*:much: but   74| P:time *1855*:time—   77| P:joy! for *1855*:joy!
For   78| P:great Sculptor—so you *1855*:great sculptor *1863*:so, you
79| *1855*:to art *1863*:to Art   80| P:your Venus—whence *1865*:your Venus, whence
81| P:burn: *1855*:burn!   82| P:acquiesce and *1863*:acquiesce, and   83| P:
you, grown *1865*:you grown   85| P:this the sole praise of your friend, *1855*:this
your sole praise from a friend,   86| P:"Greatly this Opera's *1855*:"Greatly his
opera's   87| P:in Music *1855*:in music   88| P:youth—but *1865*:youth;
but *1888*:fine DC, BrU:fine. *1889*:fine.   91| P:being; if I *1855*:being; had I
1865:being—had   92| P:Why, one *1855*:Still one   93| P:—Have < > dim-

I sink back shuddering from the quest.
Earth being so good, would heaven seem best?
    Now, heaven and she are beyond this ride.

X

100 And yet—she has not spoke so long!
What if heaven be that, fair and strong
At life's best, with our eyes upturned
Whither life's flower is first discerned,
    We, fixed so, ever should so abide?
105 What if we still ride on, we two
With life for ever old yet new,
Changed not in kind but in degree,
The instant made eternity,—
And heaven just prove that I and she
110   Ride, ride together, for ever ride?

descried: *1855:*dim-descried. *1865:*Have   ⁹⁷| P:quest— *1865:*quest.   ⁹⁸| P:
would Heaven *1868:*would heaven   ⁹⁹| *1855:*Now, Heaven *1868:*Now, heaven
¹⁰⁰| *1888:*long DC, BrU:long! *1889:*long!   ¹⁰¹| P:If Heaven be, that, most fair,
most strong, *1855:*What if < > be, that, fair and strong *1863:*be that *1868:*if heaven
¹⁰³| P:Where life's full flower *1855:*Whither life's flower   ¹⁰⁵| P:If we keep riding
on, we two, *1855:*What if we still ride on *1888:*two   ¹⁰⁸| P:eternity, *1855:*
eternity,—   ¹⁰⁹| P:And Heaven prove just that *1855:*And Heaven just prove that
*1868:*And heaven   ¹¹⁰| P:together, and ever *1855:*together, for ever *1863:* § line
not indented § *1865:* § line indented §

THE PATRIOT

AN OLD STORY

I

It was roses, roses, all the way,
    With myrtle mixed in my path like mad:
The house-roofs seemed to heave and sway,
    The church-spires flamed, such flags they had,
5   A year ago on this very day.

II

The air broke into a mist with bells,
    The old walls rocked with the crowd and cries.
Had I said, "Good folk, mere noise repels—
    But give me your sun from yonder skies!"
10   They had answered, "And afterward, what else?"

III

Alack, it was I who leaped at the sun
    To give it my loving friends to keep!
Nought man could do, have I left undone:
    And you see my harvest, what I reap
15   This very day, now a year is run.

THE PATRIOT § Subsequent placement: *1863*:DR §   *Title* P:*THE OLD STORY 1855:THE PATRIOT / AN OLD STORY* ¹| P:way *1855*:way,
²| P:mad, *1855*:mad. *1863*:mad: ⁵| P:day! *1868*:day.   ⁷| P:crowds and cries: *1855*:cries. *1863*:crowd   ⁸| P:said "Good folks mere *1855*:said, "Good folks, mere *1863*:folk   ¹⁰| P:afterward what *1855*:afterward, what   ¹¹| *1855:* sun, *1863*:sun   ¹²| P:keep: *1855*:keep. *1863*:keep!   ¹³| P:do, surely, I < > undone, *1855*:do, have I < > undone *1863*:undone: ¹⁵| P:day now *1855*:day,

IV

There's nobody on the house-tops now—
　　Just a palsied few at the windows set;
For the best of the sight is, all allow,
　　At the Shambles' Gate—or, better yet,
20　By the very scaffold's foot, I trow.

V

I go in the rain, and, more than needs,
　　A rope cuts both my wrists behind;
And I think, by the feel, my forehead bleeds,
　　For they fling, whoever has a mind,
25　Stones at me for my year's misdeeds.

VI

Thus I entered, and thus I go!
　　In triumphs, people have dropped down dead.
"Paid by the world, what dost thou owe
　　Me?"—God might question; now instead,
30　'Tis God shall repay: I am safer so.

---

now 　　¹⁶| P:now　*1855:*now— 　　¹⁷| P:Save the palsied < > set— 　　*1855:*Just a
palsied　*1863:*set; 　　¹⁹| P:or better yet　*1855:*or, better yet, 　　²¹| P:rain and < >
needs　*1855:*rain, and < > needs, 　　²²| P:behind,　*1863:*behind; 　　²³| P:bleeds
*1855:*bleeds, 　　²⁶| P:I entered this Brescia and quit it so!　*1855:*Thus I entered
Brescia, and thus I go!　*1863:*entered, and 　　²⁷| P:In such triumphs some people
< > dead:　*1855:*triumphs, people < > dead.　*1863:*In triumphs 　　²⁸| P:"Thou,
paid by the World,—what　*1863:*"Paid by　*1868:*the world, what 　　²⁹| P:Me!"—God
might have questioned—but now, instead　*1855:*Me?" God < > questioned: but now
instead　*1863:*might question: now instead,　*1868:*Me?"—God < > question; now
³⁰| P:'Tis God who requites: I　*1855:*'Tis God shall requite! I　*1863:*shall repay! I
*1868:*repay: I

284

MASTER HUGUES OF SAXE-GOTHA

I

Hist, but a word, fair and soft!
　　Forth and be judged, Master Hugues!
Answer the question I've put you so oft:
　　What do you mean by your mountainous fugues?
5　See, we're alone in the loft,—

II

I, the poor organist here,
　　Hugues, the composer of note,
Dead though, and done with, this many a year:
　　Let's have a colloquy, something to quote,
10　Make the world prick up its ear!

III

See, the church empties apace:
　　Fast they extinguish the lights.
Hallo there, sacristan! Five minutes' grace!
　　Here's a crank pedal wants setting to rights,
15　Baulks one of holding the base.

IV

See, our huge house of the sounds,
　　Hushing its hundreds at once,
Bids the last loiterer back to his bounds!
　　—O you may challenge them, not a response
20　Get the church-saints on their rounds!

MASTER HUGUES OF SAXE-GOTHA § Subsequent placement: *1863*:DL §
1| P:soft— *1855*:soft! 　 3| P:oft— *1865*:oft: 　 5| P:loft— *1855*:loft,
1863:loft,— 　 7| P:Hugues the <> note— *1855*:Hugues, the *1865*:note,
8| P:Dead, though <> with this <> year— *1855*:with, this *1863*:year: *1865*:Dead
though 　 11| P:a-pace, *1855*:a-pace. *1863*:apace: 　 12| P:lights— *1865*:
lights. 　 13| P:Hallo, there, sacristan! five minutes *1855*:minutes' *1863*:Hallo there
1868:sacristan! Five 　 15| P:base! *1855*:base. 　 16| P:See our huge House <>
sounds *1855*:See, our huge house *1863*:sounds, 　 18| P:bounds *1863*:bounds!
19| P:—Oh, you *1868*:—O you 　 20| P:church saints *1863*:church-saints

285

(Saints go their rounds, who shall doubt?
    —March, with the moon to admire,
Up nave, down chancel, turn transept about,
    Supervise all betwixt pavement and spire,
25 Put rats and mice to the rout—

VI

Aloys and Jurien and Just—
    Order things back to their place,
Have a sharp eye lest the candlesticks rust,
    Rub the church-plate, darn the sacrament-lace,
30 Clear the desk-velvet of dust.)

VII

Here's your book, younger folks shelve!
    Played I not off-hand and runningly,
Just now, your masterpiece, hard number twelve?
    Here's what should strike, could one handle it cunningly:
35 Help the axe, give it a helve!

VIII

Page after page as I played,
    Every bar's rest, where one wipes
Sweat from one's brow, I looked up and surveyed,
    O'er my three claviers, yon forest of pipes
40 Whence you still peeped in the shade.

21| P:rounds who *1855*:rounds, who   26| P:and Just, *1855*:and Just—
29| P:church plate <> sacrament lace, *1863*:church-plate <> sacrament-lace,
30| P:desk velvet *1863*:desk-velvet   31| P:shelve: *1855*:shelve!   33| P:
twelve, *1855*:twelve?   34| P:strike,—could <> cunningly. *1863*:cunningly:
1865:strike, could   36-40| § stanza VIII misnumbered III in 1888 and 1889 §
37| P:rest where *1863*:rest, where   38| P:brow I <> surveyed *1855*:brow, I
1863:surveyed,   39| P:pipes, *1855*:pipes   41| P:speak! *1855*:speak,

IX

Sure you were wishful to speak?
    You, with brow ruled like a score,
Yes, and eyes buried in pits on each cheek,
    Like two great breves, as they wrote them of yore,
45 Each side that bar, your straight beak!

X

Sure you said—"Good, the mere notes!
    Still, couldst thou take my intent,
Know what procured me our Company's votes—
    A master were lauded and sciolists shent,
50 Parted the sheep from the goats!"

XI

Well then, speak up, never flinch!
    Quick, ere my candle's a snuff
—Burnt, do you see? to its uttermost inch—
    I believe in you, but that's not enough:
55 Give my conviction a clinch!

XII

First you deliver your phrase
    —Nothing propound, that I see,
Fit in itself for much blame or much praise—
    Answered no less, where no answer needs be:
60 Off start the Two on their ways.

---

*1888:*speak?   42| P:You with *1855:*You, with   43| P:cheek *1855:*cheek,
44| P:breves as < > yore *1865:*breves, as < > yore,   45| P:beak. *1855:*beak!
46| P:said—"Good the *1855:*said—"Good, the   47| P:Still couldst *1855:*Still, couldst   48| P:votes! *1855:*votes—   49| P:Masters were lauded *1855:* Masters being lauded *1865:*A master were lauded   50| P:Parting *1855:*Parted 52| P:Quick ere *1855:*Quick, ere   43| P:enough, *1855:*enough. *1863:*enough: 55| P:clinch. *1855:*clinch!   59| P:be— *1855:*be: 60| P:ways! *1865:*ways.

XIII

Straight must a Third interpose,
   Volunteer needlessly help;
In strikes a Fourth, a Fifth thrusts in his nose,
   So the cry's open, the kennel's a-yelp,
65   Argument's hot to the close.

XIV

One dissertates, he is candid;
   Two must discept,—has distinguished;
Three helps the couple, if ever yet man did;
   Four protests; Five makes a dart at the thing wished:
70   Back to One, goes the case bandied.

XV

One says his say with a difference;
   More of expounding, explaining!
All now is wrangle, abuse, and vociferance;
   Now there's a truce, all's subdued, self-restraining:
75   Five, though, stands out all the stiffer hence.

XVI

One is incisive, corrosive;
   Two retorts, nettled, curt, crepitant;
Three makes rejoinder, expansive, explosive;
   Four overbears them all, strident and strepitant:
80   Five . . . O Danaides, O Sieve!

62| P:help— *1865*:help;   65| P:close! *1865*:close.   66| P:disertates < >
candid— *1863*:dissertates < > candid;   67| P:distinguished! *1863*:distinguished;
68| P:did, *1855*:did: *1863*:did;   69| P:protests, Five < > wished— *1863*:protests;
Five < > wished: 70| P:to One goes < > bandied! *1855*:to One, goes *1863:*
bandied.   71| P:difference— *1865*:difference;   72| P:expounding explaining!
1855:expounding, explaining!   73| P:vociferance— *1863*:abuse and *1865:*
vociferance; *1888*:abuse, and   74| P:self restraining— *1855*:self-restraining—
1865:self-restraining; *1888*:self-restraining: *1889:* § punctuation at end of line decayed;
emended to § self-restraining: § see Editorial Notes §   75| P:hence! *1855*:hence.
76| P:corrosive— *1863*:corrosive;   77| P:crepitant— *1863*:crepitant;
78| P:explosive— *1863*:explosive;   79| P:strepitant— *1863*:strepitant:
80| P:Five . . . oh, Danaides, oh, Sieve! *1855*:Five . . . O Danaides, O Sieve!

Now, they ply axes and crowbars;
    Now, they prick pins at a tissue
Fine as a skein of the casuist Escobar's
    Worked on the bone of a lie. To what issue?
⁸⁵ Where is our gain at the Two-bars?

Est fuga, volvitur rota.
    On we drift: where looms the dim port?
One, Two, Three, Four, Five, contribute their quota;
    Something is gained, if one caught but the import—
⁹⁰ Show it us, Hugues of Saxe-Gotha!

What with affirming, denying,
    Holding, risposting, subjoining,
All's like . . . it's like . . . for an instance I'm trying . . .
    There! See our roof, its gilt moulding and groining
⁹⁵ Under those spider-webs lying!

So your fugue broadens and thickens,
    Greatens and deepens and lengthens,
Till we exclaim—"But where's music, the dickens?
    Blot ye the gold, while your spider-web strengthens
¹⁰⁰ —Blacked to the stoutest of tickens?"

---

^{81|} P:crowbars— *1863*:crowbars;   ^{84|} P:lie: To *1855*:lie. To   ^{86|} P:*rota!*
1865:rota.   ^{87|} P:On I drift, where *1855*:On we drift. Where *1865*:drift: where
^{88|} P:quota— *1865*:quota;   ^{90|} P:of Saxe-Gotha. *1855*:of Saxe-Gotha!
^{92|} P:risposting *1855*:risposting   ^{94|} P:its gold moulding *1855*:its gilt moulding
^{98|} P:Till one exclaims <>where's Music *1855*:where's music *1865*:Till we exclaim
^{99|} P:strengthens, *1863*:strengthens   ^{100|} P:Blacked *1863*:—Blacked

XXI

I for man's effort am zealous:
  Prove me such censure unfounded!
Seems it surprising a lover grows jealous—
  Hopes 'twas for something, his organ-pipes sounded,
105 Tiring three boys at the bellows?

XXII

Is it your moral of Life?
  Such a web, simple and subtle,
Weave we on earth here in impotent strife,
  Backward and forward each throwing his shuttle,
110 Death ending all with a knife?

XXIII

Over our heads truth and nature—
  Still our life's zigzags and dodges,
Ins and outs, weaving a new legislature—
  God's gold just shining its last where that lodges,
115 Palled beneath man's usurpature.

101| *1855:*zealous. *1863:*zealous: 102| P:censures *1855:*censure's *1865:*censure
104| P:something his *1868:*something, his   108| P:strife *1855:*strife,   110| P:
with his knife? *1855:*with a knife?   111| P:heads Truth and Nature— *1868:*heads
truth and nature—   113| P:outs weaving *1863:*outs, weaving   115| P:beneath
Art's usurpature! *1855:*beneath Man's usurpature! *1868:*beneath man's usurpature.

XXIV

So we o'ershroud stars and roses,
    Cherub and trophy and garland;
Nothings grow something which quietly closes
    Heaven's earnest eye: not a glimpse of the far land
120 Gets through our comments and glozes.

XXV

Ah but traditions, inventions,
    (Say we and make up a visage)
So many men with such various intentions,
    Down the past ages, must know more than this age!
125 Leave we the web its dimensions!

XXVI

Who thinks Hugues wrote for the deaf,
    Proved a mere mountain in labour?
Better submit; try again; what's the clef?
    'Faith, 'tis no trifle for pipe and for tabor—
130 Four flats, the minor in F.

116| P:So men o'erweave stars *1855:*So we o'ershroud stars   117| P:garland,
*1855:*garland. *1865:*garland;   119| P:eye,—not *1865:*eye: not   121| P:Ah, but
*1865:*Ah but   123| P:intentions *1865:*intentions,   124| P:ages must *1865:*
ages, must   125| P:Leave the web all its *1865:*Leave we the web its   126| P:
Think you Hugues <> deaf? *1855:*Who thinks Hugues *1863:*deaf,   127| P:Proves
*1855:*Proved   128| P:submit—try again—what's *1865:*submit; try again; what's
129| P:it's *1865:*'tis   130| P:flats—the minor's *1855:*minor *1863:*flats, the

Friend, your fugue taxes the finger:
    Learning it once, who would lose it?
Yet all the while a misgiving will linger,
    Truth's golden o'er us although we refuse it—
135 Nature, thro' cobwebs we string her.

Hugues! I advise *meâ poenâ*
    (Counterpoint glares like a Gorgon)
Bid One, Two, Three, Four, Five, clear the arena!
    Say the word, straight I unstop the full-organ,
140 Blare out the *mode Palestrina*.

While in the roof, if I'm right there,
    . . . Lo you, the wick in the socket!
Hallo, you sacristan, show us a light there!
    Down it dips, gone like a rocket.
145 What, you want, do you, to come unawares,
Sweeping the church up for first morning-prayers,
And find a poor devil has ended his cares
At the foot of your rotten-runged rat-riddled stairs?
    Do I carry the moon in my pocket?

131| P:finger— *1855:*finger. *1863:*finger: 133| P:linger— *1863:*linger,
135| P:Art's crowned—for Nature—unking her! *1855:*Nature, thro' dust-clouds we fling
her! *1868:*thro' cobwebs we string her.   139| P:the Full-Organ, *1868:*the full-
organ,   141| P:there— *1863:*there,   142| P: . . . Lo, you *1868:* . . . Lo
you   143| P:you Sacristan *1855:*you sacristan   144| P:rocket! *1868:*
rocket.   146| P:morning prayers, *1855:*morning-prayers,   147| P:devil
at end of his *1863:*devil has ended his   148| P:your rotten-planked rat-riddled
*1863:*your rotten-runged rat-riddled

No more wine? then we'll push back chairs and talk.
A final glass for me, though: cool, i' faith!
We ought to have our Abbey back, you see.
It's different, preaching in basilicas,
5   And doing duty in some masterpiece
Like this of brother Pugin's, bless his heart!
I doubt if they're half baked, those chalk rosettes,
Ciphers and stucco-twiddlings everywhere;
It's just like breathing in a lime-kiln: eh?
10   These hot long ceremonies of our church
Cost us a little—oh, they pay the price,
You take me—amply pay it! Now, we'll talk.

So, you despise me, Mr. Gigadibs.
No deprecation,—nay, I beg you, sir!
15   Beside 'tis our engagement: don't you know,
I promised, if you'd watch a dinner out,
We'd see truth dawn together?—truth that peeps
Over the glasses' edge when dinner's done,
And body gets its sop and holds its noise
20   And leaves soul free a little. Now's the time:
Truth's break of day! You do despise me then.
And if I say, "despise me,"—never fear!
I know you do not in a certain sense—
Not in my arm-chair, for example: here,
25   I well imagine you respect my place

BISHOP BLOUGRAM'S APOLOGY § Subsequent placement: 1863:MW §
¹| P:wine? Then *1855*:wine? then   ²| P:tho' *1863*:though   ³| P:see;
1855:see.   ¹³| P:me, Mr. Gigadibs! *1855*:me, Mr. Gigadibs.   ¹⁸| P:glass's
1888:glasses'   ²⁰| P:little; now's the time— *1855*:little. Now's
1868:time: ²¹| P:'Tis break DC,BrU:Truth's break *1889*:Truth's break
²²| P:But if < > fear— *1855*:And if *1868*:fear!   ²⁴| P:arm-chair for
1865:arm-chair, for   ²⁵| P:I will imagine *1855*:I well imagine

293

(*Status, entourage,* worldly circumstance)
Quite to its value—very much indeed:
—Are up to the protesting eyes of you
In pride at being seated here for once—
30　　You'll turn it to such capital account!
When somebody, through years and years to come,
Hints of the bishop,—names me—that's enough:
"Blougram? I knew him"—(into it you slide)
"Dined with him once, a Corpus Christi Day,
35　　All alone, we two; he's a clever man:
And after dinner,—why, the wine you know,—
Oh, there was wine, and good!—what with the wine . . .
'Faith, we began upon all sorts of talk!
He's no bad fellow, Blougram; he had seen
40　　Something of mine he relished, some review:
He's quite above their humbug in his heart,
Half-said as much, indeed—the thing's his trade.
I warrant, Blougram's sceptical at times:
How otherwise? I liked him, I confess!"
45　　*Che che,* my dear sir, as we say at Rome,
Don't you protest now! It's fair give and take;
You have had your turn and spoken your home-truths:
The hand's mine now, and here you follow suit.

　　　Thus much conceded, still the first fact stays—
50　　You do despise me; your ideal of life
Is not the bishop's: you would not be I.
You would like better to be Goethe, now,
Or Buonaparte, or, bless me, lower still,
Count D'Orsay,—so you did what you preferred,

26| P:(Status *1865:*(Status　　　27| P:indeed *1865:*indeed:　　　32| P:the Bishop <>
enough— *1855:*the bishop *1868:*enough:　　　35| P:two—he's <> man— *1865:*two;
he's <> man:　　　37| P:wine! and <> the wine . . . *1855:*was wine, and
*1888:*the wine . . § emended to § the wine . . . § see Editorial Notes §　　　39| P:fellow,
Blougram—he *1865:*fellow, Blougram; he　　　40| P:relished—some review—
*1865:*relished, some review:　　　41| P:heart *1855:*heart,　　　42| P:trade— *1865:*trade.
43| P:times— *1855:*times:　　　45| P:*Che ch'é 1863:Che che*　　　46| P:take,—
*1855:*take;　　　47| P:home-truths— *1863:*home-truths:　　　51| P:the Bishop's—you
<> I— *1855:*the bishop's *1865:*bishop's: you <> I.　　　53| P:Or

55   Spoke as you thought, and, as you cannot help,
     Believed or disbelieved, no matter what,
     So long as on that point, whate'er it was,
     You loosed your mind, were whole and sole yourself.
     —That, my ideal never can include,
60   Upon that element of truth and worth
     Never be based! for say they make me Pope—
     (They can't—suppose it for our argument!)
     Why, there I'm at my tether's end, I've reached
     My height, and not a height which pleases you:
65   An unbelieving Pope won't do, you say.
     It's like those eerie stories nurses tell,
     Of how some actor on a stage played Death,
     With pasteboard crown, sham orb and tinselled dart,
     And called himself the monarch of the world;
70   Then, going in the tire-room afterward,
     Because the play was done, to shift himself,
     Got touched upon the sleeve familiarly,
     The moment he had shut the closet door,
     By Death himself. Thus God might touch a Pope
75   At unawares, ask what his baubles mean,
     And whose part he presumed to play just now.
     Best be yourself, imperial, plain and true!

     So, drawing comfortable breath again,
     You weigh and find, whatever more or less
80   I boast of my ideal realized

Buonaparte—or <> still— *1855:*still, *1865:*Or Buonaparte, or   [56] P:what;
*1855:*what,   [59] P:include— *1855:*include,   [60] P:worth, *1855:*worth
[61] P:me Pope *1888:*me Pope—   [62] P:argument) *1888:*argument!)
[63] P:end—I've *1865:*end, I've   [64] P:you, *1855:*you. *1865:*you:
[65] P:—An <> say— *1855:*An <> say.   [66] P:tell *1855:*tell,
[67] P:actor played Death on a stage *1865:*stage, *1888:*actor on a stage played Death,
[68] P:orb, and *1863:*orb and   [69] P:the Monarch <> world,— *1855:*the
monarch <> world, *1865:*world;   [70] P:Who going <> afterward
*1855:*Then going *1863:*Then, going *1865:*afterward,   [72] P:familiarly
*1865:*familiarly,   [73] P:door *1865:*door,   [74] P:himself: so God *1855:*himself.
Thus God   [76] P:now? DC,BrU:now. *1889:*now.   [78] P:So drawing
*1855:*So, drawing   [79] P:find whatever *1865:*find, whatever   [80] P:realised

Is nothing in the balance when opposed
To your ideal, your grand simple life,
Of which you will not realize one jot.
I am much, you are nothing; you would be all,
85 I would be merely much: you beat me there.

No, friend, you do not beat me: hearken why!
The common problem, yours, mine, every one's,
Is—not to fancy what were fair in life
Provided it could be,—but, finding first
90 What may be, then find how to make it fair
Up to our means: a very different thing!
No abstract intellectual plan of life
Quite irrespective of life's plainest laws,
But one, a man, who is man and nothing more,
95 May lead within a world which (by your leave)
Is Rome or London, not Fool's-paradise.
Embellish Rome, idealize away,
Make paradise of London if you can,
You're welcome, nay, you're wise.

                              A simile!
100 We mortals cross the ocean of this world
Each in his average cabin of a life;
The best's not big, the worst yields elbow-room.
Now for our six months' voyage—how prepare?
You come on shipboard with a landsman's list
105 Of things he calls convenient: so they are!
An India screen is pretty furniture,
A piano-forte is a fine resource,

1863:realized 1865:realized, DC,BrU:realized 1889:realized   83| P:realise
<>jot,— 1855:jot. 1863:realize   85| P:much—you 1865:much: you
86| P:me,—listen why: 1855:me,—hearken why. 1865:me: hearken
1888:why!   87| P:your's 1855:yours   88| P:Is not 1865:Is—not
89| P:first, 1855:first   91| P:means—a 1865:means: a   93| P:of Life's
1855:of life's   96| P:or London—not Fool's-paradise; 1855:not Fool's-paradise.
1865:or London, not   97| P:idealise 1863:idealize   98| P:Make Paradise
1868:Make paradise   101| P:life— 1865:life;   102| P:elbow room; 1855:elbow-
room.   105| P:convenient—so 1865:convenient: so   107| P:a great resource;

All Balzac's novels occupy one shelf,
The new edition fifty volumes long;
110 And little Greek books, with the funny type
They get up well at Leipsic, fill the next:
Go on! slabbed marble, what a bath it makes!
And Parma's pride, the Jerome, let us add!
'Twere pleasant could Correggio's fleeting glow
115 Hang full in face of one where'er one roams,
Since he more than the others brings with him
Italy's self,—the marvellous Modenese!—
Yet was not on your list before, perhaps.
—Alas, friend, here's the agent . . . is't the name?
120 The captain, or whoever's master here—
You see him screw his face up; what's his cry
Ere you set foot on shipboard? "Six feet square!"
If you won't understand what six feet mean,
Compute and purchase stores accordingly—
125 And if, in pique because he overhauls
Your Jerome, piano, bath, you come on board
Bare—why, you cut a figure at the first
While sympathetic landsmen see you off;
Not afterward, when long ere half seas over,
130 You peep up from your utterly naked boards
Into some snug and well-appointed berth,
Like mine for instance (try the cooler jug—
Put back the other, but don't jog the ice!)
And mortified you mutter "Well and good;
135 He sits enjoying his sea-furniture;

---

*1855:*a fine resource,   110| P:books with *1863:*books, with   111| P:at
Leipsic fill the next— *1863:*at Leipsic, fill *1865:*next: 113| P:And Parma' <>
add, *1855:*And Parma's <>add!   115| P:roams *1855:*roams,
117| P:self, the marvellous Modenese! *1855:*self,—the *1888:*marvellous Modenese!—
118| P:Yet 'twas not *1865:*Yet was not   119| P:—Alas! friend <> the Agent
*1855:*the agent *1865:*—Alas friend *1888:*—Alas, friend   120| P:here,
*1855:*here—   125| P:if in <> because they overhaul *1855:*because he overhauls
*1868:*if, in   126| P:piano and bath *1888:*piano, bath   127| P:why you <>
first! *1855:*first *1863:*why, you   129| P:afterwards when, long <> o'er,
*1855:*afterwards, when *1863:*over, *1865:*afterward, when long   131| P:berth
*1863:*berth,   132| P:mine, for *1865:*mine for   133| P:ice) *1865:*ice!)
134| P:Then mortified <> good— *1855:*And mortified *1865:*good;   135| P:sea-

'Tis stout and proper, and there's store of it:
Though I've the better notion, all agree,
Of fitting rooms up. Hang the carpenter,
Neat ship-shape fixings and contrivances—
140　I would have brought my Jerome, frame and all!"
And meantime you bring nothing: never mind—
You've proved your artist-nature: what you don't
You might bring, so despise me, as I say.

　　　　Now come, let's backward to the starting-place.
145　See my way: we're two college friends, suppose.
Prepare together for our voyage, then;
Each note and check the other in his work,—
Here's mine, a bishop's outfit; criticize!
What's wrong? why won't you be a bishop too?

150　　　　Why first, you don't believe, you don't and can't,
(Not statedly, that is, and fixedly
And absolutely and exclusively)
In any revelation called divine.
No dogmas nail your faith; and what remains
155　But say so, like the honest man you are?
First, therefore, overhaul theology!
Nay, I too, not a fool, you please to think,
Must find believing every whit as hard:
And if I do not frankly say as much,
160　The ugly consequence is clear enough.

　　　　Now wait, my friend: well, I do not believe—
If you'll accept no faith that is not fixed,

---

furniture— *1865:*sea-furniture; 　¹³⁶| P:it, *1865:*it: 　¹³⁷| P:Still,
I've *1855:*Though I've 　¹³⁸| P:up: hang *1855:*up! hang *1865:*up. Hang
¹⁴¹| P:nothing—never *1855:*nothing: never 　¹⁴²| P:artist-nature—what you
don't, *1855:*artist-nature: what *1868:*don't 　¹⁴⁴| P:starting place.
*1863:*starting-place. 　¹⁴⁵| P:suppose— *1865:*suppose. 　¹⁴⁶| P:then, *1865:*then;
¹⁴⁸| P:a Bishop's < > criticise! *1855:*a bishop's *1863:*criticize! *1868:*criticise!
*1888:*criticize! 　¹⁴⁹| P:a Bishop *1855:*a bishop 　¹⁵⁰| P:Why, first
*1865:*Why first 　¹⁵³| P:divine— *1855:*divine. 　¹⁵⁴| P:faith—and
*1865:*faith; and 　¹⁵⁵| P:are! *1855:*are? 　¹⁵⁶| P:theology— *1855:*theology!
¹⁵⁸| P:hard, *1865:*hard: 　¹⁶⁰| P:enough! *1855:*enough. 　¹⁶¹| P:Now, wait

Absolute and exclusive, as you say.
You're wrong—I mean to prove it in due time.
165 Meanwhile, I know where difficulties lie
I could not, cannot solve, nor ever shall,
So give up hope accordingly to solve—
(To you, and over the wine). Our dogmas then
With both of us, though in unlike degree,
170 Missing full credence—overboard with them!
I mean to meet you on your own premise:
Good, there go mine in company with yours!

And now what are we? unbelievers both,
Calm and complete, determinately fixed
175 To-day, to-morrow and for ever, pray?
You'll guarantee me that? Not so, I think!
In no wise! all we've gained is, that belief,
As unbelief before, shakes us by fits,
Confounds us like its predecessor. Where's
180 The gain? how can we guard our unbelief,
Make it bear fruit to us?—the problem here.
Just when we are safest, there's a sunset-touch,
A fancy from a flower-bell, some one's death,
A chorus-ending from Euripides,—
185 And that's enough for fifty hopes and fears
As old and new at once as nature's self,
To rap and knock and enter in our soul,
Take hands and dance there, a fantastic ring,
Round the ancient idol, on his base again,—
190 The grand Perhaps! We look on helplessly.

*1865:*Now wait   163| P:say *1855:*say.   164| P:to show you in *1855:*(You're
<> to prove it in due time) *1863:*time.) *1868:*You're <> time.   165| P:
Meanwhile I *1855:*Meanwhile, I   166| P:solve; nor *1855:*solve, nor
167| P:solve *1855:*solve—   169| P:In both <> tho' *1855:*With both
*1863:*though   171| P:premise— *1868:*premise: 175| P:to-morrow, and
*1865:*to-morrow and   176| *1855:*think. *1863:*think!   177| P:no-wise *1865:*nowise
*1868:*no wise   178| P:fits— *1855:*fits,   179| P:predecessor—where's
*1855:*predecessor. Where's   180| P:unbelief? *1855:*unbelief,   181| P:us,—the
<> here— *1855:*us?—the <> here.   183| P:flower bell *1855:*flower-bell
184| P:chorus ending from Euripides, *1855:*chorus-ending from Euripides,—
186| P:self *1855:*as Nature's self, *1868:*as nature's   187| P:in one's soul, *1855:*in
our soul,   190| P:grand Perhaps: we <> helplessly,— *1855:*grand Perhaps!

There the old misgivings, crooked questions are—
This good God,—what he could do, if he would,
Would, if he could—then must have done long since:
If so, when, where and how? some way must be,—
195   Once feel about, and soon or late you hit
Some sense, in which it might be, after all.
Why not, "The Way, the Truth, the Life?"

                                        —That way
Over the mountain, which who stands upon
Is apt to doubt if it be meant for a road;
200   While, if he views it from the waste itself,
Up goes the line there, plain from base to brow,
Not vague, mistakeable! what's a break or two
Seen from the unbroken desert either side?
And then (to bring in fresh philosophy)
205   What if the breaks themselves should prove at last
The most consummate of contrivances
To train a man's eye, teach him what is faith?
And so we stumble at truth's very test!
All we have gained then by our unbelief
210   Is a life of doubt diversified by faith,
For one of faith diversified by doubt:
We called the chess-board white,—we call it black.

"Well," you rejoin, "the end's no worse, at least;
We've reason for both colours on the board:

---

we   *1868:*grand Perhaps! We <> helplessly.   191| P:misgivings—crooked
*1855:*misgivings, crooked   192| *1863:*what He <> if He   *1868:*what he <> if he
193| *1863:*if He   *1868:*if he   194| P:where, and   *1865:*where and
195-196| P:feel for it, and soon you hit upon / Some <> all,   *1855:*feel about, and
soon or late you hit / Some <> all.   199| P:if it's a road at all,   *1855:*if
it's indeed a road;   *1863:*if it be indeed   *1888:*be meant for a   200| P:While if <>
itself   *1855:*itself,   *1865:*view   *1888:*While, if he views   201| P:there plain
*1855:*there, plain   204| P:then—to <> philosophy—   *1855:*then (to <>
philosophy)   207| P:faith,—   *1863:*faith?   208| P:test?   *1863:*test!
209| P:What have we gained, then, by   *1855:*gained then by   *1863:*All we have gained
210-212| P:But a <> faith— / We <> black!   *1855:*faith, / For one of faith
diversified by doubt. / We <> black.   *1863:*Is a <> / <> doubt: / We
213| P:least,   *1863:*least   *1865:*least;   214| P:board—   *1855:*board.   *1863:*board:

300

²¹⁵ Why not confess then, where I drop the faith
And you the doubt, that I'm as right as you?"

Because, friend, in the next place, this being so,
And both things even,—faith and unbelief
Left to a man's choice,—we'll proceed a step,
²²⁰ Returning to our image, which I like.

A man's choice, yes—but a cabin-passenger's—
The man made for the special life o' the world—
Do you forget him? I remember though!
Consult our ship's conditions and you find
²²⁵ One and but one choice suitable to all;
The choice, that you unluckily prefer,
Turning things topsy-turvy—they or it
Going to the ground. Belief or unbelief
Bears upon life, determines its whole course,
²³⁰ Begins at its beginning. See the world
Such as it is,—you made it not, nor I;
I mean to take it as it is,—and you,
Not so you'll take it,—though you get nought else.
I know the special kind of life I like,
²³⁵ What suits the most my idiosyncrasy,
Brings out the best of me and bears me fruit
In power, peace, pleasantness and length of days.
I find that positive belief does this
For me, and unbelief, no whit of this.
²⁴⁰ —For you, it does, however?—that, we'll try!
'Tis clear, I cannot lead my life, at least,
Induce the world to let me peaceably,
Without declaring at the outset, "Friends,

---

^{215|} P:confess, then, when I   *1855*:then, where I   *1865*:confess then
^{216|} P:Which you retain, that   *1855*:And you the doubt, that   ^{221|} P:choice—yes
1855:choice, yes   ^{222|} P:of   *1888*:o'   ^{224|} P:Consult the ship's   *1855*:Consult our
ship's   ^{225|} P:all,   *1868*:all;   ^{226|} P:choice that   *1855*:prefer
1863:choice, that < > prefer,   ^{230|} P:world,   *1855*:world   ^{232|} P:you
1888:you,   ^{237|} P:pleasantness, and < > days;   *1855*:days.   *1863*:pleasantness and
^{238|} P:this,   *1855*:this   ^{240|} P:however—that we'll   *1863*:however?—that
1868:that, we'll   ^{241|} *1855*:least   *1863*:least,   ^{243|} P:outset, "Friends—

I absolutely and peremptorily

245 Believe!"—I say, faith is my waking life:
One sleeps, indeed, and dreams at intervals,
We know, but waking's the main point with us
And my provision's for life's waking part.
Accordingly, I use heart, head and hand
250 All day, I build, scheme, study, and make friends;
And when night overtakes me, down I lie,
Sleep, dream a little, and get done with it,
The sooner the better, to begin afresh.
What's midnight doubt before the dayspring's faith?
255 You, the philosopher, that disbelieve,
That recognize the night, give dreams their weight—
To be consistent you should keep your bed,
Abstain from healthy acts that prove you man,
For fear you drowse perhaps at unawares!
260 And certainly at night you'll sleep and dream,
Live through the day and bustle as you please.
And so you live to sleep as I to wake,
To unbelieve as I to still believe?
Well, and the common sense o' the world calls you
265 Bed-ridden,—and its good things come to me.
Its estimation, which is half the fight,
That's the first-cabin comfort I secure:
The next . . . but you perceive with half an eye!
Come, come, it's best believing, if we may;
270 You can't but own that!

Next, concede again,
If once we choose belief, on all accounts

1855:outset, "Friends,   245| P:say faith <> life— 1855:life. 1863:say, faith
1868:life: 247| P:us, 1888:us   248| P:So my <> part— 1855:And my <>
part.   249| P:hands, 1855:hands 1865:hand   250| P:study and <> friends,
1855:friends; 1868:study, and   252| P:little and 1855:little, and
253| P:sooner, the better to <> afresh— 1855:sooner the better, to <> afresh.
254| P:midnight's 1868:midnight   256| P:recognise 1888:recognize
258| P:you a man, 1868:you man,   259| P:unawares 1855:unawares!
261| P:please, 1855:please.   263| P:believe. 1855:believe?   264| P:of
1888:o'   266| P:fight— 1855:fight,   267| P:first cabin-comfort I secure—
1865:first-cabin comfort I secure: 269| P:we can— 1863:we may— 1865:may;
270| P:that. § ¶ § Next<>again— 1863:that! § ¶ § Next 1865:again,

We can't be too decisive in our faith,
Conclusive and exclusive in its terms,
To suit the world which gives us the good things.
275　In every man's career are certain points
Whereon he dares not be indifferent;
The world detects him clearly, if he dare,
As baffled at the game, and losing life.
He may care little or he may care much
280　For riches, honour, pleasure, work, repose,
Since various theories of life and life's
Success are extant which might easily
Comport with either estimate of these;
And whoso chooses wealth or poverty,
285　Labour or quiet, is not judged a fool
Because his fellow would choose otherwise:
We let him choose upon his own account
So long as he's consistent with his choice.
But certain points, left wholly to himself,
290　When once a man has arbitrated on,
We say he must succeed there or go hang.
Thus, he should wed the woman he loves most
Or needs most, whatsoe'er the love or need—
For he can't wed twice. Then, he must avouch,
295　Or follow, at the least, sufficiently,
The form of faith his conscience holds the best,
Whate'er the process of conviction was:
For nothing can compensate his mistake
On such a point, the man himself being judge:
300　He cannot wed twice, nor twice lose his soul.

Well now, there's one great form of Christian faith
I happened to be born in—which to teach

276| P:indifferent—　1855:indifferent;　277| P:he is,　1863:he dares,
1865:dare,　283| P:these,　1863:these;　286| P:fellows < > otherwise—
1855:otherwise.　1863:otherwise:　1865:fellow　291| P:or be lost.　1855:or go hang.
292| P:most—　1855:most　293| P:most whatsoe'er　1855:most, whatsoe'er
294| P:avouch　1868:avouch,　295| P:sufficiently　1855:sufficiently,　296| P:best
1855:best,　297| P:was,　1855:was.　1863:was:　299| P:judge—
1865:judge:　300| P:twice nor　1855:twice, nor　301| P:now—there's　1863:now,

Was given me as I grew up, on all hands,
As best and readiest means of living by;
305   The same on examination being proved
The most pronounced moreover, fixed, precise
And absolute form of faith in the whole world—
Accordingly, most potent of all forms
For working on the world. Observe, my friend!
310   Such as you know me, I am free to say,
In these hard latter days which hamper one,
Myself—by no immoderate exercise
Of intellect and learning, but the tact
To let external forces work for me,
315   —Bid the street's stones be bread and they are bread;
Bid Peter's creed, or rather, Hildebrand's,
Exalt me o'er my fellows in the world
And make my life an ease and joy and pride;
It does so,—which for me's a great point gained,
320   Who have a soul and body that exact
A comfortable care in many ways.
There's power in me and will to dominate
Which I must exercise, they hurt me else:
In many ways I need mankind's respect,
325   Obedience, and the love that's born of fear:
While at the same time, there's a taste I have,
A toy of soul, a titillating thing,
Refuses to digest these dainties crude.
The naked life is gross till clothed upon:
330   I must take what men offer, with a grace

---

there's   303| P:hands   *1855:*hands,   304| P:by—   *1855:*by;
306| P:pronounced, moreover < > precise,   *1855:*pronounced moreover < >
precise   309| P:friend,   *1868:*friend!   312| P:Myself, by   *1868:*Myself—by
313| P:learning, and the   *1888:*learning, but the   315| P:Bid < > are bread.
*1855:*are bread,   *1863:*—Bid   *1865:*are bread;   316| P:creed—or, rather,
Hildebrand's   *1855:*creed, or < > Hildebrand's,   *1868:*or rather   318| P:And let
them make < > joy,   *1855:*And make < > joy and pride,   *1868:*pride;
319| P:gained   *1855:*gained,   321| P:ways—   *1855:*ways.   323| P:exercise,
it hurts me else—   *1855:*exercise, they hurt me else: 325| P:fear—   *1855:*fear:
328| P:crude—   *1855:*crude.   329| P:upon—   *1855:*upon: 330| P:offer

As though I would not, could I help it, take!
An uniform I wear though over-rich—
Something imposed on me, no choice of mine;
No fancy-dress worn for pure fancy's sake
335   And despicable therefore! now folk kneel
And kiss my hand—of course the Church's hand.
Thus I am made, thus life is best for me,
And thus that it should be I have procured;
And thus it could not be another way,
340   I venture to imagine.

                    You'll reply,
So far my choice, no doubt, is a success;
But were I made of better elements,
With nobler instincts, purer tastes, like you,
I hardly would account the thing success
345   Though it did all for me I say.

                    But, friend,
We speak of what is; not of what might be,
And how 'twere better if 'twere otherwise.
I am the man you see here plain enough:
Grant I'm a beast, why, beasts must lead beasts' lives!
350   Suppose I own at once to tail and claws;
The tailless man exceeds me: but being tailed
I'll lash out lion fashion, and leave apes

---

with *1855:*offer, with   331| P:take— *1855:*take!   332| P:uniform to wear
*1855:*A *1863:*An uniform I wear   333| P:mine, *1855:*mine;   334| P:fancy
dress < > pure fashion's sake *1855:*fancy-dress *1863:*pure fancy's sake
335| P:therefore—now men kneel *1855:*therefore! now *1888:*now folk kneel
337| P:made, thus is life best *1855:*made, thus life is best   338| P:be, I < >
procured, *1855:*be I < > procured;   340| P:reply— *1865:*reply,
342| P:elements *1855:*elements,   343| P:you *1855:*you,   345| P:do < > me you
say, § ¶ § *1855:*me I say. § ¶ § *1863:*did   346| P:is—not< >be *1855:*be, *1865:*is; not
347| P:otherwise: *1855:*otherwise.   348| P:enough— *1865:*enough:
349| P:why beasts< >lives— *1855:*lives! *1863:*why, beasts   350| P:claws—
*1865:*claws;   351| P:me, but *1855:*me; but *1865:*me: but   352| P:lash mine
lion's-fashion and *1855:*lash out lion-fashion, and *1868:*lion fashion

To dock their stump and dress their haunches up.
My business is not to remake myself,
355   But make the absolute best of what God made.
Or—our first simile—though you prove me doomed
To a viler berth still, to the steerage-hole,
The sheep-pen or the pig-stye, I should strive
To make what use of each were possible;
360   And as this cabin gets upholstery,
That hutch should rustle with sufficient straw.

But, friend, I don't acknowledge quite so fast
I fail of all your manhood's lofty tastes
Enumerated so complacently,
365   On the mere ground that you forsooth can find
In this particular life I choose to lead
No fit provision for them. Can you not?
Say you, my fault is I address myself
To grosser estimators than should judge?
370   And that's no way of holding up the soul,
Which, nobler, needs men's praise perhaps, yet knows
One wise man's verdict outweighs all the fools'—
Would like the two, but, forced to choose, takes that.
I pine among my million imbeciles
375   (You think) aware some dozen men of sense
Eye me and know me, whether I believe
In the last winking Virgin, as I vow,
And am a fool, or disbelieve in her
And am a knave,—approve in neither case,
380   Withhold their voices though I look their way:

353| P:their buttocks up— *1855*:their haunches up.   354| P:myself *1855*:myself,
356| P:proved *1888*:prove   357| P:steerage hole, *1855*:steerage-hole,
359| P:possible— *1855*:possible;   364| P:complacently *1855*:complacently,
365| P:can see *1855*:can find   369| P:than I need— *1855*:need, *1863*:need? *1868*:
than should judge?   370-372| § Proof prints two consecutive versions of these lines;
they are here designated P1 and P2 §   370| P1:soul; P2:soul— *1865*:soul,
371| P1:perhaps, but knows *1855*:perhaps, yet knows   372| P2:fools'?
1855:fools',— *1865*:fools'—   373| P:that? *1888*:that.   375| P:You think, aware
1855:(You think) aware   376| P:know me: whether *1855*:know me, whether
379| P:knave, approve *1855*:knave,—approve   380| P:way *1855*:way:

Like Verdi when, at his worst opera's end
(The thing they gave at Florence,—what's its name?)
While the mad houseful's plaudits near out-bang
His orchestra of salt-box, tongs and bones,
385   He looks through all the roaring and the wreaths
Where sits Rossini patient in his stall.

Nay, friend, I meet you with an answer here—
That even your prime men who appraise their kind
Are men still, catch a wheel within a wheel,
390   See more in a truth than the truth's simple self,
Confuse themselves. You see lads walk the street
Sixty the minute; what's to note in that?
You see one lad o'erstride a chimney-stack;
Him you must watch—he's sure to fall, yet stands!
395   Our interest's on the dangerous edge of things.
The honest thief, the tender murderer,
The superstitious atheist, demirep
That loves and saves her soul in new French books—
We watch while these in equilibrium keep
400   The giddy line midway: one step aside,
They're classed and done with. I, then, keep the line
Before your sages,—just the men to shrink
From the gross weights, coarse scales and labels broad
You offer their refinement. Fool or knave?
405   Why needs a bishop be a fool or knave
When there's a thousand diamond weights between?
So, I enlist them. Your picked twelve, you'll find,

381| P:when at   *1855:*when, at   384| P:tongs, and   *1855:*tongs and
387| P:answer there—   *1855:*answer here—   388| P:For even   *1863:*That
even   389| P:a thing within a thing,   *1863:*a wheel within a wheel,
392| P:minute, what's <> in such?   *1855:*minute; what's <> in that?   393| P:lad
stand on a chimney-stack—   *1855:*lad o'erstride a chimney-stack;   394| P:stands.
*1855:*stands!   395| P:things—   *1855:*things.   397| P:demireps
*1868:*demirep   398| P:love and save their souls   *1868:*loves and saves her soul
400| P:midway—one <> aside   *1855:*midway: one <> aside,   401| P:with: I
*1855:*with. I   403| P:scales, and   *1868:*scales and   404| P:refinement;
fool   *1855:*refinement. Fool   407| P:So I <> them—your picked Twelve

Profess themselves indignant, scandalized
At thus being held unable to explain
410 How a superior man who disbelieves
May not believe as well: that's Schelling's way!
It's through my coming in the tail of time,
Nicking the minute with a happy tact.
Had I been born three hundred years ago
415 They'd say, "What's strange? Blougram of course believes;"
And, seventy years since, "disbelieves of course."
But now, "He may believe; and yet, and yet
How can he?" All eyes turn with interest.
Whereas, step off the line on either side—
420 You, for example, clever to a fault,
The rough and ready man who write apace,
Read somewhat seldomer, think perhaps even less—
You disbelieve! Who wonders and who cares?
Lord So-and-so—his coat bedropped with wax,
425 All Peter's chains about his waist, his back
Brave with the needlework of Noodledom—
Believes! Again, who wonders and who cares?
But I, the man of sense and learning too,
The able to think yet act, the this, the that,
430 I, to believe at this late time of day!
Enough; you see, I need not fear contempt.

—Except it's yours! Admire me as these may,
You don't. But whom at least do you admire?
Present your own perfection, your ideal,

*1855:*them. Your   *1868:*picked twelve   *1888:*So, I   408| P:scandalised   *1863:*
scandalized   410| P:man, who disbelieves,   *1855:*man who disbelieves
411| P:well—that's   *1855:*well: that's   412| P:through one's coming
*1855:*through my coming   415| P:strange? the man of   *1855:*strange? Blougram of
417| P:believe—and yet, and yet   *1855:*believe; and yet, and yet   418| P:he?"—All
< > interest—   *1855:*interest.   *1868:*he?" All   421| P:man that write apace   *1855:*
apace,   *1865:*man who write   422| P:Think somewhat seldomer, read perhaps
*1855:*Read somewhat seldomer, think perhaps   423| P:disbelieve—who
*1855:*disbelieve! Who   424| P:Lord So-and-So < > bedropt   *1863:*Lord So-and-so
*1868:*bedropped   425| P:his throat, his   *1855:*his waist, his   426| P:of
Noodledom,   *1865:*of Noodledom—   427| P:Believes—again   *1855:*Believes!
Again   428| P:But I the < > too—   *1855:*But I, the < > too,   429| P:act—the
this, the that—   *1855:*act, the this, the that,   430| P:day?   *1855:*day!
431| P:contempt   *1855:*contempt.   431-432| *1868:* § no space before new ¶ §   *1888:* §
space restored §   432| P:yours! admire < >may   *1855:*may,   *1868:*yours! Admire
433| P:don't. But what at   *1863:*don't. But whom at   434| P:perfections < > ideal.

⁴³⁵ Your pattern man for a minute—oh, make haste,
Is it Napoleon you would have us grow?
Concede the means; allow his head and hand,
(A large concession, clever as you are)
Good! In our common primal element
⁴⁴⁰ Of unbelief (we can't believe, you know—
We're still at that admission, recollect!)
Where do you find—apart from, towering o'er
The secondary temporary aims
Which satisfy the gross taste you despise—
⁴⁴⁵ Where do you find his star?—his crazy trust
God knows through what or in what? it's alive
And shines and leads him, and that's all we want.
Have we aught in our sober night shall point
Such ends as his were, and direct the means
⁴⁵⁰ Of working out our purpose straight as his,
Nor bring a moment's trouble on success
With after-care to justify the same?
—Be a Napoleon, and yet disbelieve—
Why, the man's mad, friend, take his light away!
⁴⁵⁵ What's the vague good o' the world, for which you dare
With comfort to yourself blow millions up?
We neither of us see it! we do see
The blown-up millions—spatter of their brains
And writhing of their bowels and so forth,
⁴⁶⁰ In that bewildering entanglement
Of horrible eventualities

1855:ideal, *1865*:perfection ⁴³⁵| P:pattern Man <> haste! *1855*:pattern man
1888:haste DC,BrU:haste, *1889*:haste, ⁴³⁷| P:means—allow <> hand
1855:means; allow <> hand, ⁴³⁹| P:Good!—in *1855*:Good!—In
1868:Good! In ⁴⁴⁰| P:believe you *1855*:believe, you ⁴⁴¹| P:that concession,
recollect) *1855*:that admission, recollect) *1888*:recollect!) ⁴⁴²| P:find—(apart <>
towering-o'er *1855*:find—apart *1863*:towering o'er ⁴⁴⁴| P:tastes you
despise)— *1855*:despise— *1865*:taste ⁴⁴⁵| P:star, his *1855*:star?—his
⁴⁴⁶| P:in what—it's alive, *1855*:in what? it's alive ⁴⁴⁷| P:Shines <> him and
1855:And shines *1865*:him, and ⁴⁴⁹| P:were—and *1855*:were, and
⁴⁵⁰| P:as he, *1855*:as his, ⁴⁵³| P:a Napoleon and yet disbelieve?
1855:disbelieve! *1868*:disbelieve— *1888*:a Napoleon, and ⁴⁵⁴| *1855*:away.
1868:away! ⁴⁵⁵| P:of the world for <> you'd *1865*:world, for *1868*:you
1888:o' ⁴⁵⁷| P:it—we *1855*:it! we ⁴⁵⁹| P:forth *1855*:forth,

Past calculation to the end of time!
Can I mistake for some clear word of God
(Which were my ample warrant for it all)
His puff of hazy instinct, idle talk,
"The State, that's I," quack-nonsense about crowns,
And (when one beats the man to his last hold)
A vague idea of setting things to rights,
Policing people efficaciously,
More to their profit, most of all to his own;
The whole to end that dismallest of ends
By an Austrian marriage, cant to us the Church,
And resurrection of the old *régime*?
Would I, who hope to live a dozen years,
Fight Austerlitz for reasons such and such?
No: for, concede me but the merest chance
Doubt may be wrong—there's judgment, life to come!
With just that chance, I dare not. Doubt proves right?
This present life is all?—you offer me
Its dozen noisy years, without a chance
That wedding an archduchess, wearing lace,
And getting called by divers new-coined names,
Will drive off ugly thoughts and let me dine,
Sleep, read and chat in quiet as I like!
Therefore I will not.

Take another case;

Fit up the cabin yet another way.

462| P:time. 1855:time!   463| P:of God, 1855:of God   465| P:instincts <> talk
1855:talk, 1865:instinct   466| P:"The state <> quack nonsense about Fate,
1855:quack-nonsense about kings, 1863:"The State <> about crowns,   467| P:And,
(when 1855:And (when   468| P:The vague 1863:A vague   469| P:efficaciously
1855:efficaciously,   470| P:his, 1855:his own;   472| P:marriage—cant
<> the church— 1855:marriage, cant <> church, 1863:the Church,
473| P:régime. 1865:régime: 1868:régime?   476| P:No—for 1855:No: for
477| P:come— 1855:come!   478| P:not: doubt <> right! 1855:not. Doubt <>
right?   479| P:all—you 1855:all? you 1863:all?—you   480-481| P:dozen years
with not a chance at all / That <> an Arch-Duchess <> lace 1855:dozen
noisy years <> chance / That <> lace, 1863:years without a 1865:an arch-duchess
1868:years, without 1888:archduchess   482| P:by half a dozen names
1855:by divers new-coined names,   484| P:like— 1855:like!   485| P:not.
§ ¶ § Try another case— 1855:Therefore, I <> not. § ¶ § Take another case;

310

What say you to the poets? shall we write
Hamlet, Othello—make the world our own,
Without a risk to run of either sort?
490   I can't!—to put the strongest reason first.
"But try," you urge, "the trying shall suffice;
The aim, if reached or not, makes great the life:
Try to be Shakespeare, leave the rest to fate!"
Spare my self-knowledge—there's no fooling me!
495   If I prefer remaining my poor self,
I say so not in self-dispraise but praise.
If I'm a Shakespeare, let the well alone;
Why should I try to be what now I am?
If I'm no Shakespeare, as too probable,—
500   His power and consciousness and self-delight
And all we want in common, shall I find—
Trying for ever? while on points of taste
Wherewith, to speak it humbly, he and I
Are dowered alike—I'll ask you, I or he,
505   Which in our two lives realizes most?
Much, he imagined—somewhat, I possess.
He had the imagination; stick to that!
Let him say, "In the face of my soul's works
Your world is worthless and I touch it not
510   Lest I should wrong them"—I'll withdraw my plea.
But does he say so? look upon his life!

---

*1865:*Therefore I   ⁴⁸⁷| P:the Poet's *1855:*the poet's *1865:*poets
⁴⁸⁸| P:Hamlets, Othellos <> own *1855:*own, *1868:*Hamlet, Othello   ⁴⁹¹| P:
suffice— *1855:*suffice: *1863:*suffice;   ⁴⁹²| P:life. *1863:*life: ⁴⁹³| P:be
Shakspeare *1863:*be Shakespeare   ⁴⁹⁵| P:self *1855:*self,   ⁴⁹⁶| P:so, not
*1855:*so not   ⁴⁹⁷| P:a Shakspeare <> alone— *1863:*a Shakespeare
*1865:*alone;   ⁴⁹⁹| not Shakspeare <> probable, *1855:*no <> probable,— *1863:*no
Shakespeare   ⁵⁰⁰| P:power, and consciousness, and self delight, *1855:*power
and consciousness and self-delight   ⁵⁰¹| P:all me want <> find
*1855:*all we want <> find—   ⁵⁰²| P:tastes *1855:*taste   ⁵⁰⁵| P:realises
*1863:*realizes   ⁵⁰⁶| P:Much he <> somewhat I *1855:*Much, he <> somewhat,
I *1865:*somewhat I *1868:*somewhat, I   ⁵⁰⁷| P:that— *1855:*that!
⁵⁰⁸| P:say "in *1855:*say "In *1865:*say, "In   ⁵¹⁰| P:them"—I should yield my
cause: *1855:*them"—I withdraw my plea. *1863:*them"—I'll withdraw

Himself, who only can, gives judgment there.
He leaves his towers and gorgeous palaces
To build the trimmest house in Stratford town;
515   Saves money, spends it, owns the worth of things,
Giulio Romano's pictures, Dowland's lute;
Enjoys a show, respects the puppets, too,
And none more, had he seen its entry once,
Than "Pandulph, of fair Milan cardinal."
520   Why then should I who play that personage,
The very Pandulph Shakespeare's fancy made,
Be told that had the poet chanced to start
From where I stand now (some degree like mine
Being just the goal he ran his race to reach)
525   He would have run the whole race back, forsooth,
And left being Pandulph, to begin write plays?
Ah, the earth's best can be but the earth's best!
Did Shakespeare live, he could but sit at home
And get himself in dreams the Vatican,
530   Greek busts, Venetian paintings, Roman walls,
And English books, none equal to his own,
Which I read, bound in gold (he never did).
—Terni's fall, Naples' bay and Gothard's top—
Eh, friend? I could not fancy one of these;
535   But, as I pour this claret, there they are:
I've gained them—crossed St. Gothard last July
With ten mules to the carriage and a bed
Slung inside; is my hap the worse for that?

512| P:there! *1855:*there.   514| P:town, *1855:*town;   516| P:lute— *1855:*lute;
517| P:Would see a <> respect *1855:*Enjoys a <> respects   518| P:none
more than, had *1855:*And none more, had   519| P:"I, Pandulph <> cardinal:"
*1855:*Than "Pandulph <> cardinal."   520| P:should one who plays <>
personage *1855:*should I who play <> personage,   521| P:very Pandulph
Shakspeare made so fine, *1855:*very Pandulph Shakspeare's fancy made,
*1863:*very Pandulph Shakespeare's   522| P:the Poet *1855:*the poet   523| P:now—
some *1855:*now (some   524| P:reach— *1855:*reach)   526| P:being
Pandulph to *1855:*being Pandulph, to   527| P:but the earth's best— *1855:*but the
earth's best!   528| P:Did Shakspeare *1863:*Did Shakespeare   530| P:painting
*1855:*paintings   531| P:own *1855:*own,   532| P:Which I have, bound
in gold, (he never had) *1855:*Which I read, bound <> never did). *1888:*gold (he
533| P:—Terni and Naples *1855:*and Naples' *1868:*—Terni's fall, Naples'
534| P:these— *1865:*these;   535| P:are— *1865:*are: 536| P:I've seen them

We want the same things, Shakespeare and myself,
540 And what I want, I have: he, gifted more,
Could fancy he too had them when he liked,
But not so thoroughly that, if fate allowed,
He would not have them also in my sense.
We play one game; I send the ball aloft
545 No less adroitly that of fifty strokes
Scarce five go o'er the wall so wide and high
Which sends them back to me: I wish and get.
He struck balls higher and with better skill,
But at a poor fence level with his head,
550 And hit—his Stratford house, a coat of arms,
Successful dealings in his grain and wool,—
While I receive heaven's incense in my nose
And style myself the cousin of Queen Bess.
Ask him, if this life's all, who wins the game?

555   Believe—and our whole argument breaks up.
Enthusiasm's the best thing, I repeat;
Only, we can't command it; fire and life
Are all, dead matter's nothing, we agree:
And be it a mad dream or God's very breath,
560 The fact's the same,—belief's fire, once in us,
Makes of all else mere stuff to show itself:
We penetrate our life with such a glow
As fire lends wood and iron—this turns steel,
That burns to ash—all's one, fire proves its power

*1855:*I've gained them   539| P:things—Shakspeare and myself—   *1855:*things,
Shakspeare and myself,   *1863:*things, Shakespeare   540| P:But what <> have—he
*1855:*And what <> have: he   541| P:Can fancy that he had it when he liked
*1855:*Could fancy he too had <> liked,   *1888:*had them when   542| P:that when fate
allows   *1855:*that if fate allowed   *1868:*that, if <> allowed,   543| P:have
it also   *1888:*have them also   544| P:game, I   *1855:*game. I   *1868:*game; I
546| P:Not five   *1855:*Scarce five   547| P:get—   *1855:*get.   548| P:skill
*1855:*skill,   549| P:head   *1855:*head,   551| P:wool—   *1855:*wool,—
552| P:receive the incense   *1855:*receive heaven's incense   *1863:*receive Heaven's
*1868:*receive heaven's   553| P:of Queen Bess—   *1855:*of Queen Bess.
556| P:thing I repeat—   *1855:*thing, I repeat;   557| P:it:fire   *1855:*it; fire
558| P:agree—   *1855:*agree: 559| P:dream, or   *1855:*dream or   560| P:fire once
*1868:*fire, once   561| *1855:*itself.   *1863:*itself: 562| P:You penetrate
*1855:*We penetrate   563| P:steel   *1855:*steel,   564| P:proves itself: *1855:*proves its

565   For good or ill, since men call flare success.
       But paint a fire, it will not therefore burn.
       Light one in me, I'll find it food enough!
       Why, to be Luther—that's a life to lead,
       Incomparably better than my own.
570   He comes, reclaims God's earth for God, he says,
       Sets up God's rule again by simple means,
       Re-opens a shut book, and all is done.
       He flared out in the flaring of mankind;
       Such Luther's luck was: how shall such be mine?
575   If he succeeded, nothing's left to do:
       And if he did not altogether—well,
       Strauss is the next advance. All Strauss should be
       I might be also. But to what result?
       He looks upon no future: Luther did.
580   What can I gain on the denying side?
       Ice makes no conflagration. State the facts,
       Read the text right, emancipate the world—
       The emancipated world enjoys itself
       With scarce a thank-you: Blougram told it first
585   It could not owe a farthing,—not to him
       More than Saint Paul! 'twould press its pay, you think?
       Then add there's still that plaguy hundredth chance
       Strauss may be wrong. And so a risk is run—

---

power   565| P:success— 1855:success.   566| P:burn! 1855:burn.
567| P:me, I'd find 1855:me, I'll find   569| P:own— 1855:own.
570| P:says— 1855:says,   571| P:again, by 1855:again by   572| P:done—
1855:done.   573| P:He could enjoy the <> mankind— 1855:He flared out in the
<> mankind;   574| P:was—how 1865:was: how   575| P:do— 1855:do:
576| P:well— 1855:well,   577| P:advance—all 1855:advance. All   578| P:also—
but 1855:also. But   579| 1863:no Future 1868:no future   581| P:conflagration!
State 1855:conflagration. State   584| P:With just a thank-you—since I told it
first— 1855:With scarce a thank-you—Blougram told it first 1865:thank-you:
Blougram   585| P:to me 1855:to him   586| P:than St. Paul: 'twould
1855:than St. Paul! 'twould 1863:than Saint 1868:than Saint Paul? 'twould 1888:than
Saint Paul! 'twould   587| P:plaguey 1863:plaguy   588| P:wrong—and

For what gain? not for Luther's, who secured
590 A real heaven in his heart throughout his life,
Supposing death a little altered things.

"Ay, but since really you lack faith," you cry,
"You run the same risk really on all sides,
In cool indifference as bold unbelief.
595 As well be Strauss as swing 'twixt Paul and him.
It's not worth having, such imperfect faith,
No more available to do faith's work
Than unbelief like mine. Whole faith, or none!"

Softly, my friend! I must dispute that point.
600 Once own the use of faith, I'll find you faith.
We're back on Christian ground. You call for faith:
I show you doubt, to prove that faith exists.
The more of doubt, the stronger faith, I say,
If faith o'ercomes doubt. How I know it does?
605 By life and man's free will, God gave for that!
To mould life as we choose it, shows our choice:
That's our one act, the previous work's his own.
You criticize the soil? it reared this tree—
This broad life and whatever fruit it bears!
610 What matter though I doubt at every pore,
Head-doubts, heart-doubts, doubts at my fingers' ends,

---

*1855:*wrong. And   589| P:for Luther's—who   *1855:*for Luther's, who   590| P:life
*1855:*life,   *1863:*real Heaven   *1868:*real heaven   591| P:things!   *1863:*things.
592| P:really I lack   *1863:*really you lack   593| P:"I run   *1863:*"You run
584| P:unbelief;   *1855:*unbelief.   596| P:Myself, for instance, have imperfect   *1855:*It's
not worth having, such imperfect   597| *1855:*Nor   *1865:*No   598| P:like
yours—whole   *1855:*yours. Whole   *1863:*like mine. Whole   599| *1888:*point
DC,BrU:point.   *1889:*point.   601| P:ground; you < > faith—   *1855:*ground.
You < > faith: 602| P:that Faith   *1855:*that faith   603| P:stronger
Faith   *1855:*stronger faith   604| P:If Faith < > doubt—how   *1855:*If faith < >
doubt. How   606| P:choice,   *1855:*choice: 607| P:work's His own!
*1855:*own.   *1868:*work's his   608| P:criticise the soil? it   *1863:*criticize   *1888:*the
soul? it § emended to § soil § see Editorial Notes §   609| P:bears.   *1855:*bears!

Doubts in the trivial work of every day,
Doubts at the very bases of my soul
In the grand moments when she probes herself—
615 If finally I have a life to show,
The thing I did, brought out in evidence
Against the thing done to me underground
By hell and all its brood, for aught I know?
I say, whence sprang this? shows it faith or doubt?
620 All's doubt in me; where's break of faith in this?
It is the idea, the feeling and the love,
God means mankind should strive for and show forth
Whatever be the process to that end,—
And not historic knowledge, logic sound,
625 And metaphysical acumen, sure!
"What think ye of Christ," friend? when all's done and said,
Like you this Christianity or not?
It may be false, but will you wish it true?
Has it your vote to be so if it can?
630 Trust you an instinct silenced long ago
That will break silence and enjoin you love
What mortified philosophy is hoarse,
And all in vain, with bidding you despise?
If you desire faith—then you've faith enough:
635 What else seeks God—nay, what else seek ourselves?
You form a notion of me, we'll suppose,
On hearsay; it's a favourable one:
"But still" (you add), "there was no such good man,
Because of contradiction in the facts.
640 One proves, for instance, he was born in Rome,
This Blougram; yet throughout the tales of him

612| *1868:*day. *1888:*day,   616| P:did,—brought <> evidence— *1855:*did,
brought <> evidence   618| P:By Hell <> know. *1855:*know? *1868:*By
hell   619| P:it Faith *1855:*it faith   620| P:me, where's *1855:*me; where's
621| P:love *1865:*love,   622| P:forth, *1865:*forth   625| P:sure. *1855:*sure!
626| P:friend! when *1855:*friend? when   627| P:You like this *1863:*Like
you this   629| P:vote, to *1855:*vote to   632| P:mortified Philosophy is hoarse
*1855:*mortified philosophy is hoarse,   633| P:vain with *1855:*vain, with
634| P:enough— *1855:*enough: *1863:*enough: 637| P:one. *1855:*one:
638| P:still," (you add) "there *1888:*still" (you add), "there   639| P:contradictions
<> facts— *1855:*facts. *1865:*contradiction   641| P:This Blougram—yet *1865:*This

I see he figures as an Englishman."
Well, the two things are reconcileable.
But would I rather you discovered that,
645   Subjoining—"Still, what matter though they be?
Blougram concerns me nought, born here or there."

Pure faith indeed—you know not what you ask!
Naked belief in God the Omnipotent,
Omniscient, Omnipresent, sears too much
650   The sense of conscious creatures to be borne.
It were the seeing him, no flesh shall dare.
Some think, Creation's meant to show him forth:
I say it's meant to hide him all it can,
And that's what all the blessed evil's for.
655   Its use in Time is to environ us,
Our breath, our drop of dew, with shield enough
Against that sight till we can bear its stress.
Under a vertical sun, the exposed brain
And lidless eye and disemprisoned heart
660   Less certainly would wither up at once
Than mind, confronted with the truth of him.
But time and earth case-harden us to live;
The feeblest sense is trusted most; the child
Feels God a moment, ichors o'er the place,
665   Plays on and grows to be a man like us.
With me, faith means perpetual unbelief
Kept quiet like the snake 'neath Michael's foot
Who stands calm just because he feels it writhe.
Or, if that's too ambitious,—here's my box—

Blougram; yet   642| P:an Englishman. *1855*:an Englishman."
643| P:reconcileable— *1855*:reconcileable.   644| P:that *1855*:that,
645| P:be?— *1855*:be?   646| P:there?" *1855*:there."   650| P:borne,
1855:borne.   651| P:him no <> dare— *1855*:him, no <> dare. *1863*:seeing Him
1868:seeing him *1888*:dare DC,BrU:dare. *1889*:dare.   652| P:think
Creation's <> forth— *1855*:think, Creation's <> forth: *1863*:show Him *1865*:forth
1868:show him forth: 653| P:can *1855*:say, it's <> can, *1863*:hide Him *1865*:say
it's *1868*:hide him   654| P:blessed Evil's for, *1855*:for. *1868*:blessed evil's
655| P:in time *1863*:in Time   657| P:stress: *1855*:stress.   658| P:sun the <>
brain, *1855*:sun, the <> brain   659| P:The lidless eye, the disemprisoned
heart, *1855*:And lidless eye and disemprisoned heart   661| P:Than we, confronted
<> of Him. *1855*:Than mind, confronted *1868*:of him.   662| P:But
Time and Earth *1855*:But time and earth   663| P:most—the *1855*:most; the

317

670 I need the excitation of a pinch
     Threatening the torpor of the inside-nose
     Nigh on the imminent sneeze that never comes.
     "Leave it in peace" advise the simple folk:
     Make it aware of peace by itching-fits,
675 Say I—let doubt occasion still more faith!

          You'll say, once all believed, man, woman, child,
     In that dear middle-age these noodles praise.
     How you'd exult if I could put you back
     Six hundred years, blot out cosmogony,
680 Geology, ethnology, what not,
     (Greek endings, each the little passing-bell
     That signifies some faith's about to die),
     And set you square with Genesis again,—
     When such a traveller told you his last news,
685 He saw the ark a-top of Ararat
     But did not climb there since 'twas getting dusk
     And robber-bands infest the mountain's foot!
     How should you feel, I ask, in such an age,
     How act? As other people felt and did;
690 With soul more blank than this decanter's knob,
     Believe—and yet lie, kill, rob, fornicate
     Full in belief's face, like the beast you'd be!

          No, when the fight begins within himself,
     A man's worth something. God stoops o'er his head,
695 Satan looks up between his feet—both tug—
     He's left, himself, i' the middle: the soul wakes
     And grows. Prolong that battle through his life!

671| P:inside nose *1855*:inside-nose   672| P:comes *1855*:comes.
673| P:folk— *1865*:folk: 675| P:Say I, give still occasion for more *1855*:
Say I—let doubt occasion still more   676| P:Why, once we all *1855*:You'll
say, once all   677| P:praise— *1855*:praise.   680| P:ethnology—what
not— *1855*:ethnology, what not, *1888*:not DC, BrU:not, *1889*:not,   681| P:
endings with the *1865*:endings each the *1868*:endings, each   682| P:die)
1888:die),   683| P:again? *1855*:again,—   684| P:news *1855*:news,
685| P:the Ark <> of Ararat,— *1855*:the ark <> of Ararat   686| P:dusk,
1855:dusk   687| P:foot— *1855*:foot!   688| P:feel I ask in <> age? *1855*:feel,
I ask, in <> age,   689| P:act? as <> did— *1855*:act? As <> did;
690| P:knob— *1855*:knob,   692| P:face like *1855*:face, like   694| P:something—
God *1855*:something. God   696| P:in *1888*:i'   697| P:grows: prolong

Never leave growing till the life to come!
Here, we've got callous to the Virgin's winks
700 That used to puzzle people wholesomely:
Men have outgrown the shame of being fools.
What are the laws of nature, not to bend
If the Church bid them?—brother Newman asks.
Up with the Immaculate Conception, then—
705 On to the rack with faith!—is my advice.
Will not that hurry us upon our knees,
Knocking our breasts, "It can't be—yet it shall!
Who am I, the worm, to argue with my Pope?
Low things confound the high things!" and so forth.
710 That's better than acquitting God with grace
As some folk do. He's tried—no case is proved,
Philosophy is lenient—he may go!

You'll say, the old system's not so obsolete
But men believe still: ay, but who and where?
715 King Bomba's lazzaroni foster yet
The sacred flame, so Antonelli writes;
But even of these, what ragamuffin-saint
Believes God watches him continually,
As he believes in fire that it will burn,
720 Or rain that it will drench him? Break fire's law,
Sin against rain, although the penalty
Be just a singe or soaking? "No," he smiles;
"Those laws are laws that can enforce themselves."

The sum of all is—yes, my doubt is great,
725 My faith's still greater, then my faith's enough.

<> life *1855:*grows. Prolong <> life!   700| P:wholesomely— *1865:*wholesomely:
702| P:of Nature <> bend? *1855:*bend *1868:*of nature   703| P:them,
brother <> asks; *1855:*asks. *1863:*them?—brother   704| P:Out with *1855:*
Up with   705| P:faith—is my advice— *1855:*advice! *1863:*faith!—is my
advice.   706| P:knees *1863:*knees,   711| P:As folks do now—he's *1855:*
As some folks do. He's *1888:*folk   712| *1855:*lenient—He *1868:*lenient—he
713| P:say—the *1865:*say, the   714| P:But some men *1855:*But men   716| P:
flame—so <> writes— *1855:*flame, so <> writes;   717| P:these what *1855:*these,
what   718| P:continually *1855:*continually,   722| P:soaking? No, he
smiles— *1855:*smiles; *1868:*soaking? "No," he   723| P:Those
<> themselves! *1855:*themselves. *1868:*"Those <> themselves."   724| P:all, is
*1855:*all is   725| P:faith's the greater—then *1863:*faith's still greater <>

319

I have read much, thought much, experienced much,
Yet would die rather than avow my fear
The Naples' liquefaction may be false,
When set to happen by the palace-clock
730   According to the clouds or dinner-time.
I hear you recommend, I might at least
Eliminate, decrassify my faith
Since I adopt it; keeping what I must
And leaving what I can—such points as this.
735   I won't—that is, I can't throw one away.
Supposing there's no truth in what I hold
About the need of trial to man's faith,
Still, when you bid me purify the same,
To such a process I discern no end.
740   Clearing off one excrescence to see two,
There's ever a next in size, now grown as big,
That meets the knife: I cut and cut again!
First cut the Liquefaction, what comes last
But Fichte's clever cut at God himself?
745   Experimentalize on sacred things!
I trust nor hand nor eye nor heart nor brain
To stop betimes: they all get drunk alike.
The first step, I am master not to take.

You'd find the cutting-process to your taste
750   As much as leaving growths of lies unpruned,
Nor see more danger in it,—you retort.

---

enough, *1865:*greater, then <> enough.   726| P:experienced much—
*1855:*experienced much,   727| P:than avouch my   *1855:*than avow my
728| P:The Naples <> false   *1855:*The Naples' <> false,   729| P:palace clock
*1855:*palace-clock   730| P:dinner time.   *1855:*dinner-time.   731| P:you
interpose—"I   *1855:*you recommend, I   732| P:faith,   *1855:*faith
733| P:it: keeping <> must,   *1855:*it; keeping<>must   734| P:this!"
*1855:*this!   *1868:*this.   735| P:away!   *1855:*away.   736| P:Suppose there were no
<> what I said   *1855:*Supposing there's no   *1868:*what I hold   737| P:
trials <>faith—   *1855:*faith,   *1865:*trial   738| P:same   *1855:*same,   739| P:end,
*1868:*end.   740| P:two—   *1855:*two;   *1868:*two,   742| P:knife—I
*1865:*knife: I   743| P:First comes the   *1855:*First cut the   745| P:things?
*1863:*things!   746| P:hand, nor eye, nor heart, nor   *1855:*hand nor eye nor heart
nor   747| P:alike—   *1855:*alike.   751| P:it—you retort—   *1855:*it, you retort.

Your taste's worth mine; but my taste proves more wise
When we consider that the steadfast hold
On the extreme end of the chain of faith
755   Gives all the advantage, makes the difference
With the rough purblind mass we seek to rule:
We are their lords, or they are free of us,
Just as we tighten or relax our hold.
So, other matters equal, we'll revert
760   To the first problem—which, if solved my way
And thrown into the balance, turns the scale—
How we may lead a comfortable life,
How suit our luggage to the cabin's size.

Of course you are remarking all this time
765   How narrowly and grossly I view life,
Respect the creature-comforts, care to rule
The masses, and regard complacently
"The cabin," in our old phrase. Well, I do.
I act for, talk for, live for this world now,
770   As this world prizes action, life and talk:
No prejudice to what next world may prove,
Whose new laws and requirements, my best pledge
To observe then, is that I observe these now,
Shall do hereafter what I do meanwhile.
775   Let us concede (gratuitously though)
Next life relieves the soul of body, yields
Pure spiritual enjoyment: well, my friend,

1865:it,—you   752| P:mine—but   *1855*:mine; but   754| P:Of
the extreme   *1855*:On the extreme   755| P:difference, *1865*:difference
756| P:rule—   *1855*:rule. *1865*:rule: 757| P:us *1865*:us,   758| P:
relax that hold—   *1855*:hold. *1865*:relax our hold.   759| P:other *1888:*
others § emended to § other § see Editorial Notes §   760| P:which if *1863*:which,
if   761| P:balance turns the scale. *1855*:scale—   *1863*:balance, turns   768| P:
cabin"—in<>phrase! Well, I do—   *1855*:cabin," in<>do. *1865*:phrase. Well
769| P:talk of, live in, this <> now—   *1855*:talk for, live for this <> now,
770| P:world calls for action <> talk—   *1868*:world prizes action <> talk:
771| P:prove—   *1855*:prove,   772| *1855*:requirements my *1863*:requirements, my
773| P:observe, then *1855*:observe then   774| P:Doing hereafter
1863:Shall do hereafter   775| P:gratuitously, though) *1855*:gratuitously though)
777| P:Pure, spiritual enjoyments *1855*:Pure spiritual *1865*:enjoyment:

Why lose this life i' the meantime, since its use
May be to make the next life more intense?

780   Do you know, I have often had a dream
(Work it up in your next month's article)
Of man's poor spirit in its progress, still
Losing true life for ever and a day
Through ever trying to be and ever being—
785 In the evolution of successive spheres—
Before its actual sphere and place of life,
Halfway into the next, which having reached,
It shoots with corresponding foolery
Halfway into the next still, on and off!
790 As when a traveller, bound from North to South,
Scouts fur in Russia: what's its use in France?
In France spurns flannel: where's its need in Spain?
In Spain drops cloth, too cumbrous for Algiers!
Linen goes next, and last the skin itself,
795 A superfluity at Timbuctoo.
When, through his journey, was the fool at ease?
I'm at ease now, friend; worldly in this world,
I take and like its way of life; I think
My brothers, who administer the means,
800 Live better for my comfort—that's good too;
And God, if he pronounce upon such life,
Approves my service, which is better still.
If he keep silence,—why, for you or me

well my *1868:*well, my ⁷⁷⁸| P:in *1888:*i' ⁷⁷⁹| P:the contrast more
*1855:*the next life more ⁷⁸²| P:progress still, *1855:*still *1868:*progress,
still ⁷⁸³| P:Losing its life <> day, *1855:*Losing true life <> day
⁷⁸⁴| P:be, and <> being *1855:*be and *1865:*being— ⁷⁸⁵| P:
spheres, *1865:*spheres— ⁷⁸⁶| P:Before *1865:Before* ⁷⁸⁷| P:Half way
*1863:*Halfway ⁷⁹⁰| P:from north to south, *1863:*from North to South,
⁷⁹¹| P:in Russia—what's *1865:*in Russia; what's *1888:*in Russia: what's
⁷⁹²| P:flannel—where's *1865:*flannel; where's *1888:*flannel: where's
⁷⁹³| P:cloth—too <> for Algiers— *1855:*for Algiers! *1865:*cloth, too
⁷⁹⁵| P:at Timbuctoo— *1855:*at Timbuctoo. ⁷⁹⁶| *1865:*ease *1868:*ease?
⁷⁹⁷| P:friend—worldly <> world; *1855:*this world *1863:*Im *1865:*I'm <>
friend; worldly <> world, ⁷⁹⁹| P:brothers who <> means *1865:*brothers,
who <> means, ⁸⁰⁰| P:too— *1855:*too; ⁸⁰¹| P:And God if <> upon
it all *1855:*And God, if <> all, *1863:*if He *1868:*if he <> upon such life,
⁸⁰²| P:service which *1855:*service, which ⁸⁰³| P:If He <> why for *1863:*

Or that brute beast pulled-up in to-day's "Times,"
805 What odds is't, save to ourselves, what life we lead?

You meet me at this issue: you declare,—
All special-pleading done with—truth is truth,
And justifies itself by undreamed ways.
You don't fear but it's better, if we doubt,
810 To say so, act up to our truth perceived
However feebly. Do then,—act away!
'Tis there I'm on the watch for you. How one acts
Is, both of us agree, our chief concern:
And how you'll act is what I fain would see
815 If, like the candid person you appear,
You dare to make the most of your life's scheme
As I of mine, live up to its full law
Since there's no higher law that counterchecks.
Put natural religion to the test
820 You've just demolished the revealed with—quick,
Down to the root of all that checks your will,
All prohibition to lie, kill and thieve,
Or even to be an atheistic priest!
Suppose a pricking to incontinence—
825 Philosophers deduce you chastity
Or shame, from just the fact that at the first
Whoso embraced a woman in the field,
Threw club down and forewent his brains beside,
So, stood a ready victim in the reach

why, for *1868*:If he   804| P:brute-beast <> to-day's "Times"—
1855:to-day's "Times,"   *1863*:to-day's 'Times,'   *1868*:to-day's "Times,"
1888:brute beast   806| P:issue—you declare,   *1865*:issue: you   *1868*:
declare,—   807| P:with, truth is   *1888*:with—truth is   808| P:ways—
1855:ways.   810| P:acting   *1865*:act   811| P:feeble; do that then   *1855*:
feebly. Do then   812| P:you—how   *1855*:you! How   *1865*:you. How
815| P:person that you are,   *1855*:person you appear,   818| P:counterchecks—
1855:counterchecks.   822| P:kill, and thieve   *1863*:kill and   *1888*:thieve,
823| P:atheistic Priest!   *1855*:atheistic priest!   826| P:shame from   *1855*:
shame, from   827| P:the plain,   *1865*:the field,   828| P:Used both arms, and
<> beside—   *1855*:Threw club down, and <> beside,   *1865*:down and
829| P:So lay a <> the sight   *1855*:So stood a <> the reach   *1865*:So, stood

830   Of any brother savage, club in hand;
       Hence saw the use of going out of sight
       In wood or cave to prosecute his loves:
       I read this in a French book t'other day.
       Does law so analysed coerce you much?
835   Oh, men spin clouds of fuzz where matters end,
       But you who reach where the first thread begins,
       You'll soon cut that!—which means you can, but won't,
       Through certain instincts, blind, unreasoned-out,
       You dare not set aside, you can't tell why,
840   But there they are, and so you let them rule.
       Then, friend, you seem as much a slave as I,
       A liar, conscious coward and hypocrite,
       Without the good the slave expects to get,
       In case he has a master after all!
845   You own your instincts? why, what else do I,
       Who want, am made for, and must have a God
       Ere I can be aught, do aught?—no mere name
       Want, but the true thing with what proves its truth,
       To wit, a relation from that thing to me,
850   Touching from head to foot—which touch I feel,
       And with it take the rest, this life of ours!
       I live my life here; yours you dare not live.

       —Not as I state it, who (you please subjoin)
       Disfigure such a life and call it names,
855   While, to your mind, remains another way
       For simple men: knowledge and power have rights,
       But ignorance and weakness have rights too.
       There needs no crucial effort to find truth

830| P:brother-savage club in hand—   1865:hand;   1868:brother-savage,
club 1888:brother savage   831| P:the good of 1855:the use of
832| P:to set about the same—   1855:to prosecute his loves—   1865:loves:
834| P:analyzed 1863:analysed   837| P:won't—   1855:won't 1888:won't,
841| 1865:Then friend 1868:Then, friend   842| P:hypocrite. 1855:hypocrite,
843| P:get. 1855:get,   844| P:Suppose he<>all, 1855:all! 1865:In case he
845| P:instincts—why what<>do I— 1855:do I, 1863:why, what 1865:instincts:
why 1868:instincts? why   847| P:do aught!—no 1855:do aught?—no
849| P:me— 1855:me,   851| P:ours. 1855:ours!   852| P:here—yours you cannot
live— 1855:here; yours you dare not live.   853| P:Not 1863:—Not
854| P:names 1855:names,   855| P:While, in your 1865:While, to your   858| P:

If here or there or anywhere about:
860 We ought to turn each side, try hard and see,
And if we can't, be glad we've earned at least
The right, by one laborious proof the more,
To graze in peace earth's pleasant pasturage.
Men are not angels, neither are they brutes:
865 Something we may see, all we cannot see.
What need of lying? I say, I see all,
And swear to each detail the most minute
In what I think a Pan's face—you, mere cloud:
I swear I hear him speak and see him wink,
870 For fear, if once I drop the emphasis,
Mankind may doubt there's any cloud at all.
You take the simple life—ready to see,
Willing to see (for no cloud's worth a face)—
And leaving quiet what no strength can move,
875 And which, who bids you move? who has the right?
I bid you; but you are God's sheep, not mine:
"*Pastor est tui Dominus.*" You find
In this the pleasant pasture of our life
Much you may eat without the least offence,
880 Much you don't eat because your maw objects,
Much you would eat but that your fellow-flock
Open great eyes at you and even butt,
And thereupon you like your mates so well

truth— *1855*:truth   859| P:about *1855*:about— *1865*:about:
862-865| P:more. / Men are not Gods, but, if you like, are brutes / To < >
pasturage: / Something < > cannot see— *1855*:more, / To < > pasturage. / Men
are not gods, but, properly, are brutes. / Something *1863*:not angels, neither are
they brutes. / Something *1865*:brutes: / Something < > cannot see.   866| P:all
1855:all,   868| P:a man's face < > cloud,— *1855*:cloud: *1863*:a Pan's face
869| P:speak, and < > wink *1855*:speak and < > wink,   870| P:if I once drop
1855:if once I drop   871| P:doubt if there's a cloud *1863*:doubt there's
any cloud   872| P:simpler < > see— *1855*:see, *1868*:simple   873| P:see—for
< > a race— *1855*:a face— *1865*:see (for < > face) *1888*:face)—   875| P:move?
who, with the *1855*:move? who has the   876| P:mine— *1865*:mine:
877| P:tui Dominus"—you find, *1855*:tui Dominus." You find   878| P:In these
the < > pastures of this life, *1855*:life *1865*:In this the < > pasture of our life
879| P:offence— *1855*:offence,   880| P:eat, because < > objects— *1855*:eat
because < > objects,   881| P:eat, but *1855*:eat but   882| P:butt—
1855:butt,   883| P:Well, in the main you < > your friends so much *1855*:And

You cannot please yourself, offending them;
885 Though when they seem exorbitantly sheep,
You weigh your pleasure with their butts and bleats
And strike the balance. Sometimes certain fears
Restrain you, real checks since you find them so;
Sometimes you please yourself and nothing checks:
890 And thus you graze through life with not one lie,
And like it best.

　　　　　　　　But do you, in truth's name?
If so, you beat—which means you are not I—
Who needs must make earth mine and feed my fill
Not simply unbutted at, unbickered with,
895 But motioned to the velvet of the sward
By those obsequious wethers' very selves.
Look at me, sir; my age is double yours:
At yours, I knew beforehand, so enjoyed,
What now I should be—as, permit the word,
900 I pretty well imagine your whole range
And stretch of tether twenty years to come.
We both have minds and bodies much alike:
In truth's name, don't you want my bishopric,
My daily bread, my influence and my state?
905 You're young. I'm old; you must be old one day;
Will you find then, as I do hour by hour,
Women their lovers kneel to, who cut curls

---

thereupon you　*1863:*your mates so well　　　884| P:them—　*1865:*them;
885| P:Though sometimes, when they seem to exact too much,　*1855:*Though when
they seem exorbitantly sheep,　　　886| P:their kicks and butts,　*1855:*their butts
and kicks　*1863:*and bleats　　　888| P:Will stay you—real fears, since <> so—
*1855:*Restrain you—real checks since　*1865:*you, real <> so;　　　889| P:checks,　*1855:*
checks;　*1865:*checks:　　　892| P:means—you　*1863:*means, you　*1868:*means
you　　　893| P:Who cannot make <> mine so, feed　*1855:*Who needs must make
<> mine and feed　　　896| P:By the obsequious short horns' very
*1855:*By those obsequious wethers' very　　　897| *1855:*yours.　*1863:*yours:
898| P:enjoyed　*1855:*enjoyed,　　　899| P:be—while, permit　*1855:*be—as, permit
902| P:alike—　*1855:*alike.　*1865:*alike:　　　904| P:influence, and
*1855:*influence and　　　905| P:young, I'm old, you <> day,　*1855:*day;
*1888:*young. I'm old; you　　　907| P:to, that cut　*1865:*to, who cut

326

From your fat lap-dog's ear to grace a brooch—
Dukes, who petition just to kiss your ring—
910   With much beside you know or may conceive?
Suppose we die to-night: well, here am I,
Such were my gains, life bore this fruit to me,
While writing all the same my articles
On music, poetry, the fictile vase
915   Found at Albano, chess, Anacreon's Greek.
But you—the highest honour in your life,
The thing you'll crown yourself with, all your days,
Is—dining here and drinking this last glass
I pour you out in sign of amity
920   Before we part for ever. Of your power
And social influence, worldly worth in short,
Judge what's my estimation by the fact,
I do not condescend to enjoin, beseech,
Hint secrecy on one of all these words!
925   You're shrewd and know that should you publish one
The world would brand the lie—my enemies first,
Who'd sneer—"the bishop's an arch-hypocrite
And knave perhaps, but not so frank a fool."
Whereas I should not dare for both my ears
930   Breathe one such syllable, smile one such smile,
Before the chaplain who reflects myself—
My shade's so much more potent than your flesh.
What's your reward, self-abnegating friend?
Stood you confessed of those exceptional
935   And privileged great natures that dwarf mine—

908| P:From yonder lap-dog's ears   1855:From your fat lap-dog's   1865:ear
909| P:Dukes that petition <> kiss my ring—   1855:Dukes, that <> kiss your ring—
1865:Dukes, who petition   910| P:conceive!   1855:conceive?   912| P:me
1855:me,   915| P:at Albano, or Anacreon's   1863:at Albano, chess, or
1865:chess, Anacreon's   917| P:with all   1855:with, all   921| P:worth, in short
1855:worth in short,   922| P:fact—   1863:fact,   924| P:secresy <> words—
1855:words!   1863:secrecy   925| P:publish it 1863:publish one
926| P:first—   1855:first,   927| P:Who'd laugh—the Bishop's an arch-hypocrite—
1855:"Who'd sneer—the bishop's an arch-hypocrite,   1865:Who'd sneer—"the
<> arch-hypocrite   928| P:perhaps—but <> fool.   1855:perhaps, but <> fool."
930| P:such smile   1855:such smile,   931| P:Before my chaplain
1865:Before the chaplain   934| P:these   1855:those   935| P:natures dwarfing

A zealot with a mad ideal in reach,
A poet just about to print his ode,
A statesman with a scheme to stop this war,
An artist whose religion is his art—
940 I should have nothing to object: such men
Carry the fire, all things grow warm to them,
Their drugget's worth my purple, they beat me.
But you,—you're just as little those as I—
You, Gigadibs, who, thirty years of age,
945 Write statedly for Blackwood's Magazine,
Believe you see two points in Hamlet's soul
Unseized by the Germans yet—which view you'll print—
Meantime the best you have to show being still
That lively lightsome article we took
950 Almost for the true Dickens,—what's its name?
"The Slum and Cellar, or Whitechapel life
Limned after dark!" it made me laugh, I know,
And pleased a month, and brought you in ten pounds.
—Success I recognize and compliment,
955 And therefore give you, if you choose, three words
(The card and pencil-scratch is quite enough)
Which whether here, in Dublin or New York,
Will get you, prompt as at my eyebrow's wink,
Such terms as never you aspired to get
960 In all our own reviews and some not ours.
Go write your lively sketches! be the first
"Blougram, or The Eccentric Confidence"—

---

mine— *1855:*natures that dwarf mine—   937| P:ode— *1855:*ode,
938| P:war— *1855:*war,   939| P:art, *1865:*art—   940| P:object, such
*1855:*object! such *1865:*object: such   942| P:purple, these beat me— *1855:*purple,
they beat me.   943| P:these *1855:*those   945| P:for Blackwood's Magazine—
*1855:*for Blackwood's Magazine,   947| P:views *1855:*view   950| P:what's
the name? *1863:*what's its name?   951| P:and Cellar—or *1865:*and
Cellar, or   952| P:dark" it <> know— *1855:*dark!" it <> know,   953| P:month
and *1868:*month, and   954| P:recognise and compliment *1855:*compliment,
*1865:*recognize   955| P:if you please, three words— *1855:*words
*1863:*if you choose, three   956| P:(The simple card and pencil scratch's enough)
1855:(The card and pencil-scratch is quite enough)   957| P:in Dublin, or
*1863:*in Dublin or   958| P:you prompt <> wink *1855:*you, prompt <> wink,
961| P:sketches—be *1865:*sketches! be   962| P:"Blougram—or *1855:*"Blougram, or

Or better simply say, "The Outward-bound."
Why, men as soon would throw it in my teeth
965 As copy and quote the infamy chalked broad
About me on the church-door opposite.
You will not wait for that experience though,
I fancy, howsoever you decide,
To discontinue—not detesting, not
970 Defaming, but at least—despising me!

———

Over his wine so smiled and talked his hour
Sylvester Blougram, styled *in partibus*
Episcopus, nec non—(the deuce knows what
It's changed to by our novel hierarchy)
975 With Gigadibs the literary man,
Who played with spoons, explored his plate's design,
And ranged the olive-stones about its edge,
While the great bishop rolled him out a mind
Long crumpled, till creased consciousness lay smooth.

980 For Blougram, he believed, say, half he spoke.
The other portion, as he shaped it thus
For argumentatory purposes,
He felt his foe was foolish to dispute.
Some arbitrary accidental thoughts
985 That crossed his mind, amusing because new,
He chose to represent as fixtures there,
Invariable convictions (such they seemed
Beside his interlocutor's loose cards
Flung daily down, and not the same way twice)

———

963| P:say, "The Outward bound." *1855:*say, "The Outward-bound."
964| P:will *1855:*would 965| P:quote, the *1855:*quote the 966| P:church
door *1855:*church-door 967| P:though *1855:*though, 969| P:discontinue not
detesting—not *1855:*discontinue—not detesting, not 970| P:Degrading, but
*1855:*Defaming, but 973| P:*nee 1855:nec* 974| P:by the novel
heirarchy)— *1855:*by our novel heirarchy) 975| P:man *1855:*man,
977| P:Arranged its olive stones *1855:*And ranged the olive *1863:*olive-stones
978-980| P:great Bishop<>out his mind./ § ¶ § For<>half he said. *1855:*great
bishop<>§ ¶ §<>half he spoke. *1888:*out a mind/Long crumpled, till
creased consciousness lay smooth./ § ¶ § For 986| P:there *1855:*there,
987| P:convictions—such *1855:*convictions (such 989| P:twice; *1855:*twice)

990　While certain hell-deep instincts, man's weak tongue
　　　Is never bold to utter in their truth
　　　Because styled hell-deep ('tis an old mistake
　　　To place hell at the bottom of the earth)
　　　He ignored these,—not having in readiness
995　Their nomenclature and philosophy:
　　　He said true things, but called them by wrong names.
　　　"On the whole," he thought, "I justify myself
　　　On every point where cavillers like this
　　　Oppugn my life: he tries one kind of fence,
1000　I close, he's worsted, that's enough for him.
　　　He's on the ground: if ground should break away
　　　I take my stand on, there's a firmer yet
　　　Beneath it, both of us may sink and reach.
　　　His ground was over mine and broke the first:
1005　So, let him sit with me this many a year!"

　　　He did not sit five minutes. Just a week
　　　Sufficed his sudden healthy vehemence.
　　　Something had struck him in the "Outward-bound"
　　　Another way than Blougram's purpose was:
1010　And having bought, not cabin-furniture
　　　But settler's-implements (enough for three)
　　　And started for Australia—there, I hope,
　　　By this time he has tested his first plough,
　　　And studied his last chapter of St. John.

990| P:instincts man's   1855:instincts, man's   1863:certain Hell-deep   1868:certain
hell-deep   991| P:Shall hardly dare to   1855:Is never bold to   992| P:Till one
demonstrate it an   1855:Because styled hell-deep ('tis an   1863:styled Hell-deep
1868:styled hell-deep   993| P:earth,—   1855:earth)   1863:place Hell
1868:place hell   994| P:these, not   1855:these,—not   995| P:philosophy:—
1855:philosophy: 997| P:On the whole, he thought, I   1855:"On the whole," he
thought, "I   999| P:life—he <> fence—   1855:life: he   1865:fence,
1000| P:close—he's <> him!   1855:him;   1865:close, he's   1868:him.
1001| P:if the ground   1855:on the ground! if   1865:on the ground: if   1888:if ground
1002| P:took   1855:take   1004| P:first.   1863:first: 1005| P:So let <> me,
this <> year!   1855:me this <> year!"   1865:So, let   1006| P:minutes;
for a   1855:minutes. Just a   1008| P:(Something <> the "Outward bound"
1855:the "Outward-bound"   1865:Something   1009| P:was)   1865:was:
1010| P:bought not cabin furniture—   1855:bought, not cabin-furniture
1011| P:settler's implements   1855:settler's-implements   1012| P:there I hope
1855:there, I hope,

MEMORABILIA

I

Ah, did you once see Shelley plain,
    And did he stop and speak to you
And did you speak to him again?
    How strange it seems and new!

II

5   But you were living before that,
    And also you are living after;
And the memory I started at—
    My starting moves your laughter.

III

I crossed a moor, with a name of its own
10   And a certain use in the world no doubt,
Yet a hand's-breadth of it shines alone
    'Mid the blank miles round about:

IV

For there I picked up on the heather
    And there I put inside my breast
15 A moulted feather, an eagle-feather!
    Well, I forget the rest.

MEMORABILIA § Not in Huntington proof copy. Subsequent placement: 1863:DL §
2| *1855*:you? *1865*:you, *1888*:you   4| *1855*:seems, and *1868*:seems and
6| *1855*:And you <>after, *1865*:after; *1868*:And also you   8| *1855*:laughter!
1888:laughter   DC,BrU:laughter. *1889*:laughter.   9| *1855*:moor with *1863*:moor,
with   10| *1855*:a use *1868*:a certain use   12| *1855*:about— *1863*:about:
1868:Mid *1888*:'Mid   15| *1855*:eagle-feather— *1865*:eagle-feather!

A SOUL'S TRAGEDY

Emendations to the Text

The following emendations have been made to the 1889 text:

I, 1. 95: *Provost* has been capitalized, in accordance with all other uses of the word in all editions of the play; this restores the 1846-1865 reading.

I, 1. 116: In 1888-1889, an apostrophe was ommitted before *Tis*. It has been inserted, restoring the 1846-1868 reading.

II, 1. 386: When B removed the potentially confusing exclamation point after *Not I* in 1868, he failed to supply an end-stop for the sentence. The final exclamation point, which followed *noted*, has been moved outside the parentheses.

Composition and Publication

B's description of a work in progress on 22 May 1842 very likely pertains to *A Soul's Tragedy*: "I shall . . . finish a wise metaphysical play (about a great mind and soul turning to ill) . . . " (*Robert Browning and Alfred Domett*, ed. F. G. Kenyon [London: Smith, Elder, 1906], 36). Griffin and Minchin feel that *A Soul's Tragedy* was one of the works described by B as "in a state of forwardness" in 1844 (Griffin and Minchin, 120), and B wrote to EBB on 13 February 1846 that the play "was written two or three years ago" (RB-EBB, ed. Kintner, 455). The work lay unfinished in part because it never fully pleased B; the numerous references to it in his letters to EBB reveal that he felt a need to revise the play considerably. Elizabeth asked to see the manuscript of *A Soul's Tragedy* in February of 1845, but B did not deliver it for over a year. She read *Luria* during this time, and made many suggestions which B adopted. B contrasted the two plays on 11 February 1846: "For the Soul's Tragedy—*that* will surprise you, I think—There is no trace of you there,—you have not put out the black face of *it*—it is all sneering and *disillusion* . . . " (RB-EBB, ed. Kintner, 451). When at last B brought her the play in March of 1846, Elizabeth was delighted with it. Encouraging B at every opportunity, she helped correct the proofs. Four of her suggestions for minor changes—all incorporated in 1846—are preserved in F. G. Kenyon's transcription of part of a manuscript included in the 1913 Sotheby sale of the Browning collections (*New Poems*, 140-41). These changes are described in the notes below.

A Soul's Tragedy appeared with *Luria* on 13 April 1846 as "No. VIII and last" of *Bells and Pomegranates*, occupying pages 21-32 of the pamphlet. Some bibliographies state that in the 1846 edition, Part I contained 401 lines; in fact all 402 lines were present.

Series title

Elizabeth Barrett asserted that both the placement (on the verso of the title page of *A Soul's Tragedy*) and the somewhat obscure content of this note showed that B did not really wish to explain his title phrase (RB-EBB, ed. Kintner, 619). B refers to details of two specific paintings and their explanations. A fresco portrait of Dante with a pomegranate in his hand was uncovered in 1840-41 during restorations in the Magdalen Chapel of the Bargello (formerly called the Palazzo del Podesta) in Florence. The frescoes which contain the portrait treat scenes of the Last Judgment, and were attributed to Giotto di Bondone (c. 1266-1337) by Giorgio Vasari in his life of Giotto in *Le Vite de' Più Ecellenti Architetti, Pittori, et Scultori Italiani* (*The Lives of the Most Excellent Italian Architects, Painters, and Sculptors* [Florence, 1550]). Twentieth-century art historians have established that the Magdalene Chapel frescoes were done after Giotto's death, perhaps by his students.

Raphael (Raffaello Sanzio, 1483-1520) included a personification of Theology with a crown of pomegranate leaves as one of four allegorical figures on the ceiling of the Stanza (or Camera) della Segnatura, a room in the Vatican. The great frescoes in this room (including Raphael's "The School of Athens" and "The Disputation of the Sacrament") were described and interpreted by Giovanni Pietro Bellori (misprinted as Bellari in *Bells and Pomegranates*, No. VIII) in his study of Raphael, *Descrizzione delle Imagine Dipinte da Rafaelle . . .* (*Description of the Painted Images of Raphael . . .*). B quotes incompletely from p. 5 of this work: " . . . La corona, ch'ella porta in capo, è contesta di frondi, e fiori di Pomo granato, simbolo della Carità istessa, e delle buone opere, che devono germogliare con le Virtù; il qual Pomo fù però usato nelle vesti del Pontefice apresso gl'Ebrei" (" . . . the crown, which she wears on her head, is comprised of fronds and flowers of the pomegranate, a symbol of Charity itself, and of the good works which must spring forth with the Virtues; this fruit, however, was used in the robes of the pope after the manner of the Hebrews") [see Eleanor Cook, "Browning's 'Bellari,' " *N & Q*, NS 17 (1970), 334-35]. B had visited Rome and Florence in 1844, and may have seen both paintings. For further comment on the series title, see also Vol. III of this edition, 343-44.

Persons

Ogniben, the Pope's Legate A papal legate is an emissary who represents the pope in negotiations. As the temporal power of the pope increased in the Middle Ages, legates gained considerable political influence. As tithe-collectors, fund-raisers, and diplomats, they played a large role in maintaining the pope's political authority.

Time

The fifteenth and sixteenth centuries, like the nineteenth century, were marked by constant political strife in northern Italy, where the play is set. A series of popes tried to establish the papal lands as a unified state, but they were opposed by France, Spain, and the great ruling families of the north, such as the Este and Manfredi. The shifting alliances among the major powers forced the smaller cities and towns to change their allegiances frequently and rapidly; some tried to remain neutral, and a few were so disputed as to be practically independent. *A Soul's Tragedy* takes place after 1512, when Ravenna reverted to papal control and could thus rule Faenza in the name of the pope (see I, 94-95; II, 64-65), and before 1598, when Ferrara was claimed by the pope and could no longer offer sanctuary to his political opponents (see I, 340-41 and n.).

Place

Faenza is a city in NE Italy, 30 mi. SE of Bologna and 20 mi. SW of Ravenna. Faenza had strategic value and was fought over by various powers for centuries. Except for a period of self-government in the twelfth century, the city was ruled by outsiders until the unification of Italy in the 1870s. In the fourteenth and fifteenth centuries, the despotic Manfredi family exchanged control of Faenza with various representatives of papal authority in a long series of intrigues and battles. Finally, in 1502, Cesare Borgia had the leader of the Manfredi murdered and ceded Faenza to Cesare's father, Pope Alexander VI.

ACT I

2] *ave-bell* The church bell rung when the "Ave Maria" prayer is to be said, at six A.M., noon, and six P.M.

7] *Provost* As B explains in II, 64-65, Faenza was governed by a provost (or mayor) sent from Ravenna. Thus the provost was the indirect representative of papal authority; such governors were not tyrants, but they were neither chosen by nor loyal to a local constituency.

67] *wisely passive* cf. Wordsworth, "Expostulation and Reply," 1. 24.

74] *one who won't forego* Kenyon's transcription indicates that in 1845 this phrase read *One who don't forego*. EBB suggested substituting *won't* for *don't* (*New Poems*, 140).

90] *What's "me"* Kenyon's transcription indicates that in 1845 B had written *Who's me*; EBB suggested the change to the present reading.

95] *Ravenna* A city of NE Italy, 50 mi. E of Bologna and 40 mi. SE of Ferrara. Ravenna is the capital of Ravenna province (which includes Faenza) and the seat of the archbishop of Emilia-Romagna; for much of its history, Ravenna was a center for the administration of the temporal power of the church.

153] *fascination* The power or act of bewitching; enchantment; unseen inexplicable influence (Johnson's *Dictionary*).

159-62] According to Kenyon's transcription, in 1845 these lines read, *Wast not enough that I must strive, I said, / To grow so far familiar with all you / As find and take some way to get you—which / To do, an age seemed far too little*. EBB objected to these lines as obscure in expression, and B apparently recast them at her suggestion (*New Poems*, 140-41).

194] *liking of the eye* cf. 1 John 2:16.

198] *Nor missed . . . table* In Kenyon's transcription, EBB quotes this line as *Nor missed a cloak from wardrobe, nor a dish from table* and suggests dropping *nor a* to correct the rhythm (*New Poems*, 141).

218] *Œconomy* Regulation; distribution of everything active or passive to its proper place (Johnson's *Dictionary*).

231] *Lugo* a small town 10 mi. N of Faenza, on the road to Ferrara. Like Faenza, Lugo was ruled by outsiders; at the time of the poem's action it was ruled by the Duke of Ferrara, a member of the Este family and an opponent of the expansion of papal lands.

258-59] *Spring shall . . . time* cf. Genesis 8:22.

281] *scudi* Italian coins of gold or silver.

284] *San Vitale's suburb* San Vitale is a common place-name in northern Italy, but several possibilities arise for this reference to a place to be avoided. There is a famous church called San Vitale in Ravenna, but no one fleeing Faenza in the circumstances of the reference would need to be warned away from Ravenna and its authorities. The SE part of Ferrara is called San Vitale, but it would have been on the N road from Faenza, and is excluded by context. Of the several hamlets named San Vitale within a reasonable distance of Faenza, the one probably referred to is San Vitale di Reno, NW of Bologna.

332] *glowing trip-hook, thumbscrews and the gadge* All instruments of torture. The *glowing trip-hook* may refer to red-hot metal hooks used to tear flesh from the victim's body; *thumbscrews* were elaborately developed clamps used to apply intense pressure to various parts of the body. Of *the gadge* EBB asked, "you wrote 'gag' . . . did you not? . . where the proof says 'gadge' [?]" B replied that "gadge is a real name (in Johnson, too) for a torturing iron—it is part of the horror of such things that they should be mysteriously named . . ." (RB-EBB, ed. Kintner, 591, 593). B's knowledge of torture was extensive (he had mentioned "the gag and flesh-hook, screw and whip" in *Sordello*, VI, 770—see this edition, Vol. III, 331), but his recollection of seeing the word *gadge* in Johnson's *Dictionary* appears to be faulty. Johnson does list a meaning for the word *gad*, "a wedge or ingot of steel," which may be the source of B's remark.

340-41] *Lugo, Argenta, . . . San Nicolo, Ferrara, Venice* The towns are on a route from Faenza to Venice and safety. For Lugo, see I, 231n. Argenta, 15 mi. N of Lugo, was controlled alternately by Ravenna and Ferrara; at the time of the poem's action, the Duke of Ferrara held it. San Nicolo, 10 mi. S of Ferrara, was also under the protection of Ferrara. Ferrara itself, the seat of the house of Este, was an independent city of great wealth and power. The goal of the journey, Venice, was past the pinnacle of its power, but it remained independent and was the strongest opponent of papal domination in N Italy.

ACT II

Variant Listings Variants at the beginning and end of a line of prose are treated in the same manner as with verse. Thus some first-word variants will not be capitalized, and there will be no drop-word used at the end of a line. All end-line punctuation is included.

8] *Pope's Legate from Ravenna* See *Persons* n.

24] *perdue* concealed.

25] *San Cassiano* A fairly common place-name in N Italy. There are three towns of this or similar name that B may have passed through on his 1838 and 1844 Italian journeys: San Cassiano di Controne (near Bagni di Lucca), San Casciano dei Bagni (near Siena), and San Casciano in Val di Pesa (near Florence).

29] *Brutus the Elder* Lucius Junius Brutus, who founded the Roman republic after leading a revolution which overthrew Lucius Tarquinius Superbus (Tarquin the Proud) in 510 B.C.

35] *dico vobis* Latin for "I say to you"; implies that what follows is the truth.

41-42] *St. Nepomucene of Prague* St. John Nepomucene was martyred in 1393 by Wenceslaus IV of Bohemia for opposing the Emperor's plan to seize an abbey and create a bishopric for a friend.

54] *Our . . . bile* i.e., he is irritable, quick to anger. According to the humors theory of medicine, yellow and black bile were two of the bodily secretions which controlled health and temperament. An excess of black bile caused melancholy, while too much yellow bile made one irritable and wrathful.

68] *Cur fremuere gentes* "Why do the Gentiles [or nations] cry out in turmoil?" The Latin here is a more elevated, Ciceronian version of the Vulgate's *quare fremuerunt gentes* (Ps. 2:1).

79]   *heading nor hanging* cf. *Measure for Measure*, 2.1.250, "it is but heading and hanging."

227]   *great ugly Masaccio   Masaccio* is a clipped form of the nickname *Tomasaccio*, which means "big Thomas" or "hulking Thomas." There seems to be no reference to the Italian painter called Masaccio.

256-57]   *western lands . . . Court* Spanish and Portuguese explorers in the sixteenth century returned from the West Indies with tales of immense wealth waiting to be garnered. Such stories were sometimes circulated in order to get financing for further explorations.

326-27]   *David . . . Philistine* David, the youngest of Jesse's sons, carried grain, bread, and cheeses to his brothers on the day he fought Goliath, the champion of the Philistine army. See 1 Sam. 17.

328]   *He of Gath* Goliath came from the city of Gath (1 Sam. 17:4).

330]   *sons of Jesse* David had seven brothers; by extension the reference includes all the Israelites. See 1 Sam. 16 and 1 Chron. 27:18.

337]   *Goliath* See II, 326-27n.

370]   *profane vulgar* Horace, *Odes*, 3.1.1.

401]   *Messere Stiatta* An imaginary poet.

466-67]   *"Let whoso . . . he fall."* 1 Cor. 10:12.

EDITORIAL NOTES

CHRISTMAS-EVE AND EASTER-DAY

Emendations to the Text

The following emendations have been made to the 1889 text:

CHRISTMAS-EVE

Subtitle: The hyphen in the subtitle was omitted in 1888-1889; the 1850-1868 reading has been restored.

l. 87: 1888-1889 omits a comma between *you* and *the*, though space has been left for it. The MS-1868 reading has been restored.

l. 423: 1888 omits the comma at the end of the line; B restored the comma in DC and BrU, but 1889 does not make the correction. The comma has been restored.

l. 667: In MS, 1850, 1863, and 1865, this line begins with the word *With*. 1868 alters the word to *While*, which makes neither grammatical nor poetical sense. The MS-1865 reading *With* has been restored.

l. 729: 1888-1889 omits the required comma at the end of the line; some punctuation is needed to conclude the appositive statement. The MS-1868 reading *it,* has been restored.

l. 789: The ellipsis has been emended from two points to three, in accordance with the usual practice in 1888-1889.

l. 1054: Since the sentence as a whole is a question, and the quotations are not, the question mark should be placed outside the quotation marks. The MS reading is restored.

l. 1056: See preceding note; the MS reading is restored.

l. 1092: 1888-1889 prints only a single quotation mark at the end of the quotation, where double quotation marks are required. The MS-1868 reading has been restored.

EASTER-DAY

l. 166: The grammar of the passage requires a comma at the end of this line, not the period printed in 1888-1889. The MS-1868 reading has been restored.

l. 889: The end of this line is the end of a quotation, but 1888-1889 prints no quotation marks. The 1868 reading has been restored to provide them.

l. 901: At the end of this line the narrator of the poem ends his spoken remark; another voice begins to speak in line 902. Thus quotation marks are required at the end of line 901, but 1868, 1888, and 1889 have none. MS-1865 provide a single quotation mark here; the necessary double quotation marks have been inserted.

l. 1003: The necessary double quotation marks are faultily printed in 1888-1889; the 1868 reading is restored.

Text and Publication

Christmas-Eve and *Easter-Day* were published 1 April 1850, by Chapman and Hall, London. They appeared as companion poems in a dark green, cloth-bound octavo volume of 142 pages. A printer's MS of 71 leaves, written in the hands of both B and EBB, is preserved in the Forster and Dyce Collection in the Victoria and Albert Museum. On p. 25 of the MS a hole about the size of seven lines of verse has been cut out of the page, but without apparent loss of any of the text. The hole occurs between ll. 767 and 768. If the poet were copying out the poem from an earlier "working" MS, it is possible that he copied the same seven lines twice and chose this method of excising the error. On p. 29 at l. 887 there is a small hole eliminating the initial phrase *Not joyless*, which has been restored in the left margin, but so far over that the *N* is bound into the spine of the MS. It cannot be determined whether or not the *N* is preceded by a quotation mark. Other lines in this passage (ll. 865-889) do begin with a single quotation mark; probably there is also one before the *N*.

A curiosity of the first edition of *Christmas-Eve* was that it contained an extra line in comparison to all later editions; it was 1360 lines in length, whereas later editions contain 1359 lines. The extra line occurs between ll.769 and 770 of the later versions. The rhyme word of the extra line is *night*, which is repeated at the end of l. 769; it may be that the two lines were alternate possibilities in an earlier version, both of which were inadvertently copied into this MS.

Composition and Sources

The two poems were written in Italy and belong to the early period of B's marriage. The only poem B is known to have written after his arrival in Italy with EBB in 1846 and before *Christmas-Eve* and *Easter-Day* is *The Guardian-Angel*, a description of a painting. The birth of the poet's son and the death of his mother, both occurring in the space of a few weeks in the spring of 1849, were doubtless strong personal influences on the poems. B's mood of self-examination would have been given direction by the temper of pitched battle in religious speculation at the time, a temper which was stirring literary and popular imagination to its own critical pitch.

Perhaps the most celebrated figure in mid-nineteenth century theological controversy was David Friedrich Strauss, whose *Das Leben Jesu* (1835-36) was a milestone in the development of rational theology, or "higher criticism," in Germany. George Eliot's translation of Strauss's book, which she titled *The Life of Jesus Critically Examined,* appeared in England in 1846. Strauss's book had been translated before and was widely read. B was undoubtedly familiar with it and with the school of thought it represented. In *Christmas-Eve* rational theology is associated specifically with Göttingen, which was only one, and probably not the most influential, of the centers of theological criticism in Germany. Strauss himself studied at Tübingen under F. C. Baur, the founder of the school there. Other universities of reputation, besides Göttingen, were at Berlin and Jena. The theologian who coined the term "higher criticism," J. G. Eichhorn, taught at Göttingen, but on the whole the school was more famous as the center of the *Sturm und Drang* movement in poetry at the end of the eighteenth century than as a school of rational criticism. The application of higher criticism and the "myth theory" to the life of Christ was the origin of *Das Leben Jesu.* The "myth of Christ" (see l. 859) was the legend which accumulated about Jesus between the time of his death and the writing of the Gospels in the second century. The argument in effect rejects the historical reality of all supernatural happenings in the Gospels.

B himself belonged, through the influence and early training of his mother, to the tradition of Non-Conformity in religious orthodoxies, a tradition of which the little Evangelical chapel in *Christmas-Eve* is an extreme example.

CHRISTMAS-EVE

46] *Lot . . . Gomorrah* God warned the righteous Lot and his family to flee from the destruction of the wicked cities of the plain, Sodom and Gomorrah. Lot's wife looked back and was turned to a pillar of salt, and Lot sired the tribes of the Moabites and the children of Ammon upon his daughters. Lot and his daughters were the only immediate survivors of the destruction of Gomorrah (Gen. 18:20-19:28).

52] *wreck of whalebones* In the nineteenth century umbrella frames were made from whalebone.

66] *draggled* From v. *drag*: to have become wet or soiled by dragging.

70] *pattens* Overshoes, usually with high wooden soles or metal lifts.

73] *lance in rest* The rest was a projection on the right side of a suit of armor, for the support of the lance in battle position.

81] *Penitent Thief* One of two thieves crucified with Christ, who asked Christ for remembrance and was in turn assured of salvation (Luke 23:40-43).

89] *"a Gallio!"* Gallio, proconsul of Achaia, refused to hear the case of the

Jews against Paul, arguing that this was not a question of wrong but "of words and names, and of your law." Yet he again refused to intervene in the beating of Sosthenes, chief ruler of the synagogue, by the Greeks (Acts 18:12-17).

102] *Saint John's Candlestick* A seven-stick candleholder, symbolizing the seven candlesticks in the midst of which the Son of Man appeared to the author of the book of Revelation, presumably John, and which came to represent the seven churches of the early Church (Rev. 1:12-20).

105] *Grand-Inquisitor* Chief presiding ecclesiastical judge during the inquisition instituted by Pope Gregory IX in 1232 to prevent and punish heresy. Although Torquemada, the first to hold the office in Spain (where the Inquisition lasted 1480-1820), is probably the most notorious grand inquisitor in the popular imagination, the reference in the poem may be to less despotic, earlier inquisitors.

107] *You are the men* "No doubt but ye are the people, and wisdom shall die with you" (Job 12:2).

108] *old Seven Churches* See l. 102n.

120] *vestiment* Obsolete form of *vestment*, usually an outer, ceremonial garment. See Matt. 22:11 "And when the king came in to see the guests, he saw there a man which had not on a wedding garment."

132] *pentacle* A figure such as the five-pointed star used as a symbol, especially in magic.

133] *conventicle* A religious assembly. The term frequently suggests heresy or conspiracy connected with worship outside the established Church.

135] *Christmas-Eve of Forty-nine* B stretches a point in his account of the Dissenter worship meeting; Christmas Eve fell on a Monday in 1849, and Dissenters kept Christmas Eve or Christmas Day only if it came on a Sunday.

143] *pig-of-lead* A mass of lead, as obtained directly from a smelting furnace, with a weight of 50 to 300 pounds.

147] *wit of the Sibyl* Prophetess in Greek and Roman mythology who possessed powers of divination as well as of prophecy.

170] *dew of Hermon* A figure used by David to describe the felicity of brethren dwelling together in unity. Hermon is a sacred mountain marking the northern boundary of Palestine (Ps. 133:3).

184-85] *like Eve . . . enough of it* As Milton tells the story of the Fall, Eve found the fruit of the forbidden Tree of Knowledge delicious, and "she engorged without restraint" (*Paradise Lost*, 9, 791).

232] *Pharaoh* Pharaoh's baker, imprisoned with Joseph, dreamed of three baskets of baked goods, which Joseph interpreted as indication that in three days Pharaoh would hear the baker's case and hang him, a prediction which proved true (Gen. 40:16-19,22).

261] *"Mount Zion"* A hill fortress in Jerusalem, often used in the Bible to stand for Jerusalem itself and for salvation. "But ye are come into mount

Zion, and unto the city of the living God, the heavenly Jerusalem, and to an innumerable company of angels" (Heb. 12:22).

262] *To which . . . prophecy* The word *prophecy* here has the sense of divine imperative: "And it shall come to pass, that from one new moon to another, shall all flesh come to worship before me, saith the Lord" (Is. 66:23). "Praise waiteth for thee, O God, in Sion: and unto thee shall the vow be performed. O thou that hearest prayer, unto thee shall all flesh come" (Ps. 65:1-2).

333] *Eternal First and Last* cf. Is. 44:6 and Rev. 1:11.

412-14] *Good . . . three* cf. Matt. 17:4; Mark 9:5; Luke 9:33. The images in B's rendering of the vision are similar to those of the episode of the transfiguration of Jesus.

438] *garment . . . white* cf. Matt. 17:2; Mark 9:3; Luke 9:29.

445-46] *Where two . . . midst* Matt. 18:20.

450] *vesture's hem* cf. Matt. 9:20-22, 14:36. Those who touched the hem of Jesus' garment were miraculously cured.

467-68] *spirit . . . truth* "God is a Spirit: and they that worship him must worship him in spirit and in truth" (John 4:24).

509-511] *God . . . water* "And whosoever shall give to drink unto one of these little ones a cup of cold water only in the name of a disciple, verily I say unto you he shall in no wise lose his reward" (Matt. 10:42).

529] *Dome of God* The dome of St. Peter's in Rome, designed by Michelangelo.

530-33] *angel's measuring-rod* One of seven angels who appeared to the writer of the book of Revelation used a golden reed to measure the New Jerusalem and its gates and wall (Rev. 21:15).

536-38] *colonnade . . . race* The image refers to the immense twin semicircular colonnades (designed by Giovanni Bernini) which form two sides of the piazza of St. Peter's cathedral.

564] *architrave* The lowest unit of the structural composition called as a whole the entablature; the entablature rests on top of a column.

566] *porphyry* A purplish rock composition containing crystals. Many of the papal tombs in St. Peter's are of porphyry.

572-73] *winding . . . baldachin* A canopy structure over the altar was originally made of fine silk woven with gold. The baldachin in St. Peter's, designed by Bernini in 1633 by order of Pope Urban VIII, is entirely of bronze with gilt ornaments. It weighs over 700 tons and is supported by four spiral columns ninety-five feet high cast in bronze taken from the porch roof of the Pantheon.

578] *Behemoth* A large water animal (often assumed to be the hippopotamus) adduced by God as an example of the immensity of divine power (Job 40:15-24).

579] *silver bell* In Roman Catholic communion a silver bell is rung at the elevation of the Host. The moment signifies the miracle of transubstantiation of bread and wine into the body and blood of Christ.

588-89] *signs . . . accursed tree* According to European folklore, the tree from which Jesus' cross was made fell under a curse. Typically, the fruit, flowers, or trunk of various trees are today marked or blighted as a consequence of the tree's part in the crucifixion.

593] *King . . . lords* Rev. 19:16.

595] *"I died . . . evermore"* "I am he that liveth, and was dead; and behold, I am alive for evermore." These were Christ's words in the vision which commanded John to write Revelation (Rev. 1:17-19).

652] *antique sovereign Intellect* The world of classical antiquity; probably here the Roman Empire and its cultural domain.

664] *Sallust incomplete* Caius Sallustius Crispus (86-c.34 B.C.), Roman historian. In numerous cases, early Christian writers scraped clean and re-used parchment leaves from the manuscripts of ancient authors.

674] *Terpander's bird* Terpander was reputedly the father of Greek music, and the nightingale, known for its beautiful song, was associated with him.

680] *Aphrodite* The goddess of love, who was often portrayed in the nude in Greek art.

750] *Colossus* A large statue in human form. The most famous of several known in antiquity was a statue of Helios, god of the sun, built by Chares in the harbor of Rhodes. One of the wonders of the ancient world, it was destroyed by an earthquake in 224 B.C.

792] *Halle . . . Frankfort* All seats of learning, and in B's time, cities which still showed their medieval origins in their architecture and layout.

793] *Göttingen* See *Composition and Sources* n.

834] *hake* Hook.

837] *Young England* The Tory party led by Benjamin Disraeli, Lord John Manners, and George Smythe, which in 1843 began to oppose the Conservative ministry of Sir Robert Peel. The Young England party wished to restore certain rightful powers of the crown which since the bloodless revolution of 1688 had been usurped by the aristocracy. The party revived a romantic, chivalric spirit and became associated with the religious movement then gaining strength at Oxford, the Oxford Movement, which was Anglo-Catholic in its commitment to tradition and ritual in church services.

839] *surplice-question* A surplice is a white linen garment with wide sleeves. Whether a cleric should wear a surplice or not was a subject of debate in connection with the Ritualistic movement, which supported the reintroduction of medieval or modern Roman Catholic ceremony into the Church of England.

859] *Myth of Christ* See introductory note, *Composition and Sources.*

875] *Individuum* An indivisible entity.

899] *air-bell* A glass bell-jar, from which the air may be removed when conducting scientific experiments.

900] *mephitic* Noxious.

941] *heavenly . . . Paul* The John here is the author of Revelation, who set down his visions of heaven. The apostle Paul might be termed "Attic" not only because he grew up under the influence of Greek culture, but also because of his missionary and epistolary efforts at Christianizing Greek cities, such as Thessalonika, Corinth, and Philippi.

942-45] *weather-battered . . . nets* Peter was a fisherman before he became an apostle of Jesus (Matt. 4:18; Mark 1:16; Luke 5:2-10).

944] *sinning . . . pardoned* Peter sinned in denying that he knew Jesus (Matt. 26:69-75; Luke 22:55-61; John 18:17, 25-27).

962] *When A . . . be* The Hebrew word for *ox* (aleph) has the sound of the letter *A*. The form may originally have been a figure for the head of an ox.

963] *No Camel . . . G* The Hebrew letter *G* (gimel) is also the word for camel.

973] *Harvey* William Harvey (1578-1657) discovered the circulation of the blood and the pumping function of the heart.

1003] *Euclid* Browning uses Euclid (Greek mathematician c.300 B.C.) as a figure signifying categorical knowledge and skepticism about infinity. Euclid's *Elements* arranged the mathematical knowledge of his time in such a way that each theorem follows logically from the preceding ones. Aristotle, however, is credited with the argument that "there is no proportion between something and nothing" in refutation of infinite divisibility.

1009] *Pilate* Pontius Pilate, the Roman Prefect who allowed the crowd to have its way and crucify Jesus (Matt. 27:11-26; Mark 15:1-20; Luke 23:1-25; John 18:29-19:16).

1046] *finger-post* A sign in the shape of a pointing finger.

1047] *Morality to the uttermost* Moral philosophy is concerned with the ethics of human actions without reference to divine imperative or supernatural revelation. It is distinct from moral theology, which views God as the object of life and the moral conduct of life the means to attain Him.

1077] *pearl of price* Matt. 13:45-46.

1078] *levigable* Reducible to a fine powder or dust; analyzable.

1101] *Middle Verb* The reflexive voice of the Greek verb.

1103] *anapests in comic trimeter* In classical Greek drama a line in comic trimeter would have three metra, each composed of two iambic feet. For variety and fluidity, iambic trimeter often lent itself to a resolution into anapests.

1104] *halt . . . 'Iketides'* Aeschylus play *The Suppliants* suffered from textual corruption and had a number of short lacunae; it was largely ignored by B's contemporaries.

1107] *Titus or Philemon* F. C. Baur (see introductory note, *Composition and Sources*) attempted to establish the authenticity of St. Paul's Epistles on a linguistic and stylistic basis. His list of genuine works did not include Titus and Philemon.

1111] *Paul's Epistles* See 1. 1107n.

1115] *Heine . . . fever)* Heinrich Heine (1797-1856), German writer, produced what many consider to be some of his best poetry after becoming confined to his bed, paralyzed and partially blind, in 1848. In this period he embraced a personal religion, though often in a sardonic vein.

1126] *deist's pravity* Pravity is an earlier form of *depravity*, both deriving from Lat. *pravitas*, meaning *distortion, crookedness*. The deists were rationalists of the seventeenth and eighteenth centuries who believed in a deity who created the laws of nature. The deists did not believe that the world was a theocracy, and the strictest of them denied the idea of divine intervention in human life through reward or punishment, and rejected the literal truth of the Bible. Those who called themselves deists embraced a wide range of beliefs, however.

1195] *hebetude* Obtuseness.

1242] *raree-show* "The word is formed in imitation of the foreign way of pronouncing *rare show*" (Johnson's *Dictionary*). Itinerant musicians from Savoy, called Savoyards, were the first to offer pictures viewed through a magnifying lens set into a portable box. This apparatus was also called a peep-show. *Raree-show* was often used, as here, in a figurative and belittling sense. *Peter's successor* refers to the dogma that the popes stand in a direct line of apostolic succession from St. Peter, the first pope.

1252] *milk of kindness* cf. *Macbeth*, 1. 5. 16-18.

1268] *Pascal* Blaise Pascal (1623-1662), French scientist and religious philosopher, whose religious writings, collected as *Pensées* (1670), demonstrate extreme purity and precision of style.

1270-71] *making square . . . infinity* Squaring the circle—drawing a square with exactly the same area as a given circle—is one of the geometrical tasks proven impossible by Euclid (see 1. 1003n.).

1275] *Taylor's . . . Jeremy* English theologian and devotional writer (1613-1667) whose style was noted for imagery, lucidity, and vigor. He was author of *Holy Living* (1650) and *Holy Dying* (1651).

1278] *Is God mocked* cf. Gal. 6:7.

1292] *breccia* Breccia marble appears to be composed of fragments joined by lime. The geological formation takes its name from the marble.

1308] *the seven* See 1. 102n.

1325] *petticoatings* A coinage of B's having mocking reference to a clergyman's gown.

1326] *Bourbon bully's gloatings* Ferdinand II (1810-1859), Bourbon King of the Two Sicilies, came to the throne in 1830 and became a symbol of reactionary sentiment. He was nicknamed "King Bomba" because he ordered the bombardments of Messina and Palermo during the revolution of 1848-49. In 1849 he withdrew the constitution, drawing strong protests from England and France.

1356]   *Hepzibah Tune* Isaiah prophesied that the restored Jerusalem would be called Hephzibah, meaning "My delight is in her" (Is. 62:4).

1358]   *Whitfield's collection* George Whitefield, as the name is now usually spelled, 1714-1770, was a Methodist preacher of the Evangelical Revival in England and America. His hymnbook, compiled in 1753, went through about fifty-five editions and numerous revisions. Its title was *Hymns for Social Worship Collected from Various Authors, and more particularly design'd for the use of the Tabernacle Congregation in London.* No one hymn in several editions searched corresponds exactly to B's description.

EASTER-DAY

46]   *acquist* Acquisition, gain.

52]   *flexile* Flexible, mobile.

91-92]   *"In all . . . geometrize* In the *Timaeus* Plato describes the creation as a geometrizing force. See Plutarch, *Symposiacs* 8:2 in *Moralia*, where Diogenianos states that Plato describes God as a "geometer."

116]   *cursive . . . heiroglyph* A reference to the Rosetta Stone, discovered in 1799 and deciphered in the 1820s. The text of the Rosetta Stone is written in three parallel writing systems: heiroglyphs, cursive demotic Egyptian script, and Greek.

154]   *Coleoptera* The order of insects, especially beetles, having a hard pair of anterior wings which serve as coverings for the membranous posterior wings.

160]   *a Grignon . . . crest* A snuffbox made by the jeweller Pierre Grignon (1723-1784) and bearing the insignia of the Duke of Orleans, regent to Louis XV of France.

169]   *Semitic guess* That is, a philological speculation about one of the Semitic languages (such as Hebrew), which present great difficulties even to expert linguists.

170]   *blindfold chess* Arabian and Persian experts first demonstrated blindfold chess in the eleventh century. In the eighteenth century Philidor, a Frenchman, gave exhibitions at the chess club in St. James St. in which he played three simultaneous games of blindfold chess.

180]   *Prove . . . translatable* The story that God caused Jonah to be preserved alive in the belly of a fish for three days and three nights has been variously interpreted by critics as allegory, as moral fable incorporating elements of folklore, and as a version of some unusual but natural phenomenon. See Jonah 1, 2.

193]   *Orpheus* An early, possibly legendary Greek bard, reputed founder of the Orphic religious movement. See l. 194n.

194]   *Dionysius Zagrias* Dionysus-Zagreus was also called Bacchus. He was the son of Zeus and Persephone, and was killed and eaten by the Titans at the instigation of Zeus's jealous wife Hera. However, Athena saved his heart, which Zeus swallowed and then fathered a new Dionysus-Zagreus upon Semele, having first blasted the Titans with his thunderbolt. From the ashes of the Titans sprang man, who thus incorporated both Titanic wickedness and a trace of divinity (from having devoured a god). The Orphic religion celebrated and reenacted the violent death and resurrection of Dionysus-Zagreus. In the earliest examples of the cult, at the height of the religious frenzy induced by wine, music, and dancing, worshipers became identified with the god and were called by his name, Bacchus. The ceremonies were a version of fertility rites celebrating the alternating seasons and the mystical recreative energy of nature, but in their emphasis on a suffering god, his rebirth into immortality, the divided nature of man and the possibility of his oneness with god, they clearly anticipate the Christ idea.

234-37] *the earth . . . brink* The death of Jesus was accompanied by earthquakes and darkness at mid-day (Matt. 27:45-51; Mark 15:33-38; Luke 23:44-45).

286] *Sergius* Sergius and Bacchus were two high-ranking officers in the service of Emperor Maximinus Daja of Syria (305-313) who were denounced by enemies as Christians. Bacchus was beaten to death and Sergius was later beheaded. Their fame spread and a number of monuments to them exist in both Asia and Europe. A scholarly work devoted to Sergius and Bacchus was published at Göttingen (see *Christmas-Eve*, introductory note on sources) in 1823.

308] *truck* Exchange, trade.

330-32] *leave . . . Aeschylus* St. Paul represents the certainty of immortality, while Aeschylus would represent only the hope for it. See l. 250 of *Prometheus Bound,* τυφλὰς ἐν αὐτοῖς ἐλπίδας κατῴκισα ("Blind hopes I caused to dwell in them.")

339] *curry* Indian restaurants began to appear in London in B's time, but they were expensive and mainly frequented by the moneyed classes. Line 340 plays upon the metonymy common both then and now of calling a dish containing curry simply *a curry.*

393-94] *Lucumons . . . scheme* The Tarquin family of Etruscan kings have a possibly legendary reputation for cruelty, murder, and rape; they are probably the rulers referred to by the term *Lucumons,* an Etruscan title signifying royalty. The rule of the first Tarquin began in 616 B.C. *Fourier's scheme* refers to the utopian system of cooperative living devised by Charles Fourier (1772-1837), according to which approximately 400 families of four members each were organized into groups called *phalanxes.*

476] *'At night . . . thief.'* "But the day of the lord will come as a thief in the night" (2 Pet. 3:10).

488] *Queen Mab* The folkloric provenance of Queen Mab is uncertain. The earliest literary reference to her is Shakespeare's in *Romeo and Juliet,* 1.4.53-94, where Mercutio's speech associates her with dreams. Robert Herrick

(1591-1674) makes her queen of fairyland (*Hesperides*, "The Argument of his Book" 1.12).

598] *cloud-Tophet* Tophet means "place of fire," and was the name of a place where children were sacrificed to Moloch in the Old Testament. There are numerous Biblical references to this practice, including 2 Kings 23:10 and Jer. 7:31. Is. 30:33 mentions Tophet in a more general sense, as the fire kindled by the Lord for the wicked on the Day of Judgment.

615] *great white throne* God is described as speaking from a white throne at the Last Judgment (Rev. 20:11).

641] *Sodom* The evil cities of Sodom and Gomorrah were destroyed by God by a rain of fire and brimstone (Gen. 18-19). See *Christmas-Eve*, l. 46n.

644] *dread* Cause of awe or fear.

681] *flesh . . . nerve* Early evolutionary theorists suggested that nerve capacity is developed through increased activity in an organ or member.

713] *the filthy . . . still* "He which is filthy, let him be filthy still: and he that is righteous, let him be righteous still" (Rev. 22:11). In John's vision of the Last Judgment Christ declared that every man's reward or punishment would be according to his work.

749] *bee-bird . . . aloe-flower* The hummingbird's rapid, tireless wing motion produces a buzzing sound. The aloe flower blooms at night and fades at daybreak.

799] *Buonarroti* Michelangelo (1475-1564), artist of the Italian Renaissance.

825] *appanage* Provision for the younger children of royalty; an incomplete or limited legacy.

879] *dervish-like* Mohammedan mendicants sometimes enact a spinning dance until exhaustion produces a trance-like state.

1016] *Northern Light* The Aurora Borealis, a luminous phenomenon believed to be of electrical origin, visible at night in the Northern hemisphere.

EDITORIAL NOTES

ESSAY ON SHELLEY

B's *Essay on Shelley* figured originally as an extended introduction, occupying a full quarter of the total slender volume, to *Letters of Percy Bysshe Shelley, with an Introductory Essay by Robert Browning* (London: Edward Moxon, Dover Street, 1852). Moxon, B's friend and the publisher of his plays and poems in the *Bells and Pomegranates* series in the years 1841-46, had purchased the letters at public auction in May, 1851. When the volume came out the following February, Moxon was soon apprised of the questionable nature of the letters. Sir Francis Palgrave wrote Moxon on February 23 to inform him that one letter had been "cribbed" from an article on Shelley he had published in the *Quarterly Review* in 1840. On March 6 the *Athenaeum* gave much further detail regarding the curious provenance of the letters in an article entitled "Literary Forgeries." By this time or soon after, Moxon withdrew the volume from publication. Only a few copies, most of them in the rare book rooms of eminent libraries or in private collections, have survived. The forger was the notorious "Major" George Gordon Byron, who claimed to be the unacknowledged son of Lord Byron by a Spanish countess (he was otherwise known as one De Gibler, who had come to England from the United States a few years earlier). The letters are made up in the main of a patchwork of quotations from genuine Shelley letters that had already been published in a variety of places, many of them in the *Monthly Magazine* during the years 1818-1820.

B never published the *Essay* in his own volumes, but in 1881 F. J. Furnivall, founder of the Browning Society, obtained his permission to use the work as the initial entry for the first volume of *The Browning Society's Papers*. Furnivall reproduced the *Essay* as it had read originally, adding, however, an elaborate title, *On the Poet Objective and Subjective; on the Latter's Aim; on Shelley as Man and Poet.* He also presented a "Foretalk" of two pages and "Headlines" describing the content of successive pages as they appeared (pp. 5-19) in the *Papers*. A "Second Edition, Revized" of Part I of the *Papers*, also dated 1881, employs the same plates for reproducing the *Essay*. The table of contents for both the first and the second edition specify "Essay on Shelley" as title. In a letter of May 12, 1886, B gave Furnivall permission for the Shelley Society (of which, as of the Browning Society,

Furnivall had been founder) to reissue the *Essay,* and in 1888 *An Essay on Percy Bysshe Shelley* was published for the Society as a separate volume in five hundred copies, edited by W. Tyas Harden. The title page informs us that the *Essay* is a reprint taken from the 1852 volume of the spurious *Letters.* There is no evidence in either the Browning Society or the Shelley Society reissues that the poet had made any attempt to supervise the printing or to alter his text. In July, 1886, two months after granting Furnivall permission for the Shelley Society volume, B had refused E. Rhys leave to reproduce the *Essay* independently. The reissues by the Browning and the Shelley societies are the only reproductions known to appear in the poet's lifetime. In 1895 Horace E. Scudder reprinted the *Essay* from the Shelley Society volume as an Appendix to his single-volume collected Cambridge Browning; and Charlotte Porter and Helen A. Clarke in 1898 presented the *Essay,* again apparently taking the Shelley Society volume as their text (see their note, XII, 384) in their widely used and often reprinted Florentine Edition of B's works. The Bibelot volume of 1902 employed again the Shelley Society edition, which is a careful reproduction of the 1852 original with the exception of a single error duly noted by Harden in the opening pages. The *Essay* has been frequently reproduced in succeeding years, generally under the title *Essay on Shelley* (*An Essay on Shelley* was the title Harden assigned the work as the heading for the initial page of his text of the *Essay*).

I have found nothing to suggest that the manuscript of the *Essay* survives, and it seems unlikely that it has done so. Fortunately B seems to have taken unusual care to see that his manuscript was accurately reproduced in the original printing. He had thanked Moxon, in a letter of December 17, 1851, for his liberal payment and had promised to "spare no pains with the proofs." The 1852 form of the *Essay,* which serves again for the present text, seems clear of errors save for the omission of an accent over the second eta in line 27 and a comma after *hatred* in line 354.

116-119] *the originative painters* B is apparently thinking of such early Renaissance painters as Fra Lippo Lippi (as in his *Virgin Adoring the Child*) or Leonardo da Vinci (as in his *Madonna of the Rocks*), and by "landscape painters" he is probably thinking of the Dutch landscape painters of the seventeenth century (Jacob Van Ruisdael, for example, in such paintings as his *The Wheat Field* or his *Wooded Landscape*).

149] *Homerides* Usually *Homeridae,* reputed descendants of Homer and chanters of his poetry.

166] *that mighty ladder* "And [Jacob] dreamed, and behold a ladder set up on the earth, and the top of it reached to heaven; and behold the angels of God ascending and descending on it." Genesis 28:12.

275] *"E pur si muove"* Galileo (1564-1642), according to an apocryphal legend, was supposed, after repeating for the officers of the Inquisition the formula of abjuration for his heresy regarding the movement of the earth, to have risen from his knees murmuring, "And yet it does move."

309] *the last stain of that false life* Just what B alludes to in lines 308 ff. as a "false life" that had stained Shelley's reputation and had been forced upon the public before the public "had any curiosity in the matter" is a question unlikely to be provided with a definitive answer. It seems clear from what follows that B is aware Shelley's conduct to Harriet had been considered reprehensible. He would not, however, have had to learn that fact, as has sometimes been assumed, from consulting Harriet's letters to Hookham in Hookham's bookshop or elsewhere before writing his *Essay*. A likely candidate for having written the "false life" B refers to here is Thomas Medwin, whose *The Shelley Papers: Memoir of Percy Bysshe Shelley* (London, 1833) casts mild but unequivocal blame on Shelley for his failing to keep an eye on Harriet after he had left her for Mary. B was almost certainly aware of Medwin's *Memoir* as well as of Medwin's two-volume *The Life of Percy Bysshe Shelley* (London, 1847). It is interesting that B makes no direct reference to Medwin's *Life*, though it is the most likely source of much of his information (Shelley's hallucinations in Wales and in Italy, for example). Obviously B does not consider Medwin's biography acceptable. There is still, in his opinion, a need for a "full life" that will not shrink from "a candid statement of all ambiguous passages" (lines 312-313) but will manifest greater faith than previous biographers had evinced in Shelley's progress toward "the great Abstract Light" or "First Cause" that would ultimately have made Shelley range himself "with the Christians" (lines 443, 447). Biographies destined to appear within a few years *after* the *Essay* were not of a sort to fill such a need. T. J. Hogg's two-volume *Life of Percy Bysshe Shelley* (1858) and E. J. Trelawny's *Recollections of the Last Days of Shelley and Byron*, also published in 1858, showed that these old friends of Shelley remembered him as a more egoistical and less transcendental personality than B had been inclined to believe him in December, 1851. Even William Michael Rossetti's *Memoir of Shelley* (1869) could not support B's theory of Shelley in the *Essay*. In January, 1870, B wrote Isa Blagden: "I have just been reading Shelley's life, as Rossetti tells it,—and when I think how utterly different was the fancy I had of him forty years ago [at the time of *Pauline*] from the facts as they front one to-day, I can only avoid despising myself by remembering that I judged in pure ignorance and according to the testimony of untruthful friends." By late 1851, when B was writing the *Essay*, he was already aware that biographers had "stained" Shelley's reputation, but he was in a mind to make allowances for some evidences of ambiguous conduct (such as Medwin had presented) with full faith in the general and ultimate probity of Shelley. A "full" life, he was sure, would support such an interpretation. There has been debate in recent years as to when B's sharp disillusionment with Shelley, so pronounced by 1870, took place. An interesting summary of the problems involved and a tentative conclusion (arguing for 1856) is provided by W. O. Raymond in "Browning and the Harriet Westbrook Shelley Letters," in his *The Infinite Moment and Other Essays in*

Robert Browning, Second Edition (Toronto, 1965). To the end of his life B frequently expressed his continued admiration for Shelley's poetry; but, as he informed F. J. Furnivall in December, 1885, he had been forced to make a painful contrast between "Shelley the *man*" and "the *poet*." He refused Furnivall's offer of the presidency of the Shelley Society.

390] *"One whose heart . . ." Julian and Maddalo*, ll. 409-417.

444-445] *"hate of hate"* Apparently an allusion to Tennyson's *The Poet*, line 3: "Dowered with the hate of hate, the scorn of scorn . . ."

447-448] *leaving the dead to bury their dead* "Jesus said unto him, Let the dead bury their dead; but go thou and preach the kingdom of God." Luke 9:60.

453] *and Paul likewise* B probably has in mind I Corinthians 3:16 and perhaps Acts 17:22 ff. as well.

457] *"The stars burnt out . . ." The Boat on the Serchio*, ll. 708-713.

468] *"All rose to do the task . . ." The Boat on the Serchio*, ll. 30-33.

472] *David's pregnant conclusion* Probably a reference to the Psalms, possibly to Psalm 66 or Psalm 95.

482] *Junius* The pseudonym of the author, never positively identified, of a series of letters printed in the *Public Advertiser* in 1769-1771 bitterly attacking various public figures, including George III himself. Byron in *The Vision of Judgment* depicts Junius as appearing in a fantastic range of shapes but ultimately concludes (stanza 80) "that what Junius we are wont to call/ Was *really, truly*, nobody at all."

482] *Rowley* The fictitious fifteenth-century Bristol priest whom Thomas Chatterton (1752-1770) created as the supposed originator of the manuscripts Chatterton fabricated for his poems. Browning's *Essay on Chatterton* (1842) appears in Volume III of the present edition.

B's footnote] Andrea Verrocchio A sculptor and painter (1435-1488) at Florence and later Venice. *Pisan Torre Guelfa by the Ponte a Mare*, etc. See *Julian and Maddalo*, ll. 98 ff. The madhouse is called "windowless" at line 101 of the poem. See also Shelley's poem *The Tower of Famine* with its description of Ugolino's prison, rendered famous by Dante's *Inferno*, Canto XXXII.

485] *in these very letters* In letter XIX, "Major" Byron quotes verbatim from a genuine Shelley letter addressed to Leigh Hunt that he had presumably found in the *Westminster Review* for April, 1841. The passage generalizes upon painting as a sister art to poetry that "accomplishes its share in the common labour of sympathetic expression of universal life" but does not mention the painters named by Browning in line 488.

488] *Guido* Guido Reni (1575-1642), a painter and engraver of the Bolognese school, a precursor of neoclassicism whom Browning probably considered somewhat sentimental and mannerized. Shelley on November 9, 1818, wrote to Thomas Love Peacock from Bologna with much enthusiasm for this Guido (*not* Guido Da Siena of the thirteenth century).

488] *Carlo Dolce* Usually *Dolci* (1616-1686), a Florentine painter not usually credited with any great amount of genius or originality.

488] *Michael Angelo* Shelley wrote Leigh Hunt ca. August 20, 1819: "With respect to Michael Angelo I dissent, & I think with astonishment and indignation on the common notion that he equals & in some respects exceeds Raphael. He seems to me to have no sense of moral dignity & loveliness; & the *energy* for which he has been so much praised appears to me to be a certain rude, external, mechanical, quality in comparison with any thing possessed by Raphael,—or even much inferior artists."

488-489] *A Divine Being has Himself said* "And whosoever shall speak a word against the Son of man, it shall be forgiven him: but unto him that blasphemeth against the Holy Ghost it shall not be forgiven." Luke 12:10.

499-500] *"Julian and Maddalo" by "Zastrozzi" Zastrozzi* (1810), a romance, was Shelley's first published work. *Julian and Maddalo* was written in 1818, a product of the poet's matured powers.

502-503] *attempt to vindicate him at the expense of another* Pretty clearly an allusion to Harriet. See note to l. 309 above.

515] *The nocturnal attack in Wales* Biographers (including Medwin in 1847) are generally agreed that Shelley was subject to hallucinations, and assume that the incidents B cites were such.

521] *"To thirst and find no fill . . ."* *Fragment: Unsatisfied Desires*, ll.1-7.

532] *cry of "old rags"* B was later to publish a poem in his *Pacchiarotto* volume of 1876 entitled *Cenciaja*, a sort of poetized footnote to Shelley's drama, *The Cenci* (1819), and to explain in a letter of July 27, 1876, to H. Buxton Forman that the title meant "a bundle of rags: a trifle."

546] *the Koh-i-noor* A famous diamond relinquished to the British crown in 1849 upon the annexation of the Punjab.

554] *"The spirit of the worm . . ."* *Epipsychidion*, ll. 128-129.

581] *Paris, Dec. 4th, 1851.* The Brownings had left Italy to spend the summer of 1851 in London and had left there in late September for Paris, where they remained until the spring of 1852. The *Essay* is one of several works, including *"Childe Roland to the Dark Tower Came,"* that B wrote during his winter in Paris.

EDITORIAL NOTES

MEN AND WOMEN, *Volume I*

Emendations to the Text

The following emendations have been made to the 1889 text:

Up at a Villa—Down in the City, l. 61: In 1888 the line ends with a period; B restored a comma (as in P-1868) in the Dykes Campbell copy and in the Brown University list. 1889 does not have this correction, but drops all punctuation at the end of the line. The comma is restored.

Fra Lippo Lippi, l. 60: The ellipsis has been emended from two points to three, in accordance with the usual practice in 1888-1889.

Fra Lippo Lippi, l. 269: All editions prior to 1888 end this line with a period; the comma at the end of the line in the 1888 edition reappears in 1889. Since this line ends not only a sentence but a paragraph, which is followed by a break in the line arrangement, the period has been restored.

Fra Lippo Lippi, l. 337: The P-1863 reading *God wot* has been restored. In 1865, this became *Got wot* and was not corrected in subsequent editions.

Fra Lippo Lippi, l. 387: The ellipsis has been emended from two points to three, in accordance with the usual practice in 1888-1889.

By the Fire-Side, l. 2: In all copies of the 1889 impression collated, the punctuation at the end of the line has decayed to illegibility. The semicolon of 1865-1888 has been restored.

Any Wife to Any Husband, l. 82: In P-1868, this line ends with a comma; in 1888 and 1889, a period appears. The sentence structure requires the comma, since lines 82-84 comprise a series of specifications of the "thefts" (l. 81). The P-1868 reading has been restored.

An Epistle . . . of Karshish, l. 48: The ellipsis has been emended from two points to three, in accordance with the usual practice in 1888-1889.

Instans Tyrannus, l. 39: The P-1868 reading *'Twixt* has been restored. In 1888 and 1889 the initial apostrophe is missing, though the space for it remains.

A Pretty Woman, l. 48: The P-1888 reading of an exclamation point at the end of the line has been restored. Under magnification, the earliest examples of 1889 show faint traces of this punctuation, but most copies have a mutilated period as a result of type batter.

"Childe Roland to the Dark Tower Came," l. 192: Both 1888 and 1889 omit the required double quotation marks at the end of the line. The P-1868 punctuation has been restored.

The Statue and the Bust, l. 184: Both 1888 and 1889 omit the required double quotation marks at the beginning of the line; the 1863-1868 punctuation has been restored.

How it Strikes a Contemporary, l. 70: Both 1888 and 1889 have a single quotation mark at the end of the line, where double quotation marks are required. The P-1868 punctuation has been restored.

The Last Ride Together, l. 33: Neither 1888 nor 1889 has any punctuation at the end of this line, which ends a sentence and a stanza. The 1855-1868 punctuation has been restored.

Master Hugues of Saxe-Gotha, l. 74: In all copies of the 1889 impression collated, the punctuation mark at the end of the line has decayed to a blurred and misaligned period. The 1888 punctuation has been restored.

Bishop Blougram's Apology, l. 37: The ellipsis has been emended from two points to three, in accordance with the usual practice in 1888-1889.

Bishop Blougram's Apology, l. 608: The P-1868 reading *soil* has been restored. While the 1888-1889 reading *soul* is not patently erroneous, the version in the five preceding texts is preferable, being more consistent with Blougram's metaphor here.

Bishop Blougram's Apology, l. 759: The 1888-1889 reading *others* is ungrammatical; the P-1868 reading has been restored.

Text and Publication

No complete MS of *Men and Women* is known to exist. There is, however, a textually significant MS in Browning's hand of "Love Among the Ruins," the first poem in Volume I (MSS of poems in Volume II are discussed in the notes to those poems; see Volume VI of this edition). Titled "Sicilian Pastoral," this MS in the Lowell collection of the Houghton Library has been described by John Maynard ("Browning's 'Sicilian Pastoral,' " *Harvard Library Bulletin* 20 [1972], 436-43). Variant readings from the MS are reproduced by permission of the Houghton Library.

The earliest large body of textual material for *Men and Women* is a set of proof sheets in the Huntington Library. These proofs, complete except for "Memorabilia," contain many variants from the published editions of *Men and Women*, and comprise the earliest known versions of most of the poems in the collection. The Huntington proof sheets would seem to be closely related to a now-lost manuscript, because of the numerous typographical errors (corrected in the first edition) that appear to be the result of difficulties in B's handwriting. That these proofs sheets are early is further suggested by the presence of corrections, possibly in B's hand, in volume two; and by the sheer number of changes between the surviving proofs and the first edition. At least one more set of proofs clearly did exist: that which B sold for sixty pounds to the Boston publisher James T. Fields. The relevant letters from B to Fields are preserved in the Fields Collection of the Huntington Library; in them, B arranges with Fields for an American edition of *Men and Women* to be published simultaneously with the English first edition. In one of these letters, B provides a list of thirty corrections to be made in the American edition; since there are hundreds of corrections and alterations made between the present Huntington proofs and the first edition, B must have sent Fields a later, more accurate set of proofs—probably the final set.

The list of corrections sent to Fields (all but one of which were made in subsequent editions under B's control) represents the extent of B's control over the text of the American first edition of *Men and Women*; there is no evidence that he read or corrected any further proofs from Fields. This list, and a similar one included in a letter to D. G. Rossetti (see Hood, *Ltrs.*, 42), we consider to be secondary textual materials; they are reproduced in the final volume of this edition.

Men and Women was published on 10 November 1855 (according to B in a letter to Fields), by Chapman and Hall, 193 Picadilly, London. The two green octavo volumes contained fifty-one poems, twenty-seven in Volume I and twenty-four in Volume II. This was the first appearance for all the poems except "Saul" and "The Twins"; the earlier publications are discussed in the notes to these two poems, in Volume VI of this edition.

In the rearrangement of his poems for the *Poetical Works* of 1863, B moved all but eight of the original *Men and Women* poems to other categories. The later location of each poem is indicated in the editor's note preceding the variants.

Title

Exactly when B settled on his simple but memorable title is unknown, but as early as 1845 he had used the phrase to describe his characters. He wrote to EBB, "I have some Romances and Lyrics, all dramatic, to dispatch, and *then*, I shall stoop of a sudden under and out of this dancing ring of men & women hand in hand . . . " (RB-EBB, ed. Kintner, 26). By 1855, he was proud enough of the title *Men and Women* to withhold it from Fields until it was clear that Fields would buy the proofs.

Composition

Most of the poems in *Men and Women* were written between 1850 and 1855. "The Guardian Angel" reflects the B's visit to Fano and Ancona in the summer of 1848, and some of the love poems may have originated in the years of courtship and early marriage, but most authorities agree that B wrote little poetry from 1846 to 1849. Following the publication of *Christmas-Eve and Easter-Day* (1850) and the writing of the essay on Shelley (1851), B began to work on poems that became part of *Men and Women*. In Paris, according to biographical tradition, he wrote "Love Among the Ruins," "Women and Roses," and " 'Childe Roland to the Dark Tower Came' " on 1, 2, and 3 January 1852. Whether he did indeed write these poems on those days, and if so, in what order he wrote them, has been the subject of much discussion (see, for example, DeVane, *Hbk.*, 212, 229; Johnstone Parr, "The Date of Composition of Browning's *Love Among the Ruins*," *PQ* 32 [1953], 443-46; and John Huebenthal, "The Dating of Browning's 'Love Among the Ruins,' 'Women and Roses,' and 'Childe Roland,' " *VP* 4 [1966], 51-54). B himself was the source for at least part of this story; its accuracy is not beyond question, but that he was working at poetry in early 1852 seems certain.

B's opportunities to write appear to have been dictated by circumstance and surroundings. He seems to have composed very little during most of 1852, but upon returning to Florence in November 1852 he reexerted himself. On 24 February 1853, he wrote to Joseph Milsand that the recent poems had "more music and painting than before, so as to get people to hear and see" (quoted in Irvine and Honan, 335; letter published in *Revue Germanique* 12 [1921], 251). In March, EBB wrote Miss Mitford that "Robert too is busy with another book" (*Letters of EBB*, 2, 105). The summer of 1853 was spent in Bagni di Lucca, and EBB felt that B was less than industrious: "Not a stroke has he drawn since he came here—not a line has he written!" (Heydon and Kelley, 108). But from that summer came the materials for several poems, among them "In a Balcony" and "By the Fire-Side," and by the fall EBB reported progress: "Robert especially has done a great deal of work, & will have his volume ready for the spring without fail he says" (Landis and Freeman, 200).

But publication was delayed; a winter in Rome so severely taxed the Bs' financial resources that they could not afford to go to England in 1854. By August 1854 they were resigned: the new book would have to wait a year (see Heydon and Kelley, 125). That same month, B estimated that his next collection would contain "about 5000 lines" (quoted in DeVane and Knickerbocker, 78n.). Over the next ten months he enlarged the MS considerably. In June 1855, EBB credited him with eight thousand lines of new poetry (see Gardner B. Taplin, *The Life of EBB* [New Haven: Yale University Press, 1957], 285, 288), and in September B added "One Word More" to his total. There were finally 7167 lines in the first edition of *Men and Women*, a large number of them composed between 1853 and the spring of 1855.

Many of the poems resist more precise dating; additional information is given in their individual notes.

Sources

The individual works in *Men and Women* make use of numerous diverse sources, but several aspects of B's experience affect more than a single poem. First, many details of setting and background derive from his

European travels. The Bs' first nine years in Italy—from their marriage in 1846 to the publication of *Men and Women*—were punctuated by journeys to Venice, Rimini, Siena, Bagni di Lucca, and Rome, as well as to dozens of towns and villages along the way. Their visits to London in 1851, 1852, and 1855 took them through Paris, where they witnessed the creation of the Second Empire. And above all, it is Florence—the art, architecture, history, tradition, and topography of Florence—which permeates *Men and Women*. The masterpieces of Renaissance art that B saw in Florence had a profound effect on his poetry.

B's knowledge of art history was greater than his experiences in Florence, however. In his youth he had spent many hours at the Dulwich College gallery, and he had studied books on painting (see Irvine and Honan, 8-11). Among these books was Giorgio Vasari's *Le Vite de'Più Eccellenti Architetti, Pittori, et Scultori Italiani* (*The Lives of the Most Excellent Italian Architects, Painters, and Sculptors* [Florence, 1550]), which served as a major source for several poems in *Men and Women*. B's enthusiasm for this work is indicated in EBB's comment to him in March 1846: "Then for Vasari, it is not the handbook of the whole world . . ." (RB-EBB, ed. Kintner, 553). Among the items in the 1913 Sotheby Browning Collections was B's copy of the edition of Vasari's *Lives* prepared by Gaetano Milanesi, et al. (Florence, 1846-1857); this was probably the edition B used when working on *Men and Women*. To this reading must be added the books and conversations of the art historian Anna Brownell Jameson (1794-1860), one of the Bs' closest friends.

Through English and European newspapers and magazines, and through contact with friends and visitors to Casa Guidi, B kept abreast of intellectual, political, and popular movements. References to current events are not frequent in *Men and Women*, but one subject appears several times: spiritualism. Spirit-rappings and supernatural phenomena of all kinds were of great popular interest in the 1840s and 1850s, and the Bs paid considerable attention to them. Several of their friends in Florence were believers in mediums, spiritualism, mesmerism, and reincarnation. In May 1853 a seance was attempted at the Bs' home in Florence. EBB called it a failure and characterized B's attitude: "Robert, who won't believe, he says, till he sees and hears with his own senses—Robert, who is a sceptic—observed of himself the other day, that we had received as much evidence of these spirits as of the existence of the town of Washington" (*Letters of EBB*, 2, 117). EBB accepted on trust what others told her about spiritualism; B was genuinely curious but sceptical, as his references to spiritualism in *Men and Women* show. In later years, B emphatically expressed his disbelief in spirit phenomena and his distrust of mediums (for B and spiritualism, see Katherine H. Porter, *Through a Glass Darkly: Spiritualism in the B Circle* [Lawrence, Kansas: University of Kansas Press, 1958]).

Several of the following notes derive from or are based on Paul Turner's edition of *Men and Women* (London: Oxford, 1972). Such notes are followed by the symbol [PT].

LOVE AMONG THE RUINS

Composition] Though the MS in the Lowell collection at Harvard (see *Men and Women, Text and Publication*, above) is undated, the nature of its variant readings indicates that it represents a pre-1855 version of the poem. "Love Among the Ruins" may have been written in Paris during the first days of January 1852; the matter has been disputed (see *Men and Women, Composition*, above).

7] *a city* The description of the city in this and later stanzas is a composite to which numerous real and fictional ruins contributed. B would have been aware of the many archeological discoveries made in the mid-nineteenth century; between 1845 and 1853 accounts of the excavations at Rome, Tarquinia and Veii in the Campagna near Rome, Babylon, Nineveh, and the Egyptian city of Thebes were published (see Johnstone Parr, "The Site and Ancient City of Browning's *Love Among the Ruins*," *PMLA* 68 [1953], 128-37). Several possible literary sources—none apparently a direct source—have been suggested.

21-24] *hundred gated . . . abreast* Babylon and Thebes are said by several ancient writers to have had hundred-gated walls; Nineveh reportedly had gates large enough to allow great armies to pass through.

A LOVERS' QUARREL

Date] In light of the references in ll. 2 and 29-35, probably written in the spring of 1853.

20] *ingle* "Fire; a fire burning upon the hearth; a housefire" (*OED*).

28] *church daws* Common jackdaws (*Corvus monedula*), which are agressive, noisy birds, often nest in church towers and belfries.

29-35] *the "Times" . . . gold* The *Times* of London almost always disapproved of the French emperor Louis Napoleon. It was particularly scornful of the elaborate and expensive ceremonies at the time of his marriage to Eugenie de Montijo (30 January 1853). See the issues of 31 January, and 1 and 2 February 1853.

36] *Pampas' sheen* The Pampas, vast plains in Argentina, were once covered with dense tall grass.

42] *wild horse* Horses were introduced to the Pampas in the early nineteenth century by cattle ranchers.

43-44] *table turn . . . yearn* Table-turning is a spiritualist phenomenon. The movement of the table at a seance indicates the presence of a spirit; to perform the experiment, the participants place their fingers lightly on the table top, concentrating their thoughts as the medium directs. A mania for table-turning swept Europe and America in 1852-53 (see also *Men and Women, Sources*, above).

45-48] *Till . . . burn* Spiritualists and mediums claim to see flames or auras around people and objects. Such light was supposed to be the visible form of an otherwise insubstantial fluid "force" which connected the spirit and human realms and which the medium could control. In 1845 Karl von Reichenbach named this fluid *odyl* in his *Researches on Magnetism;* EBB reported that she could see it (see *RB-EBB,* ed. Kintner, 640). For related discussion, see notes to "Mesmerism."

58] *sledging-cap* sledding cap.

69-70] *two spots . . . swan* The juvenile of the common mute swan (*Cygnus olor*) has black patches on either side of the bill at its base. In the adult, this black area covers the entire base of the bill.

72] *mesmerizer* hypnotist; see notes to "Mesmerism."

83] *ingle-glow* see l. 20n.

90-91] *power . . . tongue* adapted from Prov. 18:21.

105] *mote . . . white* cf. Matt. 7:3-5; Luke 6:41-42.

112] *brain's coat of curd* The tough outer membrane of the brain, called the *dura mater,* has a waxy, curd-like appearance. Its great sensitivity to touch was discovered in the mid-nineteenth century.

122] *We . . . word* Some copies of the 1863 *Poetical Works* erroneously omit this line; see Nathaniel I. Hart, "A Browning Letter on 'The Poetical Works' of 1863," *N & Q* 219 (1974), 213-215.

123-24] *minor third . . . cuckoo knows* The European cuckoo (*Cuculus canorus*) sings a two-note song which changes through the spring and summer. The early song may have only a semi-tone interval between the notes; the interval increases through a minor third to a fourth or more.

131-33] *valiant Thumb . . . fee-faw-fum* Tom Thumb and Hop-o'-my-Thumb are heroes in European folk tales. Tom Thumb is hardly courageous in these stories, but he does confront the giant Grumbo in his castle. Henry Fielding (1707-1754) made Tom Thumb heroic in the comedy *The Tragedy of Tragedies; or the Life and Death of Tom Thumb the Great* (1731). In two other folktales, "Jack and the Beanstalk" and "Jack the Giant-Killer," boy heroes face giants who chant "fee, fie, foh, fum."

EVELYN HOPE

19-20] *The good stars . . . fire and dew* Aristotle, Empedocles, and other classical philosophers held that all matter is composed of four elements—earth, air, fire, and water—and that the balance of these elements determines the nature and behavior of substances. Following this belief, astrologers divide the twelve signs of the zodiac into four regions, each associated with one of the elements. A person's life and behavior are determined by the balance of signs at the time of birth; thus Evelyn Hope's personality was spiritual, not earth-bound or ordinary.

29-30] *more lives . . . traverse* Theories of reincarnation were widely discussed in the mid-nineteenth century. B had probably encountered the idea in working on *The Return of the Druses,* since the Druses believe in continual reincarnation. Soul-migration is also a feature of Swedenborgianism, with which the Bs were quite familiar. B would also have encountered the idea of reincarnation in the works of Shelley, Goethe, and Carlyle.

UP AT A VILLA—DOWN IN THE CITY

Date]   After 1849, as shown by the references to political events (see ll. 44-46nn.).

9]   *shag* "A (tangled) mass of shrubs, trees, foliage, etc." (*OED*).

26-30]   *a fountain . . . sort of a sash* Some details of the description may come from real fountains. The fountain in the public square of Fano (29 mi. NW of Ancona, on the Adriatic coast), which the Bs visited in August 1848, features a statue of the goddess Fortuna, represented as a thinly-clad girl. The horses may have been suggested by those in the Trevi fountain in Rome, where the Bs spent the winter of 1853-54.

28]   *pash* "the action of beating or striking water . . ." (*OED*). This sense apparently was coined by B.

32]   *cypress . . . forefinger* The European cypress tree (*Cupressus sempervirens*) is slender and straight, growing to a height of one hundred feet or more. It is frequently planted in cemeteries and has been a symbol of death for centuries, possibly because when felled it does not sprout from the stump, or because its wood is used for coffins.

34]   *thrid* thread.

42]   *Pulcinello-trumpet* The horn announcing a performance of a puppet show. Pulcinello is the character known in England as Punch.

43]   *scene-picture* A poster advertising a play.

44]   *liberal thieves* In mid-nineteenth century Italy, liberals supported the cause of national unification and liberation from foreign domination. The Bs were in sympathy with the growing liberal movements of the 1840s. After the failures of the wars of liberation in 1848-49, conservative Italian leaders (supported by Pope Pius IX, Austria, and France) reestablished repressive governments. To be a liberal then was to be considered an enemy of the state and a common criminal comparable to a thief.

45]   *Archbishop's . . . rebukes* Though Pope Pius IX supported Italian nationalism when he became pope, he opposed the liberals when they argued for the elimination of the temporal powers of the Roman Catholic Church. After the wars of 1848-49 (see l. 44n.) the pope and his representatives reasserted their influence in civil and political matters.

46]   *his crown . . . the Duke's* The details of the Duke's coat of arms suggest the northern Italian setting of the poem. Of the six nineteenth century Italian duchies (Tuscany, Milan, Lucca, Mantua, Modena, and Parma-Piacenza), four were ruled by the Habsburg dynasty, whose crest features a lion. The crown is the symbol of a prince or ruling duke.

Coincidentally, the coat of arms of Pope Pius IX contains two crowned lions; thus B's details connect two repressive authorities. The city in the poem is probably Florence, where Leopold II (1797-1870) of the house of Habsburg ruled as Grand Duke of Tuscany. Leopold II lived in the Pitti Palace, across from which the Bs lived. After a brief exile in 1849, Leopold II ruled Florence severely until 1859.

47] *Reverend Don So-and-so Don* is the common form of address for an Italian priest.

48] *Dante . . . Cicero* These five writers, all Italian except St. Jerome, who studied and taught at Rome, represent the highest excellence in the literary arts: narrative and dramatic poetry (Dante Alighieri [1265-1321]); lyric poetry (Francesco Petrarca, or Petrarch [1304-74]); the prose tale (Giovanni Boccaccio [1313-75]); biography (Boccaccio again); translation and editing (St. Jerome [c. 347-420]); and rhetoric (Marcus Tullius Cicero [106-43 B.C.]).

49] *Saint Paul* The first great Christian theologian and missionary. As the author of fourteen of the New Testament epistles and the main figure in the book of Acts, St. Paul's importance to Christianity is usually considered second only to that of Jesus himself.

50] *six Lent-lectures* During Lent it is customary to preach one of each week's sermons on a continuing subject, thus forming a six-part discourse on an aspect of Lenten observance.

51-52] *our Lady . . . swords in her heart* Outdoor religious processions are often held during Lent. The representation of the Virgin Mary with seven swords in her heart is a variety of the *Mater Dolorosa* (sorrowful mother) theme in Roman Catholic liturgy and iconography. Each sword symbolizes one of the seven sorrows of Mary: the prophecy of Simeon (Luke 2:25-35), the flight into Egypt (Matt. 2:13-15), the disappearance of Jesus for three days (Luke 2:41-46), the bearing of the cross (John 19:17), the crucifixion (Matt. 27:33-50; Mark 15:22-37; Luke 23:33-46; John 19:17-30), the descent from the cross (Mark 15:45-46; Luke 23:52-53), and the entombment (Matt. 27:59-61; Mark 15:46-47; Luke 23:53-55; John 19:40-42). The image itself is the result of extensive embellishment of Luke 2:35, in which Simeon prophesies to Mary that "a sword shall pierce through thy own soul also." The seven sorrows motif appears frequently in church decoration and popular religious art of the sixteenth to nineteenth centuries, though such treatments as B describes are few.

56] *tax upon salt . . . the gate* Specific taxes on staple goods like salt and flour were common in Italian cities until this century. City living was made still more expensive by the addition of the *octroi*, a general tax on nearly everything that entered a city for sale.

60] *penitents . . . shirts* Penitence, one of the major themes of Lenten observances, is sometimes dramatized by a ceremonial procession of repentent worshipers, whose white tunics symbolize their purity after confession.

A WOMAN'S LAST WORD

15-20] *Where the serpent's . . . Eve and I* That is, arguments about truth and falsity are as dangerous as the serpent's promise that Adam and Eve would know good and evil after eating the fruit of the forbidden tree. See Gen. 2:17; 3:1-24.

FRA LIPPO LIPPI

Composition] "Fra Lippo Lippi" is undoubtedly one of the poems with "more music and painting" that B mentioned to Milsand in February 1853 (see *Men and Women, Composition* n., above). EBB described B as "digging at Vasari" in April of 1853 (see Betty Miller, *Robert Browning: A Portrait* [New York: Scribner, 1953], 187), so it seems likely that the poem was written in the winter and spring of 1853.

Sources] For the story of Fra Lippo's life, B drew upon Vasari's "Fra Filippo Lippi, Painter of Florence" (Vasari, 2, 1-8) and "Masaccio di S. Giovanni of Valdarno, Painter" (Vasari, 1, 263-69). Some traits of B's Lippi may derive from the views of Anna Brownell Jameson (see *Men and Women, Sources*, above). The use of the Prior's niece may have been suggested by "Fra Filippo Lippi and Pope Eugenius the Fourth" (1846), an "Imaginary Conversation" by Walter Savage Landor (1775-1864), a close friend of the Bs.

Title] Filippo di Tommaso Lippi (c. 1406-1469) was born in Florence; he became a Carmelite friar in 1421. Following Masaccio (see ll. 273-78n.) and Masolino (Tommaso di Cristoforo Fini, c. 1383-c. 1435), Lippi employed a realistic style and emphasized the human aspects of his religious subjects. This element of his practice influenced many later artists.

3] *Zooks* Clipped form of "Gadzooks," an oath which perhaps derives from "God's hooks" (the nails used in the crucifixion of Jesus) or from "God's hocks" (following the pattern of swearing by parts of Jesus' body, as in "God's wounds").

7] *The Carmine's my cloister* In Lippi's time, the Carmelite order was housed in the church of Santa Maria del Carmine, in the Piazza del Carmine S of the Arno river in Florence. In the Brancacci chapel of the church are important frescoes by Masaccio (see ll. 273-78n.) which B knew well. The Carmelites were initially an austere ascetic order, but by the thirteenth century their practice was less rigorous. In 1431 Pope Eugenius IV relaxed the rule of the order still further, and Fra Lippo Lippi commemorated this event in a fresco at Santa Maria del Carmine.

17] *Cosimo of the Medici* Cosimo the Elder (1389-1464) was the first member of the powerful Medici family to patronize the arts extensively. Though he held no official position, Cosimo was the most powerful man in Florence. Through shrewd and ruthless commercial and political dealings, he and his family established the material basis of the Florentine Renaissance, and a large portion of his wealth was used to support painting, sculpture, architecture, music, literature, and scholarship.

18] *the house that caps the corner* The original Medici palace (sold to the Riccardi family in 1659 and now called the Palazzo Medici-Riccardi) stands at the corner of the Via de' Gori and the Via Cavour (formerly the Via Larga). One of the greatest of Florentine palaces, it was commissioned by Cosimo the Elder in 1444 and was completed in 1459.

25-26] *He's Judas . . . a face* Though no representation of Judas by Lippi is known to survive, B may be recollecting an incident from Vasari's life of Leonardo da Vinci. When Leonardo was painting his famous "Last Supper" in the monastery of Santa Maria delle Grazie in Milan, he struggled with two of the figures in particular: that of Christ and that of Judas. The prior of the monastery repeatedly urged Leonardo to finish the painting, and, when Leonardo continued to work slowly, at last complained to the artist's patron, the Duke of Milan. Leonardo then explained his difficulties with the two figures; he could not expect to find a model for Christ, he said, but for Judas he would use the Prior himself as the original. See Vasari, 2, 161.

29-30] *the munificent . . . more beside* Other recipients of Cosimo's generous commissions and gifts were the sculptors Donatello, Ghiberti, and della Robbia, and the painters Fra Angelico (see l. 235n.) and Masaccio (see ll. 273-78n.).

33-34] *the slave . . . a-dangle* John the Baptist, the forerunner of Jesus, was beheaded by King Herod at the request of his niece Salome, who was granted a wish after pleasing Herod with her dancing. The severed head of John was presented to Salome on a platter (Matt. 14:1-11; Mark 6:17-28). Lippi's fresco "The Feast of Herod" (commissioned 1452) in the cathedral at Prato portrays these incidents. The work covers more than one wall of the church, and on the wall adjoining the left side of the main scene appears a figure holding the head of the prophet by the hair.

48-49] *saints . . . again* Over half of Lippi's surviving works have saints as their subjects.

53-57] *Flower o' the broom . . . thyme* This and the other fragments of song Fra Lippo interjects were derived by B from Italian folksongs called *stornelli*. These songs always begin with a reference to a flower; B has altered the stanza from three lines to two.

67] *Saint Laurence* The church of San Lorenzo stands across from the Medici palace (see l. 18n.). Its ancient structure was rebuilt in the fifteenth century at the expense of the Medici family, and their magnificent tombs dominate the interior of the church today. Among the numerous great works of art in San Lorenzo is Lippi's "Annunciation."

72-74] *go work / On Jerome . . . round stone* St. Jerome (c. 347-420) advocated strict asceticism. He spent two years in the desert to discipline his appetites, sometimes beating himself with stones as punishment for his unruly flesh. St. Jerome in the desert was a popular Renaissance subject, and Lippi interpreted it in an altarpiece for the cathedral at Prato. This painting, of uncertain date, focuses on the death of St. Jerome; in the background are scenes from his life. At the right of the background is a desert scene showing Jerome with a stone in his left hand. Vasari (2, 6) praises a St. Jerome done by Lippi for Cosimo the Elder, but this work is not known to survive.

90-91] *over the bridge / By the . . . convent* The Ponte alla Carraia, one of the oldest bridges in Florence, crosses the Arno a few hundred yards from the church of Santa Maria del Carmine (see l. 7n.).

96-99] *Will you . . . banking-house* Compare *Book of Common Prayer*, "Ministration of Baptism": "Dost thou renounce the devil and all his works, the vain pomp and glory of the world, with all covetous desires of the same, and the carnal desires of the flesh . . . ?"

99] *banking-house* The Medici fortune was based on banking. In Lippi's time the central offices of the Medici bank were in the Medici palace.

110-11] *Flower . . . I love* see ll. 53-57n.

121] *the Eight* The *Otto di Guardia* (Eight for Defense), one of the four ruling magistracies of Renaissance Florence, coordinated civil defense, military, and police activities.

139] *Carmelites . . . Camaldolese* For Carmelites, see l. 7n. The Camaldolese friars were an independent order of Benedictine monks established near Florence in the eleventh century. They occupied the convent of Santa Maria degli Angeli, in Florence's Via degli Alfani. Several famous painters were associated with this convent: Lorenzo Monaco (see l. 235n.) was a Camaldolese monk; and Fra Angelico (see l. 235n.), Andrea del Castagno, and Sandro Botticelli all painted for Santa Maria degli Angeli.

140] *Preaching Friars* This term usually refers to members of the Dominican order, though Franciscan friars also preached in Lippi's time. The several churches of these two orders in and around Florence were remodeled and decorated by many famous artists. Here B probably refers to the Dominican convent of San Marco, at the opposite end of the Via Cavour (formerly Via Larga) from the Medici palace. That convent was overhauled in 1437-38 at the expense of Cosimo the Elder; it contains many works by the Dominican painter Fra Angelico (see l. 235n.).

145] *black and white* Some monastic orders are nicknamed for the colors of their habits, e.g.: Black Friars (Dominicans), Black Monks (Benedictines), White Friars (Carmelites), and White Monks (Cistercians).

148] *cribs* "petty theft[s]" (*OED*). In this sense, apparently a B coinage.

150] *safe and sitting there* From the fifth century until the Reformation, Christian churches in Europe had legal status as sanctuaries from arrest and prosecution. A criminal could avoid punishment for a set number of days or for an indefinite period, depending on the seriousness of the crime, by entering a church and claiming the right of sanctuary.

172] *funked* smoked.

185-86] *It's vapour . . . mouth* Such representations of the soul were common in medieval Christian art.

189] *Giotto . . . a-praising God* Giotto di Bondone (c. 1266-1337), sometimes called the father of modern art, was born near Florence. Giotto was influenced by the humanism of St. Francis of Assisi, whose life he portrayed in frescoes in the upper church at Assisi. These frescoes, mentioned in Vasari, show St. Francis at prayer; B visited the churches at Assisi in November 1853. He would also have seen works by Giotto in the galleries of Florence.

196-97] *Herodias . . . heads cut off* The Prior refers to the death of John the Baptist (see ll. 33-34n.), but he confuses Queen Herodias with her daughter Salome. Herodias convinced Salome to ask for the prophet's head, but it was Salome who danced for King Herod.

228] *rings in front* At the top of the first story of the Medici palace are several large iron rings evenly spaced along the length of the building.

235] *Brother Angelico* Guido di Pietro (c. 1400-1455), born at Fiesole (about 5 mi. from Florence), was called Fra Angelico. He was a Dominican friar whose pious devotional paintings represent a pinnacle of formal religious art.

236] *Brother Lorenzo* Piero di Giovanni (c. 1370-1425), called Lorenzo Monaco after he became a Camaldolese monk, was born at Siena, 25 mi. S of Florence. He was influenced by Giotto, and probably taught Fra Angelico; his works are formal and restrained in theme and style.

238-39] *Flower . . . to mine* see ll. 53-57n.

246] *my saints* see ll. 48-49n.

248-49] *Flower . . . for each* see ll. 53-57n.

250] *cup runs over* Adapted from Ps.23:5.

266-67] *the Garden . . . man's wife* See Gen. 2:8-25.

273-78] *a youngster . . . practice up* Tommaso di Giovanni di Simone Guidi (1401-28) was a Florentine painter who, like Lippi, was supported by Cosimo the Elder. The nickname *Masaccio*, which is always used for Guidi, is a clipped form of *Tomasaccio*, which means "big," "clumsy," or "hulking" Thomas. Masaccio was tremendously influential despite his short career. His most famous works are his portions of the frescoes in the Brancacci chapel (see l. 7n.), which were painted between 1423 and 1428. The treatment of human figures in these frescoes clearly influenced Lippi, but B reversed the master-pupil relationship because of erroneous statements in one of his sources. A footnote in the edition of Vasari that B used (see *Men and Women, Sources*, above) dates the Brancacci frescoes in the 1440s, thus making possible B's representation of Lippi as the teacher (see Johnstone Parr, "Browning's *Fra Lippo Lippi*, Baldinucci, and the Milanesi Edition of Vasari," *ELN* 3 [1966], 197-201). However, B defended his version of art history in a letter to Edward Dowden, saying "I was wide awake when I made Fra Lippo the elder practitioner of Art," and arguing the matter at some length (Hood, *Ltrs.*, 104; letter dated 13 October 1866). It was not known until this century that Masaccio died in 1428 rather than 1443.

323-28] *St. Laurence . . . toasted side* St. Laurence, a deacon of Pope

Sixtus II, was martyred c. 258 by being roasted alive on a gridiron. According to St. Ambrose, Laurence said to his judge, "Let my body be turned; one side is broiled enough." Vasari refers to a painting of St. Laurence by Lippi (Vasari, 2, 6), and the description of Lippi's painting of St. Stephen at Prato (Vasari, 2, 5) seems related to B's handling of this episode.

346] *Something in Sant' Ambrogio's* The reference is to Lippi's "Coronation of the Virgin," an altarpiece for the Augustinian convent of Sant' Ambrogio in Florence. This painting, executed between 1441 and 1447, was in the Accademia delle Belle Arti of Florence in B's time; today it hangs in the Uffizi gallery. B makes use of numerous details from the "Coronation" in the description that follows, though in some ways Lippi's projection here differs from the finished piece.

348] *her babe* The Christ-child does not appear in the finished work.

354] *Saint John . . . Florentines* John the Baptist is the patron saint of Florence. He appears in Lippi's "Coronation of the Virgin" at the extreme right, dressed in camel hair and holding a cross. See ll. 374-75n.

355] *Saint Ambrose* St. Ambrose (c. 340-97), for whom the convent of Sant' Ambrogio was named, was Bishop of Milan from 374 until his death. The large standing figure with a mitre at the extreme left of Lippi's "Coronation of the Virgin" is probably St. Ambrose.

357] *Job* The Old Testament figure who suffered his tribulations with forbearance. He appears, labeled "past mistake," in the left foreground of Lippi's painting.

358] *Uz* Job's homeland (Job 1:1).

374-75] *Saint John . . . painting-brush* When John the Baptist lived in the wilderness, he wore garments of camel hair (Matt. 3:1-4; Mark 1:4-6), which is used to make paintbrushes.

377] *Iste perfecit opus* Latin for "this man made the work," or "this man caused the work to be done." A scroll reading "is perfecit opus" appears near a figure in the right foreground of Lippi's "Coronation of the Virgin." Until this century the figure was thought to represent Lippi himself, but it is in fact a portrait of Canon Francesco Maringhi, chaplain of the convent of Sant' Ambrogio, who arranged for the decoration of the church and thus commissioned Lippi's "Coronation of the Virgin" altarpiece.

381] *hot cockles* A children's game in which a blindfolded player is struck in turn by the others; he must guess who has tagged him. The game has a flirtatious ambience, and B's sense of it may be the same as that of John Gay: "As at Hot-cockles once I laid me down, / And felt the weighty hand of many a Clown; / Buxoma gave a gentle tap, and I / Quick rose, and read soft mischief in her eye" (*The Shepherd's Week* [1714], "Monday," ll. 99-102).

387] *Saint Lucy* St. Lucy was martyred at Syracuse in 304. She refused to break her vow of virginity and was ordered to a brothel as punishment. A pretty young woman (probably modelled on Lippi's mistress, Lucretia Buti) appears in the foreground of the "Coronation of the Virgin," and this figure may have prompted B's reference.

392] *fear* fear for (an obsolete usage; *OED*).

A TOCCATA OF GALUPPI'S

Composition] It is likely that this is one of the poems with "more music and painting" that B mentioned to Milsand in February 1853 (see *Men and Women, Composition,* above). B visited Venice in 1838 and 1851.

Title] A toccata (from Italian *toccare,* "to touch") is a musical composition for keyboard instruments, characterized by rapid tempo, alternation of runs and chords, and, occasionally, fugal sections. The toccata is a specialized form of the sonata, and the two terms have sometimes been used interchangeably. Baldassare Galuppi (1706-85) was a Venetian composer known primarily for his comic operas. He did write harpsichord sonatas, though no toccatas by Galuppi are known to survive. B stated late in his life that he once had "two huge manuscript volumes almost exclusively made up of his 'Toccata pieces'—apparently a slighter form of the Sonata to be 'touched' lightly off (H. E. Greene, "Browning's Knowledge of Music," *PMLA* 62 [1947], 1099.

5] *Venice . . . the kings* The city of Venice is situated on a group of islands in the Adriatic Sea, on the NE coast of Italy. From the ninth through the sixteenth centuries, its vast trade network made the city wealthy and powerful, and the merchants of Venice controlled its economic, political, and ecclesiastical power. By Galuppi's time, however, the city was well past its period of greatness.

6] *Saint Mark's* The opulent church of San Marco is the cathedral of Venice. It stands on the Piazza San Marco, at the cultural center of the city.

6] *Doges* The Doge, or Duke of Venice, acted as chief administrator and ceremonial head of the city. During Venice's ascendancy, the Doge was elected by the merchants who controlled the Great Council of Venice.

6] *wed the sea with rings* On Ascension Day (the Thursday forty days after Easter), the Doge cast a golden ring into the Adriatic and pronounced Venice and the sea united. This elaborate ceremony originated as an offering to placate the seas, but it came to signify Venice's commercial and military domination over the eastern Mediterranean.

8] *Shylock's bridge with houses* The reference is to the Rialto bridge, although when Shakespeare's Shylock mentions "the Rialto" (*Merchant of Venice* 1. 3. 19) he means not the bridge but the district of the same name, which was the financial heart of Venice. The Rialto bridge crosses the Grand Canal in the center of the city; since its completion in 1591, the bridge has been lined with shops, not houses.

8] *they kept the carnival* The Venetian carnival, held during the week preceding Lent, was famous for elaborate entertainments, dancing, music, theater, and public celebrations. Long after other cities had reduced or eliminated carnival activities, Venice continued its extravagant festival.

14] *bell-flower on its bed* The bell-flower rises from a mat of dense foliage and swings from the top third of the stem.

18] *Toccatas* See *Title* n.

18] *clavichord* A small, stringed keyboard instrument with a very soft tone, easily overpowered by the sound of even one human voice. The instrument was popular with composers and performers from the fifteenth through the eighteenth centuries, being replaced by the piano thereafter.

19] *lesser thirds* That is, minor thirds (the Italian term *minore* means literally "lesser"). Minor keys are distinguished by the frequent use of this interval of three semitones, particularly when the lower of the two notes is the first (tonic) or fourth (subdominant) degree of the scale.

19] *sixths diminished, sigh on sigh* Technically the "diminished" sixth is not a discrete interval, since it contains seven semitones and is thus identical with a perfect fifth. Deryck Cooke explains B's terminology admirably: "Remember that B was writing of an Italian, and knew Italian; that *minore* means literally 'lesser'; and that, being a poet, he would not repeat the word, but seize on a (regrettably ambiguous) synonym—'diminished'; and his 'faulty terminology' disappears, to reveal a remarkable insight into the expressive effect of the minor third and minor sixth" (*The Language of Music* [London, 1959], 71).

20] *suspensions . . . solutions* A suspension is the holding over of one tone of an interval or chord to form a momentary dissonance with the next interval or chord. The dissonance is resolved, or finds "solution," when the held note moves up or down into a consonance. The technique is frequently employed to further harmonic and melodic flow.

21] *sevenths* The seventh note of a scale is termed the "leading tone" because it has a melodic and harmonic tendency toward the tonic. Both the minor seventh (ten semitones above the tonic) and the major seventh (eleven semitones above the tonic) create harmonic tensions that demand resolution.

24] *dominant's persistence* The fifth note in a scale is called the dominant. The sounding of this tone usually precedes a resolution to the tonic.

25] *an octave struck the answer* The sounding of the first and eighth notes of the scale together creates an interval of an octave, ending the piece with a simple resolution.

35] *Dust and ashes* Compare *Book of Common Prayer*, "Burial of the Dead": "Earth to earth, ashes to ashes, dust to dust." For the association of the images with dead lovers, see Andrew Marvell, "To His Coy Mistress," ll. 29-30: "And your quaint Honour turn to dust; / And into ashes all my Lust."

41] *they . . . fruitage* cf. Matt. 7:16-20.

BY THE FIRE-SIDE

Date] Probably late 1853, in light of autobiographical elements in the poem.

Sources]   The description of the mountain walk apparently derives from the Bs' excursion to Prato Fiorito, near Bagni di Lucca, in the summer of 1853 (See Irvine and Honan, 311; *Letters of EBB*, 2, 142-43). Some details may be drawn from a guidebook rendering of the scenery around Lake Orta, which the Bs planned to visit but did not (see Jean Stirling Lindsay, "The Central Episode of Browning's 'By the Fire-Side,' " *SP* 39 [1942], 571-79).

43]   *Pella* A small town on the W bank of Lake Orta, in the Italian Alps about 25 mi. NNW of Novara. In light of the earlier references to Greek, it is noteworthy that Pella is also the name of the ancient Macedonian city where Alexander the Great was born.

52-53]   *thorny balls . . . chestnuts throw* The bristly fruit of the European chestnut tree (*Castanea sativa*) contains two or three separate nuts.

58]   *boss* The convex decorated center of a shield.

64]   *freaked* variegated in color; streaked or flecked.

77]   *festa-day* A feast or festival day, when special church services are held.

81-82]   *charcoal-burners' huts . . . low shed* Both cottage industries in the Alps. Charcoal is made by partially burning wood; hemp-dressers comb out and straighten rotted hemp stems so that the fibers may be twisted into rope.

89]   *John in the Desert* A frequent theme in Christian art; John the Baptist lived in the deserts of Judea before beginning his ministry (Matt. 3:1; Mark 1:4; Luke 1:80).

101]   *Leonor* The loving wife in Beethoven's opera *Fidelio* (1805; final revision 1814) is named Leonore. B had seen *Fidelio* in London in 1832, and he mentioned the performance to EBB in 1845 (RB-EBB, ed. Kintner, 156).

132-33]   *great Word . . . heaven expands* That is, at the Last Judgment, when the world is ended, sin and death conquered, and the New Jerusalem created. Adapted from Rev. 21:1, 4-5, and 1 Thess. 4:16-17.

135]   *house not made with hands* "we have a building of God, a house not made with hands, eternal in the heavens" (2 Cor. 5:1).

171]   *settle* A seating place; here, a bench or ledge.

185]   *chrysolite* Both the physical nature and the symbolic associations of this mineral are significant here. Chrysolite, also known as olivine or peridot, is yellow-green to bottle-green in color and is valued as a precious stone. It is often confused with chrysoberyl (or cat's eye), which shows a light band against a dark surface when cut and polished. Furthermore, both these minerals were in ancient times called topaz, and the symbolic values of topaz were applied to all three stones. Topaz was believed to emit a ray of light under special circumstances; it also symbolized chastity, fidelity, and true love. Both topaz and chrysolite are among the twelve precious stones in the walls of the New Jerusalem (Rev. 21:20).

244-45]   *a soul . . . its fruit* cf. Matt. 7:16-20.

ANY WIFE TO ANY HUSBAND

77]   *Titian's Venus* The Urbino Venus of Titian (Titiano Vecellio, c. 1488-1576), housed in the Uffizi Gallery in Florence since 1631.

88-91] *the old mint . . . to spend* cf. John Donne's "A Valediction: of Weeping."

94] *sealing up the sum* cf. Ezek. 28:12.

AN EPISTLE CONTAINING THE STRANGE MEDICAL EXPERIENCE OF KARSHISH, THE ARAB PHYSICIAN

Sources] The story of Jesus' raising of Lazarus from the dead appears in John 11:1-44; 12:1-2, 9-11, 17. Tennyson had treated the Lazarus miracle in *In Memoriam* (1850), sec. 31-32. The deliberately archaic language of the poem is generally influenced by the style of the King James Bible; in particular, the first twenty lines of "An Epistle" follow the manner of Rom. 1:1-7.

1] *Karshish . . . crumbs* The name Karshish is a transliteration of an Arabic word meaning "one who gathers" (see Maureen Wright, *TLS* 52 [1953], 285).

4-6] *Blown . . . man's soul* "But there went up a mist from the earth, and watered the whole face of the ground. And the Lord God formed man of the dust of the ground, and breathed into his nostrils the breath of life; and man became a living soul" (Gen. 2:6-7).

17] *snakestone* Any of several substances worn as a charm to prevent snakebite or used in folk medicine as a cure for snakebite.

21] *Jericho* A city founded by Herod the Great near the N end of the Dead Sea, about 15 mi. NE of Jerusalem.

27] *marching hitherward* A Shakespearean phrase: see *Henry IV*, part 1, 4.1. 89; *King Lear*, 4.4. 21.

28] *Some . . . his son* In A.D. 67-68, Titus Flavius Vespasianus (A.D. 9-79) led Roman troops in suppressing the Jewish revolt in Palestine. Accompanied by his two sons Titus Flavius Vespasianus (A.D. 39-81) and Titus Flavius Domitianus (A.D. 51-96), he brutally subdued the countryside and advanced his armies toward Jerusalem.

34] *Jerusalem* The most important city of ancient Palestine; it is about 15 mi. W of the N end of the Dead Sea.

36] *Bethany* A small village about 1.5 mi. E of Jerusalem; Bethany was the site of the Lazarus miracle.

40] *travel-scrip* A small bag or wallet.

42] *choler* In ancient medicine, choler was one of the humors, the substances in the body which governed health and temperament. An excess of choler (later called yellow bile) was said to cause irritability and wrathfulness.

43] *tertians* Malarial fevers, which recur every third day.

44] *falling-sickness* epilepsy.

45-48] *a spider . . . drop them* Spiders were used as ingredients in drugs and medicines from ancient times to the Renaissance. The reference is probably to one of the many species of jumping spiders (*Salticidae*), which do not weave webs and display a wide range of coloration.

50-51] *sublimate . . . his nose* A sublimate is a solid substance that has been refined and powdered by being heated to a vapor and cooled back to a solid state. Medicines intended to affect the head were frequently administered through the nose.

52] *Jerusalem* See l. 34n.

55] *Judæa* The SW part of Palestine, from the Dead Sea to the Mediterranean and from Gaza and Masada in the S to Joppa and Jericho in the N.

55] *gum-tragacanth* A substance exuded from the bark of a shrub (*Astragalus gummifer*). Gum tragacanth is used as a thickener and vehicle for medicines.

57] *porphyry* A hard marble-like stone, here meant as the material of a mortar.

60] *Zoar* An ancient city mentioned in the Old Testament. It was probably located SE of the Dead Sea.

83] *exorcization* The driving out of evil spirits by magic.

100] *Nazarene physician* Jesus grew up in Nazareth, a town of Galilee in Palestine (Matt. 2:23; Luke 2:39-40).

101] *bade . . . did rise* See John 11:43-44.

137] *golden mean* The term appears in Horace (*Odes*, 2.10.5) and refers to the principle of avoidance of excess. This rule is associated with Aristotle's doctrine of the mean in Book VI of the *Nichomachean Ethics*.

222-224] *Rome . . . at once* See l. 28n.

252] *His death . . . fell* When Jesus died, the earth shook (Matt. 27:50-51).

269] *Creator . . . world* Compare *Book of Common Prayer*, "A Prayer for all Conditions of Men": "O God, the Creator and Preserver of all mankind . . . ."

281] *Aleppo* An ancient city of N Syria, important as a cultural and commercial center.

MESMERISM

Title] Mesmerism, also known as "animal magnetism" and now as hypnotism, takes its name from the Austrian physician Franz Antoine Mesmer (1734-1815), who established and promoted the practice of the art in Europe. Mesmer and his followers held that the hypnotist is a repository and conductor of a "universal magnetic fluid" (later called "odyl" and claimed as a source of power by spiritualists). Certain movements ("passes") of the hands supposedly transmit this insubstantial force to a subject, thus making control of the subject possible. The sleep-like trance so induced was claimed to be healthful. EBB learned of Mesmerism from Harriet Martineau (1802-76), who was under the care of a Mesmeric doctor. Miss Martineau was so persuasive on the matter that EBB pronounced herself "a believer" (*Letters of EBB*, 1, 197), and her letters of 1844-45 are filled with references to Mesmerism. B probably learned most of what he knew of Mesmerism from EBB, and as with spiritualism he appears to have been curious and skeptical.

8] *death-watch ticks* Two wood-boring beetles (*Xestobium rufovissosum* and *Anobium punctatum*) are popularly known as death-watch beetles. Their clicking calls supposedly presage a death in the house.

10] *water-butt* A barrel used to catch rain water.

11-15] *And the socket . . . unawares* A catalog of some of the ghostly phenomena reported at seances.

45] *calotypist's skill* The calotype, patented by W. H. Fox Talbot in 1841, was an important early form of photography.

56-57] *a gesture fit / Of my hands* That is, through the use of Mesmeric "passes" (see *Title* n.).

63-65] *hands . . . flame* The presence of the Mesmeric fluid (see *Title* n.) was supposedly detectable by the appearance of flames or auras around the hypnotist.

107] *unfilleted* Not bound up with a ribbon; hanging loose.

A SERENADE AT THE VILLA

22] *White . . . flowers* The European hemlock plant (*Conium maculatum*) bears large compound clusters of small white flowers.

37] *"So . . . worse!"* cf. *King Lear*, 4.1.25-28.

MY STAR

4] *angled spar* Several crystalline minerals are known as spar, but the reference is probably to selenite or quartz, which act as prisms.

9] *dartles* Shoots forth; apparently a B coinage.

11] *Saturn* The sixth planet from the sun; easily seen because of its size and brightness.

INSTANS TYRANNUS

Title and Source] The title and idea derive from Horace (*Odes*, 3.3.1-8): "Iustum et tenacem propositi virum / non civium ardor prava iubentium, / non vultus instantis tyranni / mente quatit solida neque Auster, / dux inquieti turbidus Hadriae, / nec fulminantis magna manus Iovis; / si fractus illabatur orbis, / impavidum ferient ruinae." ("A just man, firm in purpose, neither fellow-citizens demanding what is wrong nor the face of a threatening tyrant can shake from his solid resolve: nor the south wind, wild ruler of the stormy Adriatic, nor the great hand of thundering Jove; if the world were to break into bits, the ruins would strike him undaunted.")

15] *five wits* The five wits are common sense, imagination, fantasy, estimation, and memory.

65] *boss* The convex decorated center of a shield.

A PRETTY WOMAN

Source] DeVane (*Hbk.*, 228) speculates that the woman in the poem may have been modelled on Anna Brownell Jameson's niece (for Mrs. Jameson, see *Men and Women, Sources,* above).

23-24] *brayed you / In a mortar* "Though thou shouldst bray a fool in a mortar among wheat with a pestle, yet will not his foolishness depart from him" (Prov. 27:22).

62] *mould-flower* That is, a real flower used as a pattern for the gold one in the next line.

"CHILDE ROLAND TO THE DARK TOWER CAME"

Composition and Sources] The known facts are far fewer than the speculations. In 1866, B said that the poem was written in Paris (DeVane and Knickerbocker, 173), and Lilian Whiting quotes him in 1887 as follows: " 'Twas like this; one year in Florence I had been rather lazy; I resolved that I would write something every day. Well, the first day I wrote about some roses, suggested by a magnificent basket that some one had sent my wife. The next day 'Childe Roland' came upon me as a kind of dream. I had to write it then and there, and I finished it the same day, I believe" (*The Brownings: Their Life and Art* [Boston, 1911], 261). Biographical tradition holds that the year was 1852 and the day either 2 or 3 January (see *Men and Women, Composition,* above). Mrs. Orr, probably drawing on B's own testimony, cites four sources for " 'Childe Roland' ": Shakespeare's *King Lear,* which provided the title; an unspecified painting in Paris; the figure of a horse in a tapestry; and a tower in the area of Massa-Carrara, near Spezia in NW Italy (Orr, *Hbk.,* 274n. On the tower, see also DeVane and Knickerbocker, 173). To this diverse group has been added a steadily growing number of possible sources unacknowledged or unrecognized by B. DeVane has demonstrated that Gerard de Lairesse's *Art of Painting in All its Branches,* which B read as a child, provided details for the landscape ("The Landscape of Browning's *Childe Roland,*" *PMLA* 40 [1925], 426-32). B's knowledge of Dante came into play in writing " 'Childe Roland' " (Ruth E. Sullivan, "Browning's 'Childe Roland' and Dante's *Inferno,*" *VP* 5 [1967], 296-302), as did his familiarity with Gothic novels (Leslie M. Thompson, " 'Childe Roland to the Dark Tower Came' and the Gothic Tradition in Literature," *Browning Newsletter* 9 [1972], 17-22). The extended simile of the dying man in ll. 25-36 echoes John Donne's "A Valediction: forbidding mourning," ll. 1-4 (Robert L. Lowe, *N & Q* 198 [1953], 491). The poem also has kinships with folk tales and heroic romances (Harold Golder, "Browning's 'Childe Roland,' *PMLA* 39 [1924], 963-78), and it has striking similarities to Wordsworth's "Peter Bell" (Thomas P. Harrison, "Browning's 'Childe Roland' and Wordsworth," *TSL* 6 [1961], 119-23). Further suggestions have been and will continue to be made, their range being limited only by the extent of B's proven or proposed reading and experience.

Title and Subtitle]   The words of the title appear in *King Lear*, 3.4.185-87, as Edgar, disguised as a madman, closes the scene with a three-line song: "Child Rowland to the dark tower came, / His word was still, 'Fie, foh, and fum, / I smell the blood of a British man.' " A Childe is a young warrior who aspires to knighthood.

65]   *Judgment's fire* The purifying fire of God, which will punish sinners and consume Satan on the Day of Judgment (see Rev. 20:7-10, 14-15; 21:8).

106]   *howlet* A small owl.

114]   *bespate* spattered.

135]   *mews* An unusual plural usage of *mew*, "a place of confinement" (*OED*).

161]   *dragon-penned* "with feathers like a dragon" [PT].

179]   *nonce* moment.

182]   *blind . . . heart* Perhaps derived from Ps. 14:1 and 53:1, "The fool hath said in his heart / There is no God," or from Eph. 4:18, which characterizes non-Christians as ignorant because of the "blindness of their heart."

192]   *heft* Alternate spelling of *haft*, the handle or hilt of a knife or sword.

203]   *slug-horn* B apparently borrowed the word from Thomas Chatterton, who used *slughorne* (an early form of *slogan*) as a term for a battle-horn ("The Battle of Hastings," 2.99).

RESPECTABILITY

Source]   B was present at the ceremony referred to in l. 22 (see *Learned Lady*, ed. Edward C. McAleer [Cambridge, Mass., 1966], 92 and n.).

14]   *the Seine* The river which flows through Paris.

15]   *Boulevart* An older spelling of *boulevard*. From the other indications of the poem's locale, the reference is probably to the Boulevard Saint-Germain or the Boulevard Saint-Michel, both on the Left Bank of the Seine.

21]   *the Institute* The Institut de France houses learned societies, including the Académie Française. It stands on the Left Bank of the Seine at the Pont des Arts. Membership in the Institut is reserved for those who have reached the peak of success in a discipline.

22]   *Guizot receives Montalembert* François Pierre Guillaume Guizot (1787-1874), French historian and statesman, was a moderate conservative who had supported King Louis Philippe before the revolution of 1848. Charles Forbes René de Montalembert (1810-70) was a liberal Roman Catholic politician who opposed absolutism in both church and state. While Guizot was prime minister (1845-46), Montalembert strongly opposed him, but after Louis Philippe was deposed in 1848 the two became friends. When Montalembert was elected to membership in the Académie Française,

Guizot gave the principal address at the reception on 5 February 1852.
23] *lampions* Decorative oil lamps with colored glass sides.

A LIGHT WOMAN

28] *Eclipsing . . . disc* On 28 July 1851, a near-total solar eclipse was visible throughout most of Europe.
55-56] *Robert Browning . . . hand* The reference is a complex one: (1) between 1837 and 1846, B wrote eight plays, which met with only moderate success; (2) the ironic situation of "A Light Woman" is indeed like some of the situations in B's plays; (3) B may be referring to "In a Balcony," written in the summer of 1853 and published in *Men and Women*.

THE STATUE AND THE BUST

1] *a palace in Florence* The building referred to stands on the Piazza della Santissima Annunziata where the Via dei Servi enters the square. It was built for Ugolino Grifoni, a minor official under Cosimo de' Medici (see "Fra Lippo Lippi," l. 17n.), in the mid-sixteenth century. The palace has had several names in succeeding centuries, though today it is again called "Palazzo Grifoni." At the time of the story (between 1587 and 1609) it was still in the hands of the Grifoni, but in the first half of the nineteenth century it belonged to the Riccardi family (see l. 18n.).
2] *a statue . . . the square* In the Piazza della Santissima Annunziata is a bronze statue of the Grand Duke Ferdinand I (see l. 12n.) on horseback. Ferdinand commissioned Giovanni da Bologna (see l. 202n.) to design the statue, which was finished in 1608. The rider of the statue looks SW, in the direction of the Palazzo Grifoni.
12] *Great-Duke Ferdinand* Ferdinando de' Medici (1549-1609) was named Grand Duke of Tuscany in 1587. A beloved ruler, he eliminated much governmental corruption. B's story appears to be entirely legendary; Ferdinand was happily married to Christine of Lorraine from 1589 until his death.
18] *the Riccardi* The Riccardi were a wealthy and important Florentine family, many members of which were merchants and government officials.
22] *encolure* "French for 'neck of an animal,' here used for 'mane' " [PT].
33-35] *the pile . . . overshadows one* The reference here is to the Medici palace (see "Fra Lippo Lippi," l. 18n.). B errs slightly in having Ferdinand I live in this palace; it was closed from 1540 until 1659, when it was sold to the Riccardi family (see l. 18n.). In 1814 the building became state property, and today it houses the office of the prefect, a museum, and the Riccardi library.
36-39] *a crime . . . cursed son* The Cosimo of l. 39 is not Cosimo the Elder (see "Fra Lippo Lippi," l. 17n.), but Cosimo I (1519-74), who ruled Florence from 1537 to 1574. Cosimo I was a ruthless despot who tortured and slaughtered his opponents, who included many leading Florentines and

Cosimo's own cousin Lorenzino. Cosimo's son and successor, Francesco I (1541-87), allowed the government to become corrupt; though not so violent as his father, he ignored his duties and freely confiscated his enemies' property. However, Francesco I also patronized the arts and founded the Uffizi gallery.

57] *catafalk* "a kind of open hearse or funeral car" (*OED*); apparently B coined this sense.

72] *ave-bell* The church bell rung when the "Ave Maria" prayer is to be said, at six A.M., noon, and six P.M.

94] *Arno* The river which flows through Florence.

95] *Petraja, cool and green* Ferdinand I purchased and restored a villa at Petraja, which lies in the foothills 3 mi. NW of Florence.

101] *wind . . . Apennine* The Apennine mountains run down the center of Italy; Florence is S of the range. A cold N wind from these mountains is called a *maestrale*; it is blamed for respiratory diseases, rheumatism, and general irritability.

113] *Envoy . . . France* Ferdinand I was on good terms with France: he had married Christine, daughter of Charles III of Lorraine, and he sent large sums of money to aid Henri IV of Navarre in gaining the French throne over Spanish opposition. Henri IV later married Ferdinand's niece.

159] *serpent's tooth* That is, by being tempted as Eve was (Gen. 3:1-13). The similarity to *King Lear*, 1.4.312-13 seems coincidental.

169] *Robbia's craft . . . strange* The sculptors of the della Robbia family (Luca [1400-1482], Andrea [1435-1525], Giovanni [1469-1529]) produced bas-reliefs of glazed terra cotta. The secret of their colored glazes survived them, and della Robbia ware was still in production in Ferdinand's time. The craft is "apt" in that della Robbia figures are remarkably life-like, and "strange" because such use of color was unprecedented in Italian sculpture.

172] *a face . . . there* When Thomas Hardy asked B in 1887 about the whereabouts of the bust, B replied, "I invented it" (see Florence Emily Hardy, *The Early Life of Thomas Hardy* [N.Y., 1928], 261-262) [PT].

202] *John of Douay* Giovanni da Bologna (1529-1608), also called Giambologna, Jean Boulogne, and John of Douay, was born at Douai in Flanders. He settled in Florence and became a very successful sculptor. In 1594 he cast a bronze equestrian statue of Cosimo I (see ll. 36-39n.) at Ferdinand's request, and later he designed the similar statue for the Piazza della Santissima Annunziata (see l. 2n.). This second piece was completed by Piero Tacca (1555-1640) in 1608. Coincidentally, Giovanni da Bologna also designed the balcony of the Palazzo Grifoni, referred to in l. 1.

214] *trump of doom* On the Day of Judgment, "the trumpet shall sound, and the dead shall be raised" (I Cor. 15:52).

219] *chapel yonder* The reference is probably to the Medici chapel attached to the church of San Lorenzo. Ferdinand I (who began the construction of the mausoleum in 1604) and other Medici rulers are buried in this magnificent chapel.

234] *the very Guelph* The *Guelfo* or *Grosso Guelfo* was a Florentine silver coin of considerable value; it was struck in the fourteenth century and continued in circulation for some time. Named after a medieval political party (see this edition, Vol II, *Sordello*, I, 1. 113n.), the coin carried the arms of various noble families of Florence.

247] *unlit . . . loin* "Let your loins be girded about, and your lights burning" (Luke 12:35); the Bible passage speaks of seizing opportunities.

250] *De te, fabula* The Latin means literally, "about you, the story." It is drawn from Horace's "mutato nomine de te / fabula narratur" ("if you change the name, the story is told about you" [*Satires*, 1.1.69-70]).

HOW IT STRIKES A CONTEMPORARY

Source] The setting, the name Jacynth, and the title "Corregidor" (see l. 90n.) may come from *Gil Blas*, a romance by Alain René Le Sage (1668-1747) which B knew well.

3] *Valladolid* This ancient city in N central Spain (about 100 mi. NW of Madrid) has been a center of learning since the thirteenth century, and several poets are associated with it. Cervantes lived in Valladolid from 1603 to 1606.

19] *mouldered Moorish work* The window is in the style of Moorish (Islamic) architecture. The Moors ruled Spain from the eighth to the eleventh centuries, and their magnificent buildings survive in great numbers.

20] *ferrel* Older spelling of *ferrule*, the protective metal sleeve on the end of a walking-stick.

22] *new shop . . . fine* The Bourbon dynasty of France ruled Spain intermittently through the eighteenth and nineteenth centuries, and Napoleon's troops occupied Valladolid in 1807-8.

76] *Titians* That is, paintings by the Venetian master Tiziano Vecellio (called Titian; c. 1488-1576). Titian sent numerous paintings to the Spanish rulers Charles I and Philip II; many of these are in the Prado museum in Madrid.

84] *Jacynth* The name of a minor character in *Gil Blas* (see *Source* n.).

90] *Corregidor* The governor of the city.

115] *Prado* Since the location of the speaker of the poem is unspecified, the phrase may refer to either of two places: (1) a main boulevard and park in Madrid, and by extension any "fashionable promenade" (*OED*); or (2) the magnificent art museum of Madrid, containing some of the great art treasures of the world.

THE LAST RIDE TOGETHER

53] *petty done . . . vast* cf. *Book of Common Prayer*, "General Confession": We have left undone those things which we ought to have done . . . ."

65] *Abbey-stones* Many great figures (including B himself) are honored with inscriptions on the walls and floors of Westminster Abbey in London.

THE PATRIOT

Composition] The poem was probably written after the failure of the Italian liberal movements of 1848-49; when France, Austria, and Pope Pius IX had suppressed the liberals, they reestablished authoritarian governments immediately.

26] *Thus I . . . go* In 1855 this line reads "Thus I entered Brescia, and thus I go!" According to DeVane (*Hbk.*, 239), B dropped the reference to Brescia in order to avoid suggesting that he had Arnold of Brescia (c. 1100-1155), an anti-papal revolutionary, in mind when he wrote the poem.

MASTER HUGUES OF SAXE-GOTHA

Composition] Probably one of the poems with "more music and painting" that B mentioned to Milsand in February 1853 (see *Men and Women, Composition*, above).

Title] Hugues is B's invention. In a letter of 1887, B commented: "had he been meant for the glorious Bach it were a shame to me indeed; I had in mind one of the dry-as-dust imitators who would elaborate some such subject as [here B wrote out a simple five-note musical phrase] for a dozen pages together" (see H. E. Greene, "Browning's Knowledge of Music," *PMLA* 62 [1947], 1095-99). Saxe-Gotha was a part of one of the duchies of Saxony, in central Germany. The town of Gotha is 20 mi. E of Eisenach, the birthplace of J. S. Bach.

15] *base* "The regular form up to the [nineteenth] century of the word now spelt BASS" (*OED*).

26] *Aloys and Jurien and Just* *Aloys* is the Germanic form of Aloysius, the name of several saints; *Just* is short for Justin or Justinius, also a name shared by several saints. *Jurien* remains unidentified.

35] *help . . . helve* An adaptation of the expression "put the axe in the helve," meaning "solve the problem."

39] *three claviers* The organ being played has three keyboards ranged one above another; each keyboard controls a complete set of pipes.

44] *great breves . . . of yore* The breve (from Latin *brevis*, "short") was the shortest note value used in thirteenth-century music; it was written as a black square.

50] *Parted . . . goats* See Matt. 25:32.

67] *discept* dispute or disagree.

79] *strepitant* noisy (apparently a B coinage).

80] *O Danaides, O Sieve* The allusion suggests endless futile labor. The Danaides, daughters of King Danaüs of Argos, killed their husbands and were condemned to the underworld. Their punishment was to draw water into jars with pierced bottoms.

83]   *the casuist Escobar's* The Spanish Jesuit theologian Antonio Escobar y Mendoza (1589-1669) wrote six highly ingenious tracts. Because the French scientist and writer Blaise Pascal (1623-62) used Escobar's arguments as examples of theological hypocrisy (in *Provincial Letters* [1656-57]), Escobar's name became linked with elaborate arguments designed to prove whatever one desires.

85]   *Two-bars* The conclusion of a part or the whole of a composition is indicated in a score by two vertical lines at the end of the last measure.

86]   *Est . . . rota* Latin for "there is a flight; the wheel is turned." The phrase may be a notation on the score the speaker is using, since the term *fugue* derives from *fuga.*

92]   *risposting* Alternate spelling of *riposting.* The technical term *risposta* means "the answer to the subject of a fugue," i.e., the second voice.

94]   *groining* The decorated edge at the intersection of two ceiling vaults.

100]   *tickens* Alternate spelling of *tickings,* sturdy cloth used to cover mattresses. Here, a dust-cloth.

113]   *legislature* One obsolete meaning of the word, "the exercise of the function or power of legislation" (*OED*), perhaps applies, particularly in light of B's later use of a similar phrase for a similar treatment of the relation between human behavior and divine law: "learn earth first ere presume / To teach heaven legislation" (*Parleyings with Certain People of Importance in Their Day*, "With Chrisopher Smart," 255-56).

115]   *usurpature* Usurpation, in the sense of "unjustified assumption, arrogation, or pretension" (*OED*). B apparently coined the word in "The Flight of the Duchess," 473, though it has a slightly different meaning there.

120]   *glozes* Marginal explanations or "glosses."

127]   *mountain in labour* The image appears in Horace, *Ars Poetica* (*The Art of Poetry*), 139: "Parturient montes, nascetur ridiculus mus" ("the mountains will labor, a ridiculous mouse will be born"). This in turn probably derives from AEsop's fable, "The Mountains in Labor."

128]   *clef* key signature.

136]   *mea poena* Latin for "at the risk of being punished."

137]   *Gorgon* The Gorgons of Greek myth had brazen hands, golden wings, boar-like tusks, and nests of serpents on their heads. One glimpse of the Gorgon turned man or beast to stone.

139]   *unstop the full-organ* To play "full-organ" is to pull out a control knob ("stop") which links the several sets of pipes to the one main keyboard, thus sounding all the ranges of the instrument on each note.

140]   *mode Palestrina* Giovanni Pierluigi da Palestrina (c. 1525-94) was a great Italian composer of vocal music. As B later explained, "the 'mode Palestrina' has no reference to organ-playing; it was the name given by old Italian writers on Composition to a certain simple and severe style like that of the Master; just as, according to Byron, 'the word Miltonic means sublime' " (see H. E. Greene, "Browning's Knowledge of Music," *PMLA* 62

[1947], 1095-99). Byron's comment on Milton appears in the dedication of *Don Juan*, st. 10.

BISHOP BLOUGRAM'S APOLOGY

Date]   Certainly after 1850, when Wiseman was made Bishop of Westminster (see *Sources* n.), and probably somewhat later. Topical references in the poem (see ll. 54, 108-9, 377, 411, 704 and nn.) suggest that the poem was not completed until 1854.

Sources]   According to B, Blougram was based on Nicholas P. S. Cardinal Wiseman (1802-65), whose appointment in 1850 as Bishop of Westminster marked the restoration of the Roman Catholic hierarchy in England. In 1881 B wrote: "The most curious notice I ever had was from Cardinal Wiseman on *Blougram*—i.e. himself" (Hood, *Ltrs.*, 195. The "notice," an anonymous review in the January 1856 issue of the *Rambler*, has been shown to be not by Wiseman but by Richard Simpson. See Esther Rhoades Houghton, "Reviewer of Browning's *Men and Women* in the *Rambler* Identified," *VN* 33 [1968], 46). The poem is not a portrait of Wiseman, however; at various points Blougram sounds like John Henry Cardinal Newman (1801-1890), and the whole of "Bishop Blougram's Apology" exists in the context of the Oxford Movement and the Roman Catholic revival of the 1840s and 50s. (On Newman and Bishop Blougram, see C. R. Tracy, "Bishop Blougram," *MLR* 34 [1939], 422-25.)

Title]   *Apology* is used in the sense of "explanation" or "defense," as Cardinal Newman later used it in his autobiographical *Apologia pro Vita Sua* (1864).

3]   *our Abbey* When Wiseman was made Archbishop of Westminster, the Anglican clergy (and some of the public) feared that he would claim authority over Westminster Abbey. In his *Appeal to the Reason and Good Feeling of the English People* (1850; first published as a pamphlet and reprinted in the *Times*, 20 November 1850, 5-6), Wiseman assured his readers that he made no such claim and that the Church of England should fear no "aggression."

5-6]   *doing duty . . . Pugin's* The English architect A. W. N. Pugin (1812-52) led the Gothic revival in building design. A convert to Roman Catholicism, Pugin designed many churches, including five cathedrals. Wiseman and Pugin frequently quarrelled, but at the opening of Pugin's Cathedral of St. George in Southwark (4 July 1848) Wiseman preached the first sermon.

7-8]   *chalk . . . stucco-twiddlings* To Pugin's great dissatisfaction, his designs were often spoiled by short-cutting and inferior materials.

34]   *Corpus Christi Day* A Christian festival which falls on the Thursday after Trinity Sunday (the first Sunday after Pentecost). The festival celebrates the presence of the body of Christ in the elements of the Eucharist.

45]   *che che* An Italian phrase meaning literally "what, what"; idiomatically, an interjection meaning "no, no" or "certainly not."

52] *Goethe* Johann Wolfgang von Goethe (1749-1832), cited here as the example of supreme intellectual achievement, since he was not only the greatest writer in German literature, but a philosopher and scientist as well.

53] *Buonaparte* The allusion is as much to Napoleon's legend as to his life: his meteoric rise to power; his conquering of Europe in a series of battles won through brilliant military tactics; the establishment of the French Empire (1804); his abdication (1814) and triumphal return to power (1815); his creation of the Code Napoléon, the Banque de France, and an effective administrative system; and the sheer romance of his career.

54] *Count D'Orsay* Alfred de Grimod, Comte D'Orsay (1801-52), a French dandy and socialite, was briefly director of fine arts under Napoleon III. When D'Orsay was godfather (along with Alfred Tennyson) to one of Charles Dickens' children, B wrote to EBB: "You observe, 'Alfred' is common to both the godfather and the—devilfather, as I take the Count to be" (*RB-EBB*, ed. Kintner, 685).

61-62] *say they make me Pope— / (They can't* Though no regulation prohibits anyone from being elected pope, the only English pope was Adrian IV (Nicholas Breakspear, d. 1159), and the last non-Italian pope before the Polish John Paul II was Adrian VI, a Dutchman who was pope from 1522 to 1523.

67-69] *Death . . . the world* This representation of the figure of death is common in emblem books of the sixteenth and seventeenth centuries; it also appears in Milton's *Paradise Lost*, 2, 666-73.

96] *Fool's-paradise* Not only a stock expression for happiness based on illusions, but also a specific theological concept in medieval philosophy. As a region of the cosmos, Fool's Paradise appears in *Paradise Lost*, 3, 495-96.

106] *India screen* Indian furniture became popular in England after the Great Exhibition of 1851. The screens were usually ornately carved teak (called "Bombay furniture") or red lacquered sandalwood.

108-9] *Balzac's novels . . . long* There were many editions of the works of Honoré de Balzac (1799-1850) before 1855, but none approached fifty volumes. Since Balzac was one of B's favorite authors, he may have known in advance of the *OEuvres Complètes de Honoré de Balzac* (55 vols.: Paris, 1856-67).

110-11] *Greek books . . . Leipsic* A number of German publishers based in Leipzig, among them Teubner, Engelmann, Fleischer, and Tauchnitz, specialized in editions of the Greek and Latin classics. The German editions used a more stylized, script-like type face for Greek than their English counterparts.

113-17] *Parma's pride . . . Modenese* The reference is to an altarpiece of the Virgin with St. Jerome by Antonio Allegri (c. 1489-1534). Allegri is called Correggio after the Italian town where he was born, 12 mi. NW of Modena in northern Italy. The painting, in the city gallery of Parma (32 mi. NW of Modena), is sometimes called "The Day" to contrast it with Correggio's altarpiece of the Nativity, called "The Night" (now in Dresden, East Germany).

125] *overhauls* Unloads or sends back; B extends the nautical meaning of *overhaul*, "slacken ropes" or "release lifting tackle."

184] *chorus-ending from Euripides* Probably B refers to the lines with which Euripides (c. 484-406 B.C.) closed five of his plays—*The Bacchae, Helen, Andromache, Medea*, and *Alcestis*—and which B himself rendered as "Manifold are thy shapings, Providence! / Many a hopeless matter Gods arrange. / What we expected never came to pass: / What we did not expect, Gods brought to bear; / So have things gone, this whole experience through!" (*Balaustion's Adventure* [1871], 2392-96).

190] *grand Perhaps* A reference to the purported last words of François Rabelais (1495-1553), French physician and writer: "Je m'en vais chercher un grand peut-être" ("I am going to search for a grand perhaps"). The remark is attributed to Rabelais by Peter Motteux (1663-1718) in the preface to his translation of Rabelais.

197] *"The Way . . . Life?"* John 14:6.

294] *can't wed twice* Until the English divorce court was established in 1857, Parliament had to rule on each case, making divorce (and hence legal re-marriage) impossible for all but the very rich and powerful.

315] *Bid . . . be bread* In Matt. 4:3-4, Jesus refuses Satan's challenge to transform stones into loaves of bread.

316] *Peter's . . . Hildebrand's* St. Peter was the first pope; his creed would therefore be that of the Roman Catholic Church. Saint Gregory VII (c. 1025-85) was named Hildebrand before he became pope in 1073. Gregory VII reformed and strengthened the papacy by centralizing authority in Rome and by insisting that spiritual and ecclesiastical matters were more important than political or temporal concerns.

377] *the last winking Virgin* In an exchange of letters with the Bishop of Norwich, published in the *Morning Chronicle* on 21 October 1851 and reprinted in the *Times* the following day, Cardinal Newman reaffirmed his acceptance of the genuineness of the liquifaction of the blood of St. Januarius (see l. 728n.) and of the movement of the eyes of painted Madonnas. Newman's views first appeared in his *Lectures on Catholicism in England* (1851). The word "winking" undoubtedly was suggested by a letter in the *Times* on 24 October 1851, which sneered at Newman's belief and asked him to have chemists examine the blood of St. Januarius and to have a neutral party investigate "the next performance of a winking or bleeding statue or picture . . . ."

381] *Verdi* Giuseppe Verdi (1813-1901), Italian composer of operas and choral works, the most famous perhaps being *Rigoletto* (1851), *La Traviata* (1853), *Il Trovatore* (1853), *Don Carlos* (1867), *Aida* (1871), and *Otello* (1887).

381-82] *his worst . . . Florence* The only Verdi opera produced in Florence before 1855 was *Macbeth*, which premiered there on 14 March 1847.

Macbeth is usually regarded as one of Verdi's less successful works.

384]   *salt-box, tongs and bones* A specification of the crudeness of Verdi's orchestra: "In burlesque music, the salt-box has been used like the marrow-bones and cleaver, tongs and poker, etc." (OED)

386]   *Rossini* Gioacchino Antonio Rossini (1792-1868), the Italian compos-er of *The Barber of Seville* (1816), *Moses in Egypt* (1818), and *William Tell* (1829), was Verdi's predecessor in opera. Though Rossini lived in Florence from 1848 to 1855, there is no evidence that he attended a performance of *Macbeth*.

406]   *diamond weights* Diamonds and other precious stones are weighed in carats; one carat is equal to about .007 ounces.

407]   *Your picked twelve* See l. 375.

411]   *Schelling's way* Friedrich Wilhelm Joseph von Schelling (1775-1854), German philosopher who worked his way from Romantic nature-philosophy through neo-Platonic idealism to a rather unorthodox Chris-tianity.

425]   *Peter's chains* St. Peter was enchained while imprisoned by Herod Agrippa I (see Acts 12:3-11); thus the chains have become emblematic of the persecution of Christians in non-Christian countries.

426]   *Noodledom* A slang term meaning "folly" or "fools."

436]   *Napoleon* See l. 53n.

454]   *take . . . away* Certain kinds of madness were once treated by put-ting the patient in a darkened room; see *As You Like It*, 3.2.400-401.

466]   *"The state, that's I,"* English version of French "L'état, c'est moi," a remark usually attributed to Louis XIV. It is questionable whether Louis XIV actually said it, but Napoleon came close. In his remarks to a deputation of the *Corps législatif* (senate) on 30 December 1813, Napoleon observed "Le trône lui-même, qu'est-ce? Quatre morceaux de bois doré, recouverts de velours? Non, le trône c'est un homme et cet homme c'est moi" ("The throne itself, what is it? Four bits of gilded wood, covered with velvet? No, the throne is a man, and that man is I").

472]   *an Austrian marriage* In 1810 Napoleon divorced the Empress Jose-phine and married Marie Louise, Archduchess of Austria.

475]   *Austerlitz* In one of his most memorable battles, Napoleon employed daring and subtle tactics to lead the French army to victory over the Russian and Austrian armies at Austerlitz, in central Czechoslovakia (December 1805).

481]   *arch-duchess* See l. 472n.

482]   *divers . . . names* When Napoleon rose to power, he was given the title of First Consul. After he became emperor, he created new titles for his ministers, such as Grand Elector and Arch-Chancellor.

511 ff.]   *his life* Shakespearean biography was a matter of public interest throughout the 1840s and '50s. Charles Knight produced a bardolatrous (and sometimes fanciful) life of Shakespeare (1843) which achieved immense

popularity; this was followed in 1848 by the masterful scholarly biography by J. O. Halliwell-Phillips. On the more sensational side, John Payne Collier's numerous "discoveries" about Shakespeare's life and works were exposed as fraudulent by Halliwell-Phillips, S. W. Singer, and others, in 1853. It is noteworthy also that the Bs' friend Anna Brownell Jameson (see *Men and Women, Sources,* above) had published a highly romanticized treatment of Shakespeare's life in her *Memoirs of the Loves of the Poets* (1829).

513] *towers and gorgeous palaces* See *The Tempest,* 4.1.152.

514-15] *To build . . . things* Most of the surviving records of Shakespeare's life show him in later years as a prosperous citizen of Stratford-upon Avon. Through investments and farming, he built the money he had made in London into a sizable estate. In 1597 he purchased New Place, the second largest house in Stratford, and proceeded to make it into a fine home.

516] *Giulio Romano's pictures* Giulio Romano (c. 1499-1546) studied with Raphael and completed some of his master's works. He is praised as a sculptor in *The Winter's Tale,* 5.2.102-10.

516] *Dowland's lute* The playing of John Dowland (1563-1626), English composer and lutanist, is praised in poem VIII of *The Passionate Pilgrim* (1599), a volume of poetry attributed on its title page to Shakespeare. In fact, only five of the twenty poems are clearly Shakespeare's, and poem VIII is by Richard Barnfield (1574-1627).

519] *"Pandulph . . . cardinal." King John,* 3.1.138. Blougram would presumably find this scene memorable, since in it Pandulph demonstrates papal authority by excommunicating King John and thus turning France against England.

532] *(he never did)* Because the first publication of his plays as a group came with the First Folio (1623), seven years after Shakespeare died.

533] *Terni* A town in Umbria, about 60 mi. NNE of Rome. The main attraction of Terni is the Cascate delle Marmore, a 650 ft. waterfall; the Bs visited Terni and its falls on their way from Florence to Rome in November 1853.

533] *Naples' bay* B landed at the beautiful bay of Naples on his second visit to Italy, in the fall of 1844.

533] *Gothard's top* The St. Gothard pass through the Swiss alps affords magnificent views of the mountains; B crossed it several times.

550] *Stratford house* See ll. 514-15 n.

550] *coat of arms* The Shakespeare family was granted a coat of arms in 1596, probably at William's request. A description of the crest was first published in Alexander Pope's 1725 edition of Shakespeare.

551] *Successful . . . wool* Shakespeare used the barns at New Place (see ll. 514-15n.) to store the grain in which he traded. He also purchased land and grazing rights for sheep and cattle.

553] *cousin . . . Queen Bess* Queen Elizabeth would have addressed

Blougram as "cousin" because he would have represented a fellow-sovereign, the pope.

568] *Luther* Martin Luther (c. 1483-1546) criticized papal policy and accused the Roman Catholic hierarchy of corruption. After he was excommunicated in 1521, Luther became a leader of the Reformation in Germany.

577] *Strauss* David Friedrich Strauss (1804-1874), German scholar and theologian, applied the historian's tests of plausibility and verification to Biblical narratives. Strauss concluded that the scriptures contained more myth than fact, but he argued in *Das Leben Jesu* (*The Life of Jesus* [1835], translated into English in 1846 by George Eliot) that the truths of Christianity lay precisely in those powerful myths. Such use of literary and historical approaches in religious matters, termed "Higher Criticism," was a subject of great controversy in the nineteenth century.

585-86] *It could . . . Saint Paul* See Rom. 13:8, in which St. Paul admonishes, "Owe no man any thing, but to love one another . . . ."

626] *"What . . . Christ,"* Matt. 22:42.

640-42] *born . . . Englishman* Wiseman (see *Source* n.) was born at Seville in Spain of Anglo-Irish parents. He was educated in England and Rome, and his career as a churchman began with his London lectures in 1835-36.

664] *ichors* heals. The fluid in the veins of the Greek gods was named *ichor*; in medicine the term is used for the blood serum at a wound. B uses it as a verb.

667] *snake . . . foot* In Rev. 12:7-9, the archangel Michael battles and defeats "that old serpent, called the Devil, and Satan." Michael's conquering of a serpent or dragon is a major motif in the iconography of saints.

679-83] *blot out . . . Genesis again* Discoveries about the nature and history of the universe, the Earth, and man made it extremely difficult to maintain that Biblical narratives consisted of accurate historical truth. The apparent conflict between scientific fact and religious dogma became a major concern in the nineteenth century.

684-85] *a traveller . . . Ararat* Noah's ark came to rest on Mt. Ararat as the flood receded (Gen. 8:4). Tales of the ark's discovery appeared in travel books such as *Mandeville's Travels* (c. 1357), which claims that the ark "yet is upon that mountain and men may see it afar in clear weather" (*Mandeville's Travels*, ed. M. C. Seymour [London, 1968], 115).

699] *Virgin's winks* See l. 377n.

702-3] *What are . . . Newman asks* A somewhat oversimplified version of Newman's position, which he summarized as follows: "A miracle may be considered as an event inconsistent with the constitution of nature, that is, with the established course of things in which it is found . . . . It does not necessarily imply a violation of nature, as some have supposed,—merely the interposition of an external cause, which, we shall hereafter show, can be no other than the agency of the Deity" (*Two Essays on Scripture Miracles and on Ecclesiastical* [London, 1870], 4. This is a revision of Newman's 1826 and 1843 essays on miracles.).

704] *Immaculate Conception* This doctrine, which asserts that Mary was freed from original sin at the instant of her conception, was declared Roman Catholic dogma by Pope Pius IX in 1854.

715] *King Bomba's lazzaroni* The nickname "King Bomba" was applied to Ferdinand II (1810-1859), king of the Two Sicilies, after he suppressed the rebellions of 1849 (see "Up at a Villa—Down in the City," l. 44n.) by bombarding Sicilian cities. The *lazzaroni* were the beggars and day-laborers who supported Ferdinand II (and thus the pope) during the early years of his reign.

716] *Antonelli writes* Giacomo Cardinal Antonelli (1806-1876) was secretary of state under Pope Pius IX. Under Antonelli's guidance, the Vatican supported reactionary and tyrannical governments, including that of Ferdinand II (see l. 715n.). Since Antonelli published nothing until 1861, the reference must be to an imaginary letter to Blougram.

728] *Naples liquifaction* A vial of the alleged blood of St. Januarius (fl. c. A.D. 300) is a holy relic of the cathedral of Naples. Eighteen times a year, in connection with certain feasts and anniversaries, the relic is displayed in the presence of the purported head of St. Januarius. At these times the blood is said to liquify. The phenomenon was much discussed in the 1840s and was accepted as genuine by Newman (see l. 377n.).

732] *decrassify* "divest of what is crass, gross, or material" (*OED*); apparently a B coinage.

744] *Fichte's clever cut* The German philosopher Johann Gottlieb Fichte (1762-1814) depersonalized the idea of God by defining Deity as the moral will of the universe. In Fichte's view, individuals exist as manifestations of this moral will.

793] *Algiers* The capital city of Algeria, in N Africa.

795] *Timbuctoo* An ancient African city on the southern edge of the Sahara desert.

819-20] *natural religion . . . revealed* The affinities and conflicts between natural religion, which asserts that man can come to a sufficient knowledge of God and morality through the study of nature and the use of reason, and Christianity as revealed to man in the New Testament were staples of Victorian theological debate.

833] *a French book* Impossible to identify with certainty, but two candidates are *De l'Amour* (1822; reissued 1853), by Stendhal (pseudonym of Marie Henri Beyle, 1783-1842); and *Physiologie du Mariage* (1830) by Balzac (see ll. 108-9n.). See the letters of C. R. Tracy and R. E. N. Dodge in *TLS* 34 (1935), 48, 176.

877] *"Pastor . . . Dominus."* "The Lord is your shepherd." This appears to be B's adaptation and translation into Latin of the King James version of Ps. 23:1.

904] *daily bread* From the Lord's Prayer, Matt. 6:11 and Luke 11:3.

913-15] *my articles . . . Greek* Wiseman (see *Sources* n.) ran the *Dublin Review* from 1836 to 1862, contributing a great number of articles on a variety of subjects.

914-15] *vase / Found at Albano* Albano is an ancient Roman town 19 mi. SE of Rome along the Appian Way. A number of archeological finds were made there, including a remarkable collection of vases (see Sir William Gell, *The Topography of Rome and Its Vicinity* [London, 1834], 68).

915] *Anacreon's Greek* Anacreon was a Greek lyric poet of the sixth century B.C. whose subjects were love and drinking. His style was much imitated.

938] *stop this war* That is, the Crimean War (1854-56), in which England, France, and Turkey were allied against Russia.

945] *Blackwood's Magazine* *Blackwood's Edinburgh Magazine,* an immensely popular quarterly, was founded in 1817 by William Blackwood; John Wilson and John Gibson Lockhart served as editors. B read *Blackwood's* and felt it had ignored his work (see DeVane and Knickerbocker, 100-101, 104, 206 and n.).

946-47] *two points . . . Germans yet* After Goethe and Schiller praised Shakespeare, the German critics of the nineteenth century busily "discovered" him; they wrote volume after volume of close analysis of the plays, particularly *Hamlet.*

949-52] *article . . . after dark!"* Gigadibs' title is patterned after the titles of some of Charles Dickens' London sketches, such as "The Streets at Night," in *Sketches by Boz* (completed 1839) and "An Unsettled Neighborhood," in *Household Words,* 11 November 1854.

951] *Whitechapel* The Whitechapel district of London's East End was one of the very worst slums, largely populated by the destitute and rife with criminals.

972-73] *in partibus / Episcopus, nec non—* When Wiseman (see *Sources* n.) was consecrated bishop in 1840, he was given the title "Bishop of Melipotamus, *in partibus infedelium,"* that is, "in the lands of non-believers." The Latin fragment here may be translated, "Bishop in regions, and also—"

1011] *started for Australia* B's friend Alfred Domett (1811-87) had gone to New Zealand in 1842 and begun a new life as a farmer; he rose to the prime ministership of New Zealand in 1862. The discovery of gold in Australia in 1851 brought a rush of immigrants from all over the world; in the 1850s nearly 500,000 people left Britain for Australia.

1013] *last chapter of St. John* The allusion is ambiguous. It may refer to either John 21, in which Jesus appears to the disciples and tells Peter to "feed my sheep"; or to I John 5, which asserts that faith achieves victory over the world and closes with the admonition, "Little children, keep yourselves from idols." But the point may be that Gigadibs should read no more St. John; that is, he should give up considering theological or religious questions.

MEMORABILIA

Text] A facsimile of a manuscript of a poem similar in many ways to "Memorabilia" was published in the *Christian Science Monitor* on 17 September 1956. Nothing is reported of the history of this MS, which is in neither B's nor EBB's hand. Despite the speculations in an article accompanying the facsimile, the MS has no demonstrated textual significance.

Date and source] The poem probably dates from late 1851, when B was writing his essay on Shelley. DeVane believes that "Memorabilia" was inspired by a chance meeting between B and a man who had known Shelley (*Hbk*, 244). For a discussion of B and Shelley, see the notes to the *Essay on Shelley* in the present volume.

(Titles of long poems or of collections of short poems are capitalized.)
Any Wife to Any Husband   V, 213
Artemis Prologizes   III, 224
Bishop Blougram's Apology   V, 293
Bishop Orders his Tomb at Saint Praxed's Church, The   IV, 189
BLOT IN THE 'SCUTCHEON, A   IV, 3
Boot and Saddle   III, 200
Boy and the Angel, The   IV, 239
By the Fire-Side   V, 200
Cavalier Tunes   III, 197
"Childe Roland to the Dark Tower Came"   V, 248
CHRISTMAS-EVE AND EASTER-DAY   V, 49
Christmas-Eve   V, 53
Claret   IV, 244
COLOMBE'S BIRTHDAY   IV, 63
Confessional, The   IV, 203
Count Gismond   III, 203
Cristina   III, 239
DRAMATIC LYRICS   III, 181
DRAMATIC ROMANCES AND LYRICS   IV, 147
Earth's Immortalities   IV, 237
Easter-Day   V, 97
Englishman in Italy, The   IV, 173
Epistle Containing the Strange Medical Experience of Karshish, the Arab
  Physician, An   V, 219
ESSAY ON CHATTERTON   III, 159
ESSAY ON SHELLEY   V, 135
Evelyn Hope   V, 174
"Eyes calm beside thee"   I, 53
Flight of the Duchess, The   IV, 207
Flower's Name, The   IV, 194
Fra Lippo Lippi   V, 183

France and Spain   IV, 200
Garden Fancies   IV, 194
Give a Rouse   III, 199
Glove, The   IV, 264
"Here's to Nelson's Memory!"   IV, 245
Home Thoughts from Abroad   IV, 187
Home Thoughts from the Sea   IV, 188
How It Strikes a Contemporary   V, 274
"How They Brought the Good News from Ghent to Aix"   IV, 161
In a Gondola   III, 214
Incident of the French Camp   III, 209
Instans Tyrannus   V, 241
Italian in England, The   IV, 167
Johannes Agricola in Meditation   III, 242
KING VICTOR AND KING CHARLES   III, 83
Laboratory, The   IV, 200
Last Ride Together, The   V, 278
Life in a Love   V, 273
Light Woman, A   V, 258
Lost Leader, The   IV, 183
Lost Mistress, The   IV, 186
Love Among the Ruins   V, 163
Love in a Life   V, 272
Lovers' Quarrel, A   V, 167
LURIA   IV, 281
Marching Along   III, 197
Master Hughes of Saxe-Gotha   V, 285
Meeting at Night   IV, 243
Memorabilia   V, 331
MEN AND WOMEN, VOLUME I   V, 153
Mesmerism   V, 230
My Last Duchess   III, 201
My Star   V, 240
Nationality in Drinks   IV, 244
PAULINE   I, 3
PARACELSUS   I, 59
Parting at Morning   IV, 243
Patriot, The   V, 283
Pictor Ignotus   IV, 164
Pied Piper of Hamelin, The   III, 249
PIPPA PASSES   III, 5

Porphyria's Lover   III, 245
Pretty Woman, A   V, 244
Respectability   V, 257
RETURN OF THE DRUSES, THE   III, 263
Rudel to the Lady of Tripoli   III, 237
Saul   IV, 246
Serenade at the Villa, A   V, 237
Sidbrandus Schafnaburgensis   IV, 196
Soliloquy of the Spanish Cloister   III, 211
Song   IV, 338
SORDELLO   II, 119
SOUL'S TRAGEDY, A   V, 3
Statue and the Bust, The   V, 261
STRAFFORD   II, 3
Through the Metidja to Abd-el-Kadr   III, 247
Time's Revenges   IV, 261
Toccata of Galuppi's, A   V, 197
Tokay   IV, 244
Up at a Villa—Down in the City   V, 177
Waring   III, 228
Woman's Last Word, A   V, 181

Ah, did you once see Shelley plain,   V, 331

All I believed is true!   V, 230

All's over, then: does truth sound bitter,   IV, 186

All that I know   V, 240

As I ride, as I ride,   III, 247

Beautiful Evelyn Hope is dead!   V, 174

Boots, saddle, to horse, and away!   III, 200

Christ God who savest man, save most   III, 203

Dear, had the world in its caprice   V, 257

Escape me?   V, 273

Eyes, calm beside thee, (Lady couldst thou know!)   I, 57

Fortù, Fortù, my beloved one,   IV, 173

Gr-r-r—there go, my heart's abhorence!   III, 211

Had I but plenty of money, money enough and to spare,   V, 177

Hamelin Town's in Brunswick,   III, 249

"Heigho!" yawned one day King Francis,   IV, 264

Here's the garden she walked across,   IV, 194

Here's to Nelson's memory!   IV, 245

Hist, but a word, fair and soft!   V, 285

How very hard it is to be   V, 97

How well I know what I mean to do   V, 200

I am a goddess of the ambrosial courts,   III, 224

I am poor brother Lippo, by your leave!   V, 183

I could have painted pictures like that youth's,   IV, 164

I know a Mount the gracious Sun perceives   III, 237

I only knew one poet in my life: V, 274

I said—Then, dearest, since 'tis so,   V, 278

I send my heart up to thee, all my heart   III, 214

I sprang to the stirrup, and Joris, and he;   IV, 161

It is a lie—their Priests, their Pope,   IV, 203

It was roses, roses, all the way,   V, 283

I've a Friend, over the sea;   IV, 261

Just for a handful of silver he left us,   IV, 183

Karshish, the picker-up of learning's crumbs,   V, 219

Kentish Sir Byng stood for his King,   III, 197

King Charles, and who'll do him right now?   III, 199

Let's contend no more, Love,   V, 181

Morning, evening, noon and night,   IV, 109

My first thought was, he lied in every word,   V, 248

My heart sank with our Claret-flask,   IV, 244
My love, this is the bitterest, that thou—   V, 213
Nay, but you, who do not love her,   IV, 238
Nobly, nobly Cape Saint Vincent to the North-west died away;   IV, 188
No more wine? then we'll push back chairs and talk.   V, 293
Now that I, tying thy glass mask tightly,   IV, 200
Of the million or two, more or less,   V, 241
Oh Galuppi, Baldassaro, this is very sad to find!   V, 197
Out of the little chapel I burst   V, 53
Oh, to be in England   IV, 187
Oh, what a dawn of day!   V, 167
Plague take in all your pedants, say I!   IV, 196
Room after room,   V, 272
Round the cape of a sudden came the sea,   IV, 243
Said Abner, "At last thou art come! Ere I tell, ere thou speak,   IV, 246
See, as the prettiest graves will do in time,   IV, 237
She should not have looked at me   III, 239
So far as our story approaches the end,   V, 258
That fawn-skin-dappled hair of hers,   V, 244
That second time they hunted me   IV, 167
That's my last Duchess painted on the wall,   III, 201
That was I, you heard last night,   V, 237
The grey sea and the long black land;   IV, 243
The rain set early in to-night,   III, 245
There's a palace in Florence, the world knows well,   V, 261
There's Heaven above, and night by night,   III, 242
Up jumped Tokay on our table,   IV, 244
Vanity, saith the preacher, vanity!   IV, 187
What's become of Waring   III, 228
Where the quiet-colored end of evening smiles,   V, 163
You know, we French stormed Ratisbon: III, 209
You're my friend: IV, 207